Women's Suffrage and Prohibition:
A Comparative Study of Equality and Social Control

Women's Suffrage and Prohibition:

A Comparative Study of Equality and Social Control

ROSS EVANS PAULSON
Augustana College

SCOTT, FORESMAN AND COMPANY
Glenview, Illinois   *Brighton, England*

For Avis
— and our daughters

History creates culture, including the all-important institutions within the framework of which individuals must carry on their behavior, and comparative history is thus the most important source of hypotheses concerning the forces which operate on an individual at any time.

Arnold M. Rose
The Institutions of Advanced Societies

Library of Congress Catalog Card Number: 72-92341
ISBN: 0-673-05982-0

Regional offices of Scott, Foresman and Company are located in Dallas, Texas; Glenview, Illinois; Oakland, New Jersey; Palo Alto, California; Tucker, Georgia; and Brighton, England.

Preface

When I began the research for this book in the spring of 1968, my colleagues either expressed mild consternation over the choice of topics or they hinted that the subjects had been treated in definitive works years ago and that one hardly need bother with such matters now. Research material was hard to find except in rare book rooms and specialized collections. Then came "women's liberation," a new alcoholism and drug abuse program, and the Equal Rights Amendment. The public's insatiable appetite for new causes and dramatic confrontations was fed by television's ability to focus on the unusual and the problematic. Books and scholarly reprints flooded the academic market; magazine editors felt obligated to devote at least an entire issue or a major feature article to these current trends.

Because this atmosphere of academic overproduction and heightened public expectations still continues, it is necessary to indicate why this book was written and how it differs from other studies of the subjects. These questions are answered at length in the Prologue.

This book is primarily concerned with studying the interaction of the women's suffrage and prohibition movements in history. The broader aspects of feminism, women's rights, temperance, and total abstinence are examined to the extent that is necessary to put the women's suffrage and prohibition movements in the proper historical contexts. My contention is that the "woman question" of the nineteenth and early twentieth centuries was an aspect of the debate on the meaning of equality, and that the temperance and prohibition movements involved questions concerning the nature of democracy and the means of social control within society.

This book differs from other treatments of the same topics in that it utilizes the comparative method in studying historical problems. The selection of cases to be studied has been restricted to those countries that experienced significant interactions between the two movements, such as the United States, England, Australia-New Zealand, the Scandinavian countries, and modern India, or to those countries which showed marked variations in the general patterns of development, such as France, Russia, and republican Turkey. This attempt to survey a limited range of comparative cases has revealed the scarcity of good monographic studies, the need for better utilization of primary and printed sources, and the necessity of formulating fresh research questions and categories. What is lost in breadth of coverage by the narrowing of focus and the selection of cases, will be offset, hopefully, by the resulting depth of insight.

A number of colleagues have assisted me by translating foreign language material, loaning research notes, or guiding my reading. Most of their contributions are acknowledged in the footnotes to the appropriate sections. In addition, I wish to thank Professor Frederick Kershner for inviting me to write this book, Professors Frank Freidel and David Bien for judicious criticism of the manuscript, Professor Robert Nisbet for a stimulating discussion of the comparative method, and Professor Nils Runeby of Uppsala, Sweden, for suggestions on the section dealing with the temperance movement in Sweden. Of course, I alone am responsible for any errors or omissions that may appear in the manuscript.

The editors at Scott, Foresman and Company have helped shepherd this study to publication. I am particularly grateful to the late George Vlach and to Michael Werthman, Ms. Susan Schwartz, Thomas A. Easton, Robert Cunningham, and Phillip Martin for their tactful suggestions and respect for the author's intentions.

Emily Burgess and Constance Lundquist of the Augustana College library staff were particularly helpful in arranging interlibrary loans and in monitoring the flow of new material on the women's movement; Dr. Mildred Konan provided information on current developments within the women's movement. I am grateful for the help of student assistants Alice Hilgendorf, Katherine Milton Faust, and Dean Wilkinson and for the interest of all my students in the progress of this study. Avis (Nelson) Paulson, my wife, wrote the section on women in English literature, analyzed the Finnish parliamentary committee that enfranchised women, translated Swedish sources, and engaged in the critical dialogue, along with Anne and Stan Hauerwas, that has helped to shape the book.

Rock Island, Illinois   R.E.P.

Contents

5
The Alliance of Temperance and Women's Suffrage

6
Frontiers and Franchise

7
Nationalism and Social Control

8
Social Control, Equality, and Social Cohesion

Women's Suffrage and Prohibition:

A Comparative Study of Equality and Social Control

Prologue:
The Past in Perspective

When American writers and reporters first attempted to assess the events of the
period between 1910 and 1920, particularly the adoption of national prohibition
and of women's suffrage, they were sharply divided in their opinions. Literary
critic H. L. Mencken dismissed the prohibitionists as bluenose Puritans seeking
to impose their crabbed and pinched rural mentality onto sophisticated city
dwellers. He viewed women's suffrage as an aberration of the female psyche.[1]
Publicist Mark Sullivan, on the other hand, believed that prohibition and women's
suffrage represented a progressive extension of democracy, the righting of old
wrongs, and an attempt to purify the moral and political life of the nation in the
image of a confident middle class.[2]

When professional historians attempted to assess recent events at the end of
the 1920s and in the 1930s, they tended to accept Mark Sullivan's "progressive
interpretation." Charles and Mary Beard in their monumental work, *The Rise of
American Civilization,* took pains to refute "critics who imagined that a tyrannical minority of Puritans suddenly compelled Congress in 1917 to submit to the
states the Eighteenth Amendment" and then "browbeat local legislatures into
ratifying it within two years." The subject of women's suffrage, since it did not
fit easily into the Beards' economic interpretation of feminism, was dismissed
lightly as simply contributing to the growth of "social democracy." Frederick
Lewis Allen's popular and provocative work, *Only Yesterday: An Informal
History of the Nineteen Twenties,* published in 1931, blamed the passage of the
prohibition amendment on wartime psychology, saw women's suffrage as part
of a broader revolution in manners and morals, and expressed a gentle skepticism

---

1. See H. L. Mencken, "Puritanism as a Literary Force," in *A Book of Prefaces* (New York:
Alfred A. Knopf, Inc., 1917), pp. 197-283, and *In Defense of Women* (New York: Alfred
A. Knopf, Inc., 1918).

2. Mark Sullivan, *Our Times: The United States, 1900-1925* (New York: Charles Scribner's
Sons, 1927-1933), 2:113-16, and 4:125.

of the claims of the suffragists that women possessed a monopoly on civic virtue. After the trauma of the Great Depression and repeal of prohibition in 1933, this "progressive interpretation" became the accepted canon of textbook writers. Both women's suffrage and prohibition were treated as progressive reforms that had not fulfilled the expectations of their supporters.[3]

While historians continued to accept this consensus, other social scientists in the 1940s and early 1950s began to question it. Political scientists asked searching questions about how women actually voted. The Kinsey reports of 1946–1953 once more turned scholarly attention to the popular themes of the 1920s: feminism, sexual "emancipation," styles of life, and behavior patterns. Sociologists and social psychologists took a new look at prohibition and feminism. Far from representing a simple reflex of rural minds, the dogmatic imperatives of Puritan theology, or the desires of envious females, prohibition and women's suffrage emerged as complex responses to social change.[4]

The newer emphasis of the behavioral and social scientists, coupled with the changed political climate of the 1950s, wrought a subtle change in historical

---

3. Charles A. Beard and Mary R. Beard, *The Rise of American Civilization,* vol. 2, *The Industrial Era* (New York: The Macmillan Company, 1927), pp. 566-733; and Frederick Lewis Allen, *Only Yesterday: An Informal History of the Nineteen Twenties* (New York: Harper & Row, Publishers, 1931), pp. 20-21, 95-96.

Samuel Eliot Morison and Henry Steele Commager in a popular textbook, first written in 1930 and revised in 1936-37, 1942, and in subsequent years, called prohibition the "most notable of all reforms" of the progressive generation. Samuel Eliot Morison and Henry Steele Commager, *The Growth of the American Republic,* 3rd ed. rev. (New York: Oxford University Press, Inc., 1942), p. 376. John D. Hicks, *A Short History of American Democracy* (Boston: Houghton Mifflin Company, 1943), pp. 651-52, saw women's suffrage and prohibition as companion reforms that rested on the police power of the state "to do whatever might be necessary to promote the health, happiness, and morality of its citizens."

Mary R. Beard, in 1931, advanced what might be termed a bio-cultural interpretation of the role of women in the evolution of human society. Fifteen years later she offered an intellectual history of women's contributions to civilization. The books were diffuse, somewhat discursive, and frequently disorganized. Few historians emulated her efforts or explored her intriguing ideas. See Mary R. Beard, *On Understanding Women* (London: Longmans, Green and Co., 1931) and *Woman as Force in History: A Study in Traditions and Realities* (New York: The Macmillan Company, 1946).

For information on how textbook writers have viewed these issues, see Helen Nichols Merritt, "Certain Social Movements as Reflected in United States History Textbooks" (thesis, New York University, 1952) and Janice Law Trecker, "Women in U.S. History High School Textbooks," *Social Education* 35 (March 1971): 249-60, 338.

For a critique of recent historical works, see Ruth Rosen, "Sexism in History, or, Writing Women's History Is a Tricky Business," *Journal of Marriage and the Family* 33 (August 1971): 541-44.

4. For the evaluation of the political behavior of women, see Paul F. Lazarsfeld et al., *The People's Choice,* 3rd ed. (New York: Columbia University Press, 1968); Harold F. Gosnell, *Democracy, the Threshold of Freedom* (New York: The Ronald Press Company, 1948); V. O. Key, Arnold W. Green, and Eleanor Melnick, "What Has Happened to the Feminist Movement," in *Studies in Leadership: Leadership and Democratic Action,* Alvin W. Gouldner, ed. (New York: Harper & Row, Publishers, 1950), pp. 277-302.

For the sociological approach to prohibition, see Alfred McClung Lee, "Techniques of Social Reform: An Analysis of the New Prohibitionist Drive," *American Sociological Review* 9

interpretations. In the influential writings of historian Richard Hofstadter, prohibition was written off as one of the worst tendencies in American life, "mere
peevishness," and "a low-grade substitute for the old Social Gospel enthusiasms."
"We cannot, however, quite ignore the diagnostic significance of prohibitionism,"
Hofstadter wrote. "For Prohibition was a pseudo-reform, a pinched, parochial
substitute for reform which had a widespread appeal to a certain type of
[Yankee-Protestant] crusading mind." If the prohibitionist was a fearful rustic
trying to overcome the evils of the immigrant-dominated city, the suffragist was
a hopeless utopian or an urban idealist who was anxious about loss of social
status and about helping immigrants find humane social services in an impersonal
urban environment.[5]

Hofstadter's disciples pushed his premises to their logical conclusions.
Joseph Gusfield provided an elaborate analysis of the temperance movement in
terms of the concept of status politics. Under the pressure of status anxiety, the
temperance advocates had gradually shifted from persuasion (assimilative reform)
to restriction (coercive reform). Prohibition in its twentieth-century manifesta-
tion was seen as a fundamentalist response to change.[6] Andrew Sinclair probed
the psychology of the prohibitionist. He found that "Prohibition, an extreme
measure, forced its extremes on its supporters and its enemies." Extremists
alienated moderate supporters and worked out their bigoted frustrations on
others. "Rollin Kirby's famous caricatures of the prohibitionist as a beak-nosed,
top-hatted, etiolated, black stringbean, carrying an umbrella, seemed to be true,"
he concluded, "once the fanaticism of the victorious drys was revealed."[7]

Alan P. Grimes applied similar techniques to the granting of women's
suffrage in Wyoming, Colorado, Utah, and Idaho in the late nineteenth century.
He saw the western movement for women's suffrage not as a liberal development
but as a revival of Puritanism, an attempt by white Anglo-Saxon Protestants to
impose their morality on an increasingly urban and immigrant nation in order to

(February 1944): 65–77; Anne Roe, "A Survey of Alcohol Education in Elementary and
High Schools in the United States," Scientific Monthly 60 (January 1945): 51–54; Carney
Landis and Jane Cushman, "The Relation of National Prohibition to Mental Disease,"
Scientific Monthly 61 (December 1945): 469-73, reprinted in Social Problems in America:
A Source Book, Alfred McClung Lee and Elizabeth Briant Lee, eds. (New York: Holt, Rine-
hart & Winston, Inc., 1949).

5. Richard Hofstadter, The Age of Reform: From Bryan to F.D.R. (New York: Alfred A.
Knopf, Inc., 1955), pp. 263, 287. For Hofstadter's debt to the social sciences, see Richard
Hofstadter, "History and the Social Sciences," in The Varieties of History, Fritz Stern, ed.
(New York: World Publishing Company, 1965); American History and the Social Sciences,
Edward N. Saveth, ed. (New York: The Free Press, 1964); and Seymour M. Lipset and
Richard Hofstadter, Sociology and History: Methods (New York: Basic Books, Inc.,
Publishers, 1968).

6. Joseph R. Gusfield, Symbolic Crusade: Status Politics and the American Temperance
Movement (Urbana: University of Illinois Press, 1963).

7. Andrew Sinclair, Prohibition: The Era of Excess (Boston: Little, Brown and Company,
1962), pp. 24, 401-2. For a critique of Sinclair's views, see S. J. Mennell, "Prohibition: A
Sociological View," Journal of American Studies 3 (December 1969): 159-75.

restore their lost prestige and power. In short, women's suffrage was a nativist movement supported by men for essentially conservative purposes.[8]

After four decades of scholarly treatment, the historical evaluation of prohibition and women's suffrage had gone full circle. The newer interpretations had come down on the side of H. L. Mencken rather than on that of Mark Sullivan. The argument was back to its starting point. Indeed, there was evidence that the cycle was about to start over again. But the debate was trapped in the categories and assumptions of the 1920s. Either the prohibitionists were bluenose Puritans and redneck rural bigots or they were sincere, albeit misguided, reformers whose pet panaceas had run aground on the stubborn shoals of human personality and perversity. Either the suffragists were busybody "Aunt Sallys" in league with reactionary elements or they were crusaders for human rights smashing the last restraints to full freedom for half of the population. Neither the "progressive interpretation" nor the Hofstadter school had challenged the underlying assumption of the debate that the categories themselves were valid.[9]

If students are to achieve any fresh insights into the significance of women's suffrage and prohibition in American history, and if textbook writers are to formulate a new consensus on these topics, then the assumptions made in the traditional cycle of historical interpretations must be challenged. Faced with similar problems with other topics, some American historians have been turning to a revised version of an older historical technique, the comparative method. By comparing American experiences with those of other countries, or by viewing American developments as integral parts of general movements in western civilization or in world history, the comparative method attempts to break the intellectual isolation of American historiography.

The dual benefits of comparative history—to explain uniqueness and to emphasize similarities—have not always been fully realized by American historians. On balance, comparative history has been used mainly to reexamine the uniqueness of American experience. This one-sided use of the comparative method springs from an overreliance on a parallel model of analysis. That is, American experience is still studied in self-contained isolation and then compared to the experience of other countries.[10]

---

8. Alan P. Grimes, *The Puritan Ethic and Woman Suffrage* (New York: Oxford University Press, Inc., 1967), Chapters 1 and 6.

9. For example, James H. Timberlake, *Prohibition and the Progressive Movement, 1900–1920* (Cambridge, Mass.: Harvard University Press, 1966), revived the argument that prohibition, as an integral part of the progressive movement, drew on the same moral idealism, belief in science and efficiency, and faith in middle-class democracy as other progressive, humanitarian reforms. Indeed, Timberlake's approach was essentially old-fashioned, and the book could just as well have been written in 1922 as 1962. As Stanley M. Elkins has noted in his famous study of slavery in American life, American historiography has a tendency toward repetitive interpretations that never break out of their initial formulations. See Stanley M. Elkins, *Slavery: A Problem in American Institutional and Intellectual Life* (New York: Grosset & Dunlap, Inc., 1963), Chapter 1.

10. For criticism of the use of the comparative method in recent American history, see Richard P. McCormick, review of C. Vann Woodward, ed., *The Comparative Approach to*

The comparative method can be used to explain *both* uniqueness and similarity if an interactive model of research is used. In order to accomplish this objective, linked factors must be identified, cultural differences noted, semantic nuances (changes in the meaning of key words) clarified, and basic terms clearly defined.

Linked factors are historical developments that are causally interrelated. That is, two factors, such as the women's suffrage and prohibition movements, influence each other as well as impinge on a third factor, such as political structures. Therefore, while the similarity of one country's experience to that of another may be related to the common presence of both factors, the uniqueness of its experience may be caused by the interaction of these factors with each other within that particular cultural context.

The reason that the same linked factors can interact differently in changed cultural settings is that attitudes, behavior, and meanings are not universally constant or uniform. Thus, social scientists have discovered that "the way people comport themselves when they are drunk is determined not by alcohol's toxic assault upon the seat of moral judgment, conscience, or the like, but by what their society makes of an imparts to them concerning the state of drunkenness." Drunkenness is not simply a physiological state but is also a learned social role, a temporary suspension of certain social rules or expectations. An awareness of the fact that "drunken" behavior varies with cultural expectations can help to explain variable responses to temperance ideas.[11]

Similarly, the same words do not have identical connotations in different

---

American History (New York: Basic Books, Inc., Publishers, 1968), in *American Historical Review* 74 (February 1969): 1971-72; Carl N. Degler, "Comparative History: An Essay Review," *The Journal of Southern History* 34 (August 1968): 425-30; Oscar Handlin, review of Seymour Lipset, *The First New Nation* (New York: Basic Books, Inc., Publishers, 1963) in *American Historical Review* 70 (October 1964): pp. 180-82; and Louis Hartz, "Comparative Studies in American History: Comments," *Comparative Studies in Society and History: An International Journal* 5 (April 1963): 279-84.

For clarification of the comparative method, see Cyril E. Black, *The Dynamics of Modernization: A Study in Comparative History* (New York: Harper & Row, Publishers, 1966), Chapter 2; William Sewell, Jr., "Marc Bloch and the Logic of Comparative History," *History and Theory* 6 (1967): 208-18; Arthur L. Kalleberg, "The Logic of Comparison: A Methodological Note on the Comparative Study of Political Systems," *World Politics* 19 (October 1966): 69-82; and C. Vann Woodward, ed., *The Comparative Approach to American History* (New York: Basic Books, Inc., Publishers, 1968), Chapter 24; Arend Lijphart, "Comparative Politics and the Comparative Method," *American Political Science Review* 65 (September 1971): 682-93.

On the emergence of a common world culture based on world trade and industrialization, urbanization, specialization of function, social mobility, and secularization, see *The Institutions of Advanced Societies,* Arnold Rose, ed. (Minneapolis: University of Minnesota Press, 1958), pp. 26-29. For a counterargument, that western culture is a deviation from a common human pattern, see Jan Romein, "The Common Human Pattern: Origin and Scope of Historical Theories," *Journal of World History* 4 (1958): 449 ff., or W. F. Wertheim, *East-West Parallels: Sociological Approaches to Modern Asia* (Chicago: Quadrangle Books, Inc., 1964), Chapter 1.

11. Craig MacAndrew and Robert B. Edgerton, *Drunken Comportment: A Social Explanation* (Chicago: Aldine Publishing Company, 1969), p. 165. See also Margaret J. Sargent, "A

cultural contexts even at the same time in history. For example, the phrase "emancipation of women" might, in American history in the nineteenth century, refer to the restriction of the husband's legal control over the wife's property while, in Indian history at the same time, the phrase might be used to describe attempts to eliminate *suttee* (immolation of a widow on the funeral pyre of her husband) or *purdah* (seclusion of women from public view).

Since terms can have differing referents, precise definitions are necessary to enhance historical comparisons and minimize confusions. In this book the following definitions will be used. By *temperance* is meant any attempt to voluntarily reduce or minimize one's own consumption of alcoholic beverages and to convince others to do the same. *Teetotalism* or *total abstinence* is a more limited form of temperance in which one pledges not to drink any alcoholic beverage and to convince others to obey the same rule. The issuance of a *license* to sell alcoholic beverages is a method of controlling the vendors while *local option* refers to the delegation of authority to grant licenses to local units of government. *Prohibition* is the forbidding by law of the manufacture, transportation, or sale of alcoholic beverages (except under limited, controlled circumstances). A *prohibitionist*, therefore, is one who would use the coercive power of the state to secure compliance while a temperance advocate would rely on voluntary abstinence.

Similarly, a *suffragist* is one who advocates extending the right to vote to women. A *women's rights advocate* is one who would make changes in the legal, educational, economic, or judicial system so as to enhance, primarily, the civil, property, and political rights of women. Behind every proposal for women's rights there stands an image of what woman's position in society ought to be. These images sum up ideas about sexual roles and identities, social relations, and concepts of self. Historically, these images have ranged along a continuum between two points: orthodoxy and feminism. The orthodox image at any point in time is the socially accepted definition of woman's "place," "sphere," or "destiny." The feminist image is that projected by writers, artists, or activists to delineate an autonomous selfhood. It is a self-defining process that usually operates in negation or extension of the current orthodoxy. Not everyone who advocates a change in women's rights or position is a feminist, therefore, because such a person may be prompted by an orthodox image of woman's place. Since the content of orthodoxy is inherently dynamic over time, today's feminism may be tomorrow's orthodoxy (or today's orthodoxy may be yesterday's feminism). Since the feminist seeks changes in psychological outlook, sociological mores, and public attitudes, there is a natural affinity between feminism and imaginative art, literature, and education.[12]

Cross-Cultural Study of Attitudes and Behavior towards Alcohol and Drugs," *British Journal of Sociology* 22 (March 1971): 83–96.

12. For an excellent discussion of key terms *in the American context,* see Gerda Lerner, "Women's Rights and American Feminism," *The American Scholar* 40 (Spring 1971): 235–48.

    For the orthodox image of woman in the nineteenth century, see Barbara Welter,

The classic feminism of the nineteenth and early twentieth centuries was highly individualistic. It rested on the romantic notion that woman's true destiny was to fulfill her own potential. The neo-feminism of the late twentieth century is more group oriented. Woman's true consciousness is achieved when she sees herself as a member of a disadvantaged group. Her identity lies in her identification with her primary referent group—her "sisters." Where the public official may be willing to view women as an unused resource, the neo-feminist sees women as an oppressed class.[13]

Significantly, while the nineteenth-century feminist used the term "emancipation," the twentieth-century neo-feminist uses the term "liberation." The word "emancipation" was borrowed from the lexicon of abolitionism. It implied release from above; either the master or some superior legal power freed the slave. Abolitionists discountenanced slave revolts (forceful self-seized freedom). On the other hand, "liberation" is a term borrowed from the vocabulary of nationalism, anti-colonialism, and revolution. It implies that a subjugated group achieves self-determination through its own efforts. To read twentieth-century meanings into nineteenth-century words is to invite misunderstanding.[14]

In similar fashion, the terms "radical" and "reformer" must be defined with care. In every society there is a gap between what it professes (its institutionalized core values) and what it practices. The radical, seeing this gap, rejects the institutionalized values and projects a rhetorical alternative (usually a negation of prevailing values). The reformer, on the other hand, accepts the basic values of his society and seeks to narrow the gap between profession and practice by an appropriate plan of political action, institutional change, or intellectual innovation. Using these definitions, feminists, women's rights advocates, teetotalers, and prohibitionists can be evaluated in light of the institutionalized values *of their own societies*. What may be a reformist stance in one country may be regarded as radical in another.[15]

The theme of this book is that the "woman question" and the "temperance question" of the nineteenth and early twentieth centuries were aspects of the debates on the meaning of equality and the nature of democracy. The starting point for a comparative analysis of these developments, therefore, must be an examination of the concepts of equality and democracy in various countries at the beginning of the nineteenth century.

"The Cult of True Womanhood: 1820–1860," *American Quarterly* 18 (Summer 1966): 151–74.

13. Kate Millett, *Sexual Politics* (New York: Doubleday & Company, Inc., 1970), p. 136; Judith Hole and Ellen Levine, *Rebirth of Feminism* (Chicago: Quadrangle Books, Inc., 1971), pp. 21 and 137–52.

14. For the abolitionist content of terms, see Aileen S. Kraditor, *Means and Ends in American Abolitionism: Garrison and His Critics on Strategy and Tactics, 1834–1850* (reprint ed. New York: Vintage Books, 1970), pp. 5, 26–29. For the socialist and new-left connotations of current terms, see Roberta Salper, ed., *Female Liberation: History and Current Politics* (New York: Alfred A. Knopf, Inc., 1972), pp. 169–84.

15. Ross E. Paulson, *Radicalism and Reform: The Vrooman Family and American Social Thought, 1837–1937* (Lexington: University of Kentucky Press, 1968), Chapter 1.

The meaning of equality for a particular society can be determined by examining the interrelationship of its intellectual life (its ideas, ideals, and aspirations) and its social structure, legal codes, and institutions. To what extent does the legal code institutionalize the professed ideals of the society? To what extent does the social structure (class and status groupings, family patterns, and so forth) reinforce the values expressed in intellectual life and legal codes?

The meaning of democracy for a particular society can likewise be determined by studying the interrelationship between its social structure and political institutions and by noting the terms of political debate and the tactics of pressure groups and parties. To what extent are social divisions reflected in political divisions? Is democracy defined primarily in its social, economic, or political connotations? Do the tactics and maneuvers of political groups affirm or deny in practice the procedural or ethical implications of formal democracy?

With such questions in mind, the countries to be studied in this book can be arranged on a continuum according to the extent to which they institutionalized equality and democracy. Such a framework will not only facilitate accurate comparisons; it will also clarify the potential roles of radicals and reformers in their countries. At one end of the continuum would be England and the United States; at the other end, India, Turkey, and Russia. In between, Australia and New Zealand, France, the Scandinavian countries, and Germany. Equality in this study is considered under four aspects: legal, intellectual, economic, and ethical. Democracy is measured primarily by the extent of representation or participation in political processes as reflected in legal and constitutional, or in institutional, relationships. That is, only formal political democracy is considered, and questions about popular support of or acquiescence in authoritarian systems are laid aside. The role of informal democracy or the role of influential pressure groups is dealt with only where it is pertinent to the issue at hand.[16]

In summary, the comparative method offers the student and the historian the opportunity to gain fresh insights into old material, to formulate new research questions and categories, and to achieve a more subtle and discriminating understanding of historical experience. The opportunities offered by the comparative method are significant: (1) to clarify the meaning of key words or concepts, (2) to study linked factors in diverse settings, (3) to isolate cultural differences, and (4) to define basic terms and to utilize them in understanding ideational and institutional relationships.

This book, which relies on the comparative method, is primarily concerned with understanding the women's suffrage and prohibition movements, in studying them as linked factors held together by the Victorian ethic, and in viewing them as part of the process of modernization.

---

16. For recent debates on the question of representation as a criterion for political democracy, see J. Roland Pennock and John W. Chapman, eds., *Representation: Yearbook of the American Society for Political and Legal Philosophy: Nomos X* (Chicago: Atherton Press, Inc., 1968), particularly the essays by J. Roland Pennock, Eric A. Nordlinger, and David E. Apter.

1

Equality in a
Comparative Setting

THE WOMEN'S RIGHTS QUESTION
IN THE UNITED STATES, 1830s AND 1840s

In July 1839, antislavery newspapers in the United States carried a call from
English abolitionists for all "friends of the slave" to attend a World's Anti-Slavery
Convention in London the following year. Several antislavery organizations in the
United States elected women delegates, among them Ann Green Phillips, wife of
abolitionist Wendell Phillips, and Lucretia Mott, a Hicksite (or reform) Quaker.
When the convention opened in June 1840, the women delegates were denied
their credentials and were forced to sit in the visitors' gallery. Lucretia Mott tried
in vain to organize a parallel women's meeting, but her efforts met with rebuffs
from orthodox English Quakers and with indifference from most Englishwomen.
Wendell Phillips was defeated in his attempt to place a protest against the exclusion of women delegates into the official minutes. William Lloyd Garrison, the
militant abolitionist who had refused to take his seat at the convention in protest
over the exclusion of the women, was called to task at a post-convention tea for
speaking on women's rights, temperance, universal suffrage, and other touchy
issues.[1]

By every account the Americans encountered hostility or indifference
whenever they raised the women's rights question. The significant questions—
particularly for comparative history—are these: Why were some Americans more
willing to respond to feminist views and women's rights views in the 1830s and
1840s than were their English counterparts? Why were Englishwomen unable to
exploit ideas of women's rights in the same fashion as the Americans were able
to exploit them? How did the understanding of equality in each country influence their response to these ideas? Why did organized efforts to enhance

---

1. Douglas H. Maynard, "The World's Anti-Slavery Convention of 1840," *Mississippi Valley
Historical Review* 42 (December 1960): 452-71; Elizabeth Cady Stanton, Susan B. Anthony,
and Matilda Joslyn Gage, *History of Woman Suffrage* (Rochester, N.Y.: Charles Mann, 1887),
Chapter 3; John L. Thomas, *The Liberator: William Lloyd Garrison* (Boston: Little, Brown
and Company, 1963), pp. 295-97.

women's legal position in society take root in the United States and flounder in England and France in the 1840s and 1850s? Finally, what was the impact of these developments in other parts of the world?

At first glance, the answer to the question of why the American abolition-ist responded to feminist ideas and ideas of women's rights seems obvious. Was not the United States the most egalitarian of nations? Did not its revolutionary traditions contain strong egalitarian ideals? Had not the eminent French writer, Alexis de Tocqueville, declared after his visit to the United States that the country was characterized not only by a functioning political democracy but by a pleasing "equality of conditions" as well? Should not the abolitionist, who was most sensitive to the contradictions between the fact of slavery and ideal of equality, be the first to recognize the bondage of women to custom and law? In short, was not the United States simply more egalitarian than contemporary England?

Historian Lee Benson has suggested that, in order to determine the egalitar-ian character of any society, one must carefully distinguish between four different aspects of equality: "1) equality as a *legal* condition; 2) equality as a *value* gov-erning the way men ought to regard other men; 3) equality as an *opportunity* to obtain the 'impersonal' things valued in the society (i.e., wealth, status, power, culture, not personal beauty or artistic talent); 4) equality as a *distributional condition* (i.e., a roughly equal distribution among generational peers of the im-personal things valued in the society)."[2] On these criteria, how egalitarian was the United States in the 1830s and 1840s?

The American legal system was subjected to a number of conflicting ten-sions during the pre-Civil War era. These conflicts bore directly upon the question of the meaning of equality in American law. On the one hand, a number of influ-ential judges and commentators (for example, Chancellor Kent and Justice Storey) advocated the primacy of the English common law over American statute law. They argued that English legal principles and precedents constituted the founda-tion of American jurisprudence. They encouraged the introduction of the equity court system. Equity rules (assumed to be the guidelines of reason or the im-peratives of justice) decreased the role of juries in civil suits and increased the role of judges. The net effect of this emphasis on the common law and equity was to enhance the status of the legal profession, to institutionalize certain cases of inequality, and to minimize the "democratic" tendencies of juries and legis-latures. The law was a matter for experts, not for laymen. The security of property (and, hence, of distributional inequality) lay in the indecisiveness of the law and the unhindered discretion of the judge.

On the other hand, advocates of legal codification and judicial reform (Edward Livingston, Robert Rantoul, and David Dudley Field) argued that the traditions of monarchical England embodied in the common law were hardly

---

2. Lee Benson, "Middle Period Historiography: What Is To Be Done?" in *American History: Retrospect and Prospect,* George A. Billias and Gerald N. Grob, eds. (New York: The Free Press, 1971), p. 188.

suited to the needs of republican America. The principles of the Revolution should be the legal and logical basis for a systematic codification of the law. The procedures should be simplified. The codes should be rational, democratic (in the sense that they could be understood by anyone), and egalitarian (in the sense that one code would apply to all). Although they achieved some victories, the advocates of codification lost out in the long run to the forces of the common law tradition.

The spread of common law doctrines had important implications for the status of women. Blackstone, the English authority on the common law, treated women as little better than children and mental defectives. Where legislative enactment was silent, the legal profession read Blackstone into the texture of American law. At the same time, the growth of equity courts took over jurisdiction of annulments of marriages, divorce cases, and probate of wills. Equity courts allowed some women to escape the harsher aspects of common law legalism, but they were too expensive and cumbersome a remedy for widespread use. In summary, in the eyes of the law, all (white) men were entitled to equal justice but women, slaves, Indians, children, and idiots did not stand on the same level with them.[3]

While equality may have been becoming less of a *legal* reality in the 1830s and 1840s, it was becoming more of an ideological *value* and political goal. In a case study of New York politics, historian Lee Benson has noted that:

"By 1834, the New York Whigs and Democrats had committed themselves irrevocably to a social order based on political equality (for white men). But the Whigs translated the post-1815 egalitarian impulse into a philosophy of the *positive* liberal state, the Democrats translated it into a philosophy of the *negative* liberal state. Thus when we focus upon political economy and social legislation, we find that the parties actually stood for competing concepts of liberalism. When we focus ·upon certain types of 'moral legislation' (for example, Sunday laws, temperance), however, we find that the 'conservative-liberal' dichotomy did tend to exist."[4]

---

3. Perry Miller, *The Life of the Mind in America: From the Revolution to the Civil War* (New York: Harcourt Brace Jovanovich, Inc., 1965), Book 2; René David and John E. C. Brierly, *Major Legal Systems in the World Today: An Introduction to the Comparative Study of Law* (New York: The Free Press, 1968), pp. 335–59; Arthur M. Schlesinger, Jr., *The Age of Jackson* (Boston: Little, Brown and Company, 1945), pp. 329–33.

On the role of equity in women's rights, see Mary R. Beard, *Woman as Force in History: A Study in Traditions and Realities* (New York: The Macmillan Company, 1946), Chapters 5 and 6; Leo Kanowitz, *Women and the Law: The Unfinished Revolution* (Albuquerque: University of New Mexico Press, 1969), pp. 38–40; and Eleanor Flexner, *Century of Struggle: The Woman's Rights Movement in the United States* (Cambridge, Mass.: Harvard University Press, 1959), p. 346 n.2.

For the comparative question of the extent to which legal codes embody the ideals of a culture, see Richard A. Falk, "The Relation of Law to Culture, Power, and Justice," *Ethics* 72 (October 1961): 12–27.

4. Lee Benson, *The Concept of Jacksonian Democracy: New·York as a Test Case* (Princeton, N.J.: Princeton University Press, 1961), p. 86. Benson believed that generalizations based on New York were representative of trends elsewhere, particularly in the North.

The state was regarded as liberal (rather than paternal) because it sought to liberate men from the political and economic heritage of mercantilism and to set them free to pursue their own and society's welfare either with (positive) or without (negative) the help of the state.

The equality sought by the politically active citizen was thus rather restricted in concept. Such citizens sought primarily economic opportunity, a chance to exploit the resources of the new land or to enter business on favorable terms. Political equality was restricted to free, white males.

A few thinkers, humanitarian reformers, and abolitionists explored the wider meanings of moral equality or intellectual opportunity. Whether prompted by a rationalism lingering from the Enlightenment, by the religious fervor of evangelical revivalism, or by a romantic belief in human perfectability, the reformers operated out of a central conviction. "Salvation, however variously defined, lay open to everyone. Sin was voluntary: men were not helpless and depraved by nature but free agents and potential powers for good. Sin could be reduced to selfish preferences of individuals, and social evils, in turn, to collective sins which, once acknowledged, could be rooted out."[5] The equal worth of each individual in the sight of God, the potentiality of each converted soul, the denial of that common humanity in slavery—these were some of the glimpses of equality as a value that they proclaimed.

For the broadest spectrum of women, however, the question of equality was more a matter of economic freedom or opportunity for themselves than it was a question of the moral status of slave women or of the legal status of a married woman's property. In the United States economic opportunity for women varied regionally and even cyclically with the state of the economy as a whole. In New England, where the cotton textile mills recruited seasonal or short-term labor, a marked change occurred in the decades between 1830 and 1850. The proportion of women in the labor force in the cotton mills declined as newer, faster machines brought men into the mills as operatives. At the same time the source of women shifted from young, unmarried, educated "Yankee" farm girls of the middle class to older, married, uneducated immigrants who constituted a permanent working class.

At the same time, the proportion of women in teaching, bookbinding and bookmaking, needlework, and the tobacco industry rose while it declined in woolen and silk mills, shoe binding, paper making, and printing. Thus, while the number of women in industry was increasing, the range of opportunity was being narrowed somewhat as mechanization, intensification (speed-up of pace), and specialization took some tasks not only out of the home but out of the hands of women workers entirely.[6]

---

5. John L. Thomas, "Romantic Reform in America, 1815-1865," in *Intellectual History in America: Contemporary Essays on Puritanism, The Enlightenment, and Romanticism,* Cushing Strout, ed. (New York: Harper & Row, Publishers, 1968), p. 195.

6. Edith Abbott, "The History of Industrial Employment of Women in the United States: An Introductory Study," *Journal of Political Economy* 14 (October 1906): 480-90; Edith

In the rest of the North, the march of industrialism followed the path of transportation innovation, availability of water power, and the maturing of post-frontier economies. In the South, while the plantation wife was expected to be mistress of all skills and social graces, most of the white women on the small, marginal farms tended to be restricted to traditional agricultural pursuits or to handicraft employment as a result of the slave system.[7]

The restriction of opportunity to certain industries and professions had important implications for women and their relative position in the social structure. Recent scholarship has challenged de Tocqueville's famous observation that the United States in the 1830s was characterized by an "equality of conditions." Extremes of wealth and poverty, restrictions on social mobility related to lack of education or credit, the emergence of political and social elites, and a hardening of class lines—all of these are said to have characterized American society. The

---

Abbott, "Harriet Martineau and the Employment of Women in 1836," *Journal of Political Economy* 14 (December 1906): 614-25; Edith Abbott, "History of the Employment of Women in the American Cotton Mills," *Journal of Political Economy* 16 (November 1908): 602-16; 680-92; 17 (January 1909): 19-33. In this series of articles, Edith Abbott was primarily concerned with refuting the old canards that women workers "drove men out of jobs" and that the proportion of women employed in industry rose dramatically between 1870 and 1900. Her counter assertions, that men drove women out of certain industrial trades, particularly in the cotton mills, and that the statistics for 1870 were misleading rested on an analysis of census statistics (interpreted as proportions rather than aggregates) that was somewhat laborious. The important point demonstrated by her analysis is the narrowing of options for those who sought economic independence through employment rather than supplementary income for a short term.

Gerda Lerner has argued that this shrinking of opportunities for women, coming at a time of increased opportunity related to extended political and economic options for men, created a sense of status loss or "status displacement in an educated, white, middle-class elite" that led to an organized women's rights movement. Theories of status anxiety involve such complicated problems of historical verification that they have been increasingly abandoned in favor of more tentative, but more empirical, multifactor explanations. See Gerda Lerner, "Women's Rights and American Feminism," *The American Scholar* 40 (Spring 1971): 239; William R. Hutchison, "Cultural Strain and Protestant Liberalism," *The American Historical Review* 76 (April 1971): 386-90; Peter G. Filene, "An Obituary for 'The Progressive Movement,'" *American Quarterly* 22 (Spring 1970): 20-34.

William R. Taylor and Christopher Lasch sought to explain the "restlessness" of American women in the 1830s in terms of the loss of economic and educational functions by the family, the impact of migration on the family, and the failure of affection to maintain the social cohesion of the family. Their argument rested on assumptions that have been challenged by other students of the American family. See William R. Taylor and Christopher Lasch, "Two 'Kindred Spirits': Sorority and Family in New England, 1839-1846," *New England Quarterly* 36 (March 1963): 23-41; Edward N. Saveth, "The Problem of American Family History," *American Quarterly* 21 (Summer 1969): 311-29. In the absence of a consistent theory of family history and in face of the lack of substantial agreement among American historians, family structure has not been used here as a variable in the understanding of the meaning of equality in America. All students of this subject are awaiting the appearance of Carl N. Degler, *Women and the Family,* in the Two Centuries of American Life Series edited by Harold M. Hyman and Leonard W. Levy (New York: The Dial Press).

7. Flexner, *Century of Struggle,* pp. 52-65; William R. Taylor, *Cavalier and Yankee: the Old South and American National Character* (New York: George Braziller, Inc., 1961); Anne Firor Scott, *The Southern Lady: From Pedestal to Politics, 1830-1930* (Chicago: University of Chicago Press, 1970), Chapter 2.

simple fact was that in any social ranking based on earned income, women were placed at a disadvantage. Since they were paid less for an equal amount of service or labor, single women could not rise individually in tandem with male coworkers and married women could not contribute proportionally to the maintenance or elevation of their family's class position. In the "distribution among generational peers of the impersonal things valued in the society," women fared less than equally.[8]

In summary, in a government whose leaders boasted that it had established equality before the law, women confronted a creeping inequality in common law and a cumbersome remedy in equity. In an era of political egalitarianism that exalted equality of economic opportunity, some women faced a narrowing of economic options and unequal rewards for work. In a society that prided itself on its image of "equality of conditions" but lived easily with an extended social structure, women found themselves, and their families, at a disadvantage in translating their income into social standing commensurate with their birth rank. In the face of evangelical revivals of Protestant religion that proclaimed a universality of salvation and a uniformity of moral worth in the eyes of God, some men continued to hold black men and women slaves in body and spirit. The one social phenomenon that had caught up all these contradictions and set the stage for the "woman question" in America was the abolitionist campaign.

The antislavery crusade was thus the seedbed of the women's rights movement in the United States. It linked together white women and free Negro women with a common background and interest. Mostly Quakers and Congregationalists, or other evangelical Protestants, they organized their own female antislavery societies, defied anti-Negro prejudice, braved hostile mobs, supported the underground railroad, and, in 1837, held their own National Female Anti-Slavery convention. From their ranks emerged some of the first and most eloquent advocates of women's rights.

Foremost among these early champions of women's rights were Sarah and Angelina Grimké. Born in the South, the sisters freed their slaves, converted to Quakerism, and gravitated to the North where they became itinerant preachers for the antislavery cause.[9] When criticized by clerical opponents and women

---

8. For a summary (and critique) of recent scholarship on American social structure in the 1830s and 1840s, see Edward Pessen, *Jacksonian America: Society, Personality, and Politics* (Homewood, Ill.: Dorsey Press, 1969), Chapter 3; Lee Benson, "Middle Period Historiography: What Is to Be Done?" in *American History: Retrospect and Prospect,* George A. Billias and Gerald N. Grob, eds. (New York: The Free Press, 1971), pp. 174-90. An example of the plight of the professional woman is provided by a study of American education in 1850 by a Swedish observer. In Massachusetts in 1850 he found 2437 male teachers and 5238 females. The men were paid an average monthly salary of $25.02; the women were paid $8.12. And Massachusetts was regarded as one of the most progressive states in education at that time! P. A. Siljeström, *Educational Institutions of the United States,* trans. Frederica Rowan (1853; reprint ed., New York: Arno Press, Inc., 1969), pp. 185-89.

9. Gerda Lerner, *The Grimké Sisters from South Carolina: Rebels Against Slavery* (Boston: Houghton Mifflin Company, 1967), Chapters 1-10; Eleanor Flexner, *Century of Struggle,* Chapters 2 and 3. Angelina Grimké wrote to Theodore Dwight Weld on August 12, 1837: ". . . we are placed very unexpectedly in a very trying situation, in the forefront of an

educators for departing from their "proper sphere" by speaking before mixed audiences of men and women, Angelina retorted:

"The investigation of the rights of the slave has led me to a better understanding of my own. I have found the Anti-Slavery cause to be the high school of morals in our land—the school in which *human rights* are more fully investigated, and better understood and taught, than in any other. Here a great fundamental principle is uplifted and illuminated. . . . Human beings have *rights,* because they are *moral* beings: the rights of *all* men grow out of their moral nature; and as all men have the same moral nature, they have essentially the same rights."[10]

From this premise, she drew the further inference that the mere accident of sex did not alter one's moral nature; therefore, men and women, as moral beings, had equal rights and duties, particularly within the antislavery ranks.

Another leading advocate of women's rights was Lucretia (Coffin) Mott, whose activities at the World's Anti-Slavery Convention have been noted briefly above. Saintly, dignified, and serene, her quiet countenance counterbalanced a rationalistic mind that was searching and acute. Born on Nantucket Island and nurtured in its sea-oriented community (where women could assume considerable responsibility while their whaling or sailing husbands were off on long voyages), she had been educated in the excellent Quaker Nine Partners School. She married James Mott in 1811 and settled in Philadelphia. Within a decade she was an acknowledged minister of the Religious Society of Friends. When the Philadelphia Yearly Meeting split in 1827 into Hicksite and Orthodox factions, the Motts somewhat reluctantly went with the Hicksite party. Lucretia Mott's role in defending the Hicksites earned the enmity of English Quakers, particularly in the influential London Meeting, and this fact accounts for some of the rebuffs that she received in 1840 at the World's Anti-Slavery Convention.

Recent research has shown that the Hicksites represented more rural, moderately comfortable, traditional, and past-oriented members while the Orthodox attracted more urban, wealthy, and future-oriented members of the Quaker community. Contrary to modern expectations, the Hicksites showed more reformist

---

entirely new contest—a contest for the *rights* of *woman* as a moral, intelligent and responsible being. . . . I cannot help feeling some regret that this sh'ld have come up *before* the Anti-Slavery question was settled, so fearful am I that it may injure that blessed cause, and then again I think this must be the Lord's time and therefore the *best* time, for it seems to have been brought about by a concatenation of circumstances over which we had no control." *Letters of Theodore Dwight Weld, Angelina Grimké Weld, and Sarah Grimké, 1822-1844,* Gilbert H. Barnes and Dwight L. Dumond, eds. (New York: Appleton-Century-Crofts, 1934), 1:415. Significantly, the Grimké sisters' brother, Thomas Grimké, had been a leading advocate of "scientific" legal codification. His religious conversion, belief in education, career in law, and untimely death profoundly influenced his sisters, particularly Sarah. All the themes of equality were united in their experience. See Perry Miller, *Life of the Mind,* pp. 246-49; Gerda Lerner, *The Grimké Sisters,* pp. 27-28, 110-11.

10. Angelina Grimké to Catherine E. Beecher, Letter XII, reprinted in *Up From the Pedestal: Selected Writings in the History of American Feminism,* Aileen S. Kraditor, ed. (Chicago: Quadrangle Books, Inc., 1968), p. 62.

tendencies because their orientation toward an earlier, simpler society put them in touch with Revolutionary equalitarian ideals that were being superseded by the formalistic, hierarchical aspirations of the Orthodox. Not surprisingly, therefore, Lucretia Mott's thought emphasized the natural rights of women in a fashion reminiscent of Enlightenment rationalism rather than of Transcendental romanticism or political individualism. Like the Grimké sisters, she grounded her case for women's rights in the moral and rational nature of woman and related it to the religious egalitarianism of the abolitionist cause.[11]

The public debate on the "woman question" sparked by the activity of the Grimké sisters came at a time when American antislavery groups were dividing over questions of tactics and the clashes of personalities. On the one side stood the "moral suasionists," led by William Lloyd Garrison, who believed that the abolition of slavery was primarily a religious matter to be achieved by individual repentance, reconciliation, and reconstruction of the social and political order. On the other side stood the "political actionists," led by James G. Birney, who believed that the abolition of slavery was a political question to be settled by group action through the political process, including a third party. Espousing women's rights because they were a corollary of his views, Garrison easily achieved the support of female abolitionists and took control of the strategic Massachusetts Anti-Slavery Society and the American Anti-Slavery Society. The anti-Garrisonians withdrew from the American Society in 1840, founded the rival American and Foreign Anti-Slavery Society, and warned their friends in England that Garrison would try to take over the World's Anti-Slavery Convention unless his female legions were disqualified.[12]

Garrison's identification with the woman question in the internal power struggles among the abolitionists, clerical suspicion of the Grimké sisters' activities, and Orthodox Quaker hostility to Lucretia Mott's Hicksite affiliation would account, then, for the opposition of some American and English *men* to the seating of the women delegates at the World's Anti-Slavery Convention. In addition, several explanations have been offered to explain why a distinct and articulate debate on, and organized concern for, the rights of women had emerged in the United States in the 1830s and why some American *women* had responded, even to the point of defying custom and convention: (1) the presence of economic opportunity (although accompanied by a narrowing of options); (2) the experience of self-government in religious, charitable, and antislavery societies; (3) the sense

---

11. Otelia Cromwell, *Lucretia Mott* (Cambridge, Mass.: Harvard University Press, 1958), Chapters 1-6; Robert W. Doherty, *The Hicksite Separation: A Sociological Analysis of Religious Schism in Early Nineteenth Century America* (New Brunswick, N.J.: Rutgers University Press, 1967). Doherty sees three distinct groups among the Hicksites: (1) traditionalists, who were rural in orientation, antimodern, and antiurban; (2) sectarians, who were urban, lower and middle class, and anxious about their status (James Mott is included in this group); and (3) liberals, who were interested in reform, free inquiry, and who believed in human perfectability.

12. John L. Thomas, *The Liberator*, Chapter 13; Aileen S. Kraditor, *Means and Ends in American Abolitionism: Garrison and His Critics on Strategy and Tactics, 1834-1850*, (reprint ed., New York: Vintage Books, 1970), Chapter 3.

of incongruity between increasing legal inequalities and a heightened emphasis on political democracy and economic opportunity; (4) the revival of "natural right" and "moral worth" varieties of egalitarianism in religious and abolitionist thought; and (5) the favorable role of women in certain evangelical Protestant and Quaker subcultures. It is time to turn to the question of the status of English*women* and the contemporary meaning of equality for their lives in order to judge their response to the 1840 World Anti-Slavery Convention incident in a comparative light.

WOMEN AND ENGLISH VALUES, 1800—1840

The same categories used above will be used to understand equality in England: legal, intellectual, economic, and social. Equality before the law had long been regarded as part of an Englishman's birthright. Englishmen were fond of contrasting the absence of any special status in law for their aristocracy with the juristic status of the French nobility. Tales of peers hung for crimes against commoners in violation of law were part of English folklore. True, special hunting laws, "privilege of peerage" (the right of a peer to demand a jury excluding commoners), and property ownership as a qualification for holding the office of justice of the peace favored the aristocracy; but, to the self-confident English chauvinist, such exceptions only proved the rule of equal status under law.

The difference between the supposed absence of privilege and the existence of legal equality was wider, however, in the early nineteenth century than the popular myth would allow. The number of capital offenses, particularly for crimes against property, had been multiplied in the late eighteenth century. Habeas corpus was periodically suspended, freedom of the press curtailed, and dissent repressed with force. Transportation to penal colonies and imprisonment for debt hung like a pall over English society in the early years of the new century. Then as now, the law bore most heavily on those who could least afford to defend themselves before it; cumbersome equity proceedings limited the effectiveness of chancery courts.[13]

Reform of the harsh penal code and overworked court system proceeded slowly in the 1820s and then accelerated in the 1830s. The number of capital offenses was reduced, obsolete statutes were repealed, and transportation of criminals (including female offenders) to Australia was abolished. New rules for chancery courts and the establishment of bankruptcy courts created a measure of equal justice for some litigants. Legal reform was complicated, however, by the fact that, while the law seldom used class as an explicit legal category, it frequently used religious belief. The pursuit of civil equality for Roman Catholics,

---

13. R. H. Tawney, *Equality* (New York: Harcourt Brace Jovanovich, Inc., 1931), pp. 107-8, 110, 118; Edward Palmer Thompson, *The Making of the English Working Class* (New York: Random House, Inc., 1964), Chapter 4 and pp. 182-83; A. V. Dicey, *Law and Public Opinion in England During the Nineteenth Century* (London: Macmillan and Co., Ltd., 1920), pp. 70-125.

Jews, Protestant dissenters, and freethinkers occupied considerable public attention and achieved some limited gains in spite of preferential status of the established Church of England. By 1840, an Englishman still faced the uncertainties of the largely judge-interpreted common law; England still lacked a formal civil code; and equity was still an expensive remedy for the defects of the common law. But some improvements had been made in the efficiency of the courts, if not always in the quality of justice.[14]

A woman's standing before the law depended primarily on her marital status, secondarily on her religious community, and indirectly on her class. An unmarried woman was assumed by the common law to be under the protection and control of either her father or another male relative. However, in equity rules a *femme sole* (woman not married) had certain property rights that the courts were bound to protect. Upon marriage, according to common law, she surrendered her property—indeed her legal existence—to her husband; nevertheless, through the use of trustees and exclusion clauses in equity, she could maintain some control over her own property. By act of Parliament in 1836 civil marriages outside either the state church or dissenting chapel were made possible by the appointment of registrars of births, marriages, and deaths, although divorce still required a special act of Parliament. A Custody of Infants Act in 1839 established a prima facie claim to custody of the children for the mother (provided she had not been proved an adulteress). But even these changes indicated that the legislators and judges were more concerned with maintaining a particular social hierarchy and in protecting property than in fostering equality per se.[15]

In the intellectual and political struggles of the period 1800 to 1840, the predominate values of the reigning "religion of inequality" (R. H. Tawney's

---

14. Dicey, *Law and Opinion*, pp. 126-210; E. L. Woodward, *The Age of Reform, 1815-1870* (London: Oxford University Press, 1939), pp. 451-54; and David Thomson, *England in the Nineteenth Century, 1815-1914* (Baltimore: Penguin Books, Inc., 1950), pp. 58-62. For the importance of legal categories in comparative law studies, see David and Brierly, *Major Legal Systems*, pp. 283-85.

The reformers of the English legal system were not guided by egalitarian principles as had been the advocates of codification in the United States. John Austin, who applied utilitarianism to the concept of law in a series of influential lectures in 1828-32, defined law in terms of superiority-inferiority relationships that made the law an expression of superiority rather than a codification of customary behavior (as the German historical school advocated) or of the dictates of reason (as the French equity advocates held). In the utilitarian heritage, hierarchy and not equality was held to be the essence of law. John Austin, "Lectures on Jurisprudence," par. 61-63, 91-96 in *Readings in Recent Political Philosophy*, Margaret Spahr, ed. (New York: The Macmillan Company, 1949), pp. 108-10.

15. Dicey, *Law and Opinion*, pp. 345-47, 371-86; R. Glynn Grylls, "Emancipation of Women," in *Ideas and Beliefs of the Victorians*, Harman Grisewood, ed. (New York: E. P. Dutton & Co., Inc., 1966), p. 258; Patricia Thomson, *The Victorian Heroine: A Changing Ideal, 1837-1873* (London: Oxford University Press, 1956), p. 87.

For the status of married women in English law see Sir Montague Lush, "Changes in the Law Affecting . . . Married Women," in *A Century of Law Reform* (London: Macmillan and Company, Ltd., 1901); Sir Montague Lush, *The Law of Husband and Wife Within the Jurisdiction of the Queen's Bench and Chancery Divisions* (London: Stevens and Sons, 1884); Tapping Reeve, *The Law of Baron and Femme*, 3rd ed. (Albany, N.Y.: W. Gould, Publisher, 1862).

phrase) were challenged in turn by the ideas of political radicalism (equal political representation), Owenite socialism (equal social status), and utilitarianism (equal political and economic opportunity).

The program of the political radicals remained remarkably consistent from the 1780s to the 1830s: annual Parliaments, universal manhood suffrage, voting by ballot, equal electoral districts, no monetary prerequisites for members of Parliament, and payment of parliamentary members. While these demands implied equal civic status for and greater sharing of power by the "working classes," they coexisted with working-class values of mutualism, communalism, and deference that limited their radical impact primarily to the political realm. Spurred on by the revolutions that swept Europe in 1830, the working-class radicals supported the agitation for reform of Parliament. But the Reform Bill of 1832 was carefully drawn to extend political franchise to the upper ranks of the middle class and to bring them into power in support of the traditional system of a hierarchy of communities and "interests." The demands of radicalism were reiterated in support of the 1837 People's Charter (or Chartism). The first draft of the People's Charter contained a provision for women's suffrage, but it was dropped on grounds of inexpediency. Chartism saw the vote as a political symbol of equality of citizenship and as a means of social control by the militant and self-conscious working class.[16]

If the political radicals were primarily concerned with the values of political equality, the followers of the pioneering socialist thinker, Robert Owen, were especially attracted to his ideas of social equality. In Owen's projected cooperative communities there would be no *personal* inequalities of rank or worth; all would be regarded as equally valuable members of the community regardless of function. "Owen saw the family as the main bastion of private property and the guardian of all those qualities of individualism and self-interest to which he was opposed"; consequently, he advocated marriage based on mutual affection rather than property relationships.[17] Two of his disciples, William Thompson and Anna Wheeler, asserted new rights for women, particularly in *An Appeal of One Half the Human Race, Women, Against the Pretensions of the Other Half, Men, to*

---

16. Thompson, *English Working Class,* Chapter 16; Julius West, *A History of the Chartist Movement* (Boston: Houghton Mifflin Company, 1920), Chapter 3.

The Reform Bill of 1832 reduced the number of "rotten boroughs," redistributed some seats, set the borough franchise uniformly at householders who paid rates (certain taxes) of £10 a year or over, and allowed county voters who had 40 shillings freehold, £10 copyhold, £50 leasehold, or £50 tenant-at-will to vote. A recent author argued: "For the men who drafted the relevant legislation of the 'thirties . . . [the traditional] vertical structured and hierarchically organized communities provided the essential frame of reference"; therefore, the reform bill was not consciously egalitarian or democratic in intent. D. C. Moore, "Political Morality in Mid-Nineteenth Century England: Concepts, Norms, Violations," *Victorian Studies* 13 (September 1969): 6. In some cases, the Reform Act of 1832 actually narrowed a previously broad franchise. See W. R. Ward rev. of Malcolm I. Thomis, *Politics and Society in Nottingham, 1785-1835* (Oxford: Basil Blackwell & Mott Ltd., 1969) in *Journal of Ecclesiastical History* 21 (July 1970): 276-77.

17. John F. C. Harrison, *Quest for the New Moral Order: Robert Owen and the Owenites in Britain and America* (New York: Charles Scribner's Sons, 1969), pp. 59-60.

Retain Them in Political, and Thence in Civil and Domestic Slavery (1825). Yet there was an unresolved tension in Owen's thought between his early paternalism and his egalitarianism of the 1820s. With the failure of his New Harmony colony he became increasingly paternalistic and sectarian, thus lessening his impact on the English scene.[18]

Somewhat between the political radicals, with their emphasis on political equality, and the Owenite socialists, with their concern for social equality, was a school of thinkers variously called the philosophic radicals or the utilitarians. Followers of the views of Jeremy Bentham, Adam Smith, and Robert Malthus, they accepted the necessity of political democracy but on their own grounds. Whereas the political radicals had based their case for democracy on natural rights (i.e., that men are born free and equal and ought to have equal rights in society), the philosophic radicals rested their argument for political democracy on natural equality (i.e., that every man is the best judge of his own interest and that his wants ought to count equally with those of others).[19] Extension of the vote was justified on utilitarian grounds—the happiness of the greatest number— and therefore was a matter of political expediency, not of absolute right.

Along with their utilitarian premises, the philosophic radicals believed in social inequality and a hierarchy of merit. Given a chance (in a condition of liberty), this true aristocracy of intellect and talent would contribute more to society's well-being than if its members were restricted by either the arrogance of power or the tyranny of (mass) ignorance. Given equality of economic opportunity (*laissez-faire*), society would benefit more from men's enlightened pursuit of their self-interests than from government restrictions upholding class privilege. The emphasis on liberty and *laissez-faire* implied a limited concept of equality of political and economic opportunity that was increasingly subordinated to an elitist view of the good society.[20]

By the 1830s political radicalism had been stymied by the piecemeal approach of the Reform Bill and the initial failure of Chartism. Owenite socialism was marked by the failure of its colonies, changes in its tactics, and its increasing sectarianism. The philosophic radicals read their de Tocqueville on the "tyranny of the majority," had second thoughts, and modified their earlier commitments to egalitarianism.

By the 1830s English feminism, too, had come to an intellectual impasse. The Enlightenment rationalism of Mary Wollstonecraft's *A Vindication of the*

---

18. Ibid., pp. 75-76; Thompson, *English Working Class,* pp. 779-806.

19. John Plamenatz, *Man and Society: A Critical Examination of Some Important Social and Political Theories from Machiavelli to Marx* (London: Longmans, Green & Co., Ltd., 1963), 2: 21-22.

20. Elie Halévy, *The Growth of Philosophic Radicalism* (reprint ed., Boston: Beacon Press, 1955), Part 3; Gertrude Himmelfarb, *Victorian Minds* (New York: Alfred A. Knopf, Inc., 1968), Chapter 12; G. M. Young, "The Liberal Mind in Victorian England," in *Ideas and Beliefs of the Victorians,* Harman Grisewood, ed. (reprint ed., New York: E. P. Dutton & Co., Inc., 1966), pp. 334-39; R. J. Cruikshank, *The Liberal Party* (London: William Collins Sons & Co., Ltd., 1948).

Rights of Woman (1792) and Frances Wright's Owenite communitarianism seemed quaint and slightly dangerous in the post-Napoleonic era. They had based their case for women's rights on her capacity for reason rather than on her "nature" and had advocated education as the essential first step in her elevation. But the spirit of eighteenth-century rationalism, deism, and radicalism that permeated their books seemed out of place in an era of reaction, romanticism, and evangelicalism.[21] Along with the literary "bluestockings" of the previous century (those literate, witty, upper-class keepers of intellectual salons), Mary Wollstonecraft and Frances Wright had been replaced in the 1830s by the ardent, dissenting female abolitionists, by the strong-minded, middle-class women of letters, such as Harriet Martineau and Harriet Taylor (the future Mrs. John Stuart Mill), and by "lady scribblers" of popular and reform novels.

As in America, abolitionism had provided an expanded sphere of activity for some Englishwomen, particularly among nonconformists, evangelicals, and Quakers. Yet the differences between American and British feminism and women's rights movements can not, for the 1830s, be attributed simply to

---

21. R. Glynn Grylls, "Emancipation of Women," in *Ideas and Beliefs of the Victorians,* Harman Grisewood, ed., p. 255; and Harrison, *Quest for the New Moral World,* p. 87. Mary Wollstonecraft has frequently been portrayed as a pioneering advocate of equal rights for women or equality between the sexes. A close reading of her classic *Vindication,* however, reveals an argument more characteristic of the Enlightenment, one which implies, logically, an elitist and hierarchical, rather than a strictly egalitarian, view of society. The heart of her argument is contained in the following propositions:

[1] "In what does man's pre-eminence over the brute creation consist? The answer is . . . in Reason.

[2] "What acquirement *exalts one being above another?* Virtue, we spontaneously reply.

[3] "For what purpose were the passions implanted? That man by struggling with them might attain a degree of knowledge. . . .

[4] "Consequently the perfection of our nature and capability of happiness, must be estimated by the *degree of reason, virtue, and knowledge,* that distinguish the individual, and direct the laws which bind society:

[5] "and that from the exercise of reason, knowledge and virtue naturally flow, is equally undeniable, if mankind be viewed collectively" [italics added]. Mary Wollstonecraft, *A Vindication of the Rights of Woman* (reprint ed., New York: W. W. Norton & Company, Inc., 1967), p. 39.

Proposition 4 is crucial to her case and is the basis for her philosophical reaction to Rousseau. To assert that virtue depends on reason rather than "nature" is to undercut the basis of Rousseau's romantic primitivism. Woman is not naturally virtuous, says Mary Wollstonecraft; she must learn, by reason, to become so. Only reasonable people (male and female) are ultimately equal.

For Frances Wright, see Sidney Ditzion, *Marriage, Morals and Sex in America: A History of Ideas* (New York: Bookman Associates, 1953), Chapter 3; Alice Felt Tyler, *Freedom's Ferment: Phases of American Social History from the Colonial Period to the Outbreak of the Civil War* (New York: Harper & Row, Publishers, 1962), pp. 206-11; Frances Wright, *Views of Society and Manners in America,* Paul R. Baker, ed. (Cambridge, Mass.: Harvard University Press, 1963), pp. xx, 22-25, 219-22; William R. Waterman, *Frances Wright* (New York: Columbia University Studies, 1924); Harrison, *Quest for the New Moral World,* pp. 59-62, 87ff.; Walter Hugins, *Jacksonian Democracy and the Working Class: A Study of the New York Workingmen's Movement, 1829-1837* (Stanford, Calif.: Stanford University Press, 1960), pp. 131-34; Frances Wright [D'Arusmont], *Life, Letters and Lectures: 1834, 1844* (New York: Arno Press, Inc., 1972).

differences in their respective antislavery movements; for, as historian David
Brion Davis has noted, "it is a striking coincidence that both the British and
American antislavery movements had come to a crucial turning point by
1830."[22] The adoption of "immediate emancipation" as both goal and strategy,
the beginning of Parliamentary debate in July 1830 on West Indian slavery, and
the victory of West Indian emancipation in 1832 had made British abolitionism
a model for American efforts. But success in British abolitionism was not accompanied by a willingness to probe new issues. Significantly, the "woman question"
emerged in the late 1830s in the context of a divided, declining, and harassed
American abolitionist movement rather than in the more confident circles of
English abolitionism. English Baptist, Methodist, Presbyterian, and Quaker
abolitionists contented themselves with urging that their American coreligionists
follow their example.[23]

The feminism of the middle-class intellectuals was also exceedingly timo-
rous in the 1830s. Harriet Martineau made herself a female publicist and fretted

22. David Brion Davis, "The Emergence of Immediatism in British and American Anti-
slavery Thought," *American Historical Review* 49 (September 1962): 226-27.

23. Gilbert H. Barnes, *The Anti-Slavery Impulse, 1830-1844* (reprint ed., Harcourt Brace
Jovanovich, Inc., 1964), pp. 31-37; Frank Thistlethwaite, *America and the Atlantic Com-
munity: Anglo-American Aspects, 1790-1950* (reprint ed., New York: Harper & Row,
Publishers, 1963), pp. 108-9; Thomas F. Harwood, "British Evangelical Abolitionism and
American Churches in the 1830s," *Journal of Southern History* 28 (August 1962): 287-306;
and Howard R. Temperley, "British and American Abolitionists Compared" in *The Anti-
slavery Vanguard: New Essays on the Abolitionists,* Martin Duberman, ed. (reprint ed.,
Princeton, N.J.: Princeton University Press, 1965), pp. 343-61.
    Comparisons of British and American abolitionism have concentrated mainly on the
differences in their strategic situations and on the similarities of their constituencies and
ideologies since the publication of Stanley Elkins' classic study, *Slavery,* in 1959. David
Brion Davis criticized Elkins for attributing the anti-institutional bias of immediatism to the
fluid social structure of the United States when the same characteristics could be found in
British and French abolitionism without, presumably, the same kind of social structure.
Aileen S. Kraditor challenged the alleged anti-institutionalism of American abolitionists and
argued that they wanted to purify, not abolish, institutions. Howard Temperley believed
that the British abolitionist exhibited the same characteristics as the American movement
once the British had exploited the possibilities of Parliamentary action and confronted the
same hopeless task of persuasion as confronted the Americans. Frank Thistlethwaite noted
that, while the English forte was abolitionist organization, the American contribution to
antislavery tactics was the professional agitator; that Englishmen were more concerned with
their social status and hence were less willing to risk social ostracism for their beliefs; and
that, while the English contributed the factual report or "blue book" to the cause, the
Americans developed the popular novel as a means of propaganda. An attempt by Robert
Kelley to set the whole question in a new comparative framework by drawing a parallel
between American Whiggery and English dissent proved misleading.
    See Stanley Elkins, *Slavery: A Problem in American Institutional and Intellectual
Life* (New York: Grosset and Dunlap, Inc., 1963); David Brion Davis, "The Emergence of
Immediatism in British and American Antislavery Thought," *American Historical Review* 49
(September 1962): 230 n. 71; Aileen S. Kraditor, *Means and Ends in American Abolitionism:
Garrison and His Critics on Strategy and Tactics, 1834-1850* (reprint ed., New York: Ran-
dom House, Inc.), Chapter 2; Howard Temperley, "British and American Abolitionists
Compared" in Martin Duberman, *The Antislavery Vanguard,* pp. 358-61; Thistlethwaite,
America and the Atlantic Community, pp. 90-92, 115-17, 197 n. 55; D. P. Cook rev. of
Robert Kelley, *The Transatlantic Persuasion* (New York: Alfred A. Knopf, Inc., 1969) in
Victorian Studies 13 (March 1970): 360-62.

about the political subordination of women in America, but she was not prepared to defend advanced views in public.[24] John Stuart Mill and Mrs. Taylor,
in unpublished essays, attacked contemporary marriage laws and postulated a
new morality of equality for "higher natures" who needed no conventional law
to guide them. However, they rigidly observed social appearances and did not,
like some of their radical friends, defy custom and public opinion. Mill believed
that it was inexpedient to advocate women's suffrage publicly in the 1830s. The
feminism of the radical intellectuals who contributed articles to such journals as
the *Monthly Repository* was, therefore, a mild blend of utilitarian ethics (greatest
happiness of the greatest number) and romantic individualism (greatest good of
the best natures) with a touch of platonic idealism (such happiness is not possible
in this world as presently constituted but is a noble dream to be pursued and
could be realized in a properly ordered society).[25]

Probably more important in shaping public attitudes toward feminism than
the behind-the-scenes activities of women abolitionists or the private views of the
radical intellectuals were the popular novels of the "lady scribblers." The woman
novelist was not a new phenomenon in nineteenth-century England; what was
new was the number of women writers, the growing market for their books and
stories, and the gradual evolution of their role in literature and in society. Public
debate had shifted from such a question as "should a woman write?" (yes, if she
did so anonymously or under a masculine pseudonym) to "why should she
write?" (moral zeal and genteel financial distress were the most acceptable reasons) and "what should she write and how?" (she should write about family life,
history, or high society, and in a didactic and moralizing tone). By 1840, the
female writer was established in the early Victorian social setting. As long as she
did not abandon her role as moralizer, teacher of values and manners, and keeper
of the hearthside, she was accorded a measure of public respect.

When, in the 1840s and 1850s, a few highly talented women novelists
sought to achieve independence and personal autonomy through writing, to
search the darker side of the human personality, or to examine social problems
in a critical light, they were frequently accorded hostile treatment by both male
and female critics. The Brontë sisters, Mary Ann Evans (George Eliot), Mrs.

---

24. For the career of Harriet Martineau, see R. K. Webb, *Harriet Martineau: A Radical
Victorian* (New York: Columbia University Press, 1960), Chapters 3 and 4, and Seymour M.
Lipset, *Revolution and Counterrevolution: Change and Persistence in Social Structures* (New
York: Basic Books, Inc., Publishers, 1968), Chapter 10.

25. J. H. Burns, "J. S. Mill and Democracy, 1829-1861," in *Mill: A Collection of Critical
Essays,* J. B. Schneewind, ed. (Notre Dame, Ind.: University of Notre Dame Press, 1969),
pp. 280-307; Maurice Cowling, *Mill and Liberalism* (London: Cambridge University Press,
1963), pp. 36-39, 136-46.

For the debate on Mill's early feminism, see F. A. Hayek, *John Stuart Mill and Harriet Taylor: Their Correspondence and Subsequent Marriage* (Chicago: University of Chicago
Press, 1951), Chapters 1-3; H. O. Pappe, *John Stuart Mill and the Harriet Taylor Myth* (London: Cambridge University Press, 1960); Gertrude Himmelfarb, "The Other John Stuart
Mill," in *Victorian Minds* (New York: Alfred A. Knopf, Inc., 1968), pp. 113-53; Alice Rossi,
ed., *John Stuart Mill and Harriet Taylor Mill, Essays on Sex Equality* (Chicago: University of
Chicago Press, 1971).

Gaskell—all dealt with a range of experiences in a manner that would have been unthinkable for the novelist of the 1820s and 1830s. For the student seeking to understand the status of early English feminism, however, one point is clear: public opinion set rigid limits to artistic freedom, and no woman author was regarded as the equal of her male compatriots unless she somehow proved that she was by extraordinary effort.[26]

The emergence of the social novel (including the "governess novel" as a subtype) served to underline the extent to which equality in England, particularly for women, was intimately bound up with social class and the economic system. England's class system in the early nineteenth century has been characterized as "a stable and institutionalized open-class system" in which individualism reinforced rather than challenged traditional class values:[27]

"The potency of individualism in the life of nineteenth-century England was in no way inconsistent with a highly developed sense of class. Indeed the two tended to go together, for the radical changes of industrialization, stemming from individual initiatives, had the effect of altering the social structure, making men aware in a manner heretofore unknown of their relationship with their fellows. . . . It was when social mobility increased, when questions of borderline status were raised, that definition and conventional tests became necessary. 'The truth is,' said *The Economist* in 1857, 'that the sense of social inequality cannot be completely felt without the amount of common culture which is needful to give a keen feeling of where the difference begins.'"[28]

This complex system, in which society was open to social mobility yet divided into a number of fiercely guarded status groups meant that equality-as-opportunity was governed by traditional mores, family attitudes, and public expectations.

Social freedom and leisure varied directly with social status: the upper-class lady could choose the life of leisure, boredom, and ennui or the role of Lady Bountiful in paternalistic charity and good works. The upper-class lady could not, in any sense, earn her own way. The middle-class woman, however, occupied a

---

26. Inga-Stina Ewbank, *Their Proper Sphere: A Study of the Brontë Sisters as Early-Victorian Female Novelists* (Cambridge, Mass.: Harvard University Press, 1966), Chapter 1; Arthur Pollard, *Mrs. Gaskell: Novelist and Biographer* (Cambridge, Mass.: Harvard University Press, 1966); U. C. Knoepflmacher, *Religious Humanism and the Victorian Novel: George Eliot, Walter Pater, and Samuel Butler* (Princeton, N.J.: Princeton University Press, 1965); Vineta Colby, *The Singular Anomaly: Women Novelists of the Nineteenth Century* (New York: New York University Press, 1970), Introduction; and Hazel Mews, *Frail Vessels: Woman's Role in Women's Novels from Fanny Burney to George Eliot* (London: Oxford University Press, 1971).

27. Bernard Barber, "Change and the Stratification System in Russia, Great Britain, and the United States," in *European Social Class: Stability and Change,* Bernard and Elinor Barber, eds. (New York: The Macmillan Company, 1965), p. 141.

28. S. G. Checkland, *The Rise of Industrial Society in England, 1815-1885* (New York: St. Martin's Press, Inc., 1964), p. 280. See particularly Chapters 7-8 for study of changes in social structure.

more precarious position. "Out of the conflict of ideas between the supporters of Thomas Malthus and his opponents on the subject of working-class poverty, there had slowly emerged a growing awareness of the relevance of marriage and children to the middle-class standard of life." By the 1830s a middle-class consensus had evolved: one should delay marriage until he could afford to maintain a particular style of life characterized by leisure for the wife (apart from household management) and education for the children. The spinster, the governess, the genteel seamstress or milliner, the lady scribbler—these were all anomalies that sought somehow to reconcile middle-class status with the financial distress that forced them to work. Such middle-class women had to fight for the "right" to work as well as for an equal opportunity to do so.[29]

For the lower-class woman, no such conscientious qualms about working were expected by society at large. Indeed, those who did not work, whether in the home or in the mills, were regarded as public charges, a burden on the Poor Law, and candidates for either emigration or transportation to the colonies.

By the time reliable statistics were gathered in the census of 1851, about one fifth of the adult women in England had found employment in the textile, dressmaking, and millinery trades or in domestic service (which was regarded among the working class as an avenue to independence and marriage). The number in the clothing and textile industries doubled in the 1840s but the rate of growth slowed down in the 1850s.

The hazards of female employment were sometimes compounded by the mores of the British working force. Extra income beyond what was usually spent on necessities frequently was spent on drink:

"Many employers of miners, dock labourers, builders, and bricklayers paid wages in beer. Excessive drink meant also that the wife found it impossible to defend her petty savings, her only security, against her husband. Even more important the poor woman had no effective defence against her husband's physical demands and so was obliged to deal with unwanted pregnancies. In 1830 the government [had] acted so as to increase drunkenness greatly: the tax was taken off beer, and under the Beerhouse Act any householder assessed to the poor rate might open his house as a beershop, free of licence or control, on payment of two guineas. . . . No less than 31,000 new beer-sellers came into existence; the trade remained outside the jurisdiction of the magistrates down to 1869."[30]

Aside from the Mines and Collieries Act of 1842 that dealt with abuses of female labor in the coal fields and the Ten Hours Act of 1847 regulating hours of labor

---

29. J. A. Banks, *Prosperity and Parenthood: A Study of Family Planning Among the Victorian Middle Classes* (London: Routledge & Kegan Paul Ltd., 1954), Chapter 11 (quotation p. 13); M. Jeanne Peterson, "The Victorian Governess: Status Incongruence in Family and Society," *Victorian Studies* 14 (September 1970): 7-26; Thomson, *The Victorian Heroine,* pp. 13-15; Constance Rover, *Love, Morals and the Feminists* (London: Routledge & Kegan Paul Ltd., 1970).

30. Checkland, *The Rise of Industrial Society in England,* p. 234.

for women and children in specified industries, the woman worker was largely unprotected from the burdens of unequal employment conditions.[31]

The economic fate of working women was also related to the performance of the economy as a whole and, particularly, to the fate of the textile industry. The Anglo-American cotton trade had suffered depressions in 1833–34, 1836, and 1842 which, coupled with the general effect of the panic of 1837 in the United States, created a slowdown in economic growth. Some members of the American antislavery movement argued that England could be wooed away from its alliance with the slave-holding South if the Corn Laws and other trade restrictions were eased and if "free" cotton grown in British-controlled India was substituted for "slave" cotton. The idea was discussed at the World's Anti-Slavery Convention in 1840, but such an unofficial assembly could take no binding action. Parliament could take binding action, however, and in 1842 and 1846 it supported Sir Robert Peel's budgets that moved England toward free trade through the reduction of selected duties. A heady expansion followed that helped to further transform the English economy.[32]

In summary, the meaning of equality for Englishwomen between 1800 and 1840 represented an intriguing blend of disparate elements and tendencies. Equality as a legal norm was dependent on a woman's marital status, religious community, and social status. In a country that prized inequality and exalted it as the primary value of society, there were only a few intellectual traditions that raised the standard of equality. A Mary Wollstonecraft advocating natural rights in the tradition of Enlightenment rationalism, a Frances Wright exalting Owenite communitarian social equality, a Harriet Martineau expounding utilitarian conceptions of the importance of equality of economic and political opportunity, a Harriet Taylor pining for artistic freedom from the tyranny of public opinion, or a Charlotte Brontë proclaiming the ideal of independence—these women represented the gradual shift of feminism away from the radical and revolutionary egalitarianism of the 1790s and toward an accommodation with social conventions that granted woman's separateness (her "proper sphere") but exalted her moral or intellectual superiority. Since their intellectual sisters were increasingly concerned with demonstrating woman's supremacy rather than her equality, the mass of women could hardly be faulted for being more concerned with their duties than with their rights.

Equality-as-opportunity was, therefore, a "problem" that was felt most

---

31. Ibid., pp. 216-17, 248, 321.

32. Thomas P. Martin, "The Upper Mississippi Valley in Anglo-American Anti-Slavery and Free Trade Relations, 1837-1842," *Mississippi Valley Historical Review* 15 (September 1928), pp. 204-20; Douglas H. Maynard, "The World's Anti-Slavery Convention of 1840," *Mississippi Valley Historical Review* 47 (December 1960), pp. 461-62; A. J. Youngson, "The Opening Up of New Territories," in *The Industrial Revolutions and After: Incomes, Population and Technological Change*, H. J. Habakkuk and M. Postan, eds., *The Cambridge Economic History of Europe*, vol. 6 (London: Cambridge University Press, 1965), 1: 139-211; J. Gallagher and R. Robinson, "The Imperialism of Free Trade," *Economic History Review*, 2nd ser., 6 (August 1953): 1-15; Checkland, *The Rise of Industrial Society in England*, pp. 15-27, 35-51.

acutely by those middle-class women who were forced to earn their own living or who sought meaningful activities outside the home. For the working-class woman faced with technological displacement and endemic underemployment, the question of equality-as-distribution of income was somewhat more important. For the governess, spinster, or female novelist, the narrow range of prescribed duties in home, church, and charity was not enough opportunity; for the seamstress, loom tender, and needle woman, the factory acts and ten-hour laws of the day would not be enough protection to insure her an equitable income. An alliance could have been joined between the middle-class feminists and the working-class Chartists and trade unionists. Women's suffrage had been advocated by both utilitarians and Chartists and could have formed the common grounds for an alliance in the 1830s. However, the radical political character of Chartism, the outbreak of Chartist violence in 1839, and the priority of abolitionism among middle-class reformers had all served to prevent such an alliance.[33]

The 1840 World's Anti-Slavery Convention and its attendant furor over the "woman question" came at a time, then, when English advocates of women's rights were divided among themselves by status and economic issues; when feminist writers and thinkers were gradually emphasizing the moral superiority rather than the equality of women and were groping toward the concept of the autonomous personality; and when English abolitionists, although beset by economic problems, were basking in the glow of the successful emancipation campaign in the West Indies. In addition, English Quakerism had experienced tremors of dissension in the 1830s and feared a Hicksite style division in their own ranks. The few Englishmen and Englishwomen who sent notes of support to the ousted American women, who sat with them in the visitors' gallery, or who were subsequently influenced by the controversy, represented these divisions within the English scene and its confused state of affairs.[34]

An authority on Victorian England has noted that "the advance towards women's independence—emancipation—couldn't be made by outstanding indi-

---

33. Some authors argue that the Reform Bill of 1832 and the Municipal Corporations Act of 1835 *reduced the influence of women,* who had either voted by proxy or exerted influence as property owners, and thus constituted an additional grievance for women's rights advocates. See "Women in English Municipal Life," *The Outlook* 92 (November 30, 1907): 714; Thistlethwaite, *Atlantic Community,* pp. 122-23; Constance Rover, *Women's Suffrage and Party Politics, 1866-1914* (Toronto: University of Toronto Press, 1967), Chapter 1.

34. Elbert Russell, *The History of Quakerism* (New York: The Macmillan Company, 1942), Chapter 26. Those men and women who expressed sympathy for the excluded American women or who were influenced by the event, included:

Harriet Martineau, who had been selected as a delegate by the Garrison-controlled Massachusetts society but who was prevented from attending by illness. See Wendell Phillips Garrison and Francis Jackson Garrison, eds., *William Lloyd Garrison, 1805-1879: The Story of His Life,* vol. 2, *1835-1840* (New York: The Century Co., 1885), pp. 378-79.

Lady Byron (Anne Milbanke), a rich, strict, beautiful heiress who provided Harriet Martineau with £100 per year for charity work; Webb, *Harriet Martineau,* p. 196. She sat in the visitors' gallery with Garrison and C. L. Remond and Mrs. Mott; Garrison, 2: 376.

Anna Jameson, the art historian and critic who is described by a recent reviewer as a pivotal figure "between the clever, scribbling demi-mondaines of the Regency and the intel-

viduals alone . . . nor by leaders of ability and distinction, but had to come from the sustained efforts of an educated and disciplined rank and file."[35] This was precisely what the English women's rights movement did not have. The educational establishment had no intention of turning out educated and disciplined leaders but rather dutiful, dull, and virtuous followers. Yet there was room in the Victorian ethos for some change. G. M. Young has written of the average English gentleman's attitude toward women that "there is no doubt at all that he expected them to be good; and goodness, in that age of universal charity, imported the service of others, and if service then training for service."[36] Through this loophole, Englishwomen made some progress.

The issue of education for women finally came to a focus in 1847. Tennyson provided a poetic perception of the problem in *The Princess*, but it fell to others to do something about it. F. D. Maurice, the Christian Socialist, helped to found Queen's College in London in 1848 to educate governesses and to train other young women to be teachers. Bedford College for women was established

---

lectual feminists of the mid-century, avid for respectability"; Ellen Moers' review of Clara Thomas, *Love and Work Enough: The Life of Anna Jameson* (Toronto: University of Toronto Press, 1967) in *Victorian Studies* 13 (March 1970): 370-71.

Amelia Opie, a Quaker writer of didactic fiction that was "homely in content, realistic in technique, and moral in intention"; Inga-Stina Ewbank, *Their Proper Sphere,* pp. 20, 28. She conveyed her sympathy to Mrs. Mott on the exclusion of the women; Garrison, 2: 375.

Mary Howitt, a radical journalist and translator of Frederika Bremer's novels; see Amice Lee, *Laurels and Rosemary: The Life of William and Mary Howitt* (New York: Oxford University Press, 1955) or Carl Ray Woodring, *Victorian Samplers: William and Mary Howitt* (Lawrence: University of Kansas Press, 1952).

Dr. John Bowring, a Benthamite utilitarian member of Parliament who supported the women delegates; he was interested in the Chartists in the early 1840s; West, *History of the Chartist Movement,* pp. 78, 182; Garrison, 2: 378.

William Ashurst, a London solicitor, sympathetic to Chartism and abolitionism. He expressed support of women delegates and urged the lodging of a protest; West, *History of the Chartist Movement,* pp. 231-32; Garrison, 2: 371, 376.

Matilda Ashurst, the wife of William Ashurst, sympathetic to the same causes as her husband.

Elizabeth (Pease) Nichol, Darlington Quaker philanthropist and friend of Harriet Martineau; Webb, *Harriet Martineau,* p. 304. Her husband, J. P. Nichol, a Glasgow professor of astronomy, was a friend of J. S. Mill.

Mrs. Hugo Reid, "the widow of a doctor, an enthusiastic Unitarian who had followed W. J. Fox out of the faith; and one of the founders of Bedford College [for women, 1849]," and an intimate friend of Harriet Martineau. She published *A Plea for Women* in 1843; Webb, *Harriet Martineau,* p. 17.

Julia Smith, a friend of Harriet Martineau.

Ann Knight, a Quaker of "Quiet House," Chelmsford, and abolitionist who wrote a pamphlet in favor of women's suffrage in 1847; Rover, *Women's Suffrage and Party Politics,* p. 4.

35. R. Glynn Grylls, "Emancipation of Women," in *Ideas and Beliefs of the Victorians,* Harman Grisewood, ed., p. 254.

36. Young, *Victorian England: Portrait of an Age,* 2nd ed. (London: Oxford University Press, 1960), p. 90. For one aspect of contemporary opinion, see B. Bergonzi, "Feminism and Femininity in *The Princess,*" in *The Major Victorian Poets: Reconsiderations,* Isobel Armstrong, ed. (Lincoln: University of Nebraska Press, 1969), pp. 35-50.

by Mrs. Reid in 1849. England, in short, had reached the stage that American female education had reached in the 1820s and 1830s.

Comparative differences between the American and British situations, in the broader sense, can best be explained by noting the differences in goals and institutionalized values of each society, and by observing the respective roles that reformers and radicals could play in each society.

In the United States, women confronted a situation in which the legal and economic sources of inequality were primary, the social and political barriers to equality were secondary because of institutional weaknesses. A woman might defy family opposition and become a schoolteacher without too much fear of social ostracism, but the lower pay that she received was a matter of law or the decision of a local governmental body. Women did petition Congress for the ending of slavery in the District of Columbia and could exert some indirect influence as lobbyists. If the law needed changing, the remedy lay in persuading her legislator, neighbor, husband, or brother.

In England, the nature of the equality that middle-class women sought was primarily social and economic and only secondarily legal and political. The chains that bound the middle-class governess to her miserable situation were the invisible ones of social attitudes (she must not lose status by doing menial work) and economic necessity. If she was without political influence, so were the mass of her male companions. If the law needed changing, only a remote and austere judge could bend it (gradually) or an unrepresentative and hostile Parliament could amend it. In England, some social and class attitudes and self-concepts would have to change along with changes in the law.

The equality desired by the English working-class woman was more economic and political in orientation than legal and social. She shared the working-class culture that fostered political radicalism, Owenite socialism, and Chartism. The vote for her would be not only a symbol of equal civil status but also a powerful weapon to protect her against economic exploitation. Change in attitude alone would not rescue her from her situation.

The *women's rights* advocate in America who upheld equal rights for women had an advantage over her English counterpart: she could appeal from the fact of inequality to the institutionalized ideal (or value) of equality embodied in the Declaration of Independence and the natural law tradition in American thought. She seemed, therefore, much less dangerous politically and institutionally than the Englishwoman who appealed *from the fact and ideal of inequality* to a seemingly radical concept of political and economic equality embodied in one of the minor intellectual trends of English life. The American could play the role of the reformer (one who seeks to close the gap between what is professed and what is practiced in a society) while the Englishwoman frequently was forced into the stance of the radical (one who rejects the values professed by a society and postulates alternative values).[37]

---

37. The way in which an Englishwoman could assume the role of reformer without sharing feminist values was illustrated by the career of Caroline Norton, a popular novelist. When

The feminist, who envisioned a self-defined image of woman at variance with the socially accepted image, was a cultural radical in both countries. When she challenged the orthodox limits of woman's defined sphere to assert her independence or to seek self-fulfillment, she was regarded with suspicion. For example, Margaret Fuller, the American transcendentalist, published an essay in July 1843 entitled "The Great Lawsuit. Man versus Men. Woman versus Women." By basing her plea for women's freedom on her superiority to social claims, she sought an equal freedom, beyond the limits of her culture, for woman "as a nature to grow, as an intellect to discern, as a soul to live freely and unimpeded to unfold such powers as were given her" by Nature.[38] Such a plea for the right of individual self-fulfillment seemed safe when directed by Emerson to aspiring workmen; when directed to women by a woman, it seemed subversive. When Charlotte Brontë created in Jane Eyre a woman of self-assertion and direction, a critic wrote: "We do not hesitate to say that the tone of mind and thought which has overthrown authority and violated every code human and divine abroad, and fostered Chartism and rebellion at home, is the same which has also written Jane Eyre."[39]

The situation that confronted both American and English women in the 1840s was simply this: Where they encountered cultural attitudes that confined women to a particular sphere or role, the feminist had to expound alternate images through imaginative literature and polemical tracts.[40] Where they confronted equality before the law as an institutional ideal, the women's rights

---

she was named a corespondent in a notorious divorce suit, her husband claimed control of their children and of her literary earnings under English law. She fought back and, with the aid of influential friends, helped secure the passage of the Infant Custody Act. "I never pretended," she explained, "to the wild and ridiculous doctrine of equality. . . . I believe in the natural superiority of the man as I do in the existence of a God. The natural position of woman is inferiority to a man, that is a thing of God's appointing, not of man's devising." While she held the then orthodox image of woman, she played one cultural postulate (familial hierarchy) off against another (maternal priority in child rearing) to secure reform of the law. See H. L. Beales, "The Victorian Family," in *Ideas and Beliefs of the Victorians,* Harmon Grisewood, ed., p. 344.

38. Margaret Fuller, "Women in the Nineteenth Century" reprinted in *Margaret Fuller: American Romantic,* Perry Miller, ed. (New York: Doubleday & Company, Inc., 1963), p. 150. This is a revised version of the Dial essay. Criticism of Margaret Fuller was also directed at her career in journalism and her independent life. In Italy in 1848 she bore an illegitimate son; married her lover, the Marchese Giovanni Angelo Ossoli, an Italian Republican nobleman; and supported the abortive Italian Republic during the siege of Rome in 1849. For the details of this much misunderstood episode, see Joseph Jay Deiss, *The Roman Years of Margaret Fuller: A Biography* (New York: Thomas V. Crowell Company, 1969).

39. Inga-Stina Ewbank, *Their Proper Sphere,* p. 33.

40. For literary feminism in America, see Augusta Genevieve Violette, "Economic Feminism in American Literature Prior to 1848," *The Maine Bulletin* 27 (February 1925): 9-114; Bertha-Monica Stearns, "Reform Periodicals and Female Reformers, 1830-1860," *American Historical Review* 37 (July 1932): 678-99; Glenda Gates Riley, "The Subtle Subversion: Changes in the Traditionalist Image of the American Woman," *The Historian* 32 (February 1970), 210-27; and Ann D. Wood, "The 'Scribbling Women' and Fanny Fern: Why Women Wrote," *American Quarterly* 23 (Spring 1971): 3-24.

advocates could appear as reformers and call on the intellectual traditions of their countries for support and public sympathy. Where they confronted inequality before the law, women's rights advocates frequently had to assume the stance of radicals and call on dissenting or foreign intellectual traditions for support. Where their pleas for equality of opportunity (for education, employment, and social usefulness) and for equity (control of property, better pay, divorce rights) met with legal restraint, they were forced to consider the questions of political power and the means of institutional change. These distinctions will become clearer as the focus of analysis is shifted from the World's Anti-Slavery Convention of 1840 to the Seneca Falls convention of 1848.

2

Equality in a Revolutionary Age

THE SENECA FALLS CONVENTION: MYTHS, REALITIES, AND INFLUENCES

The story of the first women's rights convention, held in 1848 at Seneca Falls, New York, has taken on legendary dimensions. According to the standard accounts, a chance visit by Lucretia Mott to upstate New York provided the opportunity for her and Elizabeth Cady Stanton to put into effect the resolve they had taken earlier to someday hold a women's rights convention in America. Seated around a mahogany center table (now safely preserved as a feminist relic in the Smithsonian Institution) they drafted a short notice, published it in the local county newspaper, and turned to the task of preparing a declaration of sentiments. After rejecting as models the reports of certain temperance, peace, and abolitionist conventions, they seized upon the Declaration of Independence as a suitable literary form. With a little modification, the tyrannical George III was replaced with an impersonal "he" and, after considerable searching about in law books and pamphlets, sufficient complaints were discovered to substitute for the original grievances of the colonists.

On the appointed day, July 19, 1848, a large crowd appeared (almost miraculously for it was early harvest season) and entered into extended discussion. On the second day, July 20, the declaration of sentiments was adopted unanimously. Mrs. Stanton, throwing caution to the wind and ignoring Mrs. Mott's saintly objections—"Why, Lizzie, thee will make us ridiculous"—decided to press for a resolution demanding the vote for women. With the support of Frederick Douglass, the black abolitionist, she secured endorsement of the resolution by a narrow margin. A hundred brave souls (sixty-eight women and thirty-two men), about a third of those present, signed the declaration, and the convention ended.

Publication of the declaration and reports of the meeting unleashed an avalanche of criticism, fun-poking, and ill-humored editorials in the press. Some of the signers withdrew their endorsement, but the true believers persisted in holding another meeting on August 2, 1848, in Rochester, New York.

During the morning session of the Rochester convention, "a young bride in traveling dress" appeared mysteriously in the crowded hall. She had heard of the convention while on her way westward, she explained, and had paused between trains in order to add her mite to the proceedings. She then launched into an oration on women's rights which ended with a stirring peroration (which is still cited by historians as an example of the extreme naiveté of the early suffragists):

"[When women's rights are granted] fashion's votaries will silently fall off; dishonest exertions for rank in society will be scorned; extravagance in toilet will be detested; that meager and worthless pride of station will be forgotten; the honest earnings of dependents will be paid; popular demagogues crushed; impostors unpatronized; true genius sincerely encouraged; and above all, pawned integrity redeemed."[1]

---

1. Elizabeth Cady Stanton, Susan B. Anthony, and Matilda Joslyn Gage, eds., *History of Woman Suffrage,* 2nd ed. (Rochester, N.Y.: Charles Mann, 1887), vol. 1, *1848-1861,* p. 77. Hereinafter cited as *HWS.*

The standard sources for the Seneca Falls convention are the above-mentioned *HWS,* pp. 67-77; Elizabeth Cady Stanton, *Eighty Years and More: Reminiscences 1815-1897* (reprint ed., New York: Schocken Books, Inc., 1971), Chapter 9; Theodore Stanton and Harriot Stanton Blatch, eds., *Elizabeth Cady Stanton as Revealed in Her Letters, Diary and Reminiscences* (New York: Harper & Row, Publishers, 1922); and National Woman Suffrage Association, *Report of the International Council of Women* (Washington, D.C.: Rufus H. Darby, 1888), pp. 322-68. The *HWS* and Mrs. Stanton's memoirs have been assumed to be authoritative because written by a major participant; the edited version of her letters and the reminiscences of pioneering suffragists and abolitionists given at the 1888 convention have been regarded as valuable supplements to this basic account. Now, however, historians should look critically at these sources.

The first volume of *HWS,* for example, was written during the period 1876 to 1881 when the National Woman Suffrage Association (dominated by Elizabeth Cady Stanton and Susan B. Anthony) was at a low ebb in its struggle for influence with the American Woman Suffrage Association (dominated by Lucy Stone and Julia Ward Howe) and the new Woman's Christian Temperance Union. An "international woman's rights congress" held in July and August 1878, in Paris in conjunction with an international exhibition had created a "permanent international committee" which included representatives of both the NWSA and the AWSA, but little came of the effort. (*HWS* 3: 896-97). The editorial theme of *HWS,* vol. 1, was in keeping with this international mood and reflected the desire of its editors to enhance the prestige of their association. The text of volume 1 was organized around the argument (1) that the women's rights movement was a spontaneous, worldwide development with similar aspirations everywhere (pp. 42, 51); (2) that a new generation of leadership had emerged in Europe and America in 1848 to demand political freedom and liberty for women (p. 102); and (3) that the experiences of the leaders of the National Woman Suffrage Association from the World's Anti-Slavery Convention of 1840 to the Seneca Falls convention of 1848 to the women's rights conventions of the 1850s entitled them to priority in the women's movement (Chapters 3, 4, and 8). Matilda Joslyn Gage, coeditor of *HWS,* wrote to Lydia Becker of England in 1878 to refute the claim in an article in the *Englishwoman's Journal* that the first women's rights convention had been held in Akron, Ohio, in 1847 and that it had been called by Mrs. Francis Dana Gage. Matilda Joslyn Gage to Lydia Becker, August 30, 1878, reprinted in *Elizabeth Cady Stanton,* Stanton and Blatch, eds., 2: 38 n.1.

An International Congress of Women was finally held in 1888 as a result of a meeting in England in 1883 between Elizabeth Cady Stanton, Susan B. Anthony, and some English suffragists. The NWSA sponsored the congress to celebrate the fortieth anniversary of the Seneca Falls convention and invited a number of pioneers to reminisce at a "conference of pioneers" on March 31. Aside from the usual problems associated with oral-memory history,

Once again, the declaration of sentiments adopted at Seneca Falls was endorsed and some resolutions were passed.

Frederick Douglass secured the support of various Negro conventions in September and November 1848 and supported the new cause in his influential newspaper. The Seneca Falls convention acted as the catalyst and similar conventions were held in 1850 in Salem, Ohio, and, finally, in November the First National Woman's Rights Convention was held in Worcester, Massachusetts. The reports were read in England and Europe and attracted considerable support abroad.

The Seneca Falls legend obscures as much information as it reveals about the event by leading the reader's attention away from significant aspects of the

---

internal evidence in the stenographic record indicated that some of the speakers "refreshed their memories" by reading *HWS* before they came to the meeting. (See the comment by Frederick Douglass in NWSA, *Report of the International Council of Women*, p. 329.) Leaders of the AWSA pointedly ignored or refuted the claimed priority of the Seneca Falls convention (Lucy Stone and Henry Blackwell, for example, in NWSA, *Report of the International Council*, pp. 331, 337-39). Lucy Stone replied to an invitation to furnish a biographical sketch for *HWS* with a terse note that ended: "Yours with ceaseless regret that any 'wing' of suffragists should attempt to write the history of the other." Reprinted in Alma Lutz, *Created Equal: A Biography of Elizabeth Cady Stanton* (New York: The John Day Company, Inc., 1940), pp. 244-45.

Elizabeth Cady Stanton did not keep a diary during her busy life until her sixty-fifth year and did not publish her memoirs until she was eighty. Numerous minor discrepancies between the various sources indicate that Elizabeth Cady Stanton was a better publicist than historian. For example, she wrote that she had discussed the idea of holding a women's rights convention in America with Lucretia Mott during the 1840 World's Anti-Slavery Convention in London (*HWS*, 1: 61 and *Eighty Years*, Chapter 5). Lucretia Mott, on the other hand, had written to Mrs. Stanton in 1855 that the conversation had taken place in Boston in 1841 (Lucretia Mott to Elizabeth Cady Stanton, March 16, 1855, in *Elizabeth Cady Stanton*, Stanton and Blatch, eds., 2: 18 n.3). In her memoirs Elizabeth Cady Stanton magnified the impact of Lucretia Mott on her youthful ideas. Her reaction *in 1840* was indicated in a letter to the Grimké sisters: "Lucretia Mott has just given me a long message for you, . . . ; that you should either write for the public or speak out for *oppressed* woman. . . . She says a great struggle is at hand and that all the friends of freedom for woman must rally round the *Garrison standard.* I have had much conversation with Lucretia Mott and I think her a peerless woman. . . . Her views are many of them so new and strange that my [illegible] finds great delight in her society." Elizabeth Cady Stanton to Angelina Weld and Sarah Grimké, June 25, 1840, reprinted in *Letters of Theodore Dwight Weld, Angelina Grimké Weld, and Sarah Grimké, 1822-1844,* Gilbert H. Barnes and Dwight L. Dumond, eds. (New York: Appleton-Century-Crofts, 1934), 2: 845-49. Quotation on page 847.

There is some evidence in Mrs. Stanton's correspondence that she did not come to regard the 1840 Anti-Slavery Convention exclusion of women delegates as a *cause célèbre* and a milestone in the women's movement until *after* the Seneca Falls convention. She wrote to Susan B. Anthony in 1852 (April 2): "I have been re-reading the report of the London convention of 1840. How thoroughly humiliating it was to us! How I could have sat there quietly and listened to all that was said and done, I do not *now* understand" [italics added]. Reprinted in *Elizabeth Cady Stanton,* Stanton and Blatch, eds.. 2: 40. Her account of the 1840 convention, written at that time, contained only a perfunctory remark, "All things considered, the convention has passed off more smoothly than any of us anticipated. The woman's rights question, besides monopolizing one whole day, has by being often referred to, created some little discord, for on this point we find a difference of opinion among the men and women [in England] as well as with us in America." Elizabeth Cady Stanton to Angelina Weld and Sarah Grimké, June 25, 1840, in *Letters of T. D. Weld, A. G. Weld, and S. Grimké,* Barnes and Dumond, eds., 2: 845-46.

incident. For example, why were so many people in an out-of-the-way corner of upstate New York willing to drop everything on short notice at the sight of a terse announcement in a modest county newspaper and spend two days debating women's rights? The site of the convention was the result of the fortuitous accident of Mrs. Mott's visit and the coincidence of Mrs. Stanton's frustration with small-town life; but was there anything in the social and economic characteristics of the area that would account for the public response to the call for the convention?

Whitney R. Cross, a historian who studied closely the religious revivals of western New York state, has noted that the Finger Lakes region (including Seneca County) was somewhat of an exception to the general western New York pattern:

"According to the economic symptoms which apply elsewhere, this sector should have been fascinated with the enthusiasms of the period. Parts of it were. Three factors help to explain the fact that the appeal was not universal. The triangle of Pennsylvania migration extended into the heart of the region. Seneca County, for example, had the lowest percentage of Yankee nativity in western New York and also registered resistance to most religious and reform movements of the evangelistic type. Again, the lake villages were the country seats of gentlemen landlords, descended from the eighteenth-century aristocracy of New York, Pennsylvania, and Virginia, who generally attended the Episcopalian Church, which maintained a cool dignity amidst the fiercest storms of fervent revivalism. Finally, a sufficient number of the more substantial Yankee farmers espoused Universalism to make this the center of strength for that liberal denomination in the Burned-over District."[2]

At the same time, the relatively mature, postfrontier economy of the Seneca Falls area; the proximity of textile and other mills; and the opening in 1841 of the strategic Auburn and Rochester railroad linking the area with Albany, all these factors indicated that this was an area where women could supplement their income (by utilizing "leisure" time on their farms) or support themselves, if widowed.[3]

---

2. Whitney R. Cross, *The Burned-over District: The Social and Intellectual History of Enthusiastic Religion in Western New York, 1800–1850* (reprint ed., New York: Harper & Row, Publishers, 1965), p. 67 and map 5, p. 68. Cross used a Yankee-Yorker typology for his study in which Yankee meant New England nativity or antecedents and Yorker meant New York culture. His thesis, that enthusiastic revivalism was correlated with Yankee-Yorker types, need not be challenged here; however, his converse argument, that non-Yankee-Yorker types were more resistant to revivalism *and reform* is suspect. Furthermore, an analysis of birthplaces of residents of selected townships in Seneca County in the 1850 census revealed that his map 5 is highly misleading.

3. *Centennial Anniversary of Seneca County* (Seneca Falls Historical Society, 1904), p. 11. Andrew Sinclair noted the 1920 reminiscences of Charlotte Woodward, who attended the Seneca Falls convention and signed the declaration of sentiments, that a local glove factory was "putting out" piece work to area farm girls who felt exploited by the arrangement. Andrew Sinclair, *The Better Half: The Emancipation of the American Woman* (New York: Harper & Row, Publishers, 1965), pp. 58-61.

No record is available of all three hundred people who attended, but the signatures of the one hundred who signed the declaration have been preserved and have been checked against the 1850 census and other records for biographical information. An answer to the question of who signed must precede speculation about the question of why they signed.

Of the one hundred who signed the declaration (sixty-eight women and thirty-two men) information has been found for seventy (forty-one women and twenty-nine men). A composite profile of the signers revealed that they were a relatively young group, predominantly middle-class, of moderate to comfortable circumstances, possessing relatively more leisure, and belonging to liberal theological sects. In politics and reform, they were associated with abolitionism, temperance, free-soil parties, and Whig-Republican backgrounds. Significantly, no Democrats and no public officials signed the documents. Approximately one third of the women were single, one third had only their husband residing at home, and another third had children at home. The compiler of this profile concluded: "The Women's Rights movement at its roots does not seem to be a radicalism, but a liberal thrust from a relatively comfortable middle class tied to reform."[4]

Two findings throw an interesting light on the Seneca Falls area in contrast to Whitney R. Cross' generalizations about the region. The majority of the signers studied were born in New York and were involved in a variety of religious and reform activities, particularly antislavery and temperance. In spite of their denomination's "cool dignity," five Episcopalians signed the declaration along with four Presbyterians and four Methodist-Episcopal members. The largest single religious affiliation represented among the signers was the Society of Friends with over twenty adherents.[5] Thomas McClintock, for example, was one of the original leaders of the Hicksite separation and a key figure in a split in the Genesee Yearly Meeting in June 1848, that led to the formation of the Congregational or "Progressive Friends." Thomas McClintock wrote the liberal and universalistic *Basis of Religious Association* adopted by the "Progressive Friends" in the fall of 1848. Mary Ann McClintock helped to plan the Seneca Falls convention, the declaration of sentiments was written in the McClintock parlor, and the declaration was signed by Mary Ann McClintock, Elizabeth W. McClintock, Mary McClintock, and Thomas McClintock.[6]

---

4. Katherine Milton Faust, "The Signers of Seneca Falls" (unpublished senior honors paper, Department of History, Augustana College, 1970), p. 2. The ages are summarized in the following table (p. 9):

	Oldest	Youngest	Median	Average
Women	67	14	34	35
Men	68	18	41	39

Of twenty-two of the men, seventeen were married and five were single (some of whom lived in boardinghouses on the edge of town). "A small but intriguing inner circle [of men] included four members of the fire engine company" (p. 8).

5. Faust, "The Signers of Seneca Falls," appendix i and pp. 4-6.

6. A. Day Bradley, "Progressive Friends in Michigan and New York," *Quaker History* 52

The timing of the Seneca Falls convention is also significant in explaining why so many people attended and why they may have signed the declaration of sentiments. A state constitutional convention in 1846 had raised the issues of women's rights and a married woman's property rights. In late March of 1848 the state legislature had passed a married woman's property bill. A member of the constitutional convention, Ansel Bascom, addressed the Seneca Falls convention on the subject.[7]

The revolutions in Europe that had started with the French uprising of February 22, 1848, may have heightened expectations about social change; probably more important in the American context was the forthcoming presidential election. The annexation of Texas and the war with Mexico had contributed to an emerging realignment of political forces. The abolitionist Liberty Party had split into the Liberty League, which nominated Quaker philanthropist Gerrit Smith for President, and the Liberty Party regulars, who nominated John P. Hale of New Hampshire. On May 22, 1848, the free-soil New York Democrats (known as "barnburners") bolted their national party convention and refused to support the national ticket. The barnburners then held their own convention in Utica on June 22, 1848, and nominated Martin Van Buren. These circumstances may account for the interest of some men in the Seneca Falls convention and the prominent part taken by free-soil politicians in the Rochester women's rights convention two weeks later.[8]

The political tenor of the times and its relation to the theme of the women's rights conventions was alluded to by Mrs. Stanton in her opening address at the Seneca Falls convention:

"We have met here to-day to discuss our rights and wrongs, civil and political, and not, as some have supposed, to go into the detail of social life alone. We do not propose to petition the legislature to make our husbands just, generous, and courteous, to seat every man at the head of a cradle, and to clothe every woman in male attire. . . .

But we are assembled to protest against a form of government existing without the consent of the governed—to declare our right to be free as man is

---

(Autumn 1963): 95-101. Thomas McClintock was fifty-eight at the time of the 1850 census; Mary Ann was fifty; Elizabeth, twenty-nine; and Mary, twenty-seven.

Lucretia Mott had warned in 1846 that there was a spirit of "come-outerism" among Hicksite Quakers in western New York, that "assumed authority of men's meetings, and the admitted subordination of women's" meetings was a source of complaint, and that a radical change in discipline would result from any division. Other causes for the separation were the refusal of the Hicksite meetings to actively support antislavery, women's suffrage, teetotalism in temperance, and free speech and their refusal to modify church structures in a congregational pattern. Allan C. Thomas, "Congregational or Progressive Friends: A Forgotten Episode in Quaker History," *Bulletin of the Friends' Historical Society* 10 (November 1920): 21-31.

7. *HWS*, 1: 63, 69.

8. John L. Thomas, *The Liberator: William Lloyd Garrison* (Boston: Little, Brown and Company, 1963), pp. 344-55.

free, to be represented in the government which we are taxed to support, to have such disgraceful laws as give man the power to chastise and imprison his wife, to take the wages which she earns, the property which she inherits, and, in case of separation, the children of her love; [to have] laws which make her the mere dependent on his bounty [removed from the statute books] . . . . And, strange as it may seem to many, we now demand our right to vote according to the declaration of the government under which we live. This right no one pretends to deny."[9]

According to Mrs. Stanton's later accounts, however, a number of the participants did deny the right, and after considerable discussion, her resolution in favor of women's suffrage was passed by a "small majority."[10]

A close analysis of the Seneca Falls declaration of sentiments, however, raises questions about Mrs. Stanton's account. The first four complaints in the declaration of sentiments, which was adopted unanimously, dealt with women's suffrage and political representation:

"He has never permitted her to exercise her *inalienable right to the elective franchise.*

He has compelled her to submit to laws, in the formation of which she had no voice.

He has withheld from her rights which are given to the most ignorant and degraded men—both natives and foreigners.

Having deprived her of *this first right of a citizen, the elective franchise,* thereby leaving her without representation in the halls of legislation, he has oppressed her on all sides"[11] [italics added].

The conclusion to the declaration insisted that women "have immediate admission to all the rights and privileges which belong to them as citizens of the United States."

9. Elizabeth Cady Stanton, *Address Delivered at Seneca Falls and Rochester, New York, July 19 and August 2, 1848* (New York: Robert J. Johnson, 1870), pp. 9-10. Portions of this speech are reprinted in Houston Peterson, ed., *A Treasury of the World's Great Speeches* (New York: Simon & Schuster, Inc., 1954), pp. 389-92.

10. *HWS,* 1: 69-70; Stanton and Blatch, eds., *Elizabeth Cady Stanton,* 1: 46. Curiously, at the 1888 International Council of Women meeting, Mrs. Stanton, in her reminiscences of the Seneca Falls convention, said, ". . . in due time Douglass and I carried the whole convention, and the resolution was *passed unanimously*" [italics added]. See *Report of the International Council of Women* (1888), p. 324. The official published minutes of the Seneca Falls convention noted: ". . . the resolutions of the day before were read, and taken up separately. Some, from their self-evident truth, elicited but little remark; others, after some criticism, much debate, and some slight alterations, were finally passed by a *large majority*" [italics added]. [Mary Ann McClintock, Secretary], *Report of the Woman's Rights Convention Held at Seneca Falls, New York, July 19th and 20th, 1848* (Rochester, N.Y.: North Star, 1848), p. 9.

11. Seneca Falls declaration reprinted in Aileen S. Kraditor, ed., *Up From the Pedestal: Selected Writings in the History of American Feminism* (Chicago: Quadrangle Books, Inc., 1968), pp. 184-85.

Why, then, should there have been such opposition to Mrs. Stanton's resolution number nine—"That it is the duty *of the women* of this country to *secure to themselves* their sacred right to the elective franchise" [italics added] —and why should the vote have been so close (if, in fact, it was close)? Two possibilities are suggested by the evidence. First, the support of Frederick Douglass for the resolution, far from being the asset that Mrs. Stanton thought, may have caused suspicion among some of the participants. The 1846 New York constitutional convention had raised the question of removing the property qualification for Negro voters. Liberty party members, free-soil Democrats, and some Whigs had supported it, but the measure had been defeated. Perhaps some of the participants were reluctant to identify women's rights with Negro suffrage.[12]

Another cause for opposition may be found in the text of a resolution that Lucretia Mott offered at the closing session of the Seneca Falls convention: "Resolved, That the speedy success of our cause depends upon the zealous and untiring efforts of *both men and women,* for the overthrow of the monopoly of the pulpit, and for the securing to woman an equal participation with men in the various trades, professions, and commerce"[13] [italics added].

---

12. Kraditor, *Up From the Pedestal,* p. 188; John L. Stanley, "Majority Tyranny in Tocqueville's America: The Failure of Negro Suffrage in 1846," *Political Science Quarterly* 84 (September 1969): 412-35. Frederick Douglass endorsed the women's rights movement in a brilliant editorial in the *North Star,* July 28, 1848. Benjamin Quarles, *Frederick Douglass* (Washington, D.C.: The Associated Publishers, 1948), p. 133. Quarles wrote that Douglass "was the only man to support the suffrage resolution." He apparently based this statement on *HWS,* 1: 70-71. Douglass' support was an act of rare courage as his newspaper was heavily in debt at the time, a situation that caused grave concern to his friends in England (particularly the women abolitionists). See Erwin Palmer, "A Partnership in the Abolition Movement," *University of Rochester Library Bulletin* 26 (1970-71): 1-19.

13. [McClintock], *Report of the Seneca Falls Convention,* p. 9. The resolutions passed by the Seneca Falls convention represented an interesting combination of ideas. First, they turned Blackstone's authority into support for their cause by calling attention to his doctrine of the primacy of the natural law. Then they declared that all laws conflicting with the natural law premise (which is, the purpose of each being is to pursue its own true nature and happiness) are "of no validity." They followed these arguments with assertions that woman is man's equal by nature and ought to be informed of man-made laws which deny this equality; that man's acknowledgment of woman's *moral* superiority makes it his duty "to encourage her to speak and teach, as she has opportunity, in all religious assemblies"; that a single moral standard ought to exist in social relations; that men who criticize as improper and indecent women speaking in public ought not to frequent plays, concerts, and circuses where women appear in improper and indecent costumes. Furthermore, women "should move in the enlarged sphere which her . . . Creator has assigned her" and not defer to custom and ecclesiastical opinion. Accordingly, "it is the duty of the women of this country to secure to themselves their sacred right to the elective franchise." Since races are equal in capacities and responsibilities and, therefore, are equal in human rights, "it is demonstrably the right and duty of woman, equally with man, to promote every righteous cause by every righteous means."

Elizabeth Cady Stanton, as the author of these resolutions, used the "higher law" doctrine that the law of nature supersedes civil law. This argument was in keeping with current thinking among abolitionists but was coming under attack elsewhere in society. See Carl L. Becker, *The Declaration of Independence* (reprint ed., New York: Random House, Inc., 1942), Chapter 6.

The underlying argument of the declaration and of the resolutions can be reformu-

Mrs. Stanton's resolution envisioned an effort *by women alone* to secure their political rights; Mrs. Mott's encompassed *a joint effort by men and women* to secure equality of opportunity in religious and professional life. The differences were related partly to Lucretia Mott's Quakerism and her belief in moral persuasion. Women ought to have the right to vote, she reluctantly concluded a year later, but until governments adopted nonresistant principles of brotherly love, conscientious women should refrain from exercising it. To pursue political ends exclusively with political means ran the risk of contamination with worldly power, compromise, and sin.[14]

The dangers of a political approach to women's rights were amply illustrated at the Rochester convention held on August 2, 1848. W. C. Bloss, a leading free-soil politician, joined in the debates and alluded to the subject of the elective franchise. "The question was, not whether in the abstract it was a *right* of woman," he said, "but would she, under the circumstances and embarrassments which surrounded its exercise, think it worthwhile to assert it and go to the polls?" The care with which this veteran advocate of equal rights granted the premise of women's suffrage only to deny it on grounds of expediency indicated that, in the unsettled political climate of the day, party leaders could not afford to antagonize any potential source of support or influence.

Another member of the Rochester convention, the orator known to history as "the young bride in traveling dress," was also fishing in troubled waters for political supporters. Mrs. Rebecca Sanford (the mysterious figure) was, in fact, a roving lecturer on abolitionism and women's rights. Her husband had been trying for a year to organize a "Republican" party based on a union of Liberty League

---

lated in a series of propositions stemming from the primary assertion that women are politically disenfranchised, socially suppressed, and religiously degraded.

First, political disenfranchisement (and legal inequality) are wrong because: (a) equal civil status (citizenship) should be accompanied by equal civil rights; and (b) women are citizens by birth or residence; and (c) men and women are equal by birth—i.e., they are born into similar civil status.

Second, social degradation is wrong because: (a) men and women are equal by nature —i.e., they have the same law of being, which is to pursue their own true and substantial happiness (Margaret Fuller had stated a variation of this idea in her *Dial* essay: woman's true destiny is to develop her faculties); (b) all laws which deny this (or which prevent a woman from pursuing her true happiness) are contrary to nature and are, therefore, invalid; and (c) "the highest good of the race" demands that woman be recognized as equal to man.

Third, religious degradation is wrong because: (a) God, the author of nature, has assigned a sphere to woman and given her a conscience to discern it; (b) men "accord to woman moral superiority" and prove by their own misconduct that they are morally inferior to women; and (c) customs and scriptural arguments against woman's proper sphere are in violation of God's purposes.

The hedging on the second point under "religious degradation" was the source of the friction between Lucretia Mott and Elizabeth Cady Stanton. Lucretia Mott was logically more consistent in arguing that men and women were morally equal than was Elizabeth Cady Stanton in combining natural equality and equality of civil status with moral superiority. See note 17 below.

14. Lucretia Mott, *Discourse on Woman: Delivered at the Assembly Buildings, December 17, 1849* (Philadelphia: T. B. Peterson, 1850), pp. 14-15. This a phonographic [i.e., stenographic] report of her address corrected by Mrs. Mott before its publication.

abolitionists, Industrial Congress trade unionists, and reformers. He advocated a
platform that recognized "the right of women to have a voice in making any law
they submit to." A week after the Rochester women's rights convention, a free-
soil convention in Rochester did succeed in uniting barnburner Democrats,
conscience Whigs, and Liberty party men behind a ticket of Martin Van Buren
and Charles Francis Adams but without endorsing women's rights.[15]

In this politically charged atmosphere, the differences in outlook between
Lucretia Mott and Elizabeth Cady Stanton on organizational tactics were thus
indicative of deeper conflicts concerning the moral basis of society. Behind their
common advocacy of equal rights for women, these two leaders held different
images of woman. In criticism of a flattering speech by William Nell, Lucretia
Mott told the Rochester convention that "she did not believe in holding up
woman as superior to man." Given power, women could be as tyrannical as
men.[16] Elizabeth Cady Stanton, on the other hand, assumed the moral superiority of women. Her indignation and the sense of outraged innocence that
spurred her efforts flowed from this belief. What right had men to withhold the
franchise from (moral) women when they granted it to "drunkards, idiots, horse-
racing, rum-selling rowdies, ignorant foreigners, and silly boys"? Elizabeth Cady
Stanton represented a younger generation of feminists. They argued the moral
superiority of women *in all spheres* and condemned any social and political
arrangements that restricted women's activities.[17]

---

15. Rochester *Daily Democrat,* August 3, 1848, and Rochester *Daily Advertiser,* August 3,
1848. For Rebecca Sanford's career, see Ephriam H. Sanford to J. S. Brown, September 6,
1847, enclosed in Sanford to Birney, October 31, 1848, reprinted in Dwight L. Dumond, ed.,
Letters of James Gillespie Birney, 1831-1857 (New York: Appleton-Century-Crofts, 1938),
2: 1116-18.

16. Rochester *Daily Democrat,* August 3, 1848. The newspaper report is quoted in the text.
The official minutes recorded Lucretia Mott's remarks as follows: "She said that man was
not a tyrant by nature, but had been made tyrannical by the power which had, by general
consent, been conferred upon him; she merely wished that woman might be entitled to
equal rights, and *acknowledged* as the equal of man, not his superior. Woman is equally
tyrannical when she has irresponsible power. . . ." Amy Post, *Proceedings of the Woman's
Rights Convention Held at the Unitarian Church, Rochester, N.Y., August 2, 1848* (New
York: Robert J. Johnson, 1870), p. 4.

17. Elizabeth Cady Stanton, Speech to the Seneca Falls Convention, July 19, 1848, reprinted
in *A Treasury of the World's Great Speeches,* Houston Peterson, ed. (New York: Simon and
Schuster, Inc., 1954), p. 390. In the 1850s she turned to the question of marriage. "It is in
vain to look for the elevation of woman so long as she is degraded in marriage," she wrote.
"I hold it is a sin, an outrage on our holiest feelings, to pretend that anything but deep,
fervent love and sympathy constitute marriage." It was the mother's "prerogative . . . to set
bounds to [man's sexual] indulgence." From this concern came the tensions that later split
the women's suffrage movement in the 1860s. For her views on the marriage question, see
Elizabeth Cady Stanton to Susan B. Anthony, March 1, 1853 (quoted above); Lucy Stone
to Elizabeth Cady Stanton, October 22, 1856; and Elizabeth Cady Stanton to Susan B.
Anthony, June 14, 1860, reprinted in Stanton and Blatch, eds., *Elizabeth Cady Stanton* 2:
48-49, 67-68, 82-83. In 1856, she came across the manuscript of the speech she had given
at Seneca Falls and Rochester and wrote an inscription on it for her daughters:

"Dear Maggie and Hattie, this is my first speech. It was delivered several times after the first
Woman's Rights Convention. It contains all I knew at that time. I did not speak again for

From the conventional belief in the moral superiority of woman *in her "proper sphere,"* Lucretia Mott, a Quaker, came to the alternative position upholding the moral equality of the sexes.

Elizabeth Cady Stanton held the romantic feminist image of woman as a superior moral being whose individuality demanded freedom from social restraint. The differences between her view and the then orthodox image of woman were subtle but significant. The orthodox image acknowledged woman's moral superiority in a limited sphere in order to justify her social subordination and exclusion from public affairs. Her "purity" required her confinement and isolation from the sinful "world." The romantic feminist, on the other hand, proclaimed woman's moral superiority in order to deny social subordination and legal restraint. Thus, while both Lucretia Mott and Elizabeth Cady Stanton were feminists (cultural radicals), they were not identical in their views (Mrs. Mott was more of a rationalist in the spirit of Mary Wollstonecraft; Mrs. Stanton was more of a romantic in the spirit of Margaret Fuller). Elizabeth Cady Stanton was more of a political reformer than Lucretia Mott, and therein lay the source of many of their disagreements. Her early experiences in her father's law office had convinced Elizabeth Cady Stanton that it was the law that needed changing. Her insistence on the right to vote was a logical conclusion to this premise in the context of post-Jacksonian America.

One further question remains from this demythologized examination of the Seneca Falls legend. How "revolutionary" were the proceedings at the Seneca Falls and Rochester conventions? The press had a good bit of fun reporting on the "sex revolution," or "second revolution," and the local clergy thundered against this subversion of civilization. But the middle-class character of the proceedings was evident throughout in the nature of the resolutions passed and in the reaction to labor issues. The Rochester convention, for example, heard reports on the plight of seamstresses in Rochester who worked fourteen and fifteen hours to earn thirty-one to thirty-nine cents a day. Elizabeth Cady Stanton offered a resolution that those who employed servants *in their homes* ought to pay them higher wages; Lucretia Mott objected to the proposal that a society be organized "to redress the wrongs and hardships of laboring females." The subject was extraneous to the convention and ought to be left to the citizens of Rochester, she said. The supporters of the idea persisted, and a compromise resolution was adopted: "Resolved, That those who believe the laboring classes of women are oppressed, ought to do all in their power to raise their wages, be-

---

several years. As I recall my younger days, I weep over the apathy and indifference of women concerning their own degradation. I give this manuscript to my precious daughters, in the hope that they will finish the work which I have begun" (quoted by Mary Ormsbee Whitton, *These Were the Women: USA 1776-1860* [New York: Hastings House, Publishers, Inc., 1954], p. 145).

Historians should be careful, therefore, not to read Elizabeth Cady Stanton's later views back into the events of 1848.

ginning with their own household servants."[18] A truer test of the "revolutionary" character of the events can be found in a comparison with contemporary events in France, where a full-scale revolution had broken out earlier in the year.

FRANCE: WOMEN AND THE REVOLUTIONARY TRADITION, 1800–1850

In order to understand the comparable situation of Frenchwomen in 1848, four factors must be kept in mind: (1) the unique nature of French law, (2) the dual social and political heritage of the French Revolution, (3) the importance of socialist thought to French feminism, and (4) the slow pace of French industrialization combined with extraordinary demographic developments.

In legal matters, France belonged to a different "legal family" than the United States and England. Whereas England belonged to the common-law tradition and the United States had created a system based on both common law and constitutional law, France belonged to the civil law family derived from Roman law. In the civil law family, "the rule of law is conceived as a rule of conduct intimately linked to ideas of justice and morality. . . . The law has evolved, primarily for historical reasons, as an essentially *private* law, as a means of regulating the private relationships between individual citizens. . . ." The English common law, growing out of the struggle with royal power, was essentially a system of *public* law, "for contestations between private individuals did not interest the Common Law courts save to the extent that they involved the interest of the crown or kingdom" and such private matters were left to equity or ecclesiastical courts.[19] French law was, accordingly, more apt to intervene in relations *within* the family than English law.

The French Revolution had bequeathed a dual legal heritage to women in the nineteenth century. On the one hand, there had been an intellectual ferment and public debate during the turbulent years of 1789–99. *Cahiers* (petitions) to

---

18. Rochester *Daily Democrat,* August 3, 1848, and Rochester *Daily Advertiser,* August 8, 1848. The resolutions of the Rochester convention were (1) to petition the state legislature for the vote every year until granted; (2) to denounce denial of equal representation in government; (3) to deplore apathy and the indifference of women to their rights; (4) to denounce intestate laws (that gave the state control of the estates of men who died without written wills); (5) to decry laws giving husbands legal control of their wives' wages; (6) to "encourag women no longer to promise obedience in the marriage covenant"; (7) to denounce "the universal doctrine of the inferiority of woman" and its effect on women's aspirations; (8) to endorse the efforts of Elizabeth Blackwell to become a doctor; (9) to raise the wages of working women, beginning with household servants; and (10) to encourage women "to assume, as soon as possible, their true position of equality, in the social circle, the church, and the State."

19. René David and John E. C. Brierly, *Major Legal Systems in the World Today: An Introduction to the Comparative Study of Law* (London: Collier-Macmillan Ltd., 1968), pp. 14-16. For extended examination of the civil law tradition, see John Henry Merryman, *The Civil Law Tradition: An Introduction to the Legal Systems of Western Europe and Latin America* (Stanford, Calif.: Stanford University Press, 1970).

the Estates General, pamphlets, and feminist newspapers listed numerous grievances and proposed specific reforms. Olympe de Gouges had summed up this
tradition in her pamphlet, *Déclaration des droits de la femme et de la citoyenne:*
"Woman is born free and remains equal to man in rights," she declared. "The
goal of every political association is the conservation of the natural and impre-
scriptible rights of Woman and of Man: these are liberty, property, security, and
above all, resistance to oppression."[20] On the other hand, the revolutionary tradition contained memories of aristocratic women condemned to death, of militant
female revolutionaries who pressured the Jacobins into more radical tactics, and
of the suppression of the feminist *Société des Republicaines révolutionnaires*
and other clubs by the Revolutionary Convention.[21]

Under the *ancien régime* married women, depending on their class and
the customs of the region, had enjoyed some freedom and property rights. The
Revolutionary Convention drafted a preliminary version of a new civil code that
"recognized the equality of persons, civil marriage, divorce on grounds of incom-
patibility, adoption, inheritance by illegitimate children if recognized by the
parents, and equal division of property among the heirs."[22] The code was not
adopted although separate laws provided for easier divorce, established legal
majority for women at age twenty-one, and granted women the right to testify
in civil suits as witnesses. The coup d'état that brought Napoleon to power in

---

20. Olympe de Gouges, *Déclaration des droits de la femme et de la citoyenne* (Paris, 1794),
Articles 1 and 2. For background on this author, see Léopold Lacour, *Les Origines du
féminisme contemporain; Trois Femmes de la révolution; Olympe de Gouges, Théroigne de
Méricourt, Rose Lacombe* (Paris: Plon-Nourrit et Cie, 1900) or Jeanne Bouvier, *Les Femmes
pendant la révolution, leur action politique, sociale, économique, militaire, leur courage
devant l'échafaud . . .* (Paris: E. Figuière, 1931).

The salient points of the declaration may be summarized as follows: Men and women
are born free and equal and have the same rights (articles 1 and 2); government exists to
conserve these rights (article 2) and derives its sovereignty from the Nation, which is the
whole body of men and women (article 3); liberty and justice consist in mutual and equal
reciprocity and should be restrained by the laws of reason and nature (articles 4 and 5); law
is the expression of the General Will and is equally binding on all because all (men and
women) have consented to it (either in person or via representatives) and all are eligible alike
for the opportunities it creates and the benefits it bestows (articles 6 and 7); the law must
punish all alike on the basis of known and necessary punishments promulgated in advance
(articles 7, 8, and 9); freedom of speech and opinion is necessary for the good of all and for
the defense of woman's honor (i.e., to establish paternity) and ought to be curtailed only by
law for the sake of public order (articles 10-12); all citizens (men and women) must pay
taxes but should be equally eligible for public employment, should consent (either in person
or via representatives) to contribute, and should receive a strict accounting from public officials (articles 13-15); constitutions are void unless the majority cooperates in their drafting
and consents to them, unless they provide for guarantees of rights, and unless there is separation of powers (article 16); property (particularly in marriage) is separate and inviolable;
and no person can be deprived of property except by law and with just compensation
(article 17). (Translation by Chris [Peterson] Ahmed.)

21. Elizabeth Racz, "The Women's Rights Movement in the French Revolution," *Science
and Society* 16 (Spring 1952): 151-74; Scott H. Lytle, "Second Sex (September 1793),"
Journal of Modern History 27 (March 1955): 14-26.

22. F. M. H. Markham, "Napoleonic France," in *France: Government and Society: An
Historical Survey,* 2nd ed., J. M. Wallace-Hadrill and John McManners, eds. (London:
Methuen & Co. Ltd., 1970), p. 195.

1799 soon reversed the trend. Napoleon's personal intervention in the formulation of the new civil code gave it a reactionary cast in reference to women. The Civil Code of 1804, part of the *Code Napoléon*, made the husband as much the dictator of the home as Napoleon was of France. Women lost control over the family property and encountered more stringent rules of marriage and divorce.[23]

The Civil Code was soon followed by four other codes (penal, commercial, civil procedure, and criminal procedure) that continued the suppression of some aspects of the revolutionary understanding of equality as a legal condition. Some of the judicial practices of the *ancien régime* were reintroduced. Juries were restricted or eliminated in certain cases, arbitrary arrest and censorship reappeared, and special courts (without juries) were introduced to deal with such crimes against the state as rebellion and smuggling. The defeat and exile of Napoleon brought not only a restoration of the Bourbon monarchy but a new constitution as well. The charter of 1814, as it was known, provided:

"art. 1.   Frenchmen are equal before the law, whatever may be their rank and title.
art. 3.   They shall all be equally admissible to civil and military posts.
art. 4.   Their personal liberty is likewise guaranteed; no-one shall be prosecuted or arrested except in cases provided for by law and in the form which it prescribes."

However much these provisions were violated in later years, the charter remained the base line to which liberals appealed until the Revolution of 1830. In terms of legal concepts and institutions, the essential outlines of French developments in the nineteenth century were determined by 1815.[24]

The erosion of equality as a legal condition reflected the intellectual confusion over equality as a value. This process was indicated in the fate suffered in the early nineteenth century by the slogans of the French Revolution—Liberty, Equality, and Fraternity. In the recurring cycle of revolution, restoration, reac-

---

23. Alfred Cobban, *A History of Modern France,* revised ed. (New York: George Braziller, Inc., 1965), Book 2, pp. 30-31; J. Christopher Herold, *The Age of Napoleon* (New York: Random House, Inc., 1963), pp. 146-48, 166-67; Elaine Kuehn, "The Introduction of Divorce in the French Revolution," (unpublished essay, History Department, State University of Iowa, Iowa City, Iowa), p. 971; and Racz, *Science and Society* 16: 163.

The final version of the Civil Code of 1804 was a compromise between northern customs (equal inheritance for the children and community of property between parents) and the Roman law of the south (*régime dotal* or marriage settlement). Charles Seignobos, *The Evolution of the French People,* trans. Catherine Alison Phillips (New York: Alfred A. Knopf, Inc., 1932), p. 293. For further information, see Bernard Schwartz, ed., *The Code Napoleon and the Common-Law World* (New York: New York University Press, 1956), particularly Chapter 8.

24. Markham, "Napoleonic France," pp. 196-98; Irene Collins, ed., *Government and Society in France, 1814-1848* (New York: St. Martin's Press, 1971), p. 11 [Charter of 1814]; A. F. Thompson, "From Restoration to Republic," in *France: Government and Society: An Historical Survey,* 2nd ed., J. M. Wallace-Hadrill and John McManners, eds. (London: Methuen & Co. Ltd., 1970), p. 208.

tion, and revolution, French liberalism had to choose liberty over equality and in the process shattered fraternity along class lines. To the liberals, liberty was the triumph of individuality over authority, the freedom to pursue economic opportunity, and the presence of choice between competing centers of loyalty and authority. To grant equal political power to those who were not equal socially was to invite disaster, a return to the anarchy and terror of the Revolution. Too much democracy (political equality) was a threat to liberty (individuality, moral hierarchy, and orderly progress). Fraternity was a fruitless sense of transnational fellowship based on common humanity or a frightening search for a General Will to overcome the lack of social cohesion in society. Better to seek the *juste milieu*, the middle ground, the moderate way. The middle classes were regarded as the golden mean in society; they had property, responsibility, and stability.[25]

The French socialists emphasized equality above liberty and redefined fraternity. The watchwords of the French Revolution were thus given distinctive connotations in socialist thought. Liberty, in the Revolution of 1789, had been defined as the right to act within the restraints imposed by communally sanctioned law or by the mutual obligations of the equal rights of all citizens. To socialists such as Henri Saint-Simon or Karl Marx, this liberty was an illusion or an empty historical slogan. What men needed was emancipation, or freedom, from those conditions or social structures that created alienation.

Equality, which to the revolutionaries of 1789 had meant the equal legal status of all men in a society free from hereditary privileges, now took on various

25. J. P. Mayer, *Political Thought in France: From the Revolution to the Fourth Republic* (London: Routledge and Kegan Paul Ltd., 1949), pp. 9-44. For some of the key figures of French liberalism (Royer-Collard, Benjamin Constant, François Guizot, and Alexis de Tocqueville) see Vincent E. Starzinger, *Middlingness: Juste Milieu Political Theory in France and England, 1815-1848* (Charlottesville: University Press of Virginia, 1965); Paul Bastid, *Benjamin Constant et sa doctrine* (Paris: Colin, 1966); Marvin Zetterbaum, *Tocqueville and the Problem of Democracy* (Stanford, Calif.: Stanford University Press, 1967); and Felix Ponteil, *Les Classes bourgeoises et l'avènement de la démocratie, 1815-1914* (Paris: Michel, 1968).

During the period 1800 to 1820 the chief intellectual influence on French feminism was Madame de Staël (1766-1817), the literary critic, historian, savant, and author. In her youth she had endorsed Rousseau's view that women should be educated to please men. (What Blackstone was for English and American feminism—an authority to be refuted—so Rousseau was for French feminism.) Beginning in 1800, she had begun cautiously to posit an equal need for self-expression in women and by 1814 had repudiated her youthful adulation of Rousseau. Her mature view related "the equality of woman in the family and in marriage to the cultivation of her mind in terms of her *own* value and her capacity to endure the hardships of life . . ." [italics added]. See Madelyn Gutwirth, "Madame de Staël, Rousseau, and the Woman Question," *Publications of the Modern Language Association* 86 (January 1971): 107. Recent works on her include J. Christopher Herold, *Mistress to an Age* (New York: Bobbs-Merrill Company, 1958) and Monroe Berger, ed., *Madame de Staël on Politics, Literature, and National Character* (New York: Doubleday & Company, Inc., 1964).

After Madame de Staël, there was a marked decline in the role of women in French literature (with the exception of George Sand). See Edith Kern, "Author or Authoress?" *Yale French Studies* 27 (Summer 1961): 3-11; Micheline Herz, "The Angelism of Madame de Ségur," *Yale French Studies* 27 (Summer 1961): 12-21; Simone de Beauvoir, *The Second Sex*, trans. H. M. Parshley (New York: Alfred A. Knopf, Inc., 1953), p. 107. Even in the eighteenth century, "opinion was hostile to 'bluestockings,'" according to Simone de Beauvoir.

connotations in the hands of the "utopian" socialists of the early nineteenth century. Among them, equality meant (1) an equal obligation (or opportunity) to perform productive toil, (2) an equal (or at least equitable) share in the social product of industry and labor, and (3) an equal sharing of social roles and responsibilities.

Fraternity in the revolutionary tradition had referred to the universality of human nature and the hope that recognition of the rights of man would eliminate war. In the hands of the ardent feminist and socialist Flora Tristan, fraternity came to mean the unity of the working class across national lines, the essential equality between those who shared the burdens of productive toil, and the self-emancipation of the workers through unity or solidarity.[26]

With the *Code Napoléon* and the Bourbon Restoration limiting women's property rights and stifling any political aspirations, it fell to the socialists in the 1830s and 1840s to advocate women's social and economic equality. Saint-Simon, Fourier, and Cabet, the leading communitarian socialists, had all been concerned with a woman's right to choose a job in keeping with her talents, inclinations, or social function and with her right to receive an equitable share of the rewards of labor. They hoped to eliminate the poverty that drove some women into prostitution or premature marriage by substituting a communitarian society for a competitive capitalistic society. On the question of the future of the family, they parted company. Saint-Simon's followers advocated complete sexual freedom (the "rehabilitation of the flesh") and abolished the family for a communal love family or withdrew into monastic celibacy to await a female messiah. Fourier favored dissolution of the family in the larger circle of the phalanx and the abolition of marriage. But Cabet wanted to retain the family, with the father as head of the household, as did Proudhon, Marx' rival for socialist leadership. Nevertheless, free love, "community of wives," or abolition of marriage were part of the specter of communism that haunted the bourgeois imagination in the 1840s.[27]

---

26. Kingsley Martin, *French Liberal Thought in the Eighteenth Century: A Study of Political Ideas from Bayle to Condorcet* (reprint ed., New York: Harper & Row, Publishers, 1963), Chapters 9-10; Frank E. Manuel, *The New World of Henri Saint-Simon* (Cambridge, Mass.: Harvard University Press, 1956), p. 275; Shlomo Avineri, *The Social and Political Thought of Karl Marx* (London: Cambridge University Press, 1968), p. 46; George Lichtheim, *The Origins of Socialism* (New York: Praeger Publishers, Inc., 1969), pp. 60-75; and G. D. H. Cole, *Socialist Thought: The Forerunners, 1789-1850* (London: Macmillan & Co. Ltd., 1955), pp. 183-85.

27. William L. Langer, *Political and Social Upheaval, 1832-1852* (New York: Harper & Row, Publishers, 1969), p. 219; Cole, *Socialist Thought: Forerunners*, pp. 53, 69, 77, 216; Harry W. Laidler, *History of Socialism* (New York: Thomas Y. Crowell Company, 1968), p. 137; Christopher H. Johnson, "Communism and the Working Class Before Marx: The Icarian Experience," *American Historical Review* 76 (June 1971): 674-77.

The French Revolutionary tradition included a *sans culotte* "puritanical" emphasis on civic virtue, "simplicity in dress and manner, a proper married status, regular attendance at the local *société populaire*, the execution of guard duties whenever required, and the undertaking of useful productive work." Richard Cobb, "The Revolutionary Mentality in France, 1793-1794," *History* 42 (1957): 189.

The emphasis on economic issues and social status in socialist thought raised the question of the reality of economic freedom, of equality as opportunity, in France. Alfred Cobban, the historian, has noted that "the two countries which escaped serious trouble [in the revolutions of 1848] were the only two in which industrialization had made substantial progress—Great Britain (but not Ireland) and Belgium."[28] If the emergence of a women's rights movement is seen simply as a response to industrialism, then the French experience presents a unique problem. Approximately half the population or more worked in agriculture where women's roles were relatively fixed and traditional. The French cotton and woolen textile manufacture was still done on a small scale; these industries were somewhat slow in mechanizing and were less efficient than their English counterparts. The silk industry of Lyons operated on a home-production and putting-out system. Journeymen, women, and children worked in the home and sometimes even slept in hammocks suspended over their looms. The French proletariat was composed not primarily of factory workers in the modern sense but of skilled craftsmen organized along craft or traditional lines. The destruction of the ancient guilds in the Revolution and the suppression of trade unions in later years left craftsmen vulnerable to the "more efficient business practices and more careful exploitation of traditional labor resources" that characterized the 1830s and 1840s.[29]

A woman's role in the French economy thus was largely traditional and in significant areas was declining. The slow changes in the textile industries were undercutting the home craft system. Changes in agriculture and viticulture (grape growing) were reducing the number of peasant-owned and cultivated farms and vineyards. In the cities, where the jobs of washerwoman, shopkeeper, and seamstress had been some of the traditional occupations open to women, new pressures of insecurity arose from the periodic depressions. During the 1840s, for example, spokesmen for the seamstresses demanded day nurseries for children of working mothers; municipal or national laundries, restaurants, and lounges for workers; and national workshops to hire unemployed women. Opportunities for educated women in such fields as journalism, schoolteaching, and clerical work in business and government were slow to develop in France because of periodic suppression of the press, political contests over control of education, the small size of French enterprises, and frequent changes of governmental personnel.[30]

---

28. Cobban, *Modern France*, p. 135.

29. David S. Landes, "Technological Change and Development in Western Europe, 1750-1914," in *The Cambridge Economic History of Europe*, H. J. Habakkuk and M. Postan, eds. (London: Cambridge University Press, 1965), 6: 391-93; Folke Dovring, "The Transformation of European Agriculture," in *The Cambridge Economic History of Europe* 6: 604; Johnson, "Communism and the Working Class Before Marx," *American Historical Review* 76 (June 1971): 658-67 (quotation is from Johnson, p. 657); and Leo A. Loubère, "The Emergence of the Extreme Left in Lower Languedoc, 1848-1951: Social and Economic Factors in Politics," *American Historical Review* 73 (April 1968): 1038.

30. E. Labrousse, "1848-1830-1789: How Revolutions Are Born," trans. Max A. Lehmann, in *Essays in European Economic History, 1789-1914*, F. Crouzet, W. H. Chaloner, and

Since the limited extent of economic changes in France from 1815 to 1848 produced only slight modification of the social structure, interpretations of French history based on the notion of a rise and triumph of the middle class have fallen into disfavor among recent historians. They have called attention instead to the importance of certain demographic factors in French history. At the beginning of the nineteenth century, the proportion of single women was extremely high in Belgium, Holland, Switzerland, and most of France. "France was only exceptional in that its population married at a much younger age than did those of the other countries" although, by modern standards, they still married late. Age at first marriage declined in these countries throughout the century.[31]

The peak years of the marriage curve in France, 1809 and 1813, coincided with changes in the conscription laws that exempted newlyweds from military service. Thereafter the marriage curve declined to a low in 1832 and then remained high and steady from 1833 to 1845, "steadier and higher than for any corresponding period since the recording of the official statistics." More women were getting married and at an earlier age; yet the birth rate declined steadily from 1815 to 1855. The key to understanding the peculiar nature of French feminism, then, lies in the history of the French family.[32]

W. M. Stern, eds. (New York: St. Martin's Press, Inc., 1969), pp. 2-14; Edith Thomas, *Les Femmes de 1848* (Paris: Presses universitaires de France, 1948), pp. 54-56, 71; Johnson, "Communism and the Working Class Before Marx," *American Historical Review* 76 (June 1971): 676-77; Priscilla Robertson, *Revolutions of 1848: A Social History* (reprint ed., New York: Harper & Row, Publishers, 1960), p. 68. The remarks on the restriction of opportunity for educated women in journalism, education, and business hierarchies were derived from a reading of the following sources (which seldom mention women in history) with the data of Edith Thomas' *Les Femmes de 1848* in mind: Frederick A. de Luna, *The French Republic Under Cavaignac: 1848* (Princeton, N.J.: Princeton University Press, 1969), pp. 203-10 (control of press); pp. 238-48 (reform of education); and pp. 329-35 (Constitution of 1848, which reaffirmed basic civil rights); Langer, *Political and Social Upheaval, 1832-1852*, pp. 454-55 (the Falloux educational law strengthening the role of the Catholic Church in education); Eugene N. Anderson and Pauline R. Anderson, *Political Institutions and Social Change in Continental Europe in the Nineteenth Century* (Berkeley: University of California Press, 1967), Chapter 6 (Civil Rights); Lenore O'Boyle, "The Middle Class in Western Europe, 1815-1848," *American Historical Review* 71 (April 1966): 826-45; Alfred Cobban, *France Since the Revolution* (New York: Barnes & Noble, Inc., 1970), Chapters 1 and 2; and Landes, "Technological Change and Development in Western Europe, 1750-1914," *Cambridge Economic History of Europe* 6: 353-421. A law in 1793 had sought to promote equality of opportunity in education at the primary level, but women teachers received only two thirds of the salary of men for the same work. Racz, *Science and Society* 16: 165.

31. Etienne Van de Walle, "Marriage and Marital Fertility," *Daedalus* 97 (Spring 1968): 490, 493 (quotation).

32. Wesley D. Camp, *Marriage and Family in France Since the Revolution* (New York: Bookman Associates, 1961), pp. 21-23 (quotation p. 23). Marriage gave the middle-class woman her position in society, and widowhood (quite frequent as middle-class women married older men) gave her security and some freedom along with legal responsibilities for property. A. Daumard, *La Bourgeoisie Parisienne de 1815 à 1848* (Paris: École Pratique des Hautes Études, 1963), pp. 326-34, 357-65.
Under the July Monarchy, 1830-48, widows and divorcees could delegate the politi-

Since the publication of Philippe Ariés' speculations on the evolution of the French family, historians have taken a renewed interest in the relationship between family structure and the emergence of feminism. Ariés portrayed a medieval kin group, or "line," in which the woman had considerable power, in which children were frequently separated from the parents by apprenticeship and training programs under servants and relatives, and in which society intermingled freely with the household. Gradually, the modern "family" emerged. It was characterized by subordination of the woman, by reunion of parents and children, and by separation in privacy of this "nuclear family" from society and from the rest of the household.[33]

During the nineteenth century, the modern family pattern spread downward through the social structure and was adopted by the lower classes, among whom the medieval family pattern until then still prevailed. While the modern family brought subordination for the woman, it enhanced the equality of the children and shaped them in the images of both the father, "the incarnation of the universal and objective values" of society, and the mother, "the symbol of the expressive and particularistic values" of the home. The ideology of the French family thus provided for women the orthodox image of their role, lending to that image strong social sanctions and offering women considerable psychic rewards for their conforming behavior. Revolt against this orthodoxy gave a peculiar antibourgeois cast to alternate feminist images of woman's place in society.[34]

cal rights that accompanied ownership of taxable property (including the right to vote) to certain male members of their families. Sherman Kent, "Electoral Lists of France's July Monarchy, 1830-1848," *French Historical Studies* 7 (Spring 1971): 120 n.9.

33. Philippe Ariés, *Centuries of Childhood: A Social History of Family Life,* trans. Robert Baldick (New York: Alfred A. Knopf, Inc., 1962), pp. 353-57, 393-404.

34. François Bourricaud, "France," in *The Institutions of Advanced Societies,* Arnold M. Rose, ed. (Minneapolis: University of Minnesota Press, 1958), pp. 489-90, 492-93, 510-17 (quotation p. 517).

For basic demographic data, see J. Bourgeois-Pichat, "The General Development of The Population of France since the Eighteenth Century," trans. Peter Jimack in *Population in History,* D. V. Glass and D. E. C. Eversley, eds. (London: Edward Arnold [Publishers] Ltd., 1965), pp. 474-506; for the legal debate on the family as a basic institution of the second republic, see M. Léonard Gallois, *Histoire de la Révolution de 1848* (Paris: Naud et Gourju, 1849), 4: 21 ff. Article IV of the *Constitution Française de 1848* stated: "Elle [France] a pour base: la famille, le travail, la propriété et l'ordre public." (The principles on which France is based are the family, work, property, and public order.) For the impact of industrialization on social structure, see Donald J. Harvey, *France Since the Revolution* (New York: The Free Press, 1968), p. 68. Because of recent criticism I have not used the standard work on French demography, Charles Pouthas, *La Population française pendant la première moitié du XIXe siècle* (Paris: Cahiers de l'Institut National d'Etudes Démographique, 1956). See Paul G. Spagnoli, "The Demographic Work of Charles Pouthas," *Historical Methods Newsletter* 4 (September 1971): 126-39.

In the *History of Woman Suffrage* there is a curious passage: "Those who made the demand for political freedom in 1848, *in Europe as well as America,* were about the same age" *HWS,* 1: 102 [italics added]. Since the average age of the female signers of the Seneca Falls declaration of the rights of women was thirty-five, this would put their birth dates around 1813. (Katherine Milton Faust, "Signers of Seneca Falls," p. 9.) Applied to France, this would mean that the children of the 1809-1813 "marriage boom" would provide the

In summary, France in the first half of the nineteenth century was characterized by a significant number of young married women who had more time and leisure than their ancestors (because of the falling birth rate), who had confronted legal disabilities in the *Code Napoléon,* who had experienced some loss of economic status or who faced restricted social mobility, and who had been exposed to alternate images of woman's role in socialist writings and in literary feminism. In spite of renewed efforts by church and state to reinforce the "traditional" (i.e., modern or bourgeois) family pattern with an official ideology of home and marriage, some of these women responded to the new images and old needs. This was particularly true in the events of the February Revolution in 1848, which toppled the monarchy and proclaimed the Republic under a Provisional Government.

Universal suffrage was the ideological slogan of the Republicans in the Provisional Government, and it was not illogical for women's rights advocates to look to them for equal political rights. On March 5, 1848, the Provisional Government decreed "universal suffrage" and clarified it a few days later to exclude children, aliens, criminals, and those exiled by the courts. Soon women's groups were petitioning and lobbying for the vote and other political rights. Some left-wing supporters of the Provisional Government feared that universal suffrage with an "untutored" electorate would only benefit conservative forces. Neither Cabet, the socialist, nor Louis Blanc, an influential labor leader, believed that women could be trusted with the ballot until they had been properly "educated" and weaned away from the influence of conservative elements in the church.[35]

Prior to the elections of April 23, 1848, an article in the official *Bulletin of the Republic* caused considerable alarm among moderate elements by calling for further revolutionary upheavals "if they [the elections] do not lead to the triumph of social truth." The author of the inflammatory article was George Sand (née Aurore Dupin), the leading representative of literary feminism. Under the

---

leadership for the 1848 women's rights clubs and feminist agitation (since "a peak year in marriages, such as that in 1813, tends to produce a bumper crop of babies in the following year." Camp, *Marriage and Family in France,* pp. 21–22). A spot check of the birth dates of French feminist leaders of 1848 revealed that the *HWS* statement is somewhat impressionistic or propagandistic and would probably not be sustained by a statistical examination of a representative sample of French feminists and women's rights leaders. While no adequate statistical study has yet been conducted on the American suffrage leaders, the data for such a study can be found in Edward and Janet James, eds., *Notable American Women, 1607-1950: A Biographical Dictionary* (Cambridge, Mass.: Harvard University Press, 1971). A disappointing attempt at a collective portrait is found in Robert E. Riegel, *American Feminists* (Lawrence: The University Press of Kansas, 1963).

35. Thomas, *Les Femmes de 1848,* Chapter 4; Johnson, "Communism and the Working Class Before Marx," *American Historical Review* 76 (June 1971): 677; Léo A. Loubère, "The Evolution of Louis Blanc's Political Philosophy," *Journal of Modern History* 27 (March 1955): 44; Alfred Cobban, "Administrative Pressure in the Election of the French Constituent Assembly, April, 1848" and "The Influence of the Clergy and the 'Instituteurs Primaires' in the Election of the French Constituent Assembly, April, 1848" in Cobban, *France Since the Revolution,* pp. 29–81.

influence of Pierre Leroux, a self-styled mystic and social philosopher, she espoused socialism and a vague, utopian communism.

Like most of the Romantics, she thought of herself as an individual rather than as a representative of a class or caste. Her feminist vision was extremely limited:

"What she sought for women was not the right to vote nor to sit in Parliament, but the enjoyment of equality with men in Law and in Love. She believed that where the husband holds the wife in subjection, married happiness is impossible, that it can exist only in an atmosphere of freedom. Women would make no demands if they were loved as they wished to be. . . . 'As wives they are treated more as servants than as companions. Men do not love them: they make use of them, they exploit them, and expect, in that way, to make them subject to the law of fidelity.'"[36]

When Eugénie Niboyet's feminist journal, *La Voix des femmes,* nominated George Sand for a seat in the National Assembly, she refused the nomination.[37]

The election of April 23, 1848, seemed to confirm the fears of the left-wing critics. Instant democracy did not work as planned: "The elections were a resounding victory for the moderate and conservative elements." Even in Paris, "the workers and lower classes generally voted for the respectable, well-to-do candidates." The newly elected Assembly soon passed a law barring women from participating in the numerous clubs and associations that had sprung up since the February Revolution. Fourierist Victor Considérant proposed a constitutional amendment granting political rights for women but the constitutional committee rejected it out of hand. The old dual heritage for women of the French revolutionary tradition—of liberation and suppression—was about to be reenacted again. This turn of events was symbolized by the fate of two women, Pauline Roland and Jeanne Deroin.[38]

While George Sand represented the legalistic and personalistic tradition of French feminism, Pauline Roland and Jeanne Deroin represented the economic and fraternal aspects of French feminism. Pauline Roland, who had achieved some notice as a writer and a historian, had been influenced by Saint-Simonian doctrines and by Pierre Leroux's social ideas. After the February Revolution, she had founded the *Association fraternelle des Instituteurs, Institutrices et Professeurs socialistes.* Jeanne Deroin, a schoolteacher married to a ministerial

---

36. André Maurois, *Lélia: The Life of George Sand,* trans. Gerard Hopkins (New York: Harper & Row, Publishers, 1953), pp. 324-25. For her political views see pages 327-33.

37. Thomas, *Les Femmes de 1848,* Chapter 5; "Eugénie Mouchon Niboyet," *Larousse Grand Dictionnaire universel du XIXe siècle* (Paris: M. Pierre Larousse, 1875), 11: 977.

38. Langer, *Political and Social Upheaval,* p. 343 (quotation) and Bernhard J. Stearn, "Women," *Encyclopedia of the Social Sciences,* Edwin R. A. Seligman and Alvin Johnson, eds. (New York: The Macmillan Company, 1934), 15: 445. Pierre Leroux introduced a similar motion in 1851, and it suffered the same fate as Considérant's motion.
A more conservative proposal was made by the American educator Emma Willard,

employee, was the founder of a feminist newspaper, *La Politique des femmes et l'opinion des femmes;* the cofounder of a political club, the *Club de l'Emancipation des Femmes;* and a self-proclaimed candidate, in 1849, for the Assembly. She revived Flora Tristan's idea of a federation of workers' associations with a central committee composed of delegates from the associations. Both Jeanne Deroin and Pauline Roland served on the central committee. When the police suppressed the federation in 1850, the two women were sentenced to six months in jail for violating the law on associations, and the prosecutor made much of their socialist views on marriage.[39]

From the prison of St. Lazare in Paris, Pauline Roland and Jeanne Deroin in June 1851 addressed a latter to the second National Woman's Rights Convention at Worcester, Massachusetts, and recounted their failure to secure women's suffrage in France. The letter displays their values and their concepts of equality:

"Dear Sisters:

Your courageous declaration of Woman's Rights has resounded even to our prison, and has filled our souls with inexpressible joy. . . . But, while those selected [for the Assembly] by the half of the people—by men alone—evoke force to stifle liberty and forge restrictive laws to establish order by [oppression], woman, guided by fraternity, foreseeing incessant struggles, and in the hope of putting an end to them, makes an appeal to the laborer to found liberty and equality on fraternal solidarity. . . . The union of associations based on fraternal solidarity had for its end the organization of labor; that is to say, an equal division of labor, of instruments [of production], and of the products of labor. . . . Sisters of America! Your socialist sisters of France are united with you in the vindication of the rights of woman to civil and political equality."[40]

---

who held an orthodox image of woman's place. In a poem written in 1830 she called for a woman's council to advise men:

. . . There shall be a council held
Of matrons, having powers to legislate
In woman's province, and to recommend
To man's prime rule, acknowledged first and best,
As wife to husband, whatsoever, to her
Maternal eye, seems for the general good.

In 1848 she recommended that the French constitutional assembly invite women to send delegates to form such an advisory council. Alma Lutz, *Emma Willard: Pioneer Educator of American Women* (Boston: Beacon Press, 1964), p. 116.

39. Thomas, *Les Femmes de 1848,* Chapters 6-10; "Pauline Roland," *Larousse Grand Dictionnaire universel du XIXe siècle* (Paris: M. Pierre Larousse, 1875), 13: 1310.
    For additional information, see Edith Thomas, *Pauline Roland: socialisme et féminisme au XIXe siècle* (Paris: Librairie M. Rivière, 1956); A. Ranvier, "Une Féministe de 1848, Jeanne Deroin," *La Revolution de 1848* 4 (1907-8): 324.

40. Elizabeth Cady Stanton, Susan B. Anthony, and Matilda Joslyn Gage, eds., *History of Woman Suffrage,* vol. 1, *1848-1861,* 2nd ed. (Rochester, N.Y.: Charles Mann, 1887), pp. 234-36.

The letter was a noble gesture, but the differences between the two countries were greater than the words indicated.

The words "vindication of the rights of woman to civil and political equality" did not represent the common goal of the two movements but the common means that they advocated to achieve disparate goals. The French feminists' socialist vocabulary indicated that their goal was an alternate economic and political system. The American women, on the other hand, wanted not so much to change the system as to join it as full and equal partners with men. In tactics, the two movements also differed. The Frenchwomen were jailed because they violated a law controlling associations; the American women were free to form innumerable voluntary associations and to hold conventions unmolested by government.[41]

The alliance with the militant working-class unions achieved by some leading French feminists—Flora Tristan, Pauline Roland, Jeanne Deroin—was in marked contrast to the predominately middle-class sympathies of American leaders in the women's rights movement. The demand for the vote in France represented a grasping at a current revolutionary ideology; in the United States it was logically linked to the customary behavior of reformers.

Faith in democracy as a means of achieving equality was thus a common bond among French republicans, socialists, and feminists; among American political abolitionists, social reformers, and suffragists; and among English radicals, Chartists, and trade unionists. Their various experiences in the 1840s—revolution and repression in France, organization and education in America, defeat and disorganization in England—illustrated the fact that a common factor in comparable settings does not necessarily produce similar results. Yet the demand for political democracy remained; it reemerged in the turbulent 1850s in the context of temperance agitation, nativist hostilities, and social and economic tensions. For the nagging question was still unanswered: "For what purposes would men—and perhaps women—use the vote?"

---

41. William L. O'Neill has made the point that the American women's movement was characterized by voluntary associations while the English movement (in the 1830s) was not. The same observation would be valid for France. Arnold Rose has pointed out in his comparative study of social institutions and national character that "in France, beginning in 1791 and extending throughout the nineteenth century, there was a series of laws and court decisions which prohibited the formation of voluntary associations and punished those who led in their formation. Thousands of associations were formed—including such 'innocent' ones as organizations for the promotion of literature and student activities—but the authorities repressed them. Most Frenchmen [and Frenchwomen] learned to avoid forming or joining such groups. . . ." See William L. O'Neill, *The Woman Movement: Feminism in the United States and England* (New York: Barnes & Noble, Inc., 1969), p. 18; Arnold M. Rose, ed., *The Institutions of Advanced Societies* (Minneapolis: University of Minnesota Press, 1958), pp. 9-10. In the twentieth century, "a French women thinks of herself as part of a couple and a household before she thinks of herself as a part of some group," and women's organizations would be "unthinkable." Ménie Grégoire, "French Women Are Not Feminists," *Atlas: The Magazine of the World Press* 9 (February 1965): 85-86; John Ardagh, *The New French Revolution* (New York: Harper & Row, Publishers, 1969).

3

Prohibition: Society, the State, and the Problem of Democracy

THE BACKGROUND OF PROHIBITION
IN ENGLAND AND AMERICA, 1826–1856

In the 1830s and 1840s the debates on feminism, women's rights, and women's suffrage had raised questions about equality; in the same period the debates over temperance—and, in the 1850s, the debates over prohibition—raised questions about the nature of democracy and the role of the state. These aspects of the temperance and prohibition campaigns have been obscured by recent interpretations which see these developments as part of a struggle for power and social status between older social elites seeking to assert social control over others and newer self-help oriented groups seeking middle-class respectability and social mobility. A comparative perspective, on the other hand, shows that temperance and prohibition were crude attempts to deal with the problem of alcoholism and to use the state as a means of social control over this serious social problem.[1]

---

1. Joseph R. Gusfield, *Symbolic Crusade: Status Politics and the American Temperance Movement* (Urbana: University of Illinois Press, 1963), Chapter 2. Gusfield based his argument on two main assertions, one historical and the other methodological. The historical part of the argument rested on an analysis of the temperance movement in the 1820s that stressed its conservative, elitist leadership, particularly that of Reverend Lyman Beecher of Connecticut. Three points need to be remembered in attempting to generalize from Beecher's case: first, Connecticut was somewhat unique in that the political issue of disestablishment of the Congregational Church was a source of contention until 1818, long after separation of church and state was achieved elsewhere; second, Beecher's efforts in the 1810s and '20s to use temperance to bolster Federalism and the privileged position of the Congregational Church failed (the Federalist party disintegrated, the Congregational Church was disestablished, and temperance sentiment and legislation lagged); and, third, Lyman Beecher's "autobiography" was written from his reminiscences by his children during the Maine Law enthusiasm and, therefore, highlighted his pioneering role disproportionately. See Jarvis Means Morse, *A Neglected Period of Connecticut's History, 1818-1850* (New Haven: Yale University Press, 1933), pp. 3-53, 205-13; Barbara M. Cross, ed., *The Autobiography of Lyman Beecher* (Cambridge, Mass.: Harvard University Press, 1961), 1: *xi,* p. 196.
    Gusfield's methodological orientation toward the concept of status politics, particularly as it applied to prohibition, rested heavily on the notion that habits or behavior patterns help to establish status in society. Brian Harrison has successfully attacked this notion by pointing out that in the nineteenth century class determined dietary and drinking behavior whereas in the twentieth century behavior determines "class" (i.e., status group). Brian Harrison, *Drink and the Victorians: The Temperance Question in England, 1815-1872* (Pittsburgh: The University of Pittsburgh Press, 1971), p. 26.

A society can begin to solve a social problem only after it has been defined as such, and that is a function of its intellectual history. For example, heavy drinking was an integral part of the fabric of social custom and economic life in the eighteenth century in both England and its colonies. Only three groups defined drunkenness as a problem serious enough to warrant religious sanctions or professional, medical condemnation: Quakers, Wesleyan Methodists, and some enlightened rationalists such as Doctor Benjamin Rush. Many of these early pioneers regarded the drinking of "ardent spirits" as the chief cause of drunkenness and advocated the drinking of beer and ale as "temperance" substitutes. The evangelical revivalists of the early nineteenth century defined drunkenness as a personal sin, a failure of self-discipline and moral will, and advocated either abstinence or restriction of personal consumption to beer and light wines.[2]

Along with the definition of a problem, a society must have a heightened awareness of its presence before attempting a solution. A number of factors operated in the early part of the nineteenth century to increase public awareness of heavy drinking and public intoxication. The impact of industrialization, particularly in England, was complex and contained contradictory effects: on the one hand, it made sobriety necessary (particularly in dealing with high speed machinery) and possible (by bringing workers "indoors" under the factory roof, increasing dietary or consumption levels, and by rewarding a self-disciplined elite of working men with social mobility); on the other hand, it accentuated cyclical and technological unemployment (with enforced periods of idleness) and weakened traditional social restraints on behavior (by forcing the once migrant laborer into new urban situations).[3]

Taxation and licensing laws in England also had complicated interactions with these economic factors. "There is no doubt that *per capita* beer consumption went down between 1800 and 1830" in England, an authority has noted; "and no doubt that *per capita* consumption of tea and sugar went up; while between 1820 and 1840 there was a marked increase in the consumption of gin and whiskey."[4] These figures were largely a function of additional duties on malt and beer and the reduction of duties on spirits in 1823 and 1825. Pressure for free trade in beer and freer licensing laws led to the Licensing Act of 1828 and the Beer Act of 1830 which limited the magistrates' control of licenses and allowed any householder who paid poor rates to obtain (for two guineas a year)

---

2. John Allen Krout, *The Origins of Prohibition* (New York: Alfred A. Knopf, Inc., 1925), Chapters 3-4; Carl Binger, *Revolutionary Doctor: Benjamin Rush, 1746-1813* (New York: W. W. Norton and Company, Inc., 1966), pp. 91, 173, 198-201; Perry Miller, *The Life of the Mind in America: From the Revolution to the Civil War* (New York: Harcourt Brace Jovanovich, Inc., 1965), pp. 3-14, 78-86.

3. Brian Harrison, *Drink and the Victorians*, pp. 40-41.

4. E. P. Thompson, *The Making of the English Working Class* (New York: Random House, Inc., 1964), p. 317. Brian Harrison showed a similar increase in *wine* and spirit consumption for the same period (1820-1840) and related it to reductions in spirit duties and disproportionate increases in the number of licenses in spirit retailing. Harrison, *Drink and the Victorians*, p. 66.

a license to sell beer. Within a few years over thirty thousand beer shops secured such licenses. While the statistical evidence for the long-term impact of the Beer Act is not conclusive, the Beer Act "did temporarily increase drunkenness when it came into force."[5] Thus the state seemed to be acting in such a way as to increase drunkenness just at the time when economic change and religious pietism made certain sectors of the public acutely sensitive to the change.

In the United States, similarly complicated interactions took place. In 1810 (the date of the first official statistics) there were one hundred and thirty-two breweries producing fewer than two hundred thousand barrels of beer and ale annually for a population of over seven million people. "The American production was far from impressive in 1810, but by 1820 it appeared to have deteriorated completely. . . . In the 1820 census, individual breweries were reporting, 'Business diminished in consequence of the increased consumption of whiskey,' or 'Sales diminished,' 'Dull,' 'Sales decreased.'"[6] That the appeal of "temperance" beverages seemed to be declining in the 1810s, 1820s, and 1830s while the consumption of ardent spirits was apparently increasing could be related to a number of governmental decisions and economic factors: the removal of excise taxes on domestic spirits, the increase in imports of wines and spirits (related both to declining prices and low customs duties), and the technological innovations in distillation techniques (including the application of steam engines, the invention of the columnar or continuous process still, and the accidental discovery of the charred barrel technique). All these factors added to the increased supply.[7] As in England, the sensitive observer could not help but feel that the social problem of drunkenness was growing more acute.

Since the social problem of chronic drunkenness (or alcoholism in modern terminology) was defined as a personal moral problem, leadership in the early phases of the temperance movement fell naturally to those who claimed guardianship over the morals of the community, particularly the clergy. Their proposed solutions tended, therefore, to be individualistic and paternalistic. In his famous *Six Sermons on Temperance* (published in 1826) the Reverend Lyman Beecher,

---

5. Harrison, *Drink and the Victorians,* p. 82; Thompson, *Making of the English Working Class,* pp. 317-18. The Licensing Act of 1828 (which remained the basic law until 1872) specified the conditions under which a license would be granted: no adulteration of drinks, no public drunkenness, no unlawful games, disorders, or notorious persons allowed to assemble, and no serving during Sunday morning church service hours. Harrison, *Drink and the Victorians,* pp. 73-74.

6. Stanley Baron, *Brewed in America: A History of Beer and Ale in the United States* (Boston: Little, Brown and Company, 1962), pp. 123-24.

7. The invention of the column still by Robert Stein in Scotland in 1826 and its improvement in 1832 by Aeneas Coffey made possible continuous distillation. The application of steam and use of charred barrels also helped to revolutionize the whiskey industry prior to the Civil War. See Henry G. Crowgey, *Kentucky Bourbon: The Early Years of Whiskey-making* (Lexington: The University Press of Kentucky, 1971); "Whiskey," *Encyclopaedia Britannica,* 1968 ed., vol. 23.

The excise tax on domestic whiskey was lowered in 1792 and abolished in 1802. It was reimposed during the War of 1812 and abolished in 1817. The customs duty on molasses (used for distillation into rum) was raised in 1828 but reduced again in 1830.

an early temperance leader in Connecticut, advocated "the banishment of ardent spirits from the list of lawful articles of commerce" but relied initially on individual self-denial to accomplish this end. "It is the buyers who have created the demand for ardent spirits," he argued. "Let the temperate cease to buy, and the demand for ardent spirits will fall in the market three fourths," and the capitalist would find it unprofitable and shift to another line of endeavor. Those upper-class and middle-class community leaders who shared Beecher's preference for personal abstinence and moral persuasion formed in 1826 the American Society for the Promotion of Temperance (known as the American Temperance Society) and established their own newspaper, the *National Philanthropist*.[8]

The zeal with which temperance converts carried their message from the United States to England cannot be explained as status seeking; rather, it reflected the religious mentality of the times. Temperance was a crusade, part of the revivalistic emphasis on achieving moral order in society, and it was part of the transatlantic community of shared religious ideas. What the Americans contributed to the common concern was the technique of the voluntary association. "The American anti-spirits movement was first mentioned [in England] in the evangelical *Christian Observer* in July 1826, and by May 1828 the periodical was urging London to participate."[9] American sea captains introduced the new ideas into Liverpool in 1829. Antispirits movements appeared simultaneously in August 1829 in Belfast, Ireland, and in Glasgow, Scotland, (both influenced by American ministers). The antispirits movement was carried in 1830 from Scotland to Bradford, Warrington, Manchester, Liverpool, and Leeds in the north of England. Activity in the north forced the moderate Londoners to form the British and Foreign Temperance Society (BFTS) in July 1831, representing the paternalistic approach of aristocratic Anglicans, wealthy evangelicals, and Quaker philanthropists.[10]

New forces were at work during the 1830s on both sides of the Atlantic as middle-class and working-class elites joined the temperance cause. The logic of various positions was worked out in debate and organizational realignments. Anglo-American temperance societies divided over such issues as "short pledge" (voluntary abstinence from hard liquors but not necessarily from beer, light wines, and hard cider), "long pledge" (voluntary abstinence from all intoxicating beverages, except sacramental wine), and "American pledge" (voluntary abstinence from all intoxicating beverages, including sacramental wine). "Teetotalism," strong in the liberal-radical, nonconformist areas of northern and western England, sought to reform the drunkard, not just to set a model for his behavior.[11]

8. Barbara M. Cross, ed., *The Autobiography of Lyman Beecher*, 2: 23; Krout, *Origins of Prohibition*, pp. 105-8, 131; Gusfield, *Symbolic Crusade*, pp. 41-42.

9. Brian Harrison, *Drink and the Victorians*, p. 101.

10. Brian Harrison, *Drink and the Victorians*, pp. 101-5; E. H. Cherrington et al., *Standard Encyclopedia of the Alcohol Problem* (Westerville, O.: American Issue Publishing Company, 1926-1930), 1: 420 (hereinafter cited as Cherrington, *SEAP*).

11. For the origins of teetotalism, see Brian Harrison, *Drink and the Victorians*, Chapter 5.

The teetotal society at Preston, England, combined religious and political radicalism.

Moving beyond the tactics of moral suasion, some temperance advocates wanted to use the licensing power of the local community to control, tax, or eliminate retail sales of intoxicating beverages to certain groups. For example, James Appleton of Gloucester, Massachusetts, suggested in 1832 the total prohibition of retail sales in quantities of less than thirty gallons in order to stop lower-class tippling while leaving unregulated wholesale purchases by wealthy and politically influential citizens. Similarly, an English parliamentary committee in 1834 recommended closer municipal supervision of licenses and, as an ultimate solution, the prohibition of spirits.[12]

In the United States, antiwine ("American pledge") teetotalers split off from the moderate American Temperance Society to form their own American Temperance Union. In January 1837 the American Temperance Union began to denounce the license system as immoral traffic with sin under government sanction. Shifting their emphasis from moral persuasion to political pressure, temperance advocates petitioned their state legislatures for control of the liquor trade. The use of the petition reached a peak in 1838. In 1839 and 1840 attempts by Neal Dow and James Appleton to fasten prohibition on the city of Portland and on the state of Maine failed completely. In the 1840s a self-reformation movement among what were then called lower-class drunkards, the Washingtonian Society, challenged the middle-class control of temperance and returned the emphasis in American temperance circles from political action to moral suasion.[13]

A similar situation in England in the late 1830s and early 1840s has been aptly summarized by Brian Harrison in his monumental study of the English temperance movement:

"The anti-spirits leaders were alarmed. Teetotalism seemed to be moving in

---

12. Cherrington, *SEAP*, 1: 187-88; 3: 930-31; Krout, *Origins*, p. 285; Harrison, *Drink and the Victorians*, p. 111. On the topic of the extension of the license power for social control of drunkenness, John Allen Krout, writing in the 1920s, provided a scholarly treatment of this subject that has remained a standard reference work. While he eschewed moral judgments in historical analysis and presented a factual case, he was nevertheless hindered by the categories of the public debate on prohibition in the 1920s. He took pains to examine the licensing practices of the Puritans, dismissed the eighteenth-century prohibition experiments of Oglethorpe in Georgia, and slighted the role of race relations in the development of federal laws prohibiting sales to Indians and slaves.

For the role of race relations (Indian-White, Indian-Negro, and Negro-White) in the origins of federal prohibition laws, see Cherrington, *SEAP*, 1: 18, and Ora Brooks Peake, *A History of the United States Indian Factory System, 1795-1825* (Beverly Hills, Calif.: Sage Publications, Inc., 1954). Congress passed a law in 1802 authorizing the President "to prevent or restrain the vending or distributing of spiritous liquors among all or any of the said Indian tribes."

13. Frank L. Bryne, *Prophet of Prohibition: Neal Dow and His Crusade* (Madison: The State Historical Society of Wisconsin, 1961), pp. 25-26; Krout, *Origins*, pp. 155-59, 172, 179; and Frank Thistlethwaite, *America and the Atlantic Community: Anglo-American Aspects, 1790-1850* (New York: Harper & Row, Publishers, 1963); pp. 94-96.

secular directions, and was giving too much power to uncultivated laymen; the clergymen who dominated the B.F.T.S. found themselves losing control of the movement they had helped to establish. Furthermore the elevating tone was being drained out of the movement by the vulgarity and purely recreational character of the teetotal meeting. Nor had the anti-spirits movement originally been designed to promote social mobility or to enable working men to set an example to their superiors; once these developments were joined to radical and dissenting views, schism in the temperance movement was inevitable."

Moderationist versus teetotal pressures divided the London-based New British and Foreign Temperance Society in 1839. The adoption of the "American" or long pledge by the more democratic, middle- and working-class members drove the wealthier, short-pledge moderationists from the society.

In the 1840s a Catholic crusade swept across Ireland under the leadership of Father Mathew and spread to England and the United States. Consumption of spirits in England seemed to reach a peak in the early 1840s and then receded before the teetotal tide only to revive in the 1850s. The culmination of the decade's frenzied activities came in the World's Temperance Convention in London in 1846. An attempt to form a worldwide union failed. Too many unresolved issues divided the temperance forces to permit such a scheme to succeed.[14]

The temperance movement was plagued by the question of the proper role of the state. James Appleton had charged that to use the power of the state to license taverns did not serve the common good. A member of the Massachusetts Society for the Suppression of Intemperance disagreed and challenged him on the grounds that the proper technique of the temperance movement was moral persuasion by appeals to conscience rather than by legal coercion through resort to "the strong arm of the law." Appleton's reply went straight to the heart of the issue: "It is this 'strong arm of the law' that has opened tippling shops in every

---

14. Harrison, *Drink and the Victorians,* Chapter 6 (quotation, p. 134), Figure 3 (p. 66); Cherrington, *SEAP,* 3: 931-32; George M. Young, *Victorian England: Portrait of an Age,* 2d ed. (London: Oxford University Press, 1960), p. 77.

Brian Harrison has provided a biographical analysis of 382 leaders (teetotalers) active in the English temperance movement between 1833 and 1872. His main findings can be summarized briefly as follows: (1) three fourths were born between 1795 and 1824 and were influenced by evangelicalism; (2) their birthplaces were predominately in Lancashire and Yorkshire; (3) the urban element was strong and evangelized the surrounding rural areas; (4) the self-made man ethos was pervasive; (5) the prominent professions were nonconformist minister, professional lecturer or agent, clergyman of the established church, textile manufacturer, and newspaper proprietor; and (6) the movement attracted men of "immense energy, self-confidence and optimism" who occasionally turned to eccentricity. Significantly, he noted that "without a comparative sample from the contemporary general public, one cannot say whether teetotal leaders were in general more puritanical or more aggressive in manner than other people" (p. 159). Harrison, *Drink and the Victorians,* Chapter 7.

A comparable study of American leadership for the same period is not available, but the materials for such a study exist in the minutes of various temperance societies listed in Philip Hamer, ed., *Guide to Archives and Manuscripts in the United States* (New Haven: Yale University Press, 1961).

corner and village of the state;" he replied, "and we ask, if this 'strong arm' is raised at all, that it may be raised to save and not to destroy."[15]

Who was to determine how the strong arm of the law should strike? Historian Lee Benson has shown that a transformation in American values occurred in the 1820s and '30s among those who opposed the Masonic lodges and their place in society:

"Pushing democratic ideology to its Rousseauean logical limits, they argued that no restrictions could be placed on the will of the people. Rousseau made the 'general will' the standard of morality, but he had doubts about how best to ascertain it. The Antimasons had no such doubts. If the people were supreme, if their will must prevail over every standard and every institution, then the electoral process could properly be used to 'reform' *all aspects* of American society."[16]

Sharing this belief that evil could be defined by the majority, some temperance leaders in the 1840s advocated local-option elections as a method of determining the will of the community.[17]

But who constituted the community in pre-Civil War America? What was the relationship between society and the state? Irish victims of the great famine and German refugees from the unsuccessful revolutions of 1848 were flooding into the land. The annexation of Texas and the cessions following the Mexican War had vastly increased the territory of the United States and had exacerbated

---

15. Cherrington, *SEAP*, 1: 188.

16. Lee Benson, *The Concept of Jacksonian Democracy: New York as a Test Case* (Princeton, N.J.: Princeton University Press, 1961), p. 22. See also Charles McCarthy, "The Antimasonic Party," *Annual Report of the American Historical Association, 1902* (Washington, D.C.: Government Printing Office, 1903), 1: 544 for the links between antimasonry and temperance.

17. Krout, *Origins,* pp. 262-82; D. Leigh Colvin, *Prohibition in the United States: A History of the Prohibition Party and of the Prohibition Movement* (New York: George H. Doran Company, 1926), pp. 24-25.

This political aspect of the temperance question frequently has been slighted because of the more obvious correlation between evangelical Protestantism and prohibition. In the 1830s, however, the association between evangelicalism and temperance was complicated by orthodox versus ultraist tensions. By the 1840s, the ultraistic evangelical Protestant dominance had been challenged by Father Mathew's campaign among Irish Catholics and by the formation of a Church of England Temperance Society. Pietism was probably more important than revivalism per se or any particular theological stance. Roland Bainton's observation, that Catholic, Lutheran, and Episcopalian churches were willing to accept total abstinence but not to require it, is an apt summary of the situation in the 1840s (except for certain pietistic dissenters in Sweden and Methodists in England who divided on the issue).

For the relationship between evangelical Protestantism and temperance, cf. Krout, *Origins,* Chapter 6; Timothy V. Smith, *Revivalism and Social Reform* (Nashville, Tenn.: Abingdon Press, 1957), Chapter 1, and pp. 167-68; Roland Bainton, *Christian Unity and Religion in New England* (Boston: Beacon Press, 1964), pp. 181-82; Harrison, *Drink and Victorians,* Chapter 8; Richard Jensen, *The Winning of the Midwest: Social and Political Conflict, 1888-1896* (Chicago: The University of Chicago Press, 1971), Chapter 3.

the issue of slavery. "No union with slaveholders" was the cry of the Garrisonian abolitionists; some Southern firebrands talked of secession. Did "society" include the immigrant, the slave, the Indian, the Latin American? Could the bonds of the political state hold together the abolitionist and the slaveholder, the prohibitionist and the liquor dealer, the nativist and the immigrant?

Some social scientists have postulated that in such times of social stress, political reform becomes a means whereby a traditional elite seeks to ensure its continued social domination. Thus temperance, women's suffrage, free public education, and nativism have all recently been interpreted as devices for imposing the rural-oriented, middle-class mores of white, Anglo-Saxon, Protestant conservatives upon urban, lower-class, Catholic or free-thinking immigrants from Ireland, Germany, and Western Europe.[18] While such theories contain many plausible insights, they can break down when applied to particular historical situations.

In political ideology, for example, there should have been a natural affinity between the early Republican party and all those who wanted to extend the power of the state to free the slave, to educate the children, to redress women's legal grievances, to prohibit liquor sales, to enforce the Puritan Sabbath, to limit immigration, or to promote internal improvements and manufacturing. That is, they should have been attracted by the theory of the positive liberal state as contained in Republican party oratory. But the case for prohibition could be stated in negative terms—the state ought not to license the liquor traffic—and could appeal to the sentiments of states-rights Democrats corresponding to a theory of a negative liberal state. The prohibition issue thus cut across political party lines.[19]

Nor was the relationship between prohibition and political nativism the simple one-to-one relationship in the 1850s that some writers have claimed.[20]

---

18. Gusfield, *Symbolic Crusade,* pp. 55-56; Alan P. Grimes, *The Puritan Ethic and Woman Suffrage* (New York: Oxford University Press, Inc., 1967), pp. 130-41; Michael B. Katz, *The Irony of Early School Reform: Educational Innovation in Mid-Nineteenth Century Massachusetts* (Cambridge, Mass.: Harvard University Press, 1968); and John Higham, *Strangers in the Land: Patterns of American Nativism, 1860-1925* (New Brunswick, N.J.: Rutgers University Press, 1955), pp. 52-63, 136-44. Grimes and Higham are primarily concerned with events after the Civil War, but the situation then was similar to that of the 1850s.

Ray Allen Billington, writing in the 1930s on the nativism of 1800 to 1860 to analyze nativist tensions, used a rather vague concept of public opinion, which tended to underplay, but not to ignore, class issues. He did not find temperance to be a prime cause of nativist growth. In short, Billington saw anti-Catholic nativism as shattering society vertically along religious lines rather than horizontally along class or status lines. Ray Allen Billington, *The Protestant Crusade, 1800-1860: A Study of the Origins of American Nativism* (New York: Holt, Rinehart & Winston, Inc., 1938).

A summary of recent scholarship on the issue of nativism in pre-Civil War America is found in Ira M. Leonard and Robert D. Parmet, eds., *American Nativism, 1830-1860* (New York: Van Nostrand Reinhold Company, 1971).

19. For the ideology of the early Republican party and the temperance issue, see Eric Foner, *Free Soil, Free Labor, Free Men: The Ideology of the Republican Party before the Civil War* (London: Oxford University Press, 1970), pp. 230, 233, 237-42.

20. A recent book on alcoholism, for example (a private spin-off from a project financed by the National Institute of Mental Health) accepted the identity of temperance and nativism,

The disintegration of the major political parties over the slavery issue did provide an opportunity for those who advocated prohibition and for those who advocated nativism to make their bids for political power. In Maine, prohibitionist Neal Dow, a nominal Whig and a recent Free-Soiler, joined with antislavery Democrats and temperance Whigs to secure a stringent statewide prohibition bill in June 1851. He soon converted John Marsh, corresponding secretary of the American Temperance Union, to his cause. In August 1851 the Union endorsed prohibition. An immense, and exaggerated, propaganda campaign was launched by the Union for Maine Law bills in several states.[21]

At the same time, secret societies dedicated to antiforeign and nativist sentiments moved into the political arena at the local and state levels. Under the name of the Native American Party (known more popularly as the Know-Nothing Party), they too tried to exploit the chaotic political situation. There were important differences between the nativists and the prohibitionists, however. A close examination of three key cases—Illinois, Massachusetts, and New York—reveals some of the differences. In Illinois the partisans of both causes were separated by ethnic and cultural differences, in Massachusetts by class and by rural-urban tensions, and in New York by tactical and ideological considerations. Above all, these cases show that the prohibitionists and nativists held conflicting conceptions of the nature of the community.

---

partly on the basis of the writings of Gusfield, Hofstadter, and Higham and partly on the basis of an English M.A. thesis. See Rupert Wilkinson, *The Prevention of Drinking Problems: Alcohol Control and Cultural Influences* (New York: Oxford University Press, Inc., 1970), p. 8 and n. 14.

21. Byrne, *Neal Dow,* pp. 43-48; Gusfield, *Symbolic Crusade,* p. 55. P. Orman Ray, reporting to the American Historical Association in 1912 on archival and newspaper sources in Pennsylvania history, noted: "From an extended examination of newspapers for these years [1850s] . . . , I was much impressed with the amount of space devoted to this phase of the temperance question [Maine Law] at a time when the slavery question is commonly supposed to have been uppermost in politics. I am inclined to think that careful investigation would show that the liquor-law agitation was a factor in breaking down party lines in the North between 1850 and 1856, second in importance only to the repeal of the Missouri Compromise." P. Orman Ray, "On the History of Pennsylvania, 1815-1860," *Annual Report of the American Historical Association for the Year 1912* (Washington, D.C., Government Printing Office, 1914), pp. 152-53.

22. Arthur Charles Cole, *The Era of the Civil War, 1848-1870,* in *The Centennial History of Illinois,* vol. 3 (Springfield: Illinois Centennial Commission, 1919), Chapters 5, 6, and pp. 205-9; Alexander Davidson and Bernard Struvé, *History of Illinois* (Springfield: Illinois Journal Co., 1874), p. 549.
    Prior to 1847 the temperance movement in Illinois was a minor one localized in the northern "New England" belt and in a few cities such as Chicago, Springfield, and Jacksonville. The Sons of Temperance, a secret, ritualistic lodge, brought new life to the cause, and by 1849-50 had enrolled over six thousand members in 220 lodges. Similar Catholic societies gave the movement an ecumenical caste. No-license elections were carried successfully in 1850 in Quincy (a western Illinois river town with eastern U.S. antecedents), Rockford (a center of free-soil sentiment and Scandinavian immigration), and Springfield, the state capital. The state legislature passed a one-quart law in 1851 (prohibiting sales of spirituous and mixed liquor in quantities of less than a quart). This proved to be unenforceable and it was repealed in February 1853. Temperance advocates were found in both parties although the Whig press had been more pro-temperance than the "Whiskey" Democrats. A recent

In Illinois during the 1854 elections the nativist issue reemerged as the Democratic press claimed to have found evidence of Know-Nothing activity in various cities. The enthusiasm with which Democratic papers attempted to tar their opponents with the brush of Know-Nothingism, Maine Lawism, and abolitionism should make the student of history cautious about accepting their charges as fact. The Whig press had played the same game in 1852 by accusing their opponents of dropping a popular gubernatorial candidate because of his Catholic religion.[22]

The years 1855 and 1856 provided a test of the relative strength of prohibitionist and nativist sentiments. In January 1855, the Maine Law advocates pushed an ambitious, and ambiguous, bill through the state legislature. It provided for the total prohibition of the sale or manufacture of spirituous and malt liquors and wine (but exempted cider and products for export); suspended the issuance of licenses; and provided for a popular referendum in June. During the intervening period a Know-Nothing administration in Chicago raised the license fee, arrested thirty German saloon keepers, and touched off two days of rioting in March.

While speakers for and against prohibition toured the state, the Know-Nothing leadership gathered in Chicago in May. Serious divisions soon split the nativist ranks into two factions: the "Sams" and "Jonathans." "The Sams are anti-foreign and anti-Catholic," the Chicago *Democrat* reported. "The Jonathans are antislavery, but not against foreigners [who disavow temporal allegiance to the Pope]."[23]

In June the long awaited referendum on the prohibition law was held. The results revealed the geographical concentrations of prohibition sentiment. The northern counties, the old centers of the free-soil vote in 1852, along with some local centers of strength downstate, turned in heavy votes for prohibition, but they could not overcome the antiprohibition majorities in the central and

---

article noted that "in 1854 most of the leading antislavery advocates in Illinois were directing their efforts toward temperance and [on February 22, 1854] were attending the state convention of the Maine Law Alliance in the First Presbyterian Church at Springfield." Victor B. Howard, "The Illinois Republican Party: Part 1. A Party Organizer for the Republicans in 1854," *Journal of the Illinois State Historical Society* 64 (Summer 1971): 126. A year later, antislavery Republicans in Chicago and northern counties were denouncing the nativist movement. See Victor B. Howard, "The Illinois Republican Party: Part 2. The Party Becomes Conservative, 1855-1856," *Journal of the Illinois State Historical Society* 64 (Autumn 1971): 288, 295.

23. Chicago *Democrat*, May 5, 1855, as quoted in John P. Senning, "The Know-Nothing Movement in Illinois, 1854-1856," *Journal of the Illinois State Historical Society* 7 (April 1914): 19; Davidson and Struvé, *History of Illinois*, p. 606; Bessie Louise Pierce, *A History of Chicago*, vol. 2: *From Town to City, 1848-1871* (New York: Alfred A. Knopf, Inc., 1940), p. 211. In Chicago, the temperance candidate for mayor in 1854, Amos G. Throop, was defeated by a Democrat. A year later the Know-Nothing candidate, Levi D. Boone, was elected (Pierce, pp. 211, 437). In Chicago, the Jonathans (antislavery nativist moderates) outnumbered the Sams (antiforeign, anti-Catholic) (Pierce, p. 212).

southern counties. The turnout had been the largest in the history of the state. The majority of over 14,000 votes against the proposal was decisive.[24]

The State Council of the Illinois Native American party (Know-Nothing), meeting in Springfield in July 1855, issued a platform that attacked the repeal of the Missouri compromise, advocated various nativist proposals, and added a catchall plank on internal improvements. Significantly, there was no mention of either temperance or prohibition. On May 15, 1856, the hard-core "Sam" (antiforeign, anti-Catholic) faction backed the national pro-slavery nominee, Millard Fillmore, and offered a separate state ticket. The bolting "Jonathan" faction (antislavery, moderately nativist) joined the Anti-Nebraska convention in Bloomington. They became part of the new Illinois Republican party along with the strategic German Democrats, Anti-Nebraska Democrats and Whigs, and abolitionist free-soilers.[25]

The vote in 1856 for Fillmore and for the American party gubernatorial candidate may be regarded, therefore, as the hard-core nativist vote. It showed that the centers of nativism rested in the central counties, particularly along the Mississippi River. A comparison of the 1855 prohibition referendum and the 1856 Know-Nothing vote indicated that, while the center of prohibitionist strength lay in the free-soil or "New England" belt in the North with a secondary belt in central Illinois, the center of anti-Catholic, antiforeign nativism lay in the older regions of southwestern and central Illinois.[26]

---

24. The pro-prohibition vote has traditionally been interpreted primarily as a heritage of New England immigration because of the predominance of favorable votes in the northern counties (except for Cook County). But an analysis of the percentage of the prohibition votes in all counties showed a slightly different pattern. The northern tier of counties (Cook, LaSalle, Kane, and Winnebago), which returned the heaviest prohibition votes, was followed by a belt of counties in central and western Illinois (Fulton, Adams, Peoria, Madison, Sangamon, and McLean) that represented the heritage of river-borne migration from the border South.

25. Senning, "The Know-Nothing Movement in Illinois," pp. 21-29 and appropriate maps. The 1855 Know-Nothing platform is here printed between pages 27 and 29 as an appendix. The 1856 American party gubernatorial candidate, Buckner S. Morris, was a supporter of the Constitutional Union ticket in 1860 and accused of plotting to free Confederate prisoners during the Civil War. Theodore Calvin Pease and James G. Randall, eds., *The Diary of Orville Hickman Browning*, vol. 1: *1850-1864* (Springfield: Illinois State Historical Library, 1925), p. 56 n. 5.

26. Senning divided the Know-Nothing vote in each county by the total vote cast in that county and then ranked the counties by the percentage of the county that had voted for the Know-Nothing slate. This index showed two arcs of counties with high percentages running *from east to south* in central and southern Illinois (Piatt, Fayette, Bond, Wabash, Clay, White, Menard, Edwards, Lawrence, Alexander, and Madison). He correlated these findings with newspaper commentaries and concluded that the vote for Fillmore in 1856 came from Unionist Whigs. Daniel J. Elazar, a political scientist, has recently interpreted Illinois politics in the nineteenth century as the product of internal migration patterns and political cultures. The northern centers of prohibition strength would coincide with his Yankee-Scandinavian "moralistic" political culture while the nativist vote in the southwestern portion of the state would correlate with his middle state "individualistic" political culture. Neither Senning's index nor Elazar's migrant streams would account satisfactorily for the overlap of nativist

The situation in Massachusetts in the 1850s provided an example of nativism and prohibition working hand in hand, but even here important differences must be noticed. The apportionment system gave undue political influence to rural areas. The three-party system (Whig, Democrat, Free-Soil) and the need for a majority vote in the legislature in elections for governor and senator placed political power in the hands of party leaders. The social structure placed effective power in the hands of the upper-class Whig merchants and entrepreneurs.

The unreformed system of rural overrepresentation was in operation during the political upheavals of 1854–56. In September 1854, a Republican state nominating convention was convened at Worcester by Free-Soilers, Anti-Nebraska Democrats, and temperance men. Amasa Walker of North Brookfield, an old Van Buren Democrat, made a rousing speech that defined the issues of the day "as between Slavery, Romanism and Rum, on the one side, and Freedom, Protestantism and Temperance, on the other." The remarks were well received and the platform included a plank calling for "the prohibition by law of the sale of intoxicating liquors as a beverage." The convention nominated Henry Wilson for governor.[27]

---

and prohibitionist votes in Fulton, Sangamon, and Madison counties (which are outside the northern Yankee belt and which share in the middle-state heritage).

By dividing the Know-Nothing vote in each county in 1856 by the total Know-Nothing vote cast in the state, the numerical centers of nativist strength can be isolated. (Thus, although a county might show a high percentage of Know-Nothing votes, it might be insignificant in the overall total of Know-Nothing votes cast in the state.) By ranking the counties on this index, a different picture emerged. The numerical centers of Know-Nothing strength in 1856 lay in two bands of counties in the *southwestern* part of the state around the Mississippi and Illinois rivers (except for White county in the southeast). These counties (Madison, Sangamon, Macoupin, Pike, Hancock, St. Clair, Fulton, Morgan, McDonough) may indicate a reaction to German immigrants in the St. Louis area or the disaffection of former Whigs.

The complexity of the connection between prohibitionist and nativist sentiments can be illustrated by the careers of two men in Quincy in Adams County on the Mississippi River. Benjamin M. Prentis, who had been born in Virginia and who had moved to Missouri in 1835 before coming to Quincy in 1841, supported the Maine Law Alliance. Orville Hickman Browning, a Kentucky-born Whig and political friend of Lincoln, also supported the Maine Law in 1855. Yet in 1856 he was instrumental in creating the Republican party at a convention in Bloomington where he labored to reconcile German voters and "Jonathans." Neither Prentis nor Browning would fit the Yankee-Puritan stereotype of the prohibitionist nor the southern, hard-core "Sam" nativist. Lyman Trumbull, a Democrat leader who helped to form the Republican party, regarded both prohibitionist and nativist issues as distractions that hindered the new party.

See Daniel J. Elazar, *Cities of the Prairie: The Metropolitan Frontier and American Politics* (New York: Basic Books, Inc., Publishers, 1970), Chapters 4-8; Pease and Randall, ed., *Diary of O. H. Browning*, 1: 152, 169-70, 237; Mildred C. Stottler, "The Democratic Element in the New Republican Party in Illinois, 1856-1860," *Papers in Illinois History* (Springfield: Illinois State Historical Society, 1944), p. 37; Foner, *Free Soil, Free Labor, Free Men*, pp. 232-33, 242, 246.

27. Francis Curtis, *The Republican Party: A History of Its Fifty Years' Existence and a Record of its Measures and Leaders 1854-1904* (New York: G. P. Putnam's Sons, 1904), 1: 198-99.

In 1850, Henry Wilson, a self-made man and opportunistic leader of one wing of the Massachusetts Free-Soil party, had entered into a coalition with out-of-power, pro-labor

Party	Election of 1853	Election of 1854
Whig	60,600	27,200
Democratic (antislavery)	36,000	13,700
National Democratic (proslavery)	5,400	6,400
Free Soil	29,000	6,400
American (Know-Nothing)		81,500

Henry Wilson thought he detected the shifting of the political winds late in 1854 with the emergence of the Know-Nothings, so he declined the nomination and threw his support to the Know-Nothing candidate, Henry J. Gardner. The results are given in the accompanying table. For Massachusetts the election of 1854 was a political earthquake.[28]

The occupational composition of the new legislature was very revealing of the nature of this nativist movement. The number of farmers and lawyers in the legislature declined; the number of shopkeepers, clergymen, and skilled craftsmen increased. "Know Nothingism was popular among the farmers, but it had its greatest vogue in the towns, where it could build upon a strong class feeling among the workers at the same craft." Above all, the new legislators were inexperienced in parliamentary practices. Only two of six new senators had ever

Democrats. The coalition gained control of both houses, and inaugurated "something of a social and political revolution in Massachusetts. The proud, aristocratic Whigs were no longer the proprietors of power in the state." Henry Wilson became president of the Senate; Nathaniel Banks, antislavery Democrat, became Speaker of the House; George Boutwell, another Democrat, became governor; and, after a protracted struggle, Charles Sumner, the eloquent antislavery orator, became the United States senator. The coalition favored constitutional reform and pushed for the calling of a state constitutional convention.

In January 1852 the temperance forces marched five thousand strong to the State House to present a petition in favor of a Maine Law. The petition allegedly carried 130,000 signatures, and later additions carried the figure to 160,000. A bill was finally passed and signed by Governor Boutwell in May 1851. But the strains of the session split the coalition on the eve of the election of 1852 and Irish Catholics left the coalition.

In the fall of 1852, the voters approved the call for a constitutional convention. The election for delegates was apportioned by towns, with the net result that the rural areas were overrepresented while Boston was underrepresented. Only one Irishman was elected to the convention. The rural areas were antislavery and antiforeigner. The result of the convention's efforts was a series of proposed constitutional amendments that restricted the judiciary (under attack because of its role in upholding the Fugitive Slave law), increased the over-representation of the rural areas, and provided for plurality elections in the lower ranks of state offices. The proposals were soundly defeated, and the Whigs returned to power in 1853. See Ernest A. McKay, "Henry Wilson and the Coalition of 1851," *New England Quarterly* 36 (September 1963): 338-57 (quotation, p. 348); Samuel Shapiro, "The Conservative Dilemma: The Massachusetts Constitutional Convention of 1853," *New England Quarterly* 33 (June 1960): 207-24; Colvin, *Prohibition in the U.S.*, p. 32.

28. Henry Greenleaf Pearson, "Preliminaries of Civil War, 1850-1860," in *Commonwealth History of Massachusetts*, Albert Bushnell Hart, ed. (New York: The States History Company, 1930), 4: 490.

served before, and only one of forty-four new representatives had any previous legislative experience. Wags suggested an appropriate Biblical verse for the traditional swearing-in sermon: Job 8:9 "For we are but of yesterday, and know nothing."[29]

The Know-Nothing contingent was apparently made up of three separate factions. A Free-Soil faction, headed by Henry Wilson, was prepared to rule or ruin the Know-Nothings in the cause of antislavery and free soil. A strong nativist faction, without effective leadership but with broadly based strength in the state, wanted to restrict suffrage and office holding to native-born citizens or to naturalized citizens who had been residents for twenty-one years. A "Pro Slavery Rum Hunker" faction from lower-class wards in Boston, led by Joseph Hiss, wanted to investigate alleged antisocial behavior among Catholics and to enjoy power as a perquisite of office.

Prohibition was the one issue that cut across the lines of nativism and revealed the inner tensions of the Know-Nothing coalition. Joseph Hiss was appointed chairman of a "Nunnery Committee" to investigate alleged irregularities and anti-American activities in Catholic convents, nunneries, and parochial schools. The junketing committee created a scandal of its own by charging to state expense the cost of elaborate champagne dinners, the favors of a "woman of easy virtue," and numerous other items. Not only had they harassed Catholic citizens but they had violated an 1852 antiliquor law as well. Hiss was expelled from the legislature for mishandling state funds. Apparently the Boston wing of the Know-Nothings was less concerned with temperance than with the "temporal powers of the Pope" or the temptations of an erstwhile Maria Monk (author of a fake exposé of Catholic convents).[30]

The legislature, meanwhile, had been wrestling with the problem of the ineffectual 1852 antiliquor law. "It was stated that every member of the senate and seven-eighths of the house were opposed to its repeal." Nevertheless, after a bitter struggle, a law was framed that prohibited the manufacture or sale of liquor, beer, wine, and cider either as a beverage or as medicine except by an authorized and registered agent of the state. The passage of the law split the Know-Nothing legislative coalition, but not before it had passed a Personal Liberty law (to nullify the Fugitive Slave law) and a married woman's property bill.[31]

The perspective that emerged from this complicated picture suggested that class antagonism separated or complicated nativist and prohibitionist forces. Brahmin Whigs, for example, did not support nativism. Working-class or lower middle-class artisans supported nativism but probably were hostile to prohibition

29. George H. Haynes, "A Know Nothing Legislature," *Annual Report of the American Historical Association for the Year 1896* (Washington, D.C.: Government Printing Office, 1897), 1:178.

30. Billington, *Protestant Crusade,* pp. 414-15.

31. Pearson, in Hart, ed., *Commonwealth History,* 4: 492; Elizabeth Cady Stanton, Susan B. Anthony, and Matilda Joslyn Gage, eds., *History of Woman Suffrage* (Rochester, N.Y.: Charles Mann, 1887), 1:211 (hereinafter cited as *HWS*); Haynes, *Annual Report of the A.H.A., 1896,* 1: 182 (quotation).

if the Hiss case was representative. The rural, antislavery elements were probably the staunchest supporters of prohibition; the urban anti-Catholic nativists were probably more concerned with the immigrant's political power than with his social habits.[32]

Tactical and ideological considerations also entered the picture in New York. In the presidential election of 1852, New York voters had elected Horatio Seymour, a Democrat, as governor. The Democrats also enjoyed a majority in both the state Assembly and in the Congressional delegation. But success spelled disaster for the Democratic party as it split into three factions over the Kansas-Nebraska Act. The "hard-shell" faction favored the Kansas-Nebraska Act, enlargement of the Erie Canal, and a Maine Law; the "soft-shell" faction entertained reservations on the Kansas-Nebraska Act and upheld Governor Seymour's veto of the Maine Law bill in 1854; and the "Anti-Nebraska" faction opposed the Kansas-Nebraska Act and were divided on temperance questions. The Whigs, too, split into factions: the Seward Whigs (antislavery and antinativist) and Silver Grey Whigs (pro-unionist and nativist).

The Anti-Nebraska Democrats, Seward Whigs, temperance men, and some Catholic voters united to support a fusion ticket that ran Myron H. Clark for governor. The Silver Grey Whigs backed the Know-Nothing candidate, Daniel Ullman. Thus a vote for Clark (fusion ticket) would be a vote for temperance and against nativism; a vote for the "hard-shell" candidate would be a vote for prohibition (Maine Law); a vote for the "soft-shell" candidate would be a vote against prohibition, and a vote for the Know-Nothing candidate would be a nativist vote (antiforeign). The results of the election were that Clark (fusion) was elected with 156,804 votes while Seymour ("soft-shell") received 156,495 votes, Bronson ("hard-shell") received only 33,850 votes, and Ullman (Know-Nothing) received 122,282 votes.

The New York legislature passed a new prohibition law in 1855, and Governor Clark signed it in April. In the fall, the fusion forces reorganized to present a Republican ticket. They dropped the prohibition question and attacked the Know-Nothings. The Know-Nothings swept aside the Republicans and feuding Democrats to win control of the state. In 1856 the state court of appeals held that a portion of the 1855 prohibition law was unconstitutional. In 1857, the state returned to strict licensing when a coalition of Know-Nothings and Democrats emerged in the legislature.[33]

In summary, the prohibition issue in the politics of the 1850s, like a "free

---

32. Barbara Miller Solomon, "The Intellectual Background of the Immigration Restriction Movement in New England," *New England Quarterly* 25 (March 1952): 48. She quotes Theodore Parker to James Orton, February 22, 1855: "America should be the Asylum of Humanity for this century as well as for the seventeenth," p. 49.

33. Curtis, *The Republican Party*, 1: 216; Foner, *Free Soil, Free Labor, Free Men*, pp. 234-35, 239-41; Andrew Wallace Crandall, *The Early History of the Republican Party, 1854-1856* (reprint ed.; Gloucester, Mass.: Peter Smith, 1960), p. 24; Alexander C. Flick, ed., *History of the State of New York* (New York: Columbia University Press, 1935) 6: 273; 7: 77-89; Colvin, *Prohibition in the United States*, p. 34.

radical" in chemistry, had the capacity to combine with other elements. The strongest affinity was between prohibition and antislavery. Whether measured in Illinois, New York, or Massachusetts, political abolitionism and prohibition (or Maine Lawism) were found to be united. In Massachusetts the legislature, dominated by Know-Nothings, passed a Personal Freedom law to overcome the Fugitive Slave law. Nativism and prohibition exhibited the weakest urge to combine. In Illinois and New York, they worked at cross-purposes; the net result was that the new Republicans sought to please strategic German Democrats and Seward Whigs rather than the hard-core nativists or prohibitionists. In Massachusetts, working-class urban nativists ran afoul of prohibition laws. Nativism flourished in the South, sometimes in alliance with prohibition and sometimes in opposition to it.

The capacity of prohibition to combine with other elements was related as much to its concept of community as to the social origins of its adherents. Nativists believed that participation in government should be restricted and that government ought not to allow certain groups to participate in the political community. Some prohibitionists and abolitionists, on the other hand, wanted government to intervene actively in the commercial life of the community for the common good. This democratic element in the prohibitionist sentiment of the 1850s, its majoritarianism in morals and political strategies, rested on a desire to give the community a semblance of cohesion and order. Their effort, in short, was to *reform* the Irishman or German (literally as well as figuratively) and to make him an "acceptable" member of the evolving community, not to remove him from their midst (by restricting immigration) or to render him powerless (by restricting voting and extending naturalization periods). Ultimately, the nativist wanted to exclude the foreigner; the prohibitionist wanted to assimilate him. Some abolitionists wanted to restructure the community on a free-labor basis; the overlapping of political abolitionism and prohibitionism was, therefore, both logical and mutually beneficial.

The way in which the debates on temperance and prohibition raised questions about how the community will should be determined was illustrated by events in New York. The Maine Law propaganda had arrived at a moment of intense frustration for some elements within the temperance movement in New York. Women had participated actively in the local-option campaign of 1846, and the repeal of the local-option law in 1847 aroused their wrath. The Daughters of Temperance, a secret society, spread rapidly throughout the state. Some women "took power in their own hands, visiting saloons, breaking windows, glasses, bottles, and emptying demijohns and barrels into the street."[33] In January 1852 the New York state Sons of Temperance refused to allow Susan B. Anthony to speak before their convention. A few angry women withdrew and held their own meeting. In April 1852 they formed the Woman's State Temperance Society. Elizabeth Cady Stanton was elected president. She called for a statewide Maine Law, for divorce on the grounds of habitual drunkenness in the husband, and for a withdrawal of women from foreign mission societies so that they could concentrate on issues closer to home. The question of the proper role of the state in the prohibition issue was thus united with the question of equality in the women's rights issue.[34]

The appeal sent out by Susan B. Anthony in support of the Maine Law petition revealed the changed nuances in temperance and women's rights thought since 1848:

". . . Woman has so long been accustomed to non-intervention with law making, so long considered it man's business to regulate the liquor traffic, that it is with much cautiousness she receives the new doctrine which we preach; the doctrine that it is her right and duty to *speak out against the traffic and all men and institutions that in any way sanction, sustain or countenance it;* and, since she cannot vote, to duly instruct her husband, son, father or brother how she would have him vote, and if he longer continue to misrepresent her, take the right to march to the ballot-box and deposit a vote indicative of her highest ideas of practical temperance" [italics added].[35]

To speak out against institutions, to seek to influence the course of public policy, to seize the ballot—all these actions implied that women were an integral part of the social and political process, a part of that majority will of the community that defined evil and that moved the strong arm of the law. Neal Dow put the issue succinctly in a letter to Susan B. Anthony. "It is absurd," he wrote, "to argue that the community has no power to control this great evil; that any citizen has the right to inflict it upon society, or that society should hesitate to exercise its right and power of self-protection against it."[36]

The way in which the debates on prohibition and nativism also raised questions about who constituted society was illustrated by the diary of George Templeton Strong, a conservative New York lawyer. In April 1854, he wrote:

"Governor Seymour has vetoed the Maine Liquor Law. Whether he's right or wrong is a question on which an off-hand opinion is clearly presumptuous, for the questions involved are deep and dubious. I've no sort of sympathy with the temperance fanatics—rather a prejudice against them. But I am sure it would be better for mankind if alcohol were extinguished and annihilated. Has or has not society the right to make it contraband, as it forbids the sale or storage of gunpowder within certain limits, as it . . . assumes a right to confiscate and destroy a beauteous print brought into the custom-house from Paris?"[37]

Strong confessed he had no answer to the problem. He acquiesced in the prospect

---

34. Ida Husted Harper, *The Life and Work of Susan B. Anthony* (Indianapolis: Hollenbeck Press, 1898), 1: 64-68; *HWS*, 1: 474-85; Cherrington, *SEAP*, 5: 1952.

35. Harper, *Susan B. Anthony*, 1: 71.

36. Ibid., p. 93.

37. Allan Nevins and Milton Halsey Thomas, eds., *The Diary of George Templeton Strong* (New York: The Macmillan Company, 1952), 2: 165.

of a majority decision and postulated that popular support would be essential for enforcement. He had reached the limit of mid-nineteenth-century American political thought.

The notion of a realm of privacy inhering in the individual and protected by the courts from outside interference, including interference by government, was beyond his imagination. "The democratic despotism of a majority is a formidable element of injustice and oppression," he confessed, "but it is the power to which we are subject and which will determine this question." When a stringent prohibition law was passed in April 1855, along with a bill to tax church property, he did not regret the passage of either bill: "If the liquor prohibition can be enforced and alcohol be abolished by laws strictly executed, I'm not sure but it's best. To be sure, *it's a novel stretch of law-making power, but social reforms can only be effected by new instruments.*"[38]

By September 1854 Strong was overawed by the prospect of a religious civil war in the country and by "this awful vague, mysterious, new element of Know-Nothingism." "I'm sick of Celtism; it's nothing but imbecility, brag, and bad rhetoric," he wrote. "If the Know-Nothings were only political, not politico-religious, I'd join them." A month later, however, he reversed his opinion and decided that Know-Nothingism was a "humbug" that had already passed its peak. By the November elections he was ready to concede their political power and to endorse a change in naturalization laws.[39]

A year later Strong joined the new Republican party. He denounced the Know-Nothings as "treacherous folk" while applauding the middle-class character of his Republican ward. In a long, torturous examination of his attitude toward slavery, he finally convinced himself that "slavery as it *exists* at the South . . . is the greatest crime on the largest scale known in modern history. . . ." He voted for Frémont in 1856, denounced the threatened secession of South Carolina, and rejoiced in the creation of a truly Northern party.[40]

The intellectual and emotional struggles of George Templeton Strong indicated that, for him and for many like him, neither acquiescence in the innovation of statutory prohibition nor temporary flirtation with political nativism was as

---

38. Nevins and Thomas, eds., *George Templeton Strong*, 2: 165, 218. (quotation, italics added)

39. Ibid., 2: 183-96. Strong noted that a procession of Know-Nothings in November 1854 was composed of "some two or three thousand, mostly young men of the butcher-boy and *prentice* type; many a Simon Tappertit among them, no doubt, and many a shoulder-hitter and shortboy beside; . . ." ibid., 2: 197. The term *shortboy* referred to a gang of "desperadoes" who had disrupted a German picnic in 1851 and meant, therefore, any rowdy or tough. See *Harper's New Monthly Magazine,* July 1851, p. 276.

40. Nevins and Thomas, eds., *George Templeton Strong*, 2: 183, 186, 196, 241, 298, 303, 304-5. Strong's antipathy to the conduct of the New York Know-Nothings was shared by New York Congressman Edward B. Morgan of Aurora, New York. In the protracted deadlock of the election of Speaker of the House, December 3, 1855, to February 2, 1856, the New York Know-Nothings ended up voting for Aiken of South Carolina, a slave owner, and against the successful anti-Nebraska candidate, Nathaniel Banks. See Temple R. Hollcroft, "A Congressman's Letters on the Speaker Election in the Thirty-Fourth Congress," *Mississippi Valley Historical Review* 43 (December 1956): 444-58.

strong as a communal sense of belonging "to the insurgent plebeians of the North arming against a two-penny South Carolina aristocracy." Had prohibition or nativism been unchallenged by the slavery issue, either might have prevailed. But the slavery issue raised more fundamental questions about the nature of American society than did the nativist issue and more pressing questions about the nature of the democratic process than did the prohibition issue. To an extent the Republican party became an organization of persons who believed in free labor and entrepreneurialism and who were dedicated to the containment of slavery in the territories and to economic expansion; to that extent the Republican party was committed to a kind of "open community" that was incompatible with either extreme nativism or prohibition. Either program might hinder the free flow of labor so essential to economic progress and community development.[41]

There was a persistent ambiguity in prohibitionist democratic rhetoric. The majoritarian premise of the local-option elections and Maine Law referenda concealed an ethical predicament: what if the majority did not choose to define liquor sales as an evil not to be tolerated or sanctioned by law? The ease with which the prohibition laws of the 1850s were vetoed, repealed, emasculated, and declared unconstitutional by partisan governors, legislators, and judges after the political realignment of 1855–56 indicated that an electoral majority had not, in fact, consistently supported the effort. A similar predicament had confronted the antislavery forces in the Kansas-Nebraska act and in the Dred Scott case. A number of them took up the "higher law" doctrine of William H. Seward and argued that there was a common good, a moral law, beyond the will of the majority or of the Supreme Court. Would the temperance advocates also be forced to disavow majoritarianism? The issue lay, for the moment, in the future.

The emergence of prohibitionism from the American temperance movement had taken place in the context of a functioning political democracy. Its intellectual assumptions, political strategies, and moral premises rested on a democratic ethos that was pervasive and largely unexamined. What would happen to prohibitionism where political democracy was a goal yet to be achieved rather than an accomplished fact of society? For an answer to that question, events in Norway, Sweden, and England in the mid-nineteenth century are worth considering.

PROHIBITION AND POLITICS IN NORWAY, SWEDEN, AND ENGLAND, 1836–1866

Against a background of socialist and liberal thought, the questions of the police power of the state, the efficacy of universal suffrage, and the relationship between private opinions and public power were debated in England and the Scandinavian

---

41. Nevins and Halsey, eds., *George Templeton Strong*, 2: 281; Eric Foner, *Free Soil, Free Labor, Free Men*, pp. 234–36. Foner identifies antislavery "radicals" and followers of William Seward as the two groups most opposed to political nativism within the Republican party.

countries. The contexts of prohibitionism were thus more sharply ideological
and class oriented than in the United States. Because they confronted political
systems of incomplete democracy, the Scandinavian and English prohibitionist
movements had to rely on extraparliamentary means and pioneered in pressure-
group tactics.

Norway in the early nineteenth century illustrated the peculiar nature of
Scandinavian reform and radicalism. As a result of the Napoleonic wars, Norway
had been transferred from Danish control to Swedish control in a dual union
under the Swedish king. Norway had adopted a liberal constitution in 1814
that extended the vote to over half the adult male population, yet control of
the executive branch rested with the Swedish king. The *storting* (legislature) was
permeated with conservative civil servants. In addition, political cleavages existed
between this bureaucratic elite and the *bønder* opposition, representing a landowning rural peasant elite. "The countryside was provincial, the city cosmopolitan; the peasants tended to be rude, religious, superstitious, egalitarian; the
urbanites cultivated, worldly, rationalistic, hierarchic."[42] A profoundly rural,
religious, and bourgeois country thus found its political life dominated by
Sweden and its cultural life influenced by a Danish-oriented urban elite.

The Norwegian temperance movement was spawned in the aftermath of
misguided economic legislation amid religious revivals. A law of 1816 prohibited
the importation of liquor and legalized distillation of alcohol on small farms.
Poor transportation made it easier for the farmer to turn surplus grain and
potatoes into *brennevin* than to transport his surplus to market (much as trans-
appalachian settlers in America turned their corn into whiskey). The disruption
of the traditional market for peasant labor in the early nineteenth century
by increased grain imports, the overemphasis on potato cultivation, and greater
agricultural specialization, increased the number of landless, underemployed
peasants. Enforced idleness made excessive drinking a serious social problem.
At the same time, Haugeanism, a pietistic, "puritanical" religious revival, provided an impetus for political self-assertion among the *bønder*. The temperance
movement, inspired by religious pietism and also by letters from American immigrants, became entangled in the 1830s in the declining economic position of
the small farmers and in their rising political aspirations.[43]

In the 1840s the temperance movement created a drive for stricter liquor

---

42. Harry Eckstein, *Division and Cohesion in Democracy: A Study of Norway* (Princeton,
N.J.: Princeton University Press, 1966), p. 43. For background on Norway in the period
1814 to 1865, see Henry Valen and Daniel Katz, *Political Parties in Norway: A Community
Study* (London: Tavistock Publications, Ltd., 1964); Knut Gjerset, *History of the Norwegian
People* (New York: The Macmillan Company, 1915), 2: 406-504. For a literary evocation of
the mood of the country on the eve of the 1814 period, read Tryggve Andersen, *In the Days
of the Councillor,* trans. Beatrice H. Stroup and Stein Mathisen (New York: Twayne Publishers, Inc., 1969).

43. Theodore C. Blegen, *Norwegian Migration to America, 1825-1860* (Northfield, Minn.:
The Norwegian-American Historical Association, 1931), pp. 160-74. The standard work on
Norwegian temperance is Erling Tambs Wicklund, *Bøndene og Brennevinsspørsmålet i Norge*

control. The *storting* adopted a bill in 1842 that would have prohibited the production of brandy for ten years; however, the king vetoed the bill as too drastic.
A revised bill enacted in 1845 abolished home distillation, drove small dealers
out of business by raising licensing fees, provided for local option in rural areas,
and restricted the number of licenses in municipalities.

The victory for temperance was more apparent than real. Large-scale,
commercial distillation in larger municipalities had made home distillation un-
economical, and widespread illicit distillation had made taxing and enforcement
difficult for the government. The law of 1845 had the effect of making distillation a quasi-monopoly operating under stricter public control to the benefit of
certain wealthy groups.[44]

The ideological and class nature of the temperance issue in Norway was
underlined by the Marcus Thrane movement in the late 1840s and early 1850s.
Marcus Thrane was born into the Norwegian governing class, but when his father
was convicted of misappropriating bank funds, the family was plunged into
poverty. Thrane visited France in 1838, where he was exposed to the Socialists,
and England, where he encountered Chartism. He emerged from relative poverty
and obscurity in Norway in 1848 as a newspaper writer and editor of a radical
journal. Thrane was able to unite the minuscule groups of urban craftsmen with
the rural *husmænd* (crofters or landless agricultural wage workers) and lesser
peasantry. Their platform, adopted in July 1850, was an interesting mixture
of non-Marxian socialism, Chartism, liberalism, and temperance. They wanted
free trade, especially in grain; the right of retail purchase from ships in harbor
(to eliminate the economic middleman); freedom of trade in rural districts;
improvement of the conditions of *husmænd;* restriction of the liquor trade;
improved public education; judicial reform; compulsory military service; and,
most important of all, universal male suffrage.[45]

The role of the temperance issue in the Thrane movement was indicative
of the peculiarities of Scandinavian labor movements and socialism: liquor restrictions became an instrument of class conflict, a way of attacking the wealthy

---

1800-1850 (Oslo, 1925). An interesting recent work on the other side of the question is
Odd Nordland, *Brewing and Beer Traditions in Norway: The Social Anthropological Background for the Brewing Industry* (Oslo: Norwegian Universities Press, 1969).

For the ambivalent attitude toward America in this period, see Otto Reinert, "The
Image of the United States in Two Popular Norwegian Magazines, 1835-1865," in *Americana
Norvegica: Norwegian Contributions to American Studies,* Sigmund Skard, ed. (Philadelphia:
University of Pennsylvania Press, 1968), 2: 34-73.

For the background of Scandinavian temperance, see B. J. Hovde, *The Scandinavian
Countries, 1720-1865: The Rise of the Middle Classes* (Boston: Chapman and Grimes,
1943), 2: Chapter 18.

44. Hovde, *The Scandinavian Countries,* 2: 676-77.

45. Ibid., 638; Gjerset, *History of the Norwegian People,* 2: 508-9. The platform was based
on a petition sent to the king on May 15, 1850. This petition was written by Paul Hjelm
Hansen, editor of *Folkets Röst* (People's Voice), who gave it a strong free trade emphasis.
It was rejected by the king and presented to the *storting* in 1851. Magnus Jensen, *Norges*

classes. Thrane had been a temperance advocate in his youth but not a teetotaler, and his newspaper was open to a number of opinions on the temperance issue. The petition to the *storting* did not oppose the prohibition of home distillation but did criticize those portions of the law that dealt with the selling and serving of liquor. While upholding freedom of trade, the petition called for reduction in the number of inns and for a high tax on liquor.[46]

There were tensions within the Thrane movement as well as conflicts with the authorities. In June 1850 Thrane was arrested on charges of blasphemy (for anticlerical material in his paper) and sentenced to six months in prison. A higher court reversed the decision in December 1850. Taking a step like the Chartist movement, the Thrane forces held another parliamentary "labor congress" in the spring of 1851 to support their petition to the *storting*. Theodor Abildgaard, who prepared the address that accompanied the petition, favored cooperation with *bønder* elements. Thrane favored an independent course of action. Paul Hjelm Hansen, editor of *Folkets Röst (People's Voice)*, supported the petition and tried to act as a bridge between Thrane and the liberal, free-trade elements.[47]

The *storting* referred the petition to a select committee that agreed to meet with a delegation from the "labor congress" on June 16, 1851. The attitude of the *storting* members can be gleaned from a letter written by one of the committee members:

"I am a member of the special committee that has to do with the labor petition, the worst committee of the storting. As for me I am really no wiser now than when I left home. The laborers have much to suffer, it seems, partly through their own fault, partly not, connected with a strong desire and demands for improvement but with little understanding of how the improvement can happen, and therefore demands that are in part absolutely impossible to fulfill. Then there are agitators and leaders (Thrane, Abildgaard, and others) about whom, I fear, that they think more of themselves and seek their own advantages rather than that of the workers. If these leaders are led by others, God knows! If there

---

Historie: Unionstiden 1814-1905 (Oslo: Norwegian Universities Press, 1963), p. 85; J. B. Wist, ed., *Norsk-Amerikanernes Festskrift* (Decorah, Iowa: The Symra Company, 1919).

On the socialist character of the Thrane movement, it is helpful to recall the statement of historian G. D. H. Cole on the nature of socialism in the 1850s:

"If Utopian Socialism perished in the European conflagration of 1848, Marxian Socialism did not immediately replace it. Indeed, what new Socialist thought there was in the 1850s was for the most part singularly untouched by Marx's influence and was fully as ethical in its inspiration as the utopianism which the *Manifesto* had denounced as obsolete." G. D. H. Cole, *A History of Socialist Thought* (London: Macmillan & Co. Ltd., 1957), 2: 12.

46. Oddvar Bjørklund, *Marcus Thrane* (Oslo: Tiden Norsk Forlag, 1951), pp. 128-29. (I am indebted to Dr. Henriette C. K. Naeseth, Professor Emeritus of English, Augustana College, for translating this material from Norwegian. Dr. Naeseth is editing the plays of Marcus Thrane and graciously shared her extensive notes on the Thrane movement with me.)

47. Ibid., pp. 123, 213-16, 257-65. The petition had been referred to a committee on April 29, 1851.

were not strong leadership and active agitation, that labor agitation [would be of little significance.]"[48]

The *storting* tabled the petition without debate. Fearing rural and labor unrest, the authorities arrested Thrane and a number of his followers. After three years in jail pending a trial, Thrane was sentenced to four years in prison. When he emerged from prison in 1858, the times had changed. He emigrated to the United States and was known as a journalist, playwright, and free thinker.[49]

The Thrane movement indicated that the question of *what* the state could do about the "liquor traffic" was intimately bound up with the question of *who* controlled the state. Thrane's call for universal suffrage echoed the French revolution of 1848 and English Chartism while it also foreshadowed later socialist demands. The call for stricter temperance legislation showed how the class nature of the drink question could be related to the drive for equality. Similar questions were raised in Sweden in the 1850s by the "brandy revolt" in the southern provinces and helped to bring new groups into the drive to reform the unrepresentative *Riksdag*.[50]

In Sweden, the temperance movement had taken root in the fertile soil of pietistic revivals, rural unrest, and urban liberalism. One of the leading temperance advocates was Per Wieselgren. As a student in Växjö in 1819 he had helped to found one of the first Swedish temperance societies. As a young minister in Västerstad in the 1830s, he had converted his debt-ridden, hard-drinking parish into a model of sobriety and prosperity. In 1830, an eminent doctor, Anders Retzius, formed a total abstinence society in Stockholm on the model of the American Temperance Society. As was the case in England and the United States, the society soon split along moderationist versus teetotaler lines.[51]

The demands for temperance, abolition of the right of home distillation,

---

48. Letter of Niels Koren, July 28, 1851. Translation and copy furnished by Dr. Naeseth.

49. Edvard Bull, "The Labor Movement in Scandinavia," in Jørgen Bukdahl et al., *Scandinavia Past and Present: Through Revolutions to Liberty* (Denmark: Arnkrone, 1959), pp. 853-54; T. K. Derry, *A Short History of Norway* (London: George Allen and Unwin, Ltd., 1957), pp. 165-66.

50. Henrik Ibsen, the famous Norwegian playwright, was briefly associated with the Marcus Thrane movement. As a young student in Christiana (Oslo) in 1850, Ibsen became a friend of Theodor Abildgaard, editor of a labor newspaper who supported Marcus Thrane. Neither Abildgaard nor Ibsen was a socialist or a prohibitionist, but Ibsen burned with the romantic yearning for freedom that swept Norwegian students in the late 1840s and 1850s and supported the cause of labor. When the police raided the newspaper headquarters on July 7, 1851, to arrest Abildgaard, Thrane, and others, the foreman supposedly threw Ibsen's letters and manuscripts on the floor. The police rifled the files but ignored the "scraps" on the floor. By this narrow margin Ibsen escaped the arrest, detention, and sentencing that befell Abildgaard and Thrane. Halvdan Koht, *The Life of Ibsen* (New York: W. W. Norton & Company, Inc., 1931), 1: 53-63, 66-67; Evert Sprinchorn, ed., *Ibsen: Letters and Speeches* (New York: Hill & Wang, Inc., 1964), p. 14.

51. Hovde, *The Scandinavian Countries*, 2: 667-69; E. R. L. Gould, *The Gothenburg System of Liquor Control*, Fifth Special Report of the U.S. Commissioner of Labor (Washington, D.C.: Government Printing Office, 1893), p. 15.

and institution of high licensing fees represented, as in Norway, a convergence of religious, economic, and political pressures. Encouraged by American examples, temperance advocates in Sweden secured a law from the *Riksdag* in 1835 that discouraged the home distillation of spirits. In 1836 Robert Baird, an agent for the American Temperance Society, arrived in Sweden to spread the message of the American experience. The split in the Swedish temperance movement, between the moderates and the teetotalers, was healed in 1837 with the creation of the Swedish Temperance Society under royal patronage and with upper-class support. For the next decade the energies of the Scandinavian temperance advocates were devoted to temperance "revivals" (particularly among the peasants), Pan-Scandinavian congresses, and membership drives. The times of division in the Scandinavian temperance societies did not return until the decade 1848–58.[52]

The temperance advocates who hoped to secure further political aid for their cause confronted a formidable obstacle in the Swedish system of parliamentary estates. The *Riksdag* was composed of four estates: nobles, clergy, burghers, and farmers. In response to criticisms and out of fear of the 1848 revolutions, the government had introduced a reform bill in 1848. The proposal was debated in the next parliament, in 1851:

"The landowning aristocracy had hoped for a reform which would reduce the influence of the multitude of civil servants and army officers who outvoted them in the *Riddarhus* [Estate of the Nobles]. The ironmasters and business men resented being confined to a limited representation in a junior Estate. The farmers and urban middle class believed that they deserved a much larger share in Parliament. . . . But the European revolutions caused many liberal groups to think more cautiously about the effect of reform. It became apparent that the aims of the landowners, townsmen, and farmers did not coincide."[53]

In the 1850s these groups were further divided as Sweden's conversion to free trade (in 1846) wrought important changes in the economic life of the country.

The pietistic artisans and agricultural workers who petitioned the *Bonde-ståndet* [Farmer's Estate] for the abolition of home distilleries thus found their

52. Hovde, *The Scandinavian Countries*, 2: 662-70; Franklin D. Scott, "American Influences in Norway and Sweden," *Journal of Modern History* 18 (March 1946): 38-39; Halfdan Bengtsson, "The Temperance Movement and Temperance Legislation in Sweden," *The Annals of the American Academy of Political and Social Science* 197 (May 1938): 134-35.

For the early history of the temperance movement, the classic source is Per Wieselgren, "Historik öfver svenska brännvinslagstiftningen under 200 år," in *Per Wieselgrens samlade skrifter I nykterhetsfrågan: jubileumsupplaga utgifven af studenternas helnykterhetssällskap i Uppsala* (Stockholm: Svenska Bokfoerlaget AB, 1903), pp. 7-252.

A more recent study is Tage Larsson, *Reformen i Brännvinslagstiftningen, 1853-1854* (Stockholm: Oskar Eklunds Bokförlag, 1945).

53. Douglas V. Verney, *Parliamentary Reform in Sweden, 1866-1921* (London: Oxford University Press, 1957), p. 41. The farmer estate had admitted farmers owning tax-exempted land *(frälsehemmansägare)* in 1845 and had frightened the other estates by refusing to support the reform bill in 1851 because it was not drastic enough. Ibid., pp. 31-33.

will thwarted by the landowning and tax-paying farmers *(bönder)*, "who were loath to give up the income they derived from it." The right to operate a *brännvin* distillery was regarded as a privilege that accompanied landowning. "In some parishes opposition to the distilleries was so intense that mobs destroyed them or threatened the owners with violence." When the *Riksdag* considered a law prohibiting home distillation in the 1850s, the *Bondeståndet* opposed the law. A combination of ministerial pressure from government officials, personal support by the king, and a flood of petitions from temperance societies secured passage of the law; the royal assent was given in January 1855.[54]

The law of January 1855 prohibited home distillation but allowed controlled distillation in specially taxed establishments. Local communities were given some control over retail sales and rural areas were given a veto over new licenses. The net effect was to reduce rural distillation and retail sales, to concentrate both production and consumption in the cities, and to create windfall profits for the urban bourgeois at the expense of pietistic and humanitarian elements in the rural society. In the southern provinces, violent reaction to the new law threatened a minor insurrection. Troops were used to close illicit distilleries in some areas. Per Wieselgren was sent by the king to Blekinge to calm down the overwrought temperance forces.[55]

Continuing dissatisfaction with the unrepresentativeness of the *Riksdag* led to petitions for reform in 1860 in the burgher and farmer estates. The new chancellor, Louis de Greer, prepared new proposals and introduced various bills. The innovations, which were adopted between 1862 and 1866, included enfranchisement of the rural property-owning middle class *(ståndspersoner)* and their admission to the farmer estate; creation of new provincial councils, with enfranchisement of men and women taxpayers over twenty-three years of age; and abolition of the four estates in favor of a bicameral parliamentary system. Although membership was limited by requirements that members have a certain amount of taxable income, the changes represented a distinct advance over the older system. The "state" was recognizing that "society" had changed, but the persistence of temperance issues and the emergence of labor-socialist questions showed that the nature of the community that comprised the base of society was still undefined.[56]

54. George M. Stephenson, *The Religious Aspects of Swedish Immigration: A Study of Immigrant Churches* (Minneapolis: University of Minnesota Press, 1932), pp. 17 and 23. For the cultural aspects of Swedish immigration as they relate to these issues, see the sources listed in Ernest M. Espelie, "Bibliography of the Published Writings of Dr. O. Fritiof Ander," in *The Immigration of Ideas: Studies in the North Atlantic Community,* J. Iverne Dowie and J. Thomas Tredway, eds. (Rock Island, Ill.: Augustana Historical Society, 1968), pp. 198-200.

55. Gould, *Gothenburg System,* pp. 16-17; Hovde, *Scandinavian Countries,* 2: 678; Sten Carlsson and Jerker Rosén, *Svensk Historia: 2: Tiden efter 1718* (Stockholm: Svenska Bokfoerlaget AB, 1961), p. 395; Carl Hallendorff, *Sveriges Historia: till våra dagar tolfte delen Oskar I och Karl XV* (Stockholm: Norstedt and Soener AB, 1923), p. 159; Larsson, *Reformen i Brännvinslagstiftningen,* 1: 393 n. 2: 213.

56. Verney, *Parliamentary Reform,* pp. 33, 49-50 and 51-58. The legal and constitutional aspects are also found in Nils Herlitz, *Grunddragen av de svenska statsskickets historia* (Stockholm: Svenska Bokfoerlaget AB, 1959), pp. 181-232.

Similarly, questions about the nature of the state and the limits of its actions were raised in England in the 1850s. The Maine Law campaigns in the United States and Canada had an immediate impact in England. In 1853 Nathaniel Card, an Anglo-Irish manufacturer in Manchester, organized the United Kingdom Alliance for the Total and Immediate Suppression of the Liquor Traffic among self-help oriented workers and tradesmen. Within two years the Alliance had enrolled some twenty thousand members in over one hundred societies. Many moral suasionists, who hoped to revitalize the lagging temperance movement, embarked on a vigorous propaganda drive through the United Kingdom Alliance. Also in 1853 the Villiers committee, a select committee of the House of Commons, published a two-volume report on the laws regulating public houses (pubs) and beer shops: "It need not be a matter of surprise," the authors of the report noted, "that in view of the vast mass of evils found in connection with intemperance, it should have been suggested to *prohibit* altogether the manufacture and sale of intoxicating drinks. Laws to that effect are in force in the states of Maine, Massachusetts, Rhode Island." Parliament, however, preferred simply to amend the regulations governing sabbath closing laws and even reversed itself on this point in the face of Hyde Park riots in 1855 by workingmen.[57]

The "liquor question" and the aggressive electoral tactics of the Alliance in the late 1850s came at a time when local political lines had begun to alter. Temperance issues were traditionally attractive to some Liberals, but there could always be found enough Tory supporters to make the issue nonpartisan. In a case study of Rochdale, historian John Vincent has discovered that Tory pub keepers as well as beersellers (who had traditionally split their party allegiances) opposed Liberal party candidates in 1857 because the candidates had not supported the interest of their trade in an obscure beer bill in Parliament. Similar shifts occurred in Leicester in 1859 and 1861, Bolton in 1865 and 1868, and at Bristol in 1868. Alliance tactics pinned the label of "prohibitionist" on the Liberal party and forced the publicans to close ranks and to support the Conservative party after the debates of the 1860s and early 1870s.[58]

The tactics of the Alliance raised a number of pertinent questions for English liberalism. John Stuart Mill, in his classic treatise *On Liberty,* published in 1859, sought to illustrate the principle that "the sole end for which mankind are warranted, individually or collectively, in interfering with the liberty of action

---

57. Cherrington, *SEAP,* 3: 929-33; Brian Harrison, *Drink and the Victorians,* Chapters 9 and 10. In a survey of 234 financial contributors to the United Kingdom Alliance in 1868-69, Brian Harrison concluded that the prohibitionist Alliance "drew most of its major donors from industrial manufacturers—particularly from north-eastern England, Manchester, Glasgow, Cardiff and Dublin," (p. 220) and most of its membership from middle- and working-class elites with self-help orientations and from women with feminist leanings. The most important influence on their behavior was nonconformist religion.

58. John Vincent, *The formation of the British Liberal Party* (New York: Charles Scribner's Sons, 1966), pp. 97-99; Harrison, *Drink and the Victorians,* p. 184. See also Peter Mathias, "The Brewing Industry, Temperance and Politics," *The Historical Journal* 1 (No. 2, 1958): 112.

of any of their number, is self-protection."[59] But, did the vice of intemperance justify prohibition in the interest of societal self-protection? Mill devoted several pages to the current status of the problem:

"Under the name of preventing intemperance, the people of one English colony [New Brunswick], and of nearly half the United States, have been interdicted by law from making any use whatever of fermented drinks, except for medical purposes: for prohibition of their sale is in fact, as it is intended to be, prohibition of their use. And though the impracticability of executing the law has caused its repeal in several of the States which had adopted it, including the one from which it derives its name, an attempt has notwithstanding been commenced, and is prosecuted with considerable zeal by many of the professed philanthropists, to agitate for a similar law in this country. The association, or 'Alliance' as it terms itself, which has been formed for this purpose, has acquired some notoriety through the publicity given to a correspondence between its secretary and [Lord Stanley] one of the very few English public men who hold that a politician's opinions ought to be founded on principles."[60]

Mill then scrutinized the principles by which Lord Stanley justified prohibition. "All matters relating to thought, opinion, conscience, appear to me," Lord Stanley wrote, "to be without the sphere of legislation; all pertaining to social act, habit, relation, subject only to a discretionary power vested in the State itself, and not in the individual, to be within it."[61]

To this neat division, Mill objected that while selling fermented drink was a social act, the act of drinking it was an individual one. Lord Stanley's argument that the invasion of one's "social rights" by another justified an appeal to legisla-

---

59. Quoted by Gertrude Himmelfarb, "The Other John Stuart Mill," in *Victorian Minds* (New York: Alfred A. Knopf, Inc., 1968), p. 140.

60. John Stuart Mill, *Utilitarianism, Liberty, and Representative Government* (reprint ed., New York: E. P. Dutton & Co., Inc., 1951), pp. 194-95. Maine repealed its prohibition law in 1856 and returned to license for two years.

   J. K. Chapman, "The Mid-Nineteenth-Century Temperance Movement in New Brunswick and Maine," *The Canadian Historical Review* 35 (March 1954): 43-60, has noted that "the years between 1849 and 1852 were years of greater friendship and freer intercourse between Maine and New Brunswick than had hitherto prevailed. The adoption of free trade by Britain had temporarily weakened the links between mother country and province, and the latter had turned towards the United States for aid in her economic extremity, and to co-operation with Maine on the European and North American Railway project. That this period occurred at the same time as the temperance movement achieved success in Maine was coincidental, but the fact that New Brunswick . . . had moved even closer to Maine enabled the temperance movement to exert an even greater influence upon the province than it had in the past" (pp. 52-53). Spearheaded by the political power of the Sons of Temperance, New Brunswick in 1852 passed a prohibition bill modeled on the Maine Law and strengthened it in 1855. In general, the Liberals supported it, but not too warmheartedly; the Tories opposed it. The law was repealed in 1856 as political lines reformed following a minor constitutional crisis.

61. Mill, *Liberty,* p. 195.

tion seemed to Mill to be a monstrous principle that could justify any and all violations of liberty. One had no right to demand that the state make others perfect. Even drunkenness, in ordinary cases, was not a proper subject for legislative interference, but conviction of criminal violence while drunk would justify special restrictions or severe penalties because such drunkenness was "a crime against others."[62]

Mill observed that prohibition was an infringement on the liberty of the buyer. Therefore, it ought not to be allowed. On the other hand, the state was justified in "imposing restrictions and requiring guarantees" of the seller because only his pecuniary self-interest and not his liberty was at stake. Taxation for revenue and licensing for regulation of public order were admissible; taxation for restriction and limitation of licenses to approximate prohibition were not. What Mill ushered out the front door in the name of individual liberty, he thus partly smuggled in the back door in the name of public necessity. In his ambivalence Mill reflected the uneasy mind of mid-century liberalism as it confronted the issues raised by the new religious politics of the day.[63]

The militant tactics of the United Kingdom Alliance also brought it into conflict with the policies of William Gladstone, Chancellor of the Exchequer in the Palmerston ministry and future leader of the Liberal party. Free-trade advocates in the administration had negotiated a treaty with France in 1860 (the Cobden-Chevalier treaty) which reduced French duties on English coal and manufactured goods in exchange for lower English duties on French wine and brandy. To expedite the new arrangement, Gladstone introduced a "Shopkeepers License Act" in 1860 which would have allowed restaurant keepers to sell foreign wines for consumption on the premises and which would have allowed shopkeepers to sell bottled wine for off-premise use. The Alliance protested that this amounted to government action to encourage intemperance. They lost the battle and looked on in dismay as gross consumption of *all* intoxicants and the importation of wine increased significantly.[64]

The "drink question" was thus an index to subtle changes in political alignments and public attitudes in England. With their defeat in the Shopkeepers

---

62. Ibid., pp. 196, 206.

63. Ibid., pp. 210-11. On the emergence of religious and political forces in Parliament, see Vincent, *Liberal Party,* p. xxi; for the relation of Liberalism to temperance issues, see the fine discussion in Harrison, *Drink and the Victorians,* Chapter 13.

64. Harrison, *Drink and the Victorians,* pp. 248-50; Cherrington, *SEAP,* 3: 933-34; E. L. Woodward, *The Age of Reform, 1815-1870* (Oxford: Clarendon Press, 1939), pp. 172-73 n. 4; and Arthur Louis Dunham, *The Anglo-French Treaty of Commerce of 1860 and the Progress of the Industrial Revolution in France* (Ann Arbor: University of Michigan Press, 1930), pp. 54-55, 67-68, 88-92, 110-11, 118 n. 20, and Chapter 14. Gladstone was besieged by delegations of distillers, maltsters (who depended on beer makers), and licensed victuallers [restaurant owners] who resented the competition or increased fees. Gladstone defended the proposed duties on French wines (in a speech in the House of Commons on February 27, 1860), and the Refreshment House and Wine License bill (on March 26, 1860). In 1862 he defended a proposed brewers' license bill in the House. John Morley, *The Life of William Ewart Gladstone* (London: Macmillan and Co., Ltd., 1903), 2: 28, 655.

Act, the Alliance turned toward a different strategy. Rather than try to persuade Parliament or to influence public officials of metropolitan London, they sought local-option laws and fought for prohibition at the local level in the areas of their greatest strength. An unsuccessful attempt to secure the necessary enabling legislation (the "Permissive" bill) in 1864 compounded the frustration of the Alliance and added fuel to the fires of criticism of Parliament for its unrepresentativeness. The local-option strategy raised embarrassing questions about democracy and suffrage reform, about liberty, authority, and the proper role of the state, questions that led ultimately to the crucial Reform Bill of 1867.[65]

John Stuart Mill had foreseen the crisis of the times in 1861 when he had published his *Considerations on Representative Government.* A recent interpreter has written that Mill "was concerned not so much with the problem of making representative government more representative, more democratic, as with the problem of making it better. And making it better generally meant, in practice, devising ways of limiting it." One wonders how Mill would have reacted to this comment when one of his suggested reforms, the Hare system of proportional representation, was designed to make government better by making it more representative of the complexity of society and, at the same time, to correct one of the weaknesses of democracy, the tyranny of the majority.[66]

Mill acknowledged that there were some objections to the Hare system. "First," he noted, "it is said that undue power would be given to knots or cliques; sectarian combinations; associations for special objects, such as the Maine Law League, the Ballot or Liberation Society; or bodies united by class interests or community of religious persuasion." But, Mill countered, proportional representation would provide the means for disinterested individuals to counteract such special interest groups. "If there would be Temperance tickets, and Ragged School tickets, . . ." he asked, "would not one public-spirited person in a constituency be sufficient to put forth a 'personal merit' ticket, and circulate it through a whole neighbourhood?" In short, proportional representation would limit the ability of pressure groups, such as the prohibitionists, to coerce others; prevent them (if they constituted a majority) from exerting an unlimited tyranny; and, at the same time, encourage an individualistic antidote to their influence.[67]

---

65. The "Permissive" bill originated in an article written anonymously by brewer Charles Buxton in 1855. He recommended that five sixths of the ratepayers (taxpayers) in a locality should be able to ban drink shops. The United Kingdom Alliance changed this to two thirds but was itself criticized for advocating an "undemocratic" measure since only a small proportion of the population were ratepayers. The Permissive bill was introduced in 1864 and was defeated by 292 votes to 35. For the Alliance and democracy and its relation to the Permissive bill, see Harrison, *Drink and the Victorians,* pp. 198-201, 216-18, 254-55, 259-61.

66. Himmelfarb, *Victorian Minds,* p. 149. For Mill's discussion of the Hare system, see John Stuart Mill, "Representative Government," in *Utilitarianism, Liberty, and Representative Government* (reprint ed.; New York: E. P. Dutton and Co., Inc., 1951), Chapter 7.

67. Ibid., pp. 366-67, cf. p. 369. "Mr. Hare's system makes it impossible for partial interests to have the command of the tribunal, but it ensures them advocates. . . ." For the background of the Hare system, see Donald J. Ziegler, *Prelude to Democracy* (Lincoln: University of Nebraska Press, 1958).

Mill touched on other topics that were to preoccupy public attention throughout the world for the next half century: majority rule and minority rights; franchise extension and the temper of "populistic" democracy; moral ends and immoral means in social action; private conscience and public control; equality, equity, and justice in civic affairs; nationalism, federalism, and self-determination. Subsequent events would show how far political developments had proceeded since the heady days of the 1830s, what changes in social structures, values, and institutions had occurred, and how far the world had yet to travel to redeem the promise of these ideals.

4

Women's Suffrage and the Victorian Compromise

THE ANGLO-AMERICAN SUFFRAGE SCENE: DIVISIONS AND DIVERSIONS, 1866–1877

Just as John Stuart Mill's preoccupation with the intellectual problems of the prohibition issue displayed his understanding of liberty and democracy, his involvement in the cause of women's rights and women's suffrage threw a curious light on the liberal conception of equality as an aspect of democracy. Mill's wife, Harriet Taylor, had referred to the issue in an article published in 1851 in the influential *Westminster Review*. In reference to the Seneca Falls declaration of women's rights and the national women's rights conventions in America, she noted "the contradiction between principle and practice," between the equality asserted by the Declaration of Independence and the inferior status of women. "Not only to the democracy of America," did women's claim to civil and political equality have an irresistible appeal, "but also to those radicals and chartists in the British islands, and democrats on the Continent," who demanded universal suffrage "as an inherent right." But this had been the dilemma of mid-century liberalism. While liberals were interested in securing equal power for those "qualified" to participate in government, they had not been in favor, on the whole, of immediate, universal manhood suffrage and majoritarian democracy.[1]

The cause of suffrage reform in England had languished throughout the late 1850s and early 1860s until Gladstone reopened the issue of parliamentary reform in 1864. Gladstone's proposed reform bill was defeated in June 1866. The Liberal ministry resigned, and from the ensuing election the Conservatives emerged victorious. It was the Conservatives under Disraeli who finally carried electoral reform in 1867, and on terms more "democratic" than those advocated by the Liberals!

Why did Disraeli allow to become law a reform bill that was, in many respects, more "radical" (i.e., democratic in the extension of the franchise) than

---

1. [Harriet Taylor], "Enfranchisement of Women," *Westminster Review* 55 (July 1851): 289-311 (quotation, p. 292).

the one proposed by Gladstone? Historian Gertrude Himmelfarb has suggested that Disraeli's behavior can best be understood as an expression of his social philosophy. He believed that the Conservatives represented the true interests of the nation; that social hierarchy was more important than political systems; and that the English working class, with its traditions of respect for authority and social deference to superiors would, by and large, defer to the leadership of the aristocracy. These ideas separated "society" from "politics" in his mind and freed his political tactics from the narrower class interests that frequently lay behind Liberal proposals. "Secure in his faith in a national party and a natural social order, Disraeli could contemplate with equanimity the boldest political experiment" and could, therefore, foster a more democratic franchise with assurance.[2]

Was Disraeli willing to contemplate with equal equanimity the prospect of women's suffrage? On May 20, 1867, John Stuart Mill moved to amend the Reform Bill so as to extend the franchise to women on the same terms as men. Mill rested his case in support of the amendment on three arguments: justice— one should not discriminate against women without due cause; fitness—women were qualified to vote by virtue of education and experience; and taxation— women should be accorded representation since they also paid taxes.[3] But Disraeli, who "was by no means unfriendly to the idea" of female suffrage, "did not regard the proposal as practical politics and neither spoke nor voted on the motion, which was easily defeated by 196 to 73."[4]

Disraeli could afford to take a detached view of politics; most of his contemporaries could not. Local elections were a means of determining social relationships and social order. Political questions inevitably became social questions of class, status, and deference. In short, "society" and "politics" could not be easily separated, particularly at the local level. From bitter experience, members of Parliament were learning the great intensity of local feeling on religious issues

2. Gertrude Himmelfarb, *Victorian Minds* (New York: Alfred A. Knopf, Inc., 1968), pp. 354-55. In Himmelfarb's interpretation, Gladstone feared extending power to the working class; Disraeli accepted it secure in the knowledge of the instinctive conservatism of the bulk of the working class. J. L. Hammond and M. R. D. Foot, on the other hand, attribute the democratic character of the Second Reform Bill to Bright and Gladstone, whose drafts and amendments shaped its contents; but they credit Disraeli with superior tactics in securing passage of the bill in the House of Lords. Disraeli's modern biographer, Robert Blake, interprets his behavior as sheer expediency prompted by rather narrowly partisan and personal (including anti-Gladstone) motives. See J. L. Hammond and M. R. D. Foot, *Gladstone and Liberalism* (New York: The Macmillan Company, 1953), pp. 102-5; Robert Blake, *Disraeli* (New York: St. Martin's Press, 1967), Chapter 21.

3. Constance Rover, *Women's Suffrage and Party Politics in Britain, 1866-1914* (London: Routledge and Kegan Paul, Ltd., 1967), pp. 29-31. Mill had introduced a similar petition in June 1866, but it had been easily defeated. Rover, *Women's Suffrage*, p. 218.

4. Blake, *Disraeli*, pp. 472-73. Disraeli had supported women's suffrage in the 1848 debates; see Doris Mary Stenton, *The English Woman in History* (London: George Allen and Unwin, Ltd., 1957), p. 333.

and on matters of custom and local tradition.[5] Both prohibition and women's suffrage touched raw political nerves.

The unmistakably middle-class character of the women's suffrage movement in England as it took organizational form in 1867 bound its fate inextricably to the political destiny of the middle class. In the broadest sense, then, the fortunes of the women's movement rested on the state of public opinion; for without a clear-cut pressure group armed with bipartisan parliamentary power within the middle class, the reforms favored by the women's movement could not secure sufficient support to work changes in the law.[6]

Articles in magazines of the time suggest that the molders of English public opinion were ambivalent in their attitudes toward women's suffrage, equal rights, and feminism, particularly as these movements were developing in the United States. An article in *Blackwood's Edinburgh Magazine* in 1867 complained that American women, except in the South, were too assertive and ultrademocratic. It speculated that their forwardness might be due to too much boardinghouse living and wondered if a desire for free love wasn't at the root of the whole women's rights question. The influential *Westminster Review,* reviewing a book called *Spiritual Wives* by an Englishman, William Hepworth Dixon, echoed this suspicion of the free-love motive and excessive independence among American women and traced the origins of the women's movement to the abolitionist campaign: "The abolitionists of New England little thought, when organizing and urging on their crusade against Negro slavery, that they were loosing the marriage bonds of their own wives and daughters."[7]

The slightly hysterical tone of some of the comments, the thinly veiled sexual innuendos, the searching for extreme cases, and the impugning of motives revealed an uneasiness in the English mind and a desire to down phantoms in the Victorian conscience rather than to admonish erring American cousins. "It could happen here"—this seems to have been the unspoken fear of English Commentators. Middle-class Englishwomen *had* organized women's suffrage societies in

---

5. John Vincent, *The Formation of the British Liberal Party* (New York: Charles Scribner's Sons, 1966), p. 15. Disraeli remarked in 1868 that the new, post-Reform Bill electorate would take sides along religious lines. School board elections did become sectarian battles of intense ferocity. See G. M. Young, *Victorian England: Portrait of an Age,* 2nd ed. (London: Oxford University Press, 1953), pp. 117-21.

D. C. Moore has noted that in nineteenth-century England "voters were encouraged, and often forcibly encouraged, to be loyal to the community or group to which they belonged, or to which they were supposed to belong. . . ." D. C. Moore, "Political Morality in Mid-Nineteenth Century England: Concepts, Norms, Violations," *Victorian Studies* 13 (September 1969): 26, 20 n. 22.

6. Vincent, *Formation of the British Liberal Party,* Chapter 2; Rover, *Women's Suffrage and Party Politics,* pp. 15-17; Elie Halévy, *The Rule of Democracy, 1905-1914:* Book 2, trans. E. I. Watkin, 2nd (revised) ed. (New York: Peter Smith, 1952), pp. 490-91.

7. "Women and Children in America," *Blackwood's Edinburgh Magazine* 101 (January 1867): 82-92; "Spiritual Wives," *Westminster Review* 90 (April 1868): 456-79 (quotation, p. 469). Dixon's book was also reviewed in the *Dublin University Magazine* 69 (March 1867): 279-87.

1867–68. Women preachers were becoming an important part of revivalism and contemporary urban life. The social plight of unmarried, middle-class women and the economic status of working-class women were being examined. College education for women was being debated seriously. "We are quite ready," wrote one commentator, "to crush the gay trifler, but we are not prepared to accept in her stead the pale-faced student, poring over miserable books. We want healthy, happy, dutiful, Englishwomen; and we are persuaded that if women take to college, and examinations, and diplomas, and the rest, they will be unhealthy, unhappy, undutiful, and worst of all—American."[8]

John Stuart Mill attempted to mold public opinion on the subject with a long essay, "The Subjection of Women," published in 1869. Mill's overly long and tortuous essay set out to prove that woman's subjection to man in marriage and her restrictions in economic matters were relics of a previous stage of human evolution, a survival of the rule of might in the enlightened age of the nineteenth century. She was kept in mental chains by false education and denied an opportunity to contribute to the welfare of humanity. Woman's subjection was, in sum, an illogical, immoral, and unnecessary hindrance to progress. Mill's essay became the bible of the women's movement but had little immediate impact on political affairs in England.[9]

What had American women done since Seneca Falls to warrant such suspicion? The bloomer costume was still a subject of ridicule, but that phase of the women's rights agitation had largely passed. The social-sexual experiments of the Shakers (celibacy), Mormons (plural marriage), and Oneida Perfectionists

---

8. Emily Davis, "Some Account of a Proposed New College for Women," *Contemporary Review* 9 (December 1868): 549; Constance Rover, *Women's Suffrage*, pp. 6 and 56 n. 1; Olive Anderson, "Women Preachers in Mid-Victorian Britain: Some Reflexions on Feminism, Popular Religion and Social Change," *The Historical Journal* 12 (1969): 467–84.

R. K. Webb's interpretation of English attitudes is particularly relevant. He noted that Mary Estlin of Bristol "told Mrs. [Maria] Chapman in 1853 that the American agitation for women's rights would never be understood in England, because the oppressions of women were so merged in others where men were fellow sufferers. 'I find very few people who are aware that with you all *white men* are on a legal equality & that consequently our class restrictions, religious disabilities, landed property monopolies, etc., & all the hosts of oppressions under which we groan resolve themselves with you into distinctions of sex or of colour. If the English public had this key to the enigma they would be a little more merciful to the transatlantic Amazons as they suppose the advocates of Women's Rights to be.'" R. K. Webb, *Harriet Martineau: A Radical Victorian* (New York: Columbia University Press, 1960), p. 182 n. 1.

9. John Stuart Mill, "The Subjection of Women," in Emery E. Neff, ed., *On Liberty and Other Essays* (reprint ed., New York: The Macmillan Company, 1926), pp. 189–311. Mill's essay was a reworking of an essay on equality in marriage and divorce that he had written in 1832. Mill attributed the main ideas in his essay to his wife, Harriet Taylor, but recent scholarship has cast doubt on this assertion. See F. A. Hayek, *John Stuart Mill and Harriet Taylor: Their Correspondence and Subsequent Marriage* (Chicago: University of Chicago Press, 1951), Chapter 3; Gertrude Himmelfarb, *Victorian Minds*, Chapter 4; Alice S. Rossi, ed., *John Stuart Mill, Harriet Taylor Mill: Essays on Sex Equality* (Chicago: University of Chicago Press, 1970); Richard H. Powers, "John Stuart Mill: Morality and Inequality," *South Atlantic Quarterly* 58 (Spring 1959): 206-12; H. O. Pappe, *John Stuart Mill and the Harriet Taylor Myth* (Victoria, Australia: Melbourne University Press, 1960).

(complex marriage) had been minority phenomena hardly representative of the practices of most Americans. Women had served faithfully and valiantly in the Civil War hospitals, sanitary commissions, relief societies, and educational ventures and had supported their respective governments loyally.[10]

Four factors, acting in combination, caused English observers to raise their eyebrows in the 1860s and 1870s over American developments: the interaction of the Negro question and agitation for women's suffrage in Reconstruction; the identification of women's suffrage with the frontier; the seeming willingness of women's suffrage leaders to tolerate free-love advocates in their midst; and the ambiguities of Victorian feminist rhetoric.

The ending of the Civil War, the abolition of slavery by the Thirteenth Amendment, and the prospect of some form of Reconstruction in the South had raised the issue of the extension of the vote to the Negro by amendment of the Constitution. Theodore Tilton, an advocate of women's rights, urged the linking of the two issues by the creation of an Equal Rights Association. Accordingly, in May 1866, the leaders of the Woman's Rights Convention, Elizabeth Cady Stanton and Susan B. Anthony, converted their organization into the American Equal Rights Association, with their old ally, Frederick Douglass, as one of the vice-presidents. But the Radical Republican leadership in Congress had already drafted the proposed Fourteenth Amendment so as to insert the word "male" into the Constitution in such a way as to make it synonymous with "citizen." While the amendment became involved in the intricate struggle between President Johnson, Congress, and the southern states, the American Equal Rights Association tested its new strategy at the state level.[11]

The Kansas suffrage campaign of 1867 illustrated the complexity of postwar politics. Three issues were before the voters: women's suffrage, Negro suffrage, and a new liquor law that would have required that one-half the signatures on petitions for liquor licenses be women's. Financed by eastern funds, the impartial suffrage advocates flocked to Kansas—Henry Blackwell and Lucy Stone, Olympia Brown, Elizabeth Cady Stanton, and Susan B. Anthony. Letters from John Stuart Mill, reprints of Harriet Taylor's *Westminster Review* article of 1851, and copies of Mill's speeches on women's suffrage were circulated, read to audiences, and published in friendly journals. Influential eastern papers swung behind the campaign at the last moment. The results were meager: both women's suffrage and Negro suffrage were defeated.

10. Eleanor Flexner, *Century of Struggle: The Woman's Rights Movement in the United States* (Cambridge, Mass.: Harvard University Press, 1959), Chapters 6-8.

11. Robert E. Riegel, "The Split of the Feminist Movement in 1869," *Mississippi Valley Historical Review* 49 (December 1962): 487; Benjamin Quarles, "Frederick Douglass and the Woman's Rights Movement," *Journal of Negro History* 25 (January 1940): 39; W. R. Brock, *An American Crisis: Congress and Reconstruction, 1865-1867* (reprint ed., New York: Harper & Row, Publishers, 1966), pp. 139-43. Brock indicated that the draftsman of the second article was Senator George H. Williams of Oregon, an opponent of women's suffrage (Brock, 90, 141, 294 n.), but that Williams simply reflected the views of the "sound men" on the Reconstruction Committee.

The Equal Rights Association held its annual convention in May 1868, with Lucy Stone giving a résumé of the status of the women's suffrage movement in England and the United States. Signs of tension had appeared. Elizabeth Cady Stanton and Susan B. Anthony adamantly opposed the Fourteenth Amendment and found an outlet for their views in *The Revolution*, a newspaper established for them by a wealthy but eccentric supporter, George Francis Train. The Fourteenth Amendment was ratified in July 1868, and feelings grew bitter. Frederick Douglass explained the Stanton-Anthony attitude in a letter to a friend. "Their principle is: that no Negro shall be enfranchised while woman is not." Some women's rights advocates had used thinly concealed racist arguments in a bid for southern support or in criticism of the Reconstruction amendments. The old alliance between Negro abolitionists and women's rights advocates was shattered.[12]

The ranks of the women's suffrage movement were divided further in 1869 by the creation of rival organizations. The National Woman Suffrage Association was the vehicle of the New York–based Stanton-Anthony faction; the American Woman Suffrage Association represented the views of the Boston elite led by Lucy Stone. Each organization had its own journal—*The Revolution* for the National and the *Woman's Journal* for the American—and its own coterie of prominent male supporters. Theodore Tilton was president of the National; Henry Ward Beecher was president of the American. Whether the split between the two groups resulted from personal antagonisms, ideological differences, or sheer power politics, the net effect was a loss of political effectiveness for their common cause.

If the women's suffrage movement was weakened from within by bickering over Reconstruction issues, it was buffeted from without by criticism of the identification of the cause with frontier society and attacks on the institution of monogamous marriage. In 1869 the territory of Wyoming, barely out of the "hell-on-wheels" era of railroad construction, enacted women's suffrage to attract settlers to the territory. The subsequent stories out of Wyoming—of a six-foot Amazonian justice of the peace who dispensed justice with an even hand; of tough-minded women jurors who "cleaned up" Laramie; and of determined women who braved social stigma to cast their ballots—may have cheered supporters of women's suffrage but they also played on public stereotypes. When the Mormon hierarchy in the Utah Territory responded in 1869 to a Congressional challenge to polygamy by enfranchising women, they reinforced half-hidden Victorian fears that women's suffrage was an opening wedge for a full-fledged attack on marriage.[13]

12. Flexner, *Century of Struggle,* pp. 145-51; Elizabeth Cady Stanton, Susan B. Anthony, and Matilda Joslyn Gage, eds., *History of Woman Suffrage* (Rochester, N.Y.: Charles Mann, 1887), 2: 229-52, 309; Frederick Douglass to Josephine S. W. Griffing, September 27, 1868, reprinted in *Journal of Negro History* 33 (October 1948): 470; Henry B. Blackwell, "What the South Can Do: How the Southern States Can Make Themselves Masters of the Situation (1867)," reprinted in Aileen Kraditor, ed., *Up From the Pedestal* (Chicago, Quadrangle Books, Inc., 1968), pp. 253-57; Quarles, "Frederick Douglass . . . ," *Journal of Negro History* 25 (January 1940): 40-41.

13. Alan P. Grimes, *The Puritan Ethic and Woman Suffrage* (New York: Oxford University Press, 1967), Chapters 2, 3. Grimes, following the basic account of the editors of the *History*

The National Woman Suffrage Association, for example, was stigmatized in the public mind by the willingness of its leaders to tolerate the notorious Victoria Claflin Woodhull. "The Woodhull" was the *bête noire* of the age: a medical quack, lady stockbroker, pioneering Communist, and outspoken advocate and notorious practitioner of free love. With a stroke of cunning genius, she and her infamous sister Tennie C. Claflin had elaborated on an argument that had struck the leading suffragists with considerable force in 1870. Since the Fourteenth and Fifteenth Amendments had nationalized suffrage as a right, then no state could deny any citizen's inherent right to vote. Women did not need to petition for the right to vote; they already had it. The real culprits were, accordingly, not the women who demanded to exercise their rights but the public officials who prevented them from doing so. The burden of proof was on the oppressors, not the oppressed.[14]

In December 1870, Victoria Woodhull presented a memorial to Congress on the subject of women's suffrage. She argued her case before the House Judiciary Committee on January 11, 1871, but to no avail. The leaders of the National lionized her for publicizing their cause with so much vigor. When she attempted to seize control, however, the ever vigilant Susan B. Anthony blocked the attempt. Victoria Woodhull led her band of faithful followers out of the National and established her own Equal Rights party. (She ran for president in 1872 with Frederick Douglass listed as her vice-presidential running mate, without his consent or support.) Convinced that the new tactic of trying to claim the right to vote by judicial interpretation had failed, Susan B. Anthony drafted the text for a constitutional amendment. Introduced in 1878 by Senator Sargent, the "Anthony" amendment increased the distance between the National and the American, which emphasized state action.[15]

The association between the National and Victoria Woodhull had brought forth unfavorable comments both in the United States and abroad.[16] But the issue was not simply one of personalities or bad publicity. The English women's

---

of Woman Suffrage, stressed the hope of those who gránted the franchise that women would exert a conservative influence and would help to "civilize" the frontier society. For the view that stressed the publicity value and personality factors, see T. A. Larson, "Woman Suffrage in Wyoming," *Pacific Northwest Quarterly* 56 (April 1965): 57-66; and T. A. Larson, "Emancipating the West's Dolls, Vassals and Hopeless Drudges: The Origin of Woman Suffrage in the West," reprinted in Roger Daniels, ed., *Essays in Western History in Honor of Professor T. A. Larson, University of Wyoming Publications* 37 (October 1971): 1-16.

14. Emanie Sachs, *The Terrible Siren: Victoria Woodhull, 1838-1927* (New York: Harper & Row, Publishers, 1928); Sidney Ditzion, *Marriage, Morals and Sex in America: A History of Ideas* (New York: Bookman Associates, 1953), pp. 181-85.

15. Alma Lutz, *Susan B. Anthony: Rebel, Crusader, Humanitarian* (Boston: Beacon Press, 1959), Chapters 15 and 19.

16. For critical commentaries on the women's movement, see E. Lynn Linton, "The Modern Revolt," *Macmillan's Magazine* 23 (December 1870): 142-49; Goldwin Smith, "Female Suffrage," *Canadian Monthly* 6 (July 1874): 68-78, or "The Woman's Rights Movement," *Canadian Monthly* 1 (March 1872): 249-64. The Tilton-Beecher scandal and Miss Anthony's arrest and conviction on charges of unlawful voting in the 1872 election probably contributed to this image of irregularity and militancy. Harriet Beecher Stowe, for example, became

suffrage movement experienced similar difficulties during the same time period. The National Society for Women's Suffrage had been formed in 1868 by societies in London, Manchester, Edinburgh, Bristol, and Birmingham to carry on the campaign begun with John Stuart Mill's petitions and amendments. In 1871 the London National Society for Women's Suffrage split off from the NSWS. The issue was a campaign by Josephine Butler, a prominent suffragist, to repeal the Contagious Diseases Acts. These acts allowed police in seaports and army garrison towns to declare certain women to be common prostitutes and to require (under threat of imprisonment) periodic medical examinations for venereal disease. Josephine Butler felt that the laws were derogatory and discriminatory to women and constituted government sanction of the exploitation of a certain class of women. The London National rejoined the NSWS in 1877; but within a decade the movement had split again. The issue in 1888 was the attempt of one faction to ally the movement with the Liberal party.[17]

The tendency of the American and English women's suffrage movements to splinter on controversial side issues reflected the ambiguities of Victorian rhetoric. The prudery and conformity of the orthodox Victorian mentality cast up rigid dikes beyond which even the most forward middle-class woman could not venture with propriety.[18] The whole basis of suffragism would be undercut if feminism became identified in the public mind with the free-love doctrines of Victoria Woodhull, or with the attempt of Josephine Butler to deal honestly with an "unwholesome" public problem. To assert, as did the suffragists, that women ought to have equal rights because they were morally superior was to invite misunderstanding. If woman's moral superiority rested on her purity, why did she want to "soil" her cause with such impure activities as practical politics or attacks on the institution of marriage? If, on the other hand, women were only equal to men, then was not the attack on the "double standard of morality" in reality a secret desire to sin? Did women claim an equal right to do wrong?

Some recent historians have argued that the Woodhull affair had a serious impact on American feminism. It "literally destroyed the possibility that feminism would be able to generate a body of theory adequate to its later needs."

---

increasingly critical of women's suffrage because of the Woodhull incident. See Margaret Wyman, "Harriet Beecher Stowe's Topical Novel on Woman Suffrage," *New England Quarterly* 25 (Summer 1952): 383-91. For the background of E. Lynn Linton's antifeminism, see Vineta Colby, *The Singular Anomaly: Women Novelists of the Nineteenth Century* (New York: New York University Press, 1970), Chapter 1.

17. Rover, *Women's Suffrage*, pp. 53-61; Halévy, *Democracy*, pp. 498-99, 512-13. For background, see Glen Petrie, *A Singular Iniquity: The Campaigns of Josephine Butler* (New York: The Viking Press, Inc., 1971).

18. Walter E. Houghton, *The Victorian Frame of Mind, 1830-1870* (New Haven, Conn.: Yale University Press, 1957), pp. 353-72, 395-404. For admirable summaries of attitudes toward marriage, family, and women for the period after 1870, see David M. Kennedy, *Birth Control in America: The Career of Margaret Sanger* (New Haven, Conn.: Yale University Press, 1970), Chapter 2; and J. A. Banks, *Prosperity and Parenthood: A Study of Family Planning Among the Victorian Middle Classes* (London: Routledge and Kegan Paul Ltd., 1954), Chapters 9, 12.

By deferring to the Victorian premises of the moral superiority of women and of the sanctity of monogamous marriage (the Victorian Compromise) they had, of necessity, to refrain more and more from criticizing woman's subjection in the home or from searching for radical alternatives for basic social institutions. As a consequence of such an inadequate social analysis, the women's rights advocates placed too much reliance on palliatives such as the enfranchisement of women. In the twentieth century, these historians conclude, suffragists were doomed to disappointment because they had staked too much on an inadequate ideology in the nineteenth.[19]

Before hazarding such a conclusion about historical causation, however, the range of case studies should be expanded. The relationship between intellectual analysis (feminist rhetoric) and institutional change (women's rights or women's suffrage) was more complex than such a paradigm allows. An examination of the Scandinavian countries will illustrate other dimensions of this complex relationship.

SCANDINAVIA: LITERARY FEMINISM AND THE BEGINNING OF THE WOMEN'S RIGHTS MOVEMENT, 1846–1868

The importance of feminist rhetoric in shaping the women's rights and women's suffrage movements can be highlighted by comparing developments in England and the United States with those in the Scandinavian countries. Certain factors, however, must be kept in mind. While each Scandinavian country had its unique features, there was one common element that set those countries apart from the Anglo-American situation: they had a unique legal heritage. A legal scholar has noted:

"Lawyers in the United States with some familiarity with Continental law are accustomed to thinking of the world's legal systems as divided into two major types: common law based on judicial decisions and codes. They overlook the fact that there may be a third possible type, namely, customary law, based on the customs, usages and practices of the community rather than of the courts of the community. The Scandinavian states have such a legal basis. Despite much legislation by the parliaments and despite numerous uniform Scandinavian laws

---

19. William L. O'Neil, *Everyone Was Brave: The Rise and Fall of Feminism in America* (Chicago: Quadrangle Books, Inc., 1969), Chapters 1 and 2; William L. O'Neil, *The Woman Movement: Feminism in the United States and England* (New York: Barnes & Noble, Inc., 1969), pp. 15-32 (quotation, p. 29). For a slightly different version of the radical critique of American feminism and women's rights in the late nineteenth and early twentieth centuries, see Christopher Lasch, *The New Radicalism in America, 1889-1963* (New York: Alfred A. Knopf, Inc., 1965).

adopted during the past eighty years, much of the law, particularly private law, remains customary."[20]

Scandinavian women thus encountered a peculiar situation: the women's rights advocate confronted a private law that operated *within* rather than *upon* local customs; the suffragist wanted rights that neither custom nor public law had yet sanctioned for all men; and, in order to change customs, the feminist had to challenge images of women's role deeply embedded in Scandinavian culture.

Another distinguishing characteristic of the Scandinavian countries was their predominately rural character and agrarian economies. In Scandinavia the pace of industrialization was slower than in England, and the essentially agricultural character of the national economies persisted into the second half of the nineteenth century. By 1850 fully one fifth of the population in Sweden and Norway were landless "peasants"; in Finland, the ratio was as high as two fifths. For the women the results were paradoxical:

"Generally speaking Scandinavian women enjoyed more equality than their sex elsewhere in Europe. And where women joined with men in agriculture they usually had more freedom than in the gradually expanding urban economy, where they were relegated to the duties of the home without escape. Consequently, until the development of industry offered them employment outside the home, urban women were even more than their rural sisters subject to the mastery of some man."[21]

But the equality of agricultural life was an equality of burdens not of opportunities; the inequalities of urban life persisted in law until the late 1860s.

The interaction of the customary basis of the legal tradition and the slow pace of industrialism in Scandinavia can be seen in legal changes made in Sweden in the first half of the nineteenth century. Traditional Swedish law, for example, put both married and unmarried women under the guardianship of male relatives. It also restricted women to the simpler trades, retail merchandising, handicrafts, the keeping of public houses (beer halls), and, occasionally, the management of small factories. "As long as the guild system and the statutes in the legal code of 1734 relating to inheritance and majority remained intact, any extension of [economic] right raised such problems as spinsters' and married women's responsibility and liability, i.e., majority problems, education and trade schools, suffrage (in the towns, voting rights were in the main based on the guild system),

---

20. Lester Bernhardt Orfield, *The Growth of Scandinavian Law* (Philadelphia: University of Pennsylvania Press, 1953), p. xii. See also René David, *Major Legal Systems in the World Today: An Introduction to the Comparative Study of Law,* trans. John E. C. Brierley (London: Collier-Macmillan Limited, 1968), pp. 40-47.

21. B. J. Hovde, *The Scandinavian Countries, 1720-1865: The Rise of the Middle Classes* (Boston: Chapman & Grimes, 1943), 1: 286-90; (quotation, 2: 680-81); Orfield, *The Growth of Scandinavian Law,* pp. 170-72, 202, 256, 290; William L. Langer, *Political and Social Upheaval, 1832-1852* (New York: Harper & Row, Publishers, 1969), p. 12.

and taxation (women could not possibly fulfil the duties that went with the bur-ghership to the same extent as men)."[22] The *Riksdag* demanded in 1809–10 that the Crown issue an ordinance granting economic freedom to women in certain crafts and areas of trade. But the king, Karl Johan, a conservative Frenchman, successfully opposed such legislation until his death in 1844.

During the 1830s and 1840s the transformation of traditional agriculture, an increasing birth rate, a sharply declining marriage rate, and immigration created an acute surplus of women in Sweden. This situation was accompanied by an increase in the number of illegitimate children and a growing problem of pauperism among women. "At the same time women lost a great many opportunities of labour, especially in Stockholm, through the mechanization of the textile industry. . . . In order to relieve poverty and prevent 'immorality'— . . . the authorities in the capital had perforce to become more liberal in granting business licences—subject to a means test—in commerce and crafts."[23] In order to solve these social problems, a series of changes were made in the laws that dealt with the status of women: in 1845, a law for equal inheritance rights, and, in 1846, one for economic freedom.

The impact of the new laws was determined by the class structure. License laws favored middle-class women (through insistence on majority rights and status) and discriminated against lower-class women. "The formal and real restrictions placed most of the shop commerce in the hands of middle-class women, while street hawking . . . was mainly carried on by women from the lower classes." Other lower-class women were forced into being servants or into immigration. Significantly, these changes in the legal status of Swedish women had been prompted by economic conditions and not by ideological commitments to either current liberalism or natural rights feminist doctrines.[24]

---

22. Gunnar Qvist, *Kvinnofrågan i Sverige, 1809-1846* (Göteborg: Akademiförlaget-Gumperts, 1960), Chapter 1 (quotation, pp. 309-10). Swedish class structure was more influenced by the German *Ständestaat* (rigid status system) than were the Norwegian or Finnish structures which were less rigid, more "egalitarian" (in the sense that their peasantry was more prevalent and their middle class rather minuscule). Cf. Seymour M. Lipset, *The First New Nation: The United States in Historical and Comparative Perspective* (New York: Doubleday & Company, Inc., 1967), p. 11.
    See also Gunnar Qvist, "Kvinnan, hemmet och yrkeslivet," in *Den Svenska Historien,* vol. 8: *Karl Johanstiden och den borgerliga liberalismen 1809-1865,* Tage Nilsson and Henning Stålhane, eds. (Stockholm: Bonniers Foerlag AB, 1968), pp. 284-88.

23. Qvist, *Kvinnofrågan i Servige,* pp. 113-20, 212-63 (quotation, p. 313). The number of women engaged in textile manufacturing (at home) declined in the 1830s and revived again in the late 1840s (ibid., Appendix, Table 11).

24. Qvist, *Kvinnofrågan i Sverige,* pp. 265-85 (quotation, p. 315). For the condition of rural women and the relationship to immigration, see Florence Edith Janson, *The Background of Swedish Immigration, 1840-1930* (Chicago: University of Chicago Press, 1931), Chapters 3 and 4.
    Similar changes took place in Norway. A Norwegian law of 1842 granted widows, separated wives, and spinsters of majority age the right to operate a business. In 1845, spinsters over twenty-five were granted the same legal status as minor males aged eighteen to twenty-one. (Previously, proof of majority had required a royal letter.) Up to 1854,

Similarly, changes in political rights were sometimes granted in order to bolster current governments or to ward off revolutionary movements by reform.

In the aftermath of the revolutions in the 1830s and 1840s, a number of continental jurisdictions had decided to base suffrage on a combination of property ownership and class membership. In the process, some women taxpayers and property owners were granted the right to vote (either directly or indirectly) in parish councils, communes, or municipal councils. Austria extended proxy votes in 1849 to women of the landed class in communes; similar concessions were granted in Brunswick in 1850, Prussia and Westphalia in 1856, and Schleswig-Holstein in 1867. In Anglo-American and Scandinavian countries, men

---

daughters could inherit only half as much as sons in the settlement of estates. But such legal changes rested on traditional images of woman's place and role in society.

In Norway the turbulence of the labor crisis of the 1850s was replaced in the 1860s by a constitutional struggle that pitted nascent Norwegian nationalism against the ties of autocratic and bureaucratic union with Sweden. The crisis was precipitated in 1862-63 when Frederik Stang, a leading bureaucrat, established a commission to draft a revision of the Act of Union. Proposals for strengthening the ties between Sweden and Norway were discussed vehemently and flatly rejected in 1871. In this charged political climate, some laws were passed respecting the status of women: in 1863 spinsters were granted the same legal status as men twenty-one years old, economic access to occupations was extended in 1866 to unmarried women, and employment rights in teaching were equalized in 1869. A nascent party system emerged in the 1870s as farmers and middle-class groups formed a Liberal party *(Venstre)* in opposition to the bureaucratic Conservatives *(Höyre)*. These developments laid the basis for the eventual achievement of parliamentarism in 1884.

See Hovde, *Scandinavian Countries,* 2: 688-92; Thomas D. Eliot, Arthur Hillam, and others, *Norway's Families: Trends, Problems, Programs* (Philadelphia: University of Pennsylvania Press, 1960), p. 175; Ingrid Semmingsen, "The Norwegians and the Union with Sweden," in Jørgen Bukdahl et al., *Scandinavia Past and Present: Through Revolutions to Liberty* (Copenhagen: Arnkrone, 1959), pp. 752-53; and Henry Valen and Daniel Katz, *Political Parties in Norway: A Community Study* (London: Tavistock Publications Ltd., 1964), pp. 22-23.

Finland in the nineteenth century had found itself in a position analogous to that of Norway. In the aftermath of war, 1808-9, Finland had been transferred from Sweden to Russia and made a Grand Duchy with its own Diet and fundamental laws. Where Norway struggled to free itself of Danish cultural influence and Swedish political control, Finland fought to overcome Swedish cultural hegemony and Russian political domination. Both Norway and Finland were racked by language controversies in the process: *landsmaal* (new Norwegian) versus *riksmaal* (Dano-Norwegian) in Norway; *svensk* (Swedish) versus *finsk* (Finnish) in Finland.

Finland entered a new period of political activity when the Czar summoned the Finnish Diet to convene in September 1863, for the first time in half a century. A recent uprising by the Poles had made the Czar anxious to avoid similar troubles in Finland. During the next decade significant legislation was passed that set the terms of political life for the rest of the century: (1) an act giving the Finnish language a formal legal status, (2) a Diet Act in 1869 that defined the powers of the Diet more precisely and provided for its regular convocation, (3) a reorganization of church affairs that increased lay participation, and (4) the creation of a communal administrative structure. Changes in women's rights were achieved along the lines laid down earlier by other Scandinavian countries. Communal suffrage was extended to property-owning women in 1863; guardian rights were abolished with women being granted majority at age twenty-five; and municipal suffrage was extended to property-owning women in 1872.

See Ilmi Hallsten, *The Position of Woman in Finland* (Helsinki: The Government Printing Office, 1925), pp. 4-8; Eino Jutikkala and Kauko Pirinen, *A History of Finland,* trans. Paul Sjöblom (New York: Praeger Publishers, Inc., 1962), pp. 213-16.

were occasionally willing to extend political rights to women, particularly those who were taxpayers. For example, municipal suffrage was granted in Kansas in 1861, Sweden in 1862, England in 1869–70, New South Wales in 1867, the city of Victoria (Australia) in 1869, Western Australia in 1871, and Finland in 1872.[25]

Such concessions could be accommodated, however, within the framework of Victorian rhetoric. Woman's moral superiority (or conservative social instincts) entitled her to a special voice in matters such as education, morals, and charity that touched the home or the community most closely. Diplomacy, war, taxation, business regulation, fiscal matters, however, were broad, national matters reserved for men. Women should not soil themselves with such concerns. Before men would be willing to grant women a share in power at the highest constitutional rank, the prevailing ideology and institutional matrix would have to be modified by persuasion or political pressure. In short, if women's rights in general, and women's suffrage in particular, were to make any appreciable headway in the Anglo-American and Scandinavian cultures, these two causes had to become acceptable in the eyes of the middle-class women who were potential converts and in the eyes of the men who alone had the political power to grant what the women wanted.

The debates on economic and political changes in the law did arouse some interest in the "woman question" among literary figures in Scandinavia. The all-pervasive influence of custom was felt most keenly by those sensitive and perceptive artists and writers who had been touched by the romantic currents of European art. Stung by the criticism of provincial society, bored with the limited expectations and petty rituals of the urban middle class, they lashed out at their culture's values. Since changes in customs must ultimately flow from changes in public opinion, the novelist, playwright, and popular preacher-teacher were more important in Scandinavian feminism and the quest for women's rights

---

25. C. A. Reuterskiöld, *Politisk rösträtt för kvinnor* (Stockholm: Almqvist & Wiksell Gebers Foerlag AB, 1911), pp. 85, 99-100 (appendix 2); 236-37 (appendix 6). For the background of European suffrage changes, see Eugene N. Anderson and Pauline R. Anderson, *Political Institutions and Social Change in Continental Europe in the Nineteenth Century* (Berkeley: University of California Press, 1967), Chapter 8.

One exception to the above generalization concerning political reform occurred in Denmark where a democratic constitution, adopted in 1849, established nearly universal suffrage for male householders of thirty years of age. This liberal suffrage led to a struggle in the 1850s and 60s between the peasant representatives in the *folketing* (lower house) and the middle-class urban liberals and conservative bureaucrats in the *landsting* (upper house). Some changes in women's rights were secured—in 1857, unmarried women were made independent of guardians and occupational freedom was extended to them—but educational opportunities and employment for women developed slowly in the 1850s. In the 1860s foreign affairs disrupted normal political alliances. The National Liberals favored union between Denmark and Schleswig-Holstein, a German-speaking area. Their policies led to a disastrous war in 1864 between Denmark and Prussia (allied with Austria). The failure of the National Liberal policy threw them into the arms of the conservative elements in the *landsting*. Together they secured a constitutional revision in 1866 that reduced peasant control by raising the property qualifications for voting. Ironically, then, while Denmark moved away from unrestricted democratic suffrage, "conquered" Schleswig-Holstein granted women property holders proxy votes in communes and diets in 1867. See Hovde, *Scandinavian Countries*, 2: 551-55, 688-92; Reuterskiöld, *Politisk rösträtt för kvinnor*, p. 237 n. 6.

than were such persons in more formally democratic political systems (such as the United States and England) where the laws could be changed by more direct political and judicial means.

In the 1850s a small circle of Scandinavian feminist novelists laid the groundwork for the women's movement of the second half of the nineteenth century. Mathilde Fibiger of Denmark published *Tolv breve (Twelve Letters)* in 1850, in which she asserted a woman's right to be an individual. A storm of protest led the male members of her family to force her to stop agitating for her ideas, but the theme of feminine individuality in Danish literature was continued by Pauline Worm in *De fornuftige (Sensible People)*.[26]

In a similar fashion, Camilla Wergeland, sister of the leading Norwegian nationalistic poet, Henrik Wergeland, experienced a brief, tragic, and hopelessly one-sided romantic love for her brother's chief political and cultural rival, Johan Sebastian Welhaven. She too had to bow to social and familial pressures and deny her feelings. Eventually, in 1841, she married a professor, Peter Jonas Collett, and knew "a few years of almost perfect companionship. . . ." Widowed in 1851, she "tried vainly to adjust her nature to the narrow conditions of her lot, while she grew more and more embittered against the attitude of her country toward women."[27] Influenced somewhat by the careers and writings of Madame de Staël and George Sand, she published in 1855 an indictment of conventional marriage in *Amtmandens Døttre (The Governor's Daughters)*. This literary attack on the tyranny of convention over love (the true basis of marriage) inaugurated the Norwegian feminist movement.[28]

The most influential of the Scandinavian feminist novelists of the 1850s was Fredrika Bremer. The daughter of a wealthy Swedish iron manufacturer, she had rebelled against the constraints of her conventional, upper middle-class milieu. She spurned marriage for a life of literature and independence. In her literary efforts during the period 1828 to 1848, she gradually shifted from a consideration of the domestic plight of middle-class women to an examination of their legal, educational, and political needs. It was the latter question that prompted her to undertake a trip to America in 1849 to investigate, among other topics, the situation of women in the new world.[29]

---

26. For the ethos of the 1850s in Scandinavia and the response of the artists to provincial society, see Michael Meyer, *Ibsen: A Biography* (New York: Doubleday & Company, Inc., 1971), Part 1.
   For Danish literary feminism, see Hovde, *Scandinavian Countries,* 2: 686.

27. Hanna Astrup Larsen, "Four Scandinavian Feminists," *Yale Review,* n. s., 5 (1916): 349. See also Illit Grøndahl and Ola Raknes, *Chapters in Norwegian Literature* (Oslo: Gyldendal, 1923), Chapter 7.

28. Maurice Gravier, "Camilla Collett et la France," *Scandinavica* 4 (May 1965): 38-53; Brian W. Downs, *Modern Norwegian Literature, 1860-1918* (London: Cambridge University Press, 1966), pp. 12-14; and Hovde, *Scandinavian Countries,* 2: 686-87. For the contribution of Camilla Collett to Norwegian feminism, see Maurice Gravier, *D'Ibsen à Sigrid Undset, le féminisme et l'amour dans la littérature norvégienne, 1850-1950* (Paris: Minard, 1968).

29. Gunnar Qvist, *Fredrika Bremer och kvinnans emancipation: Opinionshistoriska studier* (Goeteborg: Akademifoerlaget-Gumperts AB, 1969), pp. 24-98. See also Gustaf Fredén,

During the year and a half tour, she met with or read the works of many of the leading women in America: Margaret Fuller, whose feminist views she did not like; Lucretia Mott, whose eloquent speech on peace, antislavery, and women's rights she found fascinating; and Catherine Sedgwick, a popular writer with "much sensible kindness and good will, but no real genius." She was inspired by the poetry of James Russell Lowell; she found the man to be witty and talkative but not as deeply earnest as she had expected. She wrote the kind of travelogue-exposé that Americans loved to read about themselves. *Hemmeŋ i nya världen (The Homes of the New World: Impressions of America)* was widely read in America and in Scandinavia.[30]

After a visit to England in 1851, Fredrika Bremer returned to Sweden. While she had discussed the situation of women in America, equality of the sexes, and even women's suffrage in *The Homes of the New World*, these topics were scattered throughout the massive three volumes amidst the usual descriptive and homiletical material. She spelled out her attitude toward the "woman question" more clearly in a classic novel, *Hertha*, published in 1856. In the character of Yngve, Hertha's suitor, she skillfully portrayed her own attitudes:

"Yngve told Hertha of the noble women with whom he had become acquainted [in the United States]; whose religious earnestness and liberal-minded fellow-citizenship had greatly influenced the development of his own mind. He made her acquainted with the movements in the Free States, which are there known under the name of "Woman's Rights Conventions," and read to her many large-minded sentiments of progress, from the lips of women during these assemblies. He justified them against the misconceptions with which they were regarded by prejudiced eyes, and showed that, what women on these occasions demanded, beyond everything else, was their right to an education and a freedom, which afforded to every one a possibility and a means of becoming that which God, by the gifts which He has bestowed upon her, calls her to be."[31]

The novel ended in a romantic fashion with the dying heroine issuing a stirring

Arvet från Fredrika Bremer: En bild av Fredrika Bremer sammanställd ur hennes skrifter (Lund, Sweden: Gleerup Bokfoerlag AB [C.W.K.], 1951).

30. Adolph B. Benson, ed., *America of the Fifties: Letters of Fredrika Bremer* (New York: American-Scandinavian Foundation, 1924), pp. 63-64, 209-10 (Margaret Fuller), 168-69, 311 (Lucretia Mott), 17 (Catherine Sedgwick quotation), 12, 52 (James Russell Lowell); Martin Duberman, *James Russell Lowell* (Boston: Houghton Mifflin Company, 1966), p. 95.
    For the American reaction to Fredrika Bremer's work and visit, see Marshall W. S. Swan, ed., *American Scandinavian Studies by Adolph Burnett Benson* (New York: The American Scandinavian Foundation, 1952), pp. 196-221, or Carl L. Anderson, "Fredrika Bremer's 'Spirit of the New World,'" *New England Quarterly* 38 (June 1965): 187-201.
    Most Americans read Fredrika Bremer in rather poor translations by Mary Howitt, particularly *Homes of the New World: Impressions of the New World,* trans. Mary Howitt (London: Arthur Hall, Virtue and Co., 1853), 3 vols.

31. Fredrika Bremer, *Hertha,* trans. Mary Howitt (London: Arthur Hall, Virtue and Co., 1866), p. 157.

challenge to the young women of her day: "Show yourselves, both by word and deed, by the whole of your conduct in life, worthy of the freedom, the self-responsibility which you have a right to demand from the laws of your country, and—it will be conceded to you or your successors."[32]

For a long time, historians and commentators on Scandinavian women's emancipation believed that the public debate on *Hertha* had a direct influence on the passage of reform legislation for women in the 1856–58 sessions of the Swedish *Riksdag*. In 1858, for example, the *Riksdag* granted unmarried women of twenty-five the right of majority upon application to a local court. Historian Gunnar Qvist has recently shown, however, that Fredrika Bremer's *Hertha* did not exert a direct influence on the public or parliamentary debates. Rather, he has concluded that she was regarded by her contemporaries as a reformer of morals rather than of laws.[33]

The granting of municipal and provincial council suffrage to Swedish women taxpayers in 1862 (which may seem like a significant extension of women's rights from the perspective of the twentieth century) was simply the codification of the customary practice and did not represent a direct attempt to rectify an unjust situation. In a review article in 1865, Fredrika Bremer maintained (much as Lucretia Mott had in 1849) that women who were armed with the municipal vote or who had indirect political influence via male proxy votes under the new constitutional system should not exercise this right. They should concentrate instead, she wrote, on creating an ennobling atmosphere for their children and husbands. Small wonder, then, that when the New Liberal party leaders proposed universal suffrage for both men and women in 1868 that the *Riksdag* could defeat the proposals without so much as a debate. Outside of a few "radicals" and liberals who looked to England and America, there was no constituency to support the effort.[34]

To the romantic individualism of Scandinavian literary feminism, Fredrika Bremer had added an emphasis on the social role of woman as redeemer-mother for society. In a letter to Charles Kingsley, the English author, she summed up her ideas:

"In almost all your works (known to me) I have observed a yearning or a hopeful look to Woman as to the redeeming Angel for the woes and wrongs of society. *Even I look to the advent of the true Woman in her fully rounded sphere of life as to the true advent of God's kingdom in social life.* But miserably narrowed by the crushing institutions and trainings of thousands of centuries she has hitherto lacked power to come forward in her true worth and dignity. . . .

---

32. Ibid., p. 387.

33. Qvist, *Fredrika Bremer*, pp. 160-82, 183-206. Elsewhere Qvist has pointed out that the granting of spinster's majority was a necessary consequence of the earlier acts extending liberty to pursue a trade to women. Qvist in *Den Svenska Historien,* Nilsson and Stålhane, eds., 8: 284-88.

34. Qvist, *Fredrika Bremer,* pp. 276, 281; Douglas V. Verney, *Parliamentary Reform in Sweden, 1866-1921* (London: Oxford University Press, 1957), p. 98.

Interest her heart, her mind, her best feelings in the cause of humanity from the time of her childhood; make her feel that she can work for it with every pulsation of her heart and you will have enlisted the most powerful worker in the redemption of society. *Then the new Woman will breed the New Man!"* [italics added].[35]

Carrying her doctrine into practice, Fredrika Bremer had worked in temperance, popular education, and orphan care programs.

Since the publication of Carl Jonas Love Almqvist's *Det går an* in 1839 (a romantic plea for replacing the conventional family with a relationship between equals), Swedish feminism had been equated in the public mind with attacks on marriage and advocacy of free love. But Fredrika Bremer's writings portrayed women as endowed with special intuitions and powers and as being called to a divine mission to save the world. She sought first the spiritual emancipation of women and, through their achievement of equality, the redemption of society. It was a moral stance that saddled women with a double burden—to achieve equality and to demonstrate moral superiority—but it fulfilled the same function for Scandinavian feminism as did the Victorian Compromise for the Anglo-American women's rights and women's suffrage movements.

In summary, the romantic English and American feminists of the 1830s and 1840s had raised the banner of individual self-fulfillment through the cultivation of woman's natural capacities. Woman's moral (i.e., natural) superiority should free her from societal restraints so that she could achieve individual self-fulfillment. The Scandinavian literary feminists of the 1850s echoed these themes in their fiction. Fredrika Bremer, however, rested her case for woman's superiority not only on her alleged moral constitution but also on her social role as homemaker and redeemer. Similar subtle shifts in emphasis had been made by Elizabeth Cady Stanton in the 1850s and by some English feminists of the 1860s. It was a shift that had important implications for the future of women's rights and women's suffrage.

---

35. Fredrika Bremer to Charles Kingsley, September 8, 1853, reprinted in Signe Alice Rooth, *Seeress of the Northland: Fredrika Bremer's American Journey 1849-1851* (Philadelphia: American Swedish Historical Foundation, 1955), pp. 217-19. Given Fredrika Bremer's emphasis on the social role of woman (with its emphasis on the subordination of self for the sake of society), her criticism of Margaret Fuller becomes more understandable. In this same letter to Charles Kingsley she noted: "Alas! for the many, many minds lost to their high mission from want of understanding it, from want of consciousness of their true relationship to God and to society!

"Marg[a]ret Fuller Ossoly [Ossoli] (whose life I have not read but whom I know a good deal of through her friends and even her writings) was, as I think, one of these. Man and [wo]man were in her in juxtaposition. Her metamorphosis was incomplete. She was and wanted to be more than a commonplace woman, but looked for that to the intellect more than to the growth of the heart from out of the selfish one in the Universal. Intellect should in woman enlarge in great sympathies else it will never be truly great in her. (Mrs. B. Stowe has written romance with true womanly intelligence and of course power.) Marg[a]ret F. is a figure strongly characteristic of the ambiguity in woman's position and consciousness in this age of transition."

5

The Alliance of Temperance and Women's Suffrage

"RESPECTABILITY" VERSUS "RADICALISM" IN SCANDINAVIA, 1879–1890

In the United States and England in the 1870s the debate over marriage, free love, and prostitution had violated Victorian proprieties and split women's rights and suffrage organizations. In Scandinavia in the 1880s literary, socialistic, and political debates on these same issues divided the ranks of feminists, prompted their critics to counter efforts, and pushed many women's rights advocates into a public defense of conventional values. Just as in English-speaking areas men and women found in renewed temperance activity a way to conform to conventional mores while creating politically powerful pressure groups, so in Scandinavia they used the temperance movement as a vehicle of protest. While these developments laid the base for modern Scandinavian feminism and welfare programs, the controversies in the 1880s also delayed change in some areas and disrupted the balance of power within various reform organizations.

The influences that triggered these developments in the 1880s can be symbolized by a number of literary events in the year 1879. In that year Henrik Ibsen, the Norwegian playwright, published his classic drama of the "woman question," *A Doll's House.* His literary compatriot, Bjørnstjerne Bjørnson, explored the question of the double standard of morality in a comedy, *Leonarda.* In Germany, the social democratic publicist, August Bebel, published his classic adaptation of the Marx-Engels analysis of marriage, *Die Frau und der Sozialismus (Woman and Socialism).* August Strindberg, the Swedish writer, unleashed a scathing attack on contemporary hypocrisy in his novel, *The Red Room.* Camilla Collett, the Norwegian feminist and novelist, called attention in 1879 to Josephine Butler's ideas on the elimination of officially sanctioned prostitution.[1]

---

1. Michael Meyer, *Ibsen: A Biography* (New York: Doubleday & Company, Inc., 1971), Chapter 19; Maurice Gravier, *D'Ibsen à Sigrid Undset: le féminisme et l'amour dans la littérature norvégienne, 1850-1950* (Paris: Minard, 1968), pp. 166-68; Jacqueline Strain, "Feminism and Political Radicalism in the German Social Democratic Movement, 1890-1914," (Ph.D. diss., University of California, Berkeley, 1964), pp. 36-38; and Martin Lamm, *August Strindberg,* trans. Harry G. Carlson (New York: Benjamin Blom, Inc., 1971), Chapter 5.

Ibsen set the framework for the public debate in the working notes for
A Doll's House:

"There are two kinds of moral laws, two kinds of conscience, one for men and
one, quite different, for women. They don't understand each other; but in practical life, woman is judged by masculine law, as though she weren't a woman but
a man. . . . *A woman cannot be herself in modern society.* It is an exclusively
male society, with laws made by men and with prosecutors and judges who assess
feminine conduct from a masculine standpoint"[2] [italics added].

The opposition of self and society, the dramatic tension between conformity
and true individuality, the elevation of self-fulfillment to the status of a moral
absolute represented a literary revolt against the constraints of traditional Scandinavian society that subordinated the desires of the individual to the prior claims
of the maintenance of the family fortune, the search for a "desirable" marriage,
and the excessive preoccupation with status and official prestige.

In *A Doll's House,* Nora Helmer, a lawyer's wife, has committed a crime
(forgery) out of love for her husband Torvald and concern for his health. When
he learns of the deed, he adopts a legalistic and conventional attitude:

"*Torvald Helmer:* It's all so incredible, I can't grasp it. But we must try and
come to some agreement. Take off that shawl. Take it off, I say! Of course, we
must find some way to appease him—the matter must be hushed up at any cost.
As far as we two are concerned, there must be no change in our way of life—
in the eyes of the world, I mean. You'll naturally continue to live here. But you
won't be allowed to bring up the children—I'd never dare trust them to you—

---

2. Meyer, *Ibsen,* p. 446. In his youth, Ibsen had read the novels of Fredrika Bremer, had
supported the Marcus Thrane labor movement with his pen, and had struggled to promote
a native Norwegian theater free of Danish cultural dominance. In his later plays, Ibsen
pursued a lonely quest for the psychological dimensions of freedom, for those conditions
and attitudes that would emancipate men and women from the ghosts of the past and the
fearful delusions of the future. Only a few critics perceived this dimension of his work;
most of his contemporaries thought of his plays as illustrated arguments on current problems and reacted to them accordingly. While such Norwegian feminists as Camilla Collett
and Amalie Skram criticized his early plays for their portrayal of women, they stoutly
defended his later plays, particularly *Ghosts,* from charges that Ibsen endorsed free love
and attacked marriage.
    One of the emancipated Norwegian women of the 1870s, Aasta Hansteen, was the
model for Lona Hessel in Ibsen's *The Pillars of Society.* Aasta Hansteen was so publicly
condemned for her feminist lectures that she emigrated to the United States in 1880.
See Meyer, *Ibsen,* p. 434; Arlow W. Andersen, "American Politics in 1880: Norwegian
Observations," *Scandinavian Studies* 40 (August 1968): 239-40; Gravier, *D'Ibsen à Sigrid
Undset,* pp. 81-84.
    In addition to memorable women characters, Ibsen sprinkled his plays with minor
temperance figures: Pastor Manders in *Ghosts,* a weak-willed clergyman more concerned
with public appearances than with private moral realities; Mr. Aslaksen in *An Enemy
of the People,* a lower-middle-class reformer of the booster type; and Professor Kroll in
Rosmersholm, a conservative molder of public opinion and a manipulator of other people.

God! to have to say this to the woman I've loved so tenderly—There can be no further thought of happiness between us. We must save what we can from the ruins—we can save appearances, at least— . . ."[3]

Once freed from the specter of disgrace by a turn of events, Torvald "magnanimously" offers to "forgive and forget"; but Nora's eyes have been opened by the experience. She leaves her husband and children—her doll-like existence in a conventional dollhouse home playing with her doll-children—and sets out to find her real self and to educate herself. "I want to find out which of us is right—society or I," she proclaims. Nora leaves her husband with a dramatic, offstage door slam.[4]

The question of the double standard of morality was taken up by Bjørnstjerne Bjørnson in a slightly different way from Ibsen. In 1883 Bjørnson wrote a play entitled *En hanske [A Gauntlet]* in which a young girl breaks her engagement when she discovers that her fiancé has had an affair with a married woman. The conventional morality was summed up in a phrase: "A woman owes a man both her past and her future; a man owes a woman only his future." The message of the play, however, was that both men and women should live "up" to the standard of morality expected of respectable women. The play sparked a literary feud that raged for five years and that divided Scandinavian writers into two antagonistic camps—the "moralists" and "immoralists." The "immoralist" writers "were in favour of a less rigid and more tolerant view of sex and marriage; they rebelled against the idea of sex as being sinful; they realized that social conditions and sexual morals were closely interlocked, and being rebels in the political field, most of them found it natural also to be rebels in the question of sexual morals."[5]

A number of Scandinavian feminists explored these themes in novels and plays. Anne Charlotte (Edgren) Leffler (the Margaret Fuller of Swedish literature) explored the erotic frustrations and moral dilemmas of women caught in conven-

---

3. Henrik Ibsen, *A Doll's House,* trans. Eva Le Gallienne, *Six Plays by Henrik Ibsen* (New York: Random House, Inc., 1951), p. 72.

4. Ibid., p. 78. An illustration of the continuing power and influence of Ibsen's drama is found in a modern Chinese novel. The heroine, idly thumbing through *New Youth* magazine, glances on a passage from *A Doll's House:* "To her they were a revelation, and her eyes grew bright. She saw clearly that her desire [for an education] was not hopeless, that it all depended on her own efforts. In other words, there was still hope, and the fulfillment of that hope rested with her, not with others." Pa Chin [Li Fei-kan], *The Family* (Peking: Foreign Language Press, 1964), p. 27. The novel was written in the late 1920s.

5. Elias Bredsdorff, "Moralist *versus* Immoralist: The Great Battle in Scandinavian Literature in the 1880s," *Scandinavica* 8 (November 1969): 91-92, 109-10 (quotation). A contemporary critic of the "immoralist" writers argued that they had not proved their main contention that the demand for premarital chastity was "contrary to nature" and therefore debilitating or unhealthful [Anon.], "Om en Reaktion mod den moderne Stræben efter større sexuel Sædelighed: Af. Forf. til 'Forholdet mellem Mand og Kvinde, belyst gennem Udviklingshypotesen,'" *Tilskueren* (Copenhagen, May 1885), 375-94 [trans. from Danish by Sonja Knutsen].

tional marriages although "in her work eroticism seemed to be a matter of abstract debate on 'women's rights' rather than a primitive, self-forgetful inner drive."[6] Nevertheless some of the bitterness and frustration of the emancipated Swedish woman can be seen, for example, in her play *Sanna kvinnor (True Women)*:

"*Berta* . . . Fortunately it is no longer the greatest virtue of woman to be like dogs.
Mrs. Bark. Dogs! Oh, Berta, how—
Berta. Yes, just dogs! The more you beat them the more devoted they become. And now that the law of the country has begun to help the women to become human beings they cannot even rid themselves of the traditions. They will rather take thrashing and hunger than they will be without a master."[7]

Anne Charlotte Leffler realized, both in her own life and in her dramas, that the greatest barrier to progress for women in Scandinavia was the predominate influence of custom over legal code.

In contrast to Anne Charlotte Leffler's intellectualism, Victoria Benedict-sson explored the emotional and psychological dimensions of contemporary marriage out of depths of her own unhappy experience. "Brought up as a child under difficult circumstances on the Skåne countryside, and living out her young womanhood in a stuffy provincial community with a husband more than twice her age and five stepchildren, she had always met with misunderstanding and opposition in her desire to develop her artistic and literary interests." Influenced by a Swedish-American radical named Quillfeldt and by the liberal-minded pastor Axel Lundegård, she contributed to the debate on marriage with her novel *Pengar [Money]* (1885), which defended divorce. Lionized by the Young Sweden group and the Danish literary circle, she nevertheless criticized their "free love" bohe-

---

6. Alrik Gustafson, *A History of Swedish Literature* (Minneapolis: University of Minnesota Press, 1961), pp. 276-77. Anne Charlotte Leffler found her "primitive, self-forgetful inner drive" in 1888 when she fell in love with a young Italian mathematician, the Duke of Cajanello. After a divorce from her Swedish husband, she remarried in 1890 and became the Duchess of Cajanello. In the joy of her new relationship she rewrote one of her earlier "abstract" works, *Womanliness and Love, I*, into a warm "existential" novel, *Womanliness and Love, II*. Her newfound creativity was cut short by her death in 1892. For biographical details see Ellen Key, *Anne Charlotte Leffler, Duchessa di Cajanello: Några biografiska meddelanden* (Stockholm: Bonniers Foerlag AB, 1893).

7. Anne Charlotte Edgren (Leffler), *True Women: A Play in Three Acts*, trans. H. L. Brækstad (London: Samuel French, 1885[?]), p. 11 [copy furnished by Harvard College Library]. Anne Charlotte Leffler also collaborated with the Russian feminist mathematician, Sonja Kovalevsky, in writing an elaborate dual drama on the theme of what was and what might have been. As she explained in a letter to a friend (February 2, 1887): "In the first piece all are unhappy, because we generally impede one another's happiness here in life; in the second, the same characters appear living for and helping one another, forming a small communistic and ideal society [of equals], where all become happy." Anne Charlotte (Edgren) Leffler, Duchessa di Cajanello, *Sonia Kovalevsky: Biography and Autobiography*, trans. Louise Von Cossel (New York: The Macmillan Company, 1895), p. 114.

mianism in her next novel, *Fru Marianne [Mrs. Marianne]* (1887). Stung by the criticism of her literary "friends," and seemingly rejected by her lover, Danish critic Georg Brandes, she knew the ultimate frustration of the creative artist: the incomprehension of the conventional; the intolerance of the unconventional. Her contribution to the marriage debate in *Fru Marianne* was to raise the concept of love to the level of a moral principle (based on loyalty and mutual attraction). "As such the supreme insult to love is the mere flirtation, the handling of love as a plaything, as something to pick up or drop as one's whims dictate."[8]

In Norway, Amalie Skram joined the debate on marriage and morality with a semiautobiographical novel, *Constance Ring,* written in 1883 but not published until 1885. In the novel a young, innocent girl from the provinces is married to an older, rich bourgeois (an "advantageous" marriage). When she later discovers that her husband is deceiving her, she seeks the counsel of her pastor, who advises against a divorce. Infidelity in the man is of little consequence, he says, but separation would be a serious wrong on her part. She returns to her husband's house "for the sake of appearances." When her husband dies, she marries a young admirer only to discover that he, too, has had a mistress and an illegitimate daughter. She decides to take a lover but realizes that he has probably "played the field" and is unworthy. In true melodramatic style, she commits suicide.[9]

To a reviewer Amalie Skram wrote:

"You know that I am terribly happy about your promise to write about *Constance.* It can be forceful. Treat it as a "human document" because out of this can be taken, as will, the doctrine that women, now as always, are exactly as men have made them and evaluated them. Women will take this up, saying: if immorality can't hurt men, it can't hurt us either! And I believe both sexes behave this way. It is the fear which emerges from this so-called immorality which has the damaging effect. I believe this, but I don't know it. And so women are everything this damned conspiracy of silence has made them."[10]

Like Anne Charlotte Leffler, Amalie Skram was preoccupied with the erotic element in marriage but from a naturalistic rather than idealistic perspective. The theme that persisted in many of her writings was "the formidable difficulty,

---

8. Gustafson, *History of Swedish Literature,* pp. 284-86. Victoria Benedictsson committed suicide on July 22, 1888, in Copenhagen at the age of thirty-eight. For biographical details, see "Victoria Benedictsson," in Nils Bohman et al., *Svenska Män och kvinnor: Biografisk uppslagbok* (Stockholm: Bonniers Foerlag AB, 1942), 1: 208-9; Holger Ahlenius, *Georg Brandes i Svensk litteratur till och med 1890* (Stockholm: Bonniers Foerlag AB, 1932), pp. 227-30, 266-93, 314-21; and Axel Lundegård, *Victoria Benedictsson: Dagboksblad och Brev* (Stockholm: Bonniers Foerlag AB, 1928).

9. Gravier, *D'Ibsen à Sigrid Undset,* pp. 150-62.

10. Amalie Skram to Arne Garborg, August 11, 1885, reprinted in *Amalie Skram: Mellom Slagene: Brev i Utvalg,* Eugenia Kielland, ed. (Oslo: Aschehoug & Co. [H.], 1955), pp. 106-7 [trans. from Norwegian by Harold Sjursen].

arising from temperament as well as convention, of adjusting passion and marriage in the social conditions of her time."[11]

Ibsen had set the terms of the debate, the "immoralists" had carried some of the arguments to their logical extremes, the feminist novelists (Leffler, Benedictsson, Skram) had related the arguments to the life situations of women. All had sought to elevate the claims of the self (to fulfillment, to love, to passion, to equality) above the claims of society (to order, "appearances," or continuity). It remained for the socialists to subject the claims of society to searching criticism and to counter the individualism of the literary critics.

The socialist interpretation of marriage, as worked out by Engels from Marx' ideas, rested on the premise that the purpose of bourgeois monogamous marriage was to preserve the property of the line by providing "certified" inheritors (i.e., children of proven parentage). Such a system reduced women to the status of property, undercut the basis of love (since freedom of choice was restricted by class interests and parental control), and re-created within the family the exploitative relationships of society (the husband represented the bourgeois, the wife the proletariat). But monogamous marriage had engendered its own internal contradictions in the form of the prostitute (who satisfied the husband, who required fidelity of his wife but not of himself) and the paramour (who satisfied the wife's desires to claim the same rights as her husband).

If private property was the root cause, then only the abolition of private property by social property through the radical restructuring of society would solve the problem. If "true love" was hampered by the woman's fear of individually bearing the results of pregnancy, then restructuring society so as to assure her of social support would create genuine "free love" (i.e., free from care, not from commitment). If women were forced into marriage by economic dependence, then ensuring their economic independence (by industrialism) or interdependence (by socialism) would free them from unequal choices. Woman's struggle, therefore, was but part of the broader struggle of the proletariat for the transformation of society.[12]

The socialist critique of women's status in capitalism was turned into specific proposals and incorporated into the party platforms of the German social democrats. In 1875 the Socialist Labor party congress had endorsed resolutions calling for the franchise for *all* citizens, for free public education for both sexes, and for prohibition of labor by women that would be harmful to their health and morals. (This was the so-called Gotha program criticized by Marx.) In a clandestine congress held in Copenhagen, Denmark, in 1883 (to escape Bismarck's

---

11. Brian W. Downs, *Modern Norwegian Literature, 1860-1918* (London: Cambridge University Press, 1966), p. 93. See also p. 95. For further biographical details, see Borghild Krane, *Amalie Skram og kvinnens problem* (Oslo: Gyldendal Norsk Forlag, 1951) or Borghild Krane, *Amalie Skrams diktning. Tema og variasjoner* (Oslo: Gyldendal Norsk Forlag, 1961).

12. A convenient selection of Marxist-Leninist ideas on marriage is found in Miriam Schneir, ed., *Feminism: The Essential Historical Writings* (New York: Random House, Inc., 1972), pp. 189-211.

antisocialist laws), the German Social Democratic party made plans to win work-ing women to socialism, and some pleas for clarification of the Gotha resolutions were heard. Some women's unions were established during the 1880s, and women delegates did attend the founding congress of the Second International in 1889, but the position of the German social democrats on the "woman question" was not without its ambiguities inasmuch as the male socialists held rather patron-izing attitudes. Finally, in the Erfurt congress of 1891 the party (now freed from the restrictive antisocialist laws and scenting victory via parliamentarianism) "de-manded universal suffrage, including women's suffrage, the secret ballot, propor-tional representation, biennial elections," and other proposals for constitutional change. But it did not demand equal pay for equal work by women, nor did it call for abolition of all restrictions on women's work.[13]

The 1883 German Social Democratic party convention in Denmark gave a boost to the diminutive Danish Social Democratic party and the trade unionists. Socialist ideas had already reached Sweden in 1881 through August Palm, a journeyman tailor, who had worked his trade in Germany and Denmark. Leader-ship in the Swedish socialist movement was shared by Palm with Axel Danielsson, a brilliant orator and advocate of direct action, and Hjalmar Branting, editor of radical and socialist newspapers. Axel Danielsson was imprisoned for eighteen months for advocating direct action. He emerged from prison a convert to parliamentarianism, but anarchist elements remained strong in Swedish socialist circles.

In Norway, Henrik Ibsen was ostracized by conservatives for calling for a "new aristocracy of character, of mind and of will" and for a reshaping of social institutions based on an emancipation of women and workers. Swedish writer August Strindberg also stirred opposition when he outlined a radical women's program in *Giftas [Married]* and hinted that the true solution of social problems, including marriage, lay in socialism. "Shortly after Volume I of *Married* was pub-lished in September, 1884, the state confiscated copies and charged the author with blasphemy. Strindberg, living in Switzerland, was shocked and frightened, and at first it appeared he might let his publisher take all the blame. He finally

13. Strain, "Feminism and Political Radicalism," pp. 20, 43-45, 71-72; G. D. H. Cole, *A History of Socialist Thought*, vol. 3, *The Second International, 1889-1914* (London: Macmillan & Co., Ltd., 1956), Part 1, pp. 254-55; Jacqueline Strain has pointed out that August Bebel's *Die Frau und der Sozialismus* was researched and written during the period 1872-1878 and that he was influenced both by Marx and by the French Utopian Socialists. A major revision in 1891 incorporated the work of the American anthropologist Lewis Henry Morgan and of Frederick Engels on the evolution of society from the primitive matriarchy to the capitalist patriarchy. It was this revised version that was translated into English and published in 1893 under the title, *Woman in the Past, Present and Future.* She also noted that, although such leading women socialists as Clara (Eissner) Zetkin were influenced by Bebel's book, there is little evidence that it prompted the debates at the Copenhagen con-gress. See Strain, "Feminism and Political Radicalism," pp. 31-39, 43 n. 92. Bebel's book has recently been republished in the Source Library of the Woman's Movement. See August Bebel, *Woman and Socialism* (New York: Source Book Press, 1970).

returned, however, and went to trial on October 21, 1884. On November 17, 1884, he was acquitted, but the ordeal had a crushing effect on him."[14]

In Sweden the Social Democratic party was formed in 1889. In Norway, two minor socialist groups had emerged in 1885 and formed a nonpolitical, educationally oriented Social Democratic party in 1887. The rapid economic changes of the 1880s fostered a sudden (and, to hostile observers, threatening) rise in socialist and feminist agitation.[15]

As disturbing as the development of literary and socialist radicalism might have been to the conservative ruling groups in Scandinavia, equally subversive of their power, in the long run, was the democratic recruitment of aspiring working-class and middle-class elements into "popular movements" by trade unions, temperance societies, and free church associations. The system of property quali-

---

14. Cole, *A History of Socialist Thought*, 3, Part 2, pp. 672-82; Meyer, *Ibsen*, pp. 549-50; Jules Mauritzson, "Strindberg and the Woman Question," *Scandinavian Studies* 1 (1911-1914): 208; and Lamm, *Strindberg*, quotation pp. 154-55. In the Preface to *Giftas* 1, Strindberg had advocated woman's equality with man in her rights to education, franchise, public office and opportunity. In the second volume, *Giftas*, 2, published in 1885, Strindberg's stories reflected a negative attitude toward women. Mauritzson believed that "whether right or wrong, [Strindberg] stoutly maintains that the champions of women's rights through their agitation had caused the indictments against him," and that the Young Sweden group had deposed him as their king and looked instead to Anne Charlotte (Edgren) Leffler for leadership. Mauritzson, *Scandinavian Studies* 1: 208-9. Lamm also credited the disintegration of Strindberg's marriage, a commitment to literary naturalism, and growing psychological stress for his reversal of views. Lamm, *Strindberg*, Chapter 7. On Strindberg and socialism, see also Herbert Tingsten, *Den svenska socialdemokratiens idéutveckling* (Stockholm: Tiden, 1941), 1: 56.

15. Cole, *A History of Socialist Thought*, 3: 672; 681-82; 698.
   By way of comparison, in Poland, intellectual currents from the West (particularly Comtean Positivism, English utilitarianism—especially John Stuart Mill—and Spencerian evolutionism) and institutional changes (industrialism, abolition of serfdom, and confiscation of insurrectionists' estates) influenced a literary school known as the Positivists. "According to the Positivists, Poland's obsolete feudal mentality, inherited from the Polish gentry, was an obstacle to her transformation into a modern capitalistic country. A strong moralistic current permeated their publicism; they attacked obscurantism, clericalism, class barriers and advocated equal rights for the downtrodden—not only for peasants, but also for Jews and for women." Czesław Milosz, *The History of Polish Literature* (New York: The Macmillan Company, 1969), p. 284.
   The Positivists produced a series of novels and books that were important to the development of the women's rights movement in Poland: E. Prądzyński, *O prawach kobiety [Concerning Woman's Rights]*, 1870; Eliza Orzeszkowa, *O kobiecie [Concerning the Woman]*, 1871; *Dziurdziowie* [the title comes from the name of a peasant family], 1885; *Cham [The Boor]*, 1888; and *Nad Niemnem [On the Banks of the Niemen]*, 1888; K. W. Wóycicki, *Niewiasta polska w początkach naszego stulecia 1800-1830 [The Polish Woman in the Beginning of our Century 1800-1830]*, 1875; Bolesław Prus, *Lalka [The Doll]*, 1887-1890; and *Emancypantki [The Emancipationists]*, 1894.
   A number of important foreign works were translated into Polish during this period and exerted considerable influence: John Stuart Mill's *Subjection of Women* in 1870, E. Reich's *Studien Über Frauen* in 1876, Theodore Stanton's *The Woman Question in Europe* in 1885, and August Bebel's *Die Frau und der Sozialismus* in 1897.
   Information for the above comments was derived from Milosz, *History of Polish Literature*, Chapter 8, and from "Stan badań nad dziejami kobiety polskiej" [Status of the Investigation of the Polish Woman], *Kultura i Społeczénstwo [Culture and Society]* 7 (No. 1, 1967): 97-101 [Translation by Professor Richard Wartman, Augustana College].

fications for voting (with multiple votes) in Sweden, for example, was weighted heavily in favor of the traditionally rich; this system tended to antagonize the "nouveaux riche" as well as the middle- and working-class elites and forced the "popular movements" to pioneer in methods of mass finance and recruitment. The historic function of these movements in the late nineteenth century was to provide the political mobilization and education necessary for the democratic breakthrough in the twentieth century. This unique characteristic of Swedish reform was indicated in 1890 by the creation of a Universal Suffrage Association from the combined action of socialist, temperance, and liberal groups.[16]

Renewed temperance activity in Scandinavia had begun in 1878-79 (sparked by American, German, and English examples and missionaries) and had led to the founding of various teetotal societies. The American-based International Order of Good Templars (a nonsectarian, teetotal society) established lodges in Sweden in 1879, Denmark in 1880, and Norway in 1884. Tensions between the nonsectarian approach of the Swedish IOGT and the church-oriented approach caused a split in 1884 with the Christian sectarians forming their own National Order of Templars. The Norwegian IOGT split in 1888 over beer drinking with the strict teetotalers staying in the IOGT while the more moderate abstainers formed the Norwegian Order of Good Templars. As teetotal and prohibition sentiment grew, temperance leaders advocated the use of local option and popular referendums. This move would culminate in 1895 in Sweden when the parliament strengthened local control of liquor rights and decreed the adoption of the Gothenburg system of public, nonprofit corporations to sell and dispense liquor.[17]

---

16. Carl Göran Andræ, "Popular Movements in Sweden: Report on a Mass-Data Research Project," *Social Science Information* 8 (1): 65-75; Bo Andersson, "Föreningsrelationer: Personsamband och åsiktsprofiler: En studie i den s. k. liberala arbetarrörelsen i Stockholm, 1880-1885," *Historisk tidskrift* [with English summary] 91 (1971): 197-245; Cole, *Socialist Thought* 3: Part 2, p. 702; Douglas V. Verney, *Parliamentary Reform in Sweden, 1866-1921* (London: Oxford University Press, 1957), pp. 110-11; G. Hilding Nordström, *Sveriges socialdemokratiska arbetareparti: Under genombrottsåren 1889-1894* (Stockholm: Kooperativa Förbundets Bokförlag, 1938), pp. 113-23 (suffrage), 135-37 (temperance), 314-22 (anarchism), and 444-55 (woman question).

An important observation is made by Carl Andræ: "If we look at the biographies of the parliamentary representatives of this period [1900-1920], we find that many of them belonged to one of the popular movements, most often a temperance movement; the left coalition of the liberals and social democrats was dominated by the teetotallers." Andræ, *Social Science Information* 8: 66.

Teetotalism was the philosophy of self-help oriented liberal and labor elites in the 1880s. Unfortunately many of them fell in with the scheme of L. O. Smith, the "liquor baron," to attack the Stockholm liquor corporation. Smith argued that free trade (including free trade in liquor) would lower the cost of living for workers. Through "self-help" they could raise themselves. Before the Smith movement collapsed in 1884 it had involved perhaps as many as fifty thousand workers and left them disillusioned and wary of organization. See John Lindgren, *Från Per Götrek till Per Albin: Några drag ur den svenska socialdemokratiens historia* (Stockholm: Bonniers Foerlag AB, 1936), pp. 40-44 [trans. Michael Setterdahl].

17. Ernest H. Cherrington et al., *Standard Encyclopedia of the Alcohol Problem* (Westerville, O.: The American Issue Publishing Company, 1924-1930), 2: 792-93; 5: 2023; 6: 2569-70 (hereinafter cited as *SEAP*); Walter Thompson, *The Control of Liquor in Sweden* (New York: Columbia University Press, 1935), pp. 14, 19-20.

Interest in democratic politics was also stimulated by a series of constitutional crises in the 1880s in the Scandinavian countries. In Denmark the more liberal and popular *Venstre* (party of the left), which controlled the lower house in the legislature, refused to cooperate with the *Höjre* (party of the right). The leader of the *Venstre*, Christen Berg, "wanted everything to wither in the hands of a cabinet which opposed general suffrage." The leadership of the *Venstre* was drawn from the "folk high school" movement (combining popular education with nationalism and democratic yearnings), from the Lutheran pietists, and from the literary radicals of the various circles in Copenhagen. In the 1884 election, *Venstre* and social democratic candidates won a majority in Copenhagen. The idea of pietistic and democratic masses being mobilized by general suffrage was repugnant to the conservative prime minister, J. B. Scavenius Estrup, who regarded universal suffrage as "one of the worst discoveries of the time."[18]

In Norway, until the passage of a constitutional amendment in 1884, no more than 7½ percent of the population enjoyed the right to vote. Furthermore the government was practically paralyzed by a constitutional crisis over the veto power of the Swedish king and his ministers. The liberal opposition forced the issue. "The first straight two-party contest in Norway, the election of 1882, produced a striking contrast between the central constituencies around the national metropolis and the provinces to the South, West and North. . . ." The conservative party, *Höjre*, was strongest in the cosmopolitan and metropolitan areas; the liberal party, *Venstre*, represented an unstable alliance of radical urban nationalists, cautious provincial farmers, and religious dissidents from rural areas. The liberal ministry began ousting the ruling ministers through a Court of the Realm (an action similar to impeachment) and the king backed down. Parliamentarianism had won. The *Venstre* "acceded to power in 1884 but did not survive as a united party for more than four years: it split up into a 'Pure' wing of radical nationalists and a 'Moderate' wing of spokesmen for traditional religious and moral values."[19]

---

18. Roar Skovmand, "The Struggle of the Danish 'Venstre' Party," in Jørgen Bukdahl, et al., *Scandinavia Past and Present;* vol. 2, *Through Revolutions to Liberty* (Copenhagen: Arnkrone, 1959), pp. 831-33 [quotations pp. 832-33]. See also John Danstrup, *Danmarks Historia: Från Äldsta tid till våra dagar* (Malmö, Sweden: Allhems Foerlag AB, 1946), 2: 140-45.

19. Johs Andenæs, "The Development of Political Democracy in Scandinavia," in *Scandinavian Democracy: Development of Democratic Thoughts and Institutions in Denmark, Norway and Sweden* (Copenhagen: The American-Scandinavian Foundation, 1958) as quoted by Johan Galtung in *Humaniora Norvegica* 5 (1957-58): 150; Stein Rokkan and Henry Valen, "Regional Contrasts in Norwegian Politics: A Review of Data From Official Statistics and From Sample Surveys," in *Cleavages, Ideologies and Party Systems: Contributions to Comparative Political Sociology*, Erik Allardt and Yrjö Littunen, eds. (Helsinki: The Academic Bookstore, 1964), pp. 162, 168 (quotations); Ingrid Semmingsen, "Parliamentarianism Wins Through in Norway," in Bukdahl, *Scandinavia Past and Present* 2: 850-52.
    Much of Bjørnson's behavior during the morality debate of the late 1880s can be accounted for by this political crisis in Norwegian politics. In late 1887 he toured the Scandinavian countries speaking before packed audiences on "monogamy and polygamy."

The split in the *Venstre* was caused, in part, by the refusal of the *storting* to grant a poet's pension to Alexander Kielland, one of the leading "immoralist" writers. But the underlying causes of the split were related to contrasting community norms and traditional religious attitudes. The "moderates" drew their support from the coastal communities in the South and West and from such cities as Stavanger and Haugesund. These areas were characterized by small farms of uniform land distribution; homogenous communities with little class cleavage; consistent support of the *landsmål* (rural folk language), temperance, and prohibition; and pietist fundamentalism within Lutheran orthodoxy. The "pures" drew strength from the Trondelag area and the North and East where the communities tended to be more polarized and hierarchical with intense class cleavages. They were indifferent to the fate of *landsmål* (the folk language) or more in favor of *riksmål* (the national literary language); more radical and socialist (particularly among the rural forestry workers); less concerned with temperance; and more likely to be followers of the pietistic theologian, Grundtvig. Thus the election of 1888 revealed a deep cultural cleavage in Norwegian life between cohesive, traditional rural communities and increasingly polarized urban areas and diversified rural communes that would persist into the twentieth century with important consequences for prohibition and women's suffrage.[20]

The entrance of temperance, labor, and free-church groups into the political arena through mass mobilization of popular support had caused consternation among those elements in society that had traditionally exercised community

---

"Bjørnson had a hero's welcome everywhere, his moral crusade was a personal triumph, and hundreds of thousands of people must have heard Bjørnson 'chanting his morality hymn,' as Oscar Levertin maliciously put it." Bjørnson seemed to be trying to identify his version of Norwegian nationalism and liberalism with the forces of respectability to allay his own religiously tortured conscience or to enhance his political power. Bredsdorff, *Scandinavica* 8 (November 1969): 108.

20. Knut Gjerset, *History of the Norwegian People* (New York: The Macmillan Company, 1915), 2: 555-56; Rokkan and Valen, "Regional Contrasts in Norwegian Politics," *Cleavages, Ideologies and Party Systems*, pp. 171-76, 184-85. Interestingly, the socialists have had their greatest difficulties in Norway's southern and western communities where the industrial units are small; where the proportion of women in the industrial force has been high; and where, even in recent times, the proportion of women in rural communes involved in religious groups has been higher than national averages. Ibid., pp. 175 n. 1, 188.

For a much criticized (but fascinating) study of the significance of community cohesion and norms for Norwegian democracy, see Harry Eckstein, *Division and Cohesion in Democracy: A Study of Norway* (Princeton, N.J.: Princeton University Press, 1966). Criticism of Eckstein's book by Ulf Torgersen and Erik Allardt is found in *Tidsskrift for Samfunnsforskning* (1967), pp. 232-46, 305-23.

For a comprehensive analysis of the language question in Norwegian politics, see Einar Haugen, *Language Conflict and Language Planning: The Case of Modern Norwegian* (Cambridge, Mass.: Harvard University Press, 1966).

Alexander Kielland (1849-1906) was born into an aristocratic commercial family in Stavanger and reared in a pietistic milieu; he later lived in self-imposed exile in Copenhagen among the radical literary circles. His novels exhibited support of feminist views, anticlericalism, hostility to classical learning, and ardent Norwegian nationalism. He wanted to reform marriage, not to abolish it, by establishing free choice, not free love. Gravier, *D'Ibsen à Sigrid Undset*, pp. 132-49.

leadership in matters of social control. This conflict can be seen most dramatically in the areas of antiprostitution, women's rights, and temperance, where institutional developments in the United States soon influenced the English and Scandinavian patterns of change.

RESPECTABILITY AND UNION, 1879–1890

The process of changing public attitudes and of building a political base of support for further extensions of women's rights and women's suffrage was symbolized by two developments in temperance organization and international cooperation: the creation of the Woman's Christian Temperance Union and the meeting of the International Council of Women. In this period of increasing international travel and communication, innovations launched in the United States or England soon found their way to Scandinavia and to the fringes of the British Empire.

An extraordinary "woman's crusade" in western New York and in the middle western states in 1873–74 had brought bands of praying, singing women into the saloons to close them (at least temporarily) through public pressure. From the crusade came the formation of the Woman's Christian Temperance Union. Under its first national president, Annie Wittenmyer (1874–79), the WCTU stressed moral suasion, religious conservatism, and cautious, paternalistic reforms. Under the second national president, Frances Willard (1879–98), the aims of the organization were broadened to include labor reform, "social purity" (antiprostitution), and women's suffrage.[21]

It was the historical role of the WCTU in the 1870s and 1880s to create a "respectable" alternative for middle-class women to the existing women's rights and suffrage organizations that had been "tainted" by their attacks on marriage and the hint of free love. The WCTU's "social purity" campaign stayed within the limits of Victorian rhetoric and stressed the theme that a woman's inherent purity was the warrant for her concern about public morality.[22]

Frances Willard soon formed an alliance between the leadership of the WCTU and the newly organized National Prohibition party. The National Prohibition party provided an outlet for the moral idealism of some Republicans who were dissatisfied with the status of their party in the gilded age. Many of the reform proposals later espoused by the Populists and other third parties were

---

21. D. Leigh Colvin, *Prohibition in the United States: A History of the Prohibition Party and of the Prohibition Movement* (New York: George H. Doran Co., 1926), p. 101; Joseph R. Gusfield, *Symbolic Crusade: Status Politics and the American Temperance Movement* (Urbana: University of Illinois Press, 1966), pp. 74-77, 88-90.

22. In Iowa, for example, an anti-free-love faction developed in 1871 in the Iowa Equal Suffrage Association. It was led by Mrs. Callahan, wife of a prominent Des Moines banker, who was later active in the WCTU. See Francis Craig, "Strong-Minded Iowa Women Won the Right to Vote" [review of Louise R. Nown, *Strong-Minded Women* (Ames: Iowa State University Press, 1970)], *Des Moines Sunday Register,* Nov. 2, 1969, sec. 6, pp. 1, 4.

first endorsed in the National Prohibition party platforms. Women's suffrage, for example, was endorsed by the National Prohibition party in 1872 and consistently supported by them in the 1870s.[23] In 1880-81 Frances Willard persuaded the National Prohibition party to change its name to the Prohibition Home Protection party. "The name Home Protection had been used for several years by the WCTU in connection with petitions in behalf of women voting on the liquor question."[24]

In the 1880s the temperance forces in the United States tested their political tactics of alliance with the women and renewed their drive for statewide prohibition amendments and laws. Such enactments were secured in Kansas (1880), Iowa (1882), Maine (1884), and Rhode Island (1886). In addition, the National Prohibition party made a spectacular campaign in the 1884 presidential election with ex-governor John P. St. John of Kansas as its standard bearer. Then the tide seemed to turn against the prohibitionists. "Between 1887 and 1890 out of fourteen states voting upon the question of the adoption of state prohibitory constitutional amendments, in twelve prohibition was defeated."[25]

Behind the antiprohibition mood of the late 1880s lay the economic chaos caused by a technological revolution. The brewing industry was being transformed by pasteurization, the use of pure culture yeast, better bottling and capping methods, the development of refrigerated railway cars, and the creation of national markets. "In those palmy days of the brewing industry between about 1880 and 1910, the number of brewers was steadily decreasing whereas the production of beer constantly—and at a quicker pace—increased. Improved methods of production and distribution meant that fewer breweries could manufacture more beer."[26]

Production of beer doubled in the decade between 1880 and 1890 while per capita annual consumption jumped from 8.2 gallons in 1880 to 13.6 gallons in 1890. The decision of a number of brewers to "go national" in the 1880s meant that the pressure of competition would force each brewer to seek an expanded market for his production. A wave of mergers, consolidations, invasions of sales territories, and price wars brought instability to the industry. Brewers bought saloons to increase and control their distribution outlets.[27]

---

23. James C. Malin, *A Concern About Humanity: Notes on Reform, 1872-1912, at the National and Kansas Levels of Thought* (Lawrence, Kansas: published by the author, 1964), pp. 5-6, 9.

24. Colvin, *Prohibition Party*, p. 132.

25. Ibid., p. 202.

26. Stanley Baron, *Brewed in America: A History of Beer and Ale in the United States* (Boston: Little, Brown and Company, 1962), pp. 240-46, 257-60 (quotation, p. 257).

27. Ibid., Chapters 29 and 30; United States Brewers Association, Inc., *Brewers Almanac: 1969* (New York: United States Brewers Association, 1969), Tables I, II, pp. 12, 13.
A similar technological and corporate revolution had taken place in the distilleries before the Civil War with the introduction of the steam process. See Henry G. Crowgey, *Kentucky Bourbon: The Early Years of Whiskeymaking* (Lexington: The University Press of Kentucky, 1971).

Small wonder, then, that the brewers began to resist local-option and state-wide prohibition campaigns. For example, in Kansas, where an important test of the constitutionality of state prohibition was pending before the United States Supreme Court in 1883, local politicians approached the Board of Trustees of the United States Brewers Association to underwrite the cost of the appeal. The board agreed to take the case and retained a prominent senator to represent them. A Kansas historian has noted that "the entrance of the Brewers' Association into the controversy converted the local brewery fight against the Kansas law into a phase of the national campaign to break down the liquor regulation of all the states, especially those following the Kansas lead to establish prohibition by constitutional amendment."[28]

Another example was provided by the Territory of Washington where the primitive technological state of the brewing industry and the poor transportation net meant that the brewery and the saloon had been localized institutions confined to the urban areas until the 1880s. "When the Northern Pacific came in the 1880s, the city brewers began to look for customers beyond the reach of horse-drawn beer wagons. Although refrigerated cars were few and shipping arrangements hazardous, the brewers saw vast new markets in the saloons in the small communities that were sprouting up along the Northern Pacific Railroad."[29]

The push of the larger brewers into the small towns antagonized the temperance forces. They responded with political pressure for a local-option law, which was secured in 1885. When the territorial supreme court invalidated both the local-option law and a women's enfranchisement law, the temperance and women's suffrage forces demanded that their causes be written into the draft of the state constitution. The constitutional convention refused but did agree to submit separate prohibition and women's suffrage amendments to the all-male electorate. Both amendments were defeated in the election on October 1, 1889. The prohibitionists blamed brewery interests and "political trickery" for the defeat; some suffrage leaders concluded that alliance with the prohibitionists was detrimental to their cause.[30]

The political alliance between the WCTU and the National Prohibition party did not bring spectacular results for either cause. Yet thousands of women had gained experience in organizational discipline and practical politics. Women's suffrage had been restored to the pantheon of "respectable" causes that middle-class men and women could support.

Frances Willard, who had an optimistic "do everything" policy, was prepared to go even further. During a visit to San Francisco's Chinatown in 1883,

28. James C. Malin, "Mugler v. Kansas and the Presidential Campaign of 1884," *Mississippi Valley Historical Review* 34 (September 1947): 276.

29. Norman Clark, "The 'Hell-Soaked Institution' and the Washington Prohibition Initiative of 1914," *Pacific Northwest Quarterly* 56 (January 1965): 3.

30. Susan B. Anthony and Ida Husted Harper, eds., *History of Woman Suffrage*, vol. 4, *1883-1900* (Rochester, N.Y.: Susan B. Anthony, 1902), 968-70; Cherrington, *SEAP*, 6: 2799.

she was struck by a compelling vision. "But for the intervention of the sea, the shores of China and the Far East would be part and parcel of our fair land," she wrote. "We are one world of tempted humanity. . . . We must be no longer hedged about by the artificial boundaries of state and nation." From this vision came the founding of the World's WCTU in 1884, a call for the worldwide prohibition of liquor and opium, and the dispatching of organizers around the world. In four years, Mary Clement Leavitt, an organizer for the World's WCTU, had established WCTUs in Hawaii, New Zealand, Japan, Australia, and China.[31]

The Scandinavian debate on marriage and morality prompted by the publication of Ibsen's *A Doll's House*, Bjørnson's *The Gauntlet*, Bebel's *Die Frau und der Sozialismus*, the translation of John Stuart Mill's *Subjection of Women*, and the prosecution of "immoralist" writers came at the same time as women's rights and suffrage associations were being formed or older organizations were being transformed by international influences. In Norway, the *Norsk kvindesaksforening* (Norwegian Society for Women's Rights) was founded in 1884 to promote women's rights by educational means. The following year, a much smaller *Norsk kvindestemmeretsforening* (Norwegian Woman Suffrage Society) was formed under the leadership of Gina Krog. In Sweden, leadership was taken by the *Fredrika Bremer—förbundet* (Fredrika Bremer Society) and the new feminist journal *Dagny*. Although the Danish Woman's Association had been founded in 1871, it was transformed in 1883 into an aggressive pressure group and, in 1885, established its own journal, *Kvinden og Samfundet (Woman and Society)*. The Finnish Woman's Association was established in 1884 and pressed for a wide variety of reforms.[32]

While a few of the literary feminists supported the "immoralist" side in the morality debate or independently explored their feminist visions of a woman's individual superiority to society's claims upon her, the bulk of the women's rights advocates accepted the conventional morality and tried to reform society in keeping with its own premises. Elizabeth Grundtvig, in a talk before a Danish audience, "warned women not to accept the philosophy of those who claimed that sex was an irrepressible force in both men and woman, and who preached the dangerous gospel that women, too, could live a full sexual life if only prejudices and conventional education did not prevent them from doing so." In

---

31. Elizabeth Putnam Gordon, *Women Torch-Bearers: The Story of the Woman's Christian Temperance Union* (Evanston, Ill.: National WCTU Publishing House, 1924), pp. 70-73 (quotation, p. 70); Hannah Whitall Smith, "The Latest Evolution of the WCTU," in *Report of the International Council of Women* (Washington, D.C.: National Woman Suffrage Association, 1888), p. 115.

32. Agnes Matilde Wergeland, *Leaders in Norway and Other Essays* (reprint ed., Freeport, N.Y.: Books for Libraries, Inc., 1966), pp. 111-13; Karen Larsen, *A History of Norway* (Princeton, N.J.: Princeton University Press, 1948), p. 472; Gunnar Qvist, "Kvinnan i yrkesliv och kamp för likställdhet," in Jan Cornell, Sten Carlsson, Jerker Rosén et al., *Den Svenska historien*, vol. 9, *Industri och folkrörelser 1866-1920* (Stockholm: Bonniers Foerlag AB, 1968), pp. 194-95; Kirstine Frederiksen, "The Danish Woman's Association" in *Report of the International Council of Women*, pp. 203-6; Alexandra Gripenberg, "Woman's Work in Finland," in *Report of the International Council of Women*, pp. 388-92.

Sweden, Anna Hierta Retzius, wife of the editor of the influential *Aftonbladet* newspaper and a pioneer in Swedish women's rights, drove suspected "immoralist" writers from the newspaper staff. But to the genuine conservatives, all such disturbers of the status quo as feminists or women's rights advocates were equally subversive of the social order.[33]

Among those elements in society that had traditionally exercised community leadership in matters of social control, particularly the clergy of the established state churches, the "social purity" issue was another uncomfortable reminder of the leadership exercised by feminists and women's rights advocates. In 1876–1877 Josephine Butler, the English advocate of abolition of government regulation of legally sanctioned prostitution, had published her ideas in an influential book and had seen them endorsed by an international congress held in Geneva, Switzerland. Her book had been translated into Danish and supported by the Norwegian feminist, Camilla Collett.

In the autumn of 1879 a small circle of Norwegian theologians considered establishing an organization to condemn officially sanctioned prostitution. The Christiana ministerial association addressed an appeal to the Ministry of Justice on the question. Meanwhile, the *arbeidersamfundet* (workers' union) held public meetings on the problem; dissenting free church communities displayed excessive zeal on the issue; and a number of women's rights advocates—Ragna Nielsen, Dorothea Schjoldager, Ida Welhaven, and Birgitte Esmark—spoke frequently at "social purity" meetings. These events dramatized the underlying question: Who spoke for the good of the community—the established clergy or the self-appointed spokesmen of the workers, the evangelists, and the feminists?

In 1881 the ministerial groups revived the idea of an organization opposed to officially sanctioned prostitution and in May 1882 they formed the *Foreningen mot den offentlige usædelighet* (Association Against Public Immorality) with women as *nonvoting* members. During the morality debate some writers explored the problem of prostitution in considerable (and naturalistic) detail and precipitated a series of "scandalous" episodes involving censorship. The Norwegian painter Christian Krogh published a novel, *Albertine,* about a woman falsely caught up in a police sweep of alleged prostitutes and forced to submit to a medical examination for venereal disease.

Amalie Skram jumped into the fray with a pamphlet attack on the double standard of morality in the prostitution question. Morally, she asked, what is the difference between the buyer and the seller? Why did the police stigmatize the prostitute but ignore the patron? Although Camilla Collett warned in an article in 1887 that the "immoralists" (writers) and their feminist supporters were hurting the cause of women's rights, Amalie Skram persisted. A conference between the theologians and the *Statsminister* on December 14, 1887, resolved the public issue by transferring control of venereal disease from the police to the public health administration. The ministers had reasserted their leadership

---

33. Bredsdorff, *Scandinavica* 8 (November 1969): 97-99, 103-9 (quotation, p. 103).

in society, but "leagues of public morality," led increasingly by women, continued to agitate throughout the 1890s.[34]

While Scandinavian men combined temperance with trade unionism, free church piety, or free-thinking sectarianism, Scandinavian women united "social purity" with women's rights or temperance. In 1886 the WCTU was introduced to Sweden at a meeting of the *Fredrika Bremer-förbundet* (Fredrika Bremer Society) by Mary Leavitt, organizer for the World's WCTU, and Natalie Anderson-Meijerhelm. The same year saw the establishment of local circles of rival societies from America, the *Sveriges Blåblandsförbund* (Blue Ribbon Society) and the *Vita Bandet* (White Ribbon Society). The White Ribbon, which was WCTU supported, spread to Denmark in 1888 and to Norway in 1892 as a result of visits by Charlotte Grey and correspondence between Birgitte Esmark, veteran of the social purity campaign, and Frances Willard of the American WCTU. The net result was an increase in prohibition sentiment in the 1890s and a growing number of women's organizations prepared to exert pressure either directly or indirectly on the political process.[35]

While Frances Willard's WCTU developed into a powerful international women's organization, Elizabeth Cady Stanton and Susan B. Anthony labored to enhance the prestige of their National Woman Suffrage Association. In the struggle for recognition and prestige, they worked for the establishment of an international women's suffrage association. At a *bon voyage* reception in their honor in Liverpool, England, in November 1883, they had joined with leaders of the English, Irish, and Scottish women's suffrage movements to set up a committee of correspondence to call an international women's rights conference. Three years later, in January 1887, the National Woman Suffrage Association decided to sponsor the conference so as to coincide with the fortieth anniversary of the Seneca Falls convention.[36]

The convening of the International Council of Women in Washington, D.C., on March 25, 1888, represented not only a personal triumph for the Stanton-Anthony wing of the women's suffrage movement in the United States but also a symbolic union of the international temperance and women's rights movements. Of the fifty-one associations represented at the 1888 convention, seven were temperance or prohibition associations, ten were suffrage leagues, and six were concerned with the "social purity" (antiprostitution) question. Representatives from the Finnish Women's Union, the Danish Woman's Association, the French Woman's Union for the Care of the Wounded, and numerous British associations gave the conference a cosmopolitan air.

---

34. Gravier, *D'Ibsen à Sigrid Undset*, pp. 75, 166-91; Glen Petrie, *A Singular Iniquity: The Campaigns of Josephine Butler* (New York: The Viking Press, Inc., 1971), pp. 184-86; Fredrikke Mørck, ed., *Norske Kvinder: En oversigt over deres stilling og livsvilkaar i hundredeaaret 1814-1914* (Kristiania: Berg & Høgh Forlag, 1914), 2: 16-18.

35. Cherrington, *SEAP*, 5: 1997; 6: 2571; Thompson, *Control of Liquor in Sweden*, p. 22.

36. "Origin of the Council," in *Report of the International Council of Women*, 1888, pp. 2-3. See above, footnote 1, Chapter 2, for the background and the circumstances of the writing of the *History of Woman Suffrage* by the leaders of the National Woman Suffrage Association.

The two sessions devoted to the political conditions of women indicated how far the women's suffrage movement had come in a decade. The remarks of Mrs. Ashton Dilke of the Women's Liberal Association of Newcastle-on-Tyne were typical:

"A great work has been done in the past by Women's Suffrage Societies all over England. They have had to pass an immense amount of ridicule and abuse; but at the present day there is more tolerance of woman suffrage. Some years ago, when I first took an interest in the matter, it certainly was not so. Opinion seemed to be very sharply divided as to whether woman should have the parliamentary suffrage or not; but at the present day there is a great deal of toleration, and I put down the toleration that it has obtained of late, very much to the action outside of the Woman Suffrage Society itself. For in England women take a very large part in politics."[37]

The creation in England of the Primrose League, the women's suffrage auxiliary of the Conservative party, provided another index of the changing times. Not everyone had been converted, of course. In 1889, Beatrice Webb, future theoretician of the Fabian socialists, signed a manifesto against women's suffrage. Bills for female enfranchisement languished in both Parliament and Congress.[38]

The presence at the International Council of Women of Baroness Alexandra Gripenberg of Finland, representing the Finnish Women's Association, indicated the status of both the suffrage movement and the growing women's rights movement in Scandinavia. The Finnish Women's Association had been formed in 1884 to raise the educational standards of women and to push for a variety of reforms: protection of married women's property rights, extension of political franchise, lowering of majority to age twenty-one, raising of age of consent to fifteen, securing entrance to teaching and other professions, and abolition of legal prostitution.

Under its second president, Baroness Gripenberg (1889–1904), the Association became the leading force for women's rights in Finland. Her social position, international reputation, and editorship of the influential journal *Koti ja Yhteiskunta (Home and Community)* made Baroness Gripenberg a leader among the women's rights advocates in Scandinavia.[39] In her report to the International Council of Women, Baroness Gripenberg summed up the status of her work in Finland and touched on the secret of its success: "Many women, who from religious or other motives do not join suffrage work, are active supporters of

---

37. *Report of the International Council of Women,* 1888, p. 385.

38. Lena Jeger, "Has It Made Any Difference?" *The New Statesman* 75 (February 16, 1968): 198. For the relative importance of women and temperance to the revival of the Liberal party in the 1880s, see Janet Howarth, "The Liberal Revival in Northamptonshire, 1880-1895: A Case Study in Late Nineteenth Century Elections," *The Historical Journal* 12 (1969): 79-118.

39. Hallsten, *The Position of Women in Finland,* pp. 10-12.

temperance or social purity work, these questions and also that of coeducation, being at present subjects of great interest for the whole country."[40]

The working alliance of prohibition, social purity, and women's rights forces in the United States, England, and the Scandinavian countries helped to facilitate the eventual reunion of the shattered women's suffrage movement and to boost its cause. In 1890, the National Woman Suffrage Association combined with the American Woman Suffrage Association to form the National American Woman Suffrage Association (NAWSA) under the presidency of Elizabeth Cady Stanton. In England the process took a bit longer, but by 1897 all the societies devoted exclusively to women's suffrage had federated into a National Union of Women's Suffrage Societies. In Norway women's voting rights were debated in the Norwegian parliament in 1890; women's suffrage secured a majority vote in 1893 but failed for lack of a two-thirds majority. The incident did arouse considerable interest in Scandinavian countries. However, not until 1906 would an international women's suffrage union be created.[41]

Once the prohibition and women's suffrage movements had joined forces in the 1880s and 1890s in the Anglo-American and Scandinavian cultures; once they had learned how to utilize the Victorian attitudes toward women and the home to their own advantage; and once they had created international institutions to exchange ideas, startling victories might have been expected in the next decades in those areas where middle-class citizens and working-class elites were most susceptible to the twin appeals of respectability and responsible, democratic citizenship. Such was not to be the case.

One of the paradoxes of the prohibition and women's suffrage movements was that, while their intellectual and financial leadership was centered in the older, established areas such as the eastern section of the United States, the evangelical-radical areas of England, and the literary centers of Scandinavia, the practical achievements of the period 1890–1910 occurred on the frontiers

---

40. *Report of the International Council of Women,* p. 392. See also Alexandra Gripenberg, *A Half Year in the New World: Miscellaneous Sketches of Travel in the United States,* trans. Ernest J. Moyne (Newark, N.J.: University of Delaware Press, 1954), Chapters 1, 2.

Literary feminism had been somewhat slower in developing in Finland than in other Scandinavian countries. The first woman author in Finland, Sara Wacklin, published stories on the hard lot of women in the 1840s in Swedish. Fredrika Runeberg, wife of the Finnish nationalist poet J. L. Runeberg, published similar articles in 1850 in a leading literary journal. It was not until the publication of Fredrika Bremer's *Hertha,* however, that a public debate was stirred on the woman question. Adelaïde Ehrnrooth, writing under the pseudonym A-i-a, took up the women's cause in the 1860s in Swedish-language newspapers and advocated equality of educational and professional opportunity, equality before the law, and a single moral standard. Later, Minna Canth, writing in Finnish, provided realistic dramas of the harsh condition of women and provoked considerable public discussion.

For additional material on women writers in Finland, see Erik Ekelund, *Finlands svenska litteratur: från Åbo brand till sekelskiftet* (Stockholm: Bonniers Foerlag AB, 1969), 2: 133-34 (Sara Wacklin), 135-42 (Fredrika Runeberg), and 338-42 (Adelaïde Ehrnrooth).

41. Constance Rover, *Women's Suffrage and Party Politics in Britain, 1866-1914* (London: Routledge and Kegan Paul, Ltd., 1967), p. 6; Mørck, *Norske Kvinder, 1814-1914,* p. 5.

of the Anglo-American and Scandinavian cultures: Australia-New Zealand, the American West, and Finland.

The connection between the American "frontier" and women's suffrage and prohibition was noted early in this century by followers of the American historian Frederick Jackson Turner. These historians attributed the extension of the franchise and willingness to engage in experiments in social control to the democratizing and liberalizing effects of the frontier environment. Recent historians, however, have challenged this argument both for its environmental determinism and for its designation of women's suffrage and prohibition as essentially liberal or "progressive" innovations.[42]

The comparative historical method offers an opportunity to reexamine the frontier question in a broader framework and with a wider range of cases. Since any analysis of social innovation must take into account both the intellectual and institutional barriers to change, the frontier can be viewed as a combination of ideological and institutional weaknesses or strengths. If belief in prohibition as a means of social control for the problem of alcoholism was a matter of enforcing social conformity, then interest in prohibition would be stimulated where the social institutions and means of enforcing conformity were unstable. Similarly, the willingness and ability to grant extension of the suffrage to women at the highest constitutional level would be inversely related to the age or "maturity" of the political institutions. That is, the older the existing political institutions, the stronger the ideological resistance to change; the newer the political institutions, the weaker the ideological resistance to change.

This hypothesis would suggest that women's suffrage was granted on the frontiers of the Anglo-American and Scandinavian cultures because the institutional barriers to ideologically sanctioned change were ineffective. This hypothesis would also indicate that an argument for social control (as advanced by prohibitionists) would seem most persuasive to its partisans and potential converts precisely in those social and institutional contexts characterized by "chaos"— that is, where institutional disorder or weakness prevailed. A closer look at the relevant cases will illustrate these factors and provide a test of the hypothesis.[43]

---

42. Alan P. Grimes, for example, has argued that in the American West "the constituency granting woman suffrage was composed of those who supported prohibition and immigration restriction and felt that woman suffrage would further their enactment." In short, women's suffrage was, paradoxically, an essentially conservative innovation adopted for reasons of political expediency, not for ideological consistency, by antilibertarian forces. Alan P. Grimes, *The Puritan Ethic and Woman Suffrage* (New York: Oxford University Press, Inc., 1967), pp. xii, 5.

Grimes in turn has been criticized for overgeneralizing from too limited a selection of cases and for underestimating the complexities of the issue. For a critical review, see Anne F. Scott's review of Alan P. Grimes, *The Puritan Ethic and Woman Suffrage,* in *American Historical Review* 73, No. 2 (1967): 608-9.

43. I am indebted to my former research assistant Dean Wilkinson for helping in this formulation of the problem. For a convenient summary of other comparative hypotheses on the "frontier" problem, see the essays by Seymour M. Lipset and Marvin W. Mikesell in *Turner and the Sociology of the Frontier,* Richard Hofstadter and Seymour M. Lipset, eds. (New York: Basic Books, Inc., Publishers, 1968).

6

Frontiers and Franchise

AUSTRALIA AND NEW ZEALAND

The society that emerged on the Australian frontier in the mid-nineteenth century was decidedly different from that of the United States. The harsh geography, the high capitalization of entrepreneurial endeavors, the early grant of political home rule, and land laws created a "big man's frontier" in which sheep-raising, pastoral oligarchs, called squatters, monopolized land and political power. The town tradesmen and the unsuccessful gold miners of the 1850s, dubbed diggers, succeeded in wresting a democratic franchise from the squatters and gradually enacted most of the Chartist and "radical" programs that they had brought with them from Ireland, Scotland, and England. But they did not succeed, on the whole, in creating a significant class of independent farmers engaged in small-scale agriculture. The net effect was to increase the urbanization of the population, to stimulate industrialism, and to foster trade unionism. By the crucial decade of the 1890s "the average Australian was not his own economic boss. He was a wage earner, like the average native of Britain, whence he had recently come."[1]

The women's suffrage question was, therefore, a complicated matter. The fact that the vote came to Australian women more or less fortuitously rather than by their own efforts or organizational skill and political pressure may help to explain their subsequent timidity about enhancing their status. More importantly, the lack of a genuine feminist movement and the rather narrow range of concerns in the area of women's rights were developments related to the

---

1. A. L. Burt, "If Turner Had Looked at Canada, Australia, and New Zealand When He Wrote About the West," in *The Frontier in Perspective,* Walker D. Wyman and Clifton B. Kroeber, eds. (Madison: University of Wisconsin Press, 1957), pp. 72-75 (quotation, p. 75); A. Griffiths, "The Irish and Australian Radicalism," *Contemporary Review* 216 (February 1970): 57-63; I. D. McNaughtan, "Colonial Liberalism, 1851-92," in *Australia: A Social and Political History,* Gordon Greenwood, ed. (New York: Praeger Publishers, Inc., 1955), pp. 102-22.

Australian concept of equality.[2] Numerous authors have noted that, whereas the American concept of equality emphasized opportunity, reward proportionate to risk or effort, and a blurring of class identity, the Australian concept of equality emphasized security, an equitable share, and strong class consciousness.[3] An essential expression of these attitudes was found in the philosophy of mateship. "The essence of mateship is the uncritical acceptance of reciprocal obligations to provide companionship and material or ego support as required." In some respects, it is the opposite of the success mentality dominant in the United States. Mateship, an essentially masculine trait of comradeship, acted to perpetuate economic and social discrimination against women.[4] At the same time, pioneering welfare laws and social services, underlining the equality-as-security theme, tended to encase women in their primary sex roles rather than to free them from the restrictions of such socially sanctioned duties.[5]

To be a feminist, to rebel against Australia's "radical culture" (in the British sense), to assert the superiority of feminine individualism against masculine mateship collectivism (or solidarity) led either backwards to England's mother culture with its emphasis on hierarchy, inequality, and Victorian mores or outwards toward America's liberal culture with its emphasis on equal opportunity, assertive individualism, and disproportionate material rewards. Australian demography operated against the first option; Australian geography against the second. The would-be feminist in the nineteenth century was isolated in advance and denied an effective organizational stance. Nor could the potential feminist find solace and strength in literature as could her Scandinavian counterpart.[6]

---

2. Ronald Taft and Kenneth F. Walker, "Australia," in *The Institutions of Advanced Societies,* Arnold M. Rose, ed. (Minneapolis: University of Minnesota Press, 1958), p. 147.

3. K. F. Walker, "The Australian Labor Movement," *South Atlantic Quarterly* 58 (Spring 1959): 185-95: "Whereas America was 'the land of opportunity,' Australia was more a 'land of equality,' where the frugal gifts of nature were at least to be fairly shared" (p. 187); Richard N. Rosecrance, "The Radical Culture of Australia," in *The Founding of New Societies: Studies in the History of the United States, Latin America, South Africa, Canada, and Australia,* Louis Hartz et al. (New York: Harcourt Brace Jovanovich, Inc., 1964), pp. 275-318: "One of the most fundamentally important facts of Australian development is that capitalism emerged in a society which had been 'born radical'" (p. 304); Taft and Walker in *Advanced Societies,* Rose, ed., pp. 144-46: "Perhaps the most important [values and beliefs] of all are the underlying class attitudes: militant equalitarian social attitudes on the part of the workers, set in the background of politico-economic class consciousness . . ." (p. 144).

4. Taft and Walker in *Advanced Societies,* Rose, ed., p. 147.

5. T. H. Kewley, "The Development of the Social Services," in *Australia,* C. Hartley Grattan, ed. (Berkeley: University of California Press, 1947), p. 253.

6. The Anglo-American and Scandinavian literary pattern (in which literary feminism preceded or accompanied the movement for women's rights and suffrage) was almost reversed in Australian history. The pioneering women novelists of the 1850s and 1860s either detailed the hardships of emigration or explored the familiar romantic theme of the triumph of woman's inherent moral character over circumstances and class restrictions. Most of the novels

To advocate women's rights, that is, to take a reformist stance in reference to Australian ideals, was a more viable organizational option. Unlike the American western frontier with its chronic shortage of women, Australia had, by the 1880s, developed a relatively balanced population (except for Queensland and the Northern Territory). Australian women married young (at 23 in the 1880s) and had a higher birth rate and fewer economic opportunities than their English counterparts. The strong ideological restraints of an essentially Victorian middle-

---

by women authors in the late nineteenth and early twentieth centuries dealt with the themes of the lonely splendor of the harsh landscape, the spiritual isolation of women, and the hearty mateship culture of the masculine pioneers. A few utopian novels in the era (by both men and women) took up the theme of women's suffrage: Harriet A. Dugdale, *A Few Hours in a Far Off Age* (1883); Sir Julius Vogel, *Anno Domini 2000, or Woman's Destiny* (1888); and M. M. Bentley [Mary Anne Moore Ling], *A Woman of Mars; or Australia's Enfranchised Woman* (1901). The flowering of Australian feminist literature, the creation of alternative images of woman's role, did not come until *after* the achievement of the vote and some welfare legislation.

The careers of some of Australia's principal women authors revealed the peculiar tensions of the cultural rebel in a "radical" political culture. Kathleen Hunt Caffyn was born in Ireland, emigrated to Australia in 1879, and returned to England in 1894. Under the pseudonym "Iota" she published *A Yellow Aster* (1894) and *The Minx* (1901) in which marriage is treated as an experiment in equality and emancipation. Stella Maria Miles Lampre Franklin, who wrote under the name Miles Franklin, published *My Brilliant Career* (1901), the story of a sensitive girl's ambitions in conflict with her environment, and edited a women's trade union magazine before emigrating to New York. Australia's first internationally known author, "Henry Handel Richardson" [Ethel Henrietta Richardson] left Australia at the age of sixteen to live in England and Europe. She returned to Australia in the 1920s to gather background material for her classic novel, *The Fortunes of Richard Mahoney* (1930). Katharine Pritchard was born on Fiji in 1884 and raised in Australia. She went to London in her twenties before writing a series of novels that celebrated mateship and condemned Australia as a primitive land where white women were not really at home. Winifred James also moved to London in the 1900s and there married an American citizen. She spelled out her alienation from Australian society in her novels and complained bitterly of the law that took away her nationality and determined it by that of her husband. Christine Stead, born in 1902, moved to New York, yet her *Seven Men of Sydney* (1934) was a celebration of the masculine demi-world of the radical left intellectuals. In short, to rebel against Australia's current values led either back to England and its values, to a rejection of the tyranny of Australian geography, to a celebration of Australia's legendary (masculine) past, or to a search for personal freedom in America at the expense of Australian equality and security.

For the role of women, and of feminism, in Australian literature, see Edmund Morris Miller, *Australian Literature: From Its Beginnings to 1935* (Melbourne: Melbourne University Press, 1940), 1: 405-8, 445-47, 503-6, 2: 513-15, 515-19, 547-50, 638; H. M. Green, "Literature" in *Australia,* C. Hartley Grattan, ed. (Berkeley: University of California Press, 1947), pp. 291-302; H. M. Green, *Australian Literature, 1900-1950* (Melbourne: Melbourne University Press, 1951); George Nadel, *Australia's Colonial Culture: Ideas, Men and Institutions in Mid-Nineteenth Century Eastern Australia* (Melbourne: F. W. Cheshire Pty. Ltd., 1957), pp. 106-10.

Political feminism also flourished after the achievement of women's suffrage. In 1903 Vida Goldstein organized the Women's Political Association to support her candidacy for the Australian federal senate. She combined feminism and socialism in one movement. On a trip to London in 1914 she recruited one of the famous English suffragettes, Adela Pankhurst, and persuaded her to come to Australia. Adela joined the Women's Political Association and participated in feminist-pacifist-socialist opposition to World War I. See David Mitchell, *The Fighting Pankhursts: A Study in Tenacity* (New York: The Macmi   Company, 1967), pp. 55-58.

class conception of female roles limited the potential scope of women's rights activities to education, temperance, and women's suffrage.[7]

In the more populous colonies such as Victoria and New South Wales, women's suffrage organizations were formed in the 1880s and by the 1890s they had secured the leadership and support of seasoned veterans of the English suffrage movement. In spite of conservative opposition, by 1890 New Zealand and all the Australian colonies (except Queensland) had granted municipal suffrage for women. But New Zealand, South Australia, and Western Australia were the first to grant women's suffrage at the highest constitutional level.[8]

These exceptions to the expected pattern of development had important long-range effects on the fate of women's suffrage. The colony of South Australia, chartered in 1834, owed its ideological origins in part to the Benthamite utilitarians and in part to the eclectic theories of Edward Gibbon Wakefield, who emphasized the recruitment of families, freehold agriculture, and compact settlement. The colony was planned in detail prior to settlement; it attempted to transplant a full-blown English society without the disadvantages of squatting, penal colony squalor, and speculative land fever. Adaptation to the Mediterranean-style climate and geography was not without its hazards and setbacks. "Despite financial distress, administrative confusion, and environmental experimentation, a solid nucleus was established in these first years which, compared with other beginnings on the continent, was quite exceptional: a family-based, self-consciously Christian, middle-class society, diverse in skills, imbued with

---

7. Robert V. Horn, "Australia's Population," in *Asia's Population Problems*, S. Chandrasekhar, ed. (New York: Praeger Publishers, Inc., 1967), p. 220; *Official Yearbook of the Commonwealth of Australia*, J. P. O'Neill, statistician (Canberra: Commonwealth Bureau of Census and Statistics, 1970), pp. 124-25, 134.

8. The chronology of women's suffrage in the Australian Colonies and New Zealand prior to 1890 was as follows:

    1867: Municipal suffrage granted in New South Wales
    1869: Municipal suffrage granted in Victoria
    1871: Municipal suffrage granted in West Australia
    1873: Colony suffrage defeated in Victoria
    1877: School board suffrage granted in New Zealand
    1878: Municipal suffrage for women ratepayers granted in New Zealand
    1878-79: Colony suffrage defeated in New Zealand
    1880: Municipal suffrage granted in South Australia
    1883: Liquor License Board suffrage granted in New Zealand
    1884: Municipal suffrage granted in Tasmania
    1885: Colony suffrage for women property holders failed in South Australia
    1886: Municipal suffrage for women property holders granted in New Zealand
    1889: Colony suffrage for women property holders failed in South Australia
    1891: Colony suffrage defeated in New Zealand and New South Wales
C. A. Reuterskiöld, *Politisk rösträtt för kvinnor* (Stockholm: Almqvist & Wiksell/Gebers Foerlag AB, 1911), Appendix 6: 237; William P. Reeves, *State Experiments in Australia and New Zealand* (London: George Allen & Unwin Ltd., 1902), 1: 109-10, 126, 135; Alice Henry, "The Australian Woman and the Ballot," *North American Review* 183 (December 21, 1906): 1272-73; and Hugh H. Lusk, "Remarkable Success of Women's Enfranchisement in New Zealand," *The Forum* 23 (March-August 1897): 177-79.

energy, untainted by either the evils of gross speculation or penal servitude."[9] One result of the unique settlement pattern in South Australia was that the colony avoided the extreme demographic imbalance between the sexes that usually characterized the "frontier" phase of colonial development. It also avoided some of the hard-drinking, free-spending binges of the roving gangs of gold seekers, sheepshearers, and cattlemen that had characterized the far western and eastern colonies.[10]

In many respects, South Australia was more like New Zealand in social and political complexion than it was like the other Australian colonies. Both South Australia and New Zealand owed some of their early laws and social institutions to the theories of Edward Gibbon Wakefield; both had strong religious communities with important dissenting elements; both had stable populations by the 1890s; both experienced political instability in the 1880s; and both had developed important agricultural export economies (wheat for South Australia, meat for New Zealand).[11]

The movement for women's suffrage in New Zealand had begun in 1877 with the formation of the Liberal party under the leadership of Sir George Grey and the passage of acts enabling women to vote in school board elections. The Liberal party, representing the interests of those opposed to the large landowners,

---

9. D. W. Meinig, *On the Margins of the Good Earth: The South Australian Wheat Frontier, 1869-1884* (Chicago: Rand McNally & Co., 1962), p. 20. See also Russel Ward, *Australia* (Englewood Cliffs, N.J.: Prentice-Hall, Inc., 1965), p. 42.

10. William Harcus, *South Australia: Its History, Resources, and Productions* (London: Sampson Low, Marston, Searle, & Rivington, 1876), pp. 319-28. In the 1871 census, South Australia had 95,408 males and 90,218 females. ". . . there were, in 1871, 30,002 married males and 30,029 married females. Married women exceed in number the married men in towns, and the reverse is the case in the country districts, where also bachelors predominate. The proportion of bachelors to spinsters at marriageable ages (all above fifteen), is as twenty-one to fifteen, but of adults as eleven to five" (p. 323). Forty-three percent of the population were adults. Fifty-five percent of the population were native-born, twenty-five percent English born, and eight percent Irish. "The proportion of males and females in the settled districts is about equal. There are more English men than English women, and more Irish women than Irish men" (p. 321). The chief alcoholic beverage in Australia was rum, either imported or distilled from native sugar grown in Queensland. H. C. Allen, *Bush and Backwoods: A Comparison of the Frontier in Australia and the United States* (East Lansing: Michigan State University Press, 1959), pp. 29-31, 35-36.

11. Meinig, *On the Margins of the Good Earth,* Chapters 2, 4, 5, 9; Leslie Lipson, *The Politics of Equality: New Zealand's Adventures in Democracy* (Chicago: The University of Chicago Press, 1948), pp. 488-93; Horace Belshaw, ed., *New Zealand* (Berkeley: University of California Press, 1947), Chapters 4, 7. For religion, the census of 1891 showed that the four main groups in New Zealand were: Church of England 40.5 percent, Presbyterian 22.6 percent, Roman Catholic 13.9 percent, and Methodist 10.1 percent. In population studies "the proportions for successive census periods exhibit on the male side a rise in the percentage of the married men and a steady increase in regard to widowers since the year 1878. On the female side the percentage of the unmarried rose with regularity until the year 1891, while the married diminished; but since that date there has been a marked increase in the percentage of the married." By 1891 the number of bachelors (aged 20 years and above) for every 100 spinsters (aged 15 years and above) had fallen to 105. *The New Zealand Official Year-Book, 1902* (Wellington: John Mackay, 1902), pp. 224, 231 (quotation).

proposed in 1878 that women ratepayers should be allowed to vote for candidates for the colonial parliament, but parliament would have none of it. The Grey ministry collapsed shortly thereafter and the party was left leaderless, weakened by the bolt of members from Auckland, and unable to provide an effective opposition. The Conservatives ruled the country in the interests of the large landowners and rode out the disastrous effects of a depression with a program of budget cutting and retrenchment until they lost control in 1884, though they had extended female suffrage to local liquor licensing board elections in 1883.

The new Liberal coalition of Sir Robert Stout, Prime Minister, and Sir Julius Vogel, Treasurer, was unstable. Stout was a political Radical (in the English sense) with an interest in progressive land taxes; Vogel was the Disraeli of New Zealand politics—a Tory democrat and a financial genius whose "pump priming" deficit spending policies in an earlier administration had been blamed for the depression. In 1887, Vogel moved a women's franchise bill that was carried through its second reading only to die in committee. The Liberal ministry went the way of previous coalitions, and the Conservatives returned to power until the traumatic events of the maritime strike in 1890.[12]

When the Liberals regained power in 1891 behind Prime Minister John Ballance, the issue of women's suffrage was suddenly and unexpectedly revived when an electoral bill was amended in the House. The new Labour party, born of the travail of widespread unemployment, massive maritime strikes, and ideological ferment, supported the issue. The electoral bill passed the lower house but failed in the Conservative-dominated upper house by two votes. Thus, in a fifteen-year span, women's suffrage had been supported by leading figures in the Liberal, Conservative, and Labour parties. Had it not been for the interposition of the temperance issue in the 1890s, however, women's suffrage might have been delayed for another decade.[13]

Women had been voting for liquor control boards in New Zealand since 1883. These boards had been somewhat conservative in refusing to renew "surplus" licenses. A strong prohibition movement, spearheaded by the New Zealand Alliance and the Woman's Christian Temperance Union, swept through the colony in the early 1890s. When women's suffrage came before the legislature in 1893, the temperance forces threw their weight behind it in the expectation that women voters would support their cause. This maneuver put them in opposition to the Liberal ministers, some of whom believed in women's suffrage but not in prohibition. The Conservative opposition was lulled into the belief that, if they supported women's suffrage, it would embarrass the Liberals by strengthening the power of the prohibitionists. The bill passed the upper house by two votes, and "so, one fine morning of September 1893, the women of New Zealand woke up and found themselves enfranchised. The privilege was theirs—

---

12. Reeves, *State Experiments,* 1: 105-9; Lipson, *The Politics of Equality,* pp. 62-72.

13. Reeves, *State Experiments,* 1: 109-10. The political instability of the period is analyzed in detail in Lipson, *The Politics of Equality,* Chapter 6.

given freely and spontaneously . . . by male politicians" whose motives ranged from sincere conviction (based on arguments derived from John Stuart Mill) to crass expediency (based on a hope of embarrassing the Liberal ministry or of strengthening the Conservatives in the face of the Labour challenge).[14]

Apart from the WCTU, no franchise leagues or equal suffrage associations had helped women secure this victory. The temperance forces used their new electoral power in referendums held over the next few years. The voters faced a threefold choice—continuance of licenses, reduction of licenses, and abolition of licenses. By the turn of the century an astute observer concluded:

"A striking feature in all the polls has been the small number of votes given for reduction only. The moderate reformers, properly so-called, are in danger of being squeezed out in the conflict between the [Liquor Trade] and total abstinence. . . . The prohibitionists, still in a distinct minority, are drawing up so fast that they may carry No License in a good many districts in the course of the next ten years."

If women voters were supporting prohibition at the polls, then the strategy of the temperance forces had worked as expected.[15]

In a similar fashion, women in South Australia received the vote in 1894. There were two differences, however. In South Australia a Women's Suffrage League had been organized in 1888, and it exercised a positive role along with the WCTU. A new licensing law had been passed in 1891, so the temperance forces did not take as antagonistic an attitude toward the ruling Liberal government as had their co-workers in New Zealand. In 1893, when the issue of women's suffrage was brought forward by the Liberal ministry, it enjoyed the support of Radical Liberals (i.e., those who favored universal suffrage), Labour, and temperance forces. When opposition to a novel referendum feature of the law brought about its defeat, the WCTU swung into action with a petition campaign

---

14. Reeves, *State Experiments*, 1: 111-12. W. P. Reeves served as Agent-General for New Zealand and was a Liberal supporter of women's suffrage. In a speech in England in 1897 he allocated credit for the passage of the bill and assessed the impact as follows: "The Liberal Government that was in and passed the Franchise is still in; the Conservatives, many of whom warmly supported the Suffrage Bill, and were then out, are still out!" There was no reference to the role of the temperance issue. When he came to write the history of the event in 1902, he published the version used in the above narrative. See W. P. Reeves, "The Working of Women's Suffrage in New Zealand and South Australia," in Reuterskiöld, *Politisk rösträt för kvinnor*, pp. 184-87.

For the history of temperance in New Zealand, see Ernest H. Cherrington et al., *Standard Encyclopedia of the Alcohol Problem* (Westerville, Ohio: American Issues Publishing Company, 1925-1930), 5: 1972-73 (hereinafter abbreviated *SEAP*). The emergence of the prohibition drive in the 1890s seemed to be related to a changed perception of the problem rather than a drastic change in the situation. Per capita consumption of beer, wine, and spirits declined from 1883 to 1893 but production of beer was increasing and there was a high rate of arrests for drunkenness. *New Zealand Year-Book, 1902*, pp. 157, 281.

15. Reeves, *State Experiments*, 2: 314-15. Strictly speaking, "no license" was not the same

that brought the issue before the parliament again in 1894 (without the controversial referendum). The opposition stalled for three months; and when they finally lost by one vote, tried to wreck the plan with what they hoped would be embarrassing amendments to allow women to run for parliament and to vote by letter if they could not, for reasons of health or distance, get to the polls. The amendments were accepted, however, and the bill passed on December 18, 1894. The royal assent was received early in 1895.[16]

---

as prohibition since private citizens could still import liquor for private use and not violate the law (p. 312).

The role of women voters in this shift of opinion may be inferred from the following statistics (Reuterskiöld, *Politisk rösträt*, p. 159; Reeves, *State Experiments*, 2: 313):

PARLIAMENTARY ELECTIONS

	1893	1896
Total population	672,265	714,162
Registered voters		
Male	193,536	196,925
Female	109,461	142,305
Votes cast		
Male	129,792	149,471
Female	90,290	108,783
Percentage voting		
Male	70%	76%
Female	85%	76%

LIQUOR REFERENDUMS

	1894	1896	1899
Votes for continuance	42,429	139,580	142,443
Votes for reduction	16,096	94,555	107,751
Votes for refusal (no license)	48,933	98,312	118,575

The peculiarities of these statistics need some explanation since the number of votes cast on the liquor question exceed the number of registered voters. A complicated system of rules provided that continuance or reduction required a simple majority while no license required a three-fifths majority. Also a double vote rule held that "all voters in the No-License division who did not also vote for Reduction are held to have voted against it, and their votes are counted with those for Continuance in defeating it" (Reeves, *State Experiments*, 2: 314).

16. Reeves, *State Experiments*, 1: 126-230; 2: 309. The text of the South Australian law is printed in Reuterskiöld, *Politisk rösträt*, Appendix 4: 167. The law is a beautiful example of male deference to Victorian images of woman's need for special privileges due to her "delicate constitution." *Every* woman was entitled to an absentee ballot, even if she was not absent from her district on polling day, if she declared "that she is resident more than three miles from the nearest polling-place, or that by reason of the state of her health she will probably be unable to vote at the polling-place on polling day."

William Reeves, contemporary historian of New Zealand's social legislation, noted: "Most of the women voters show as yet no disposition to follow the clergy in assailing the national system of free, secular, and compulsory education. They clearly favour temperance reform, but are by no means unanimous for total prohibition. On the whole, the most marked feature of their use of the franchise is their tendency to agree with their menkind. . . . There are some who connect the appearance of women in the political arena with the recent passing of an Infants' Life Protection Act, the raising of the age of consent to fifteen, the admission of women to the Bar, the appointment of female inspectors to lunatic asylums, factories, and other institutions, improvements in the laws dealing with Adoption of Children

In Western Australia the question of women's suffrage became entangled in the political struggle between the older settlers and recently arrived gold diggers (called Outlanders). "By enfranchising women the voting strength of the farming and grazing districts and of the seaports would be increased, and the influence of the Outlanders to some extent neutralized." In 1899, the conservative "old guard" overcame its earlier objections to women's suffrage and joined its supporters to pass the bill. But "those who had built their calculations upon what the women would do with their votes turned out to be mistaken." In the first election, free-trade and Labour representatives scored impressive victories and helped to turn out the ruling party.[17]

In six years, in a context of political instability, women in New Zealand, South Australia, and Western Australia had been enfranchised. In two cases the temperance issue had played an important role; in the third, demographic factors and political expediency had carried the question. In the more populous colonies such as Victoria and New South Wales, they had been less successful. In 1900, for example, a government bill in New South Wales granting women's suffrage was narrowly defeated. At this point changes in the constitutional structure facilitated further change.[18]

The subject of a federal union of the Australian colonies had been broached periodically for half a century. The final and effective drive dated, however, from a classic speech made in 1889 by Sir Henry Parkes, a respected statesman in New South Wales. Within a decade intergovernmental conferences, effective organization, and the dramatic events of the 1890s had brought the movement to maturity. The second conference in 1897–98, under the leadership of the strong, cohesive South Australian delegation, hammered out the details of the new constitution, which borrowed heavily from the American model. The new constitution was adopted in a referendum, formally enacted by the British Parliament, and inaugurated on January 1, 1901.[19]

The newly constituted Federal Parliament faced a peculiar situation. Women in South Australia and Western Australia, since they had enjoyed the colony vote, automatically acquired a federal vote. Could the Federal Parliament allow some women to have the federal vote and deny it to others? Rather than disfranchise those who had the vote, the Federal Parliament decided to extend it to those who did not have it. "Accordingly the women of New South Wales,

and Industrial Schools, a severe law against the keepers of houses of ill-fame, and with the new liquor laws and the Prohibition movement which is so prominent a feature of New Zealand public life." William Pember Reeves, *The Long White Cloud: Ao Tea Roa* (London: Horace Marshall & Son, 1898), pp. 379, 381.

17. Reeves, *State Experiments,* 1: 133-34.

18. Ibid., p. 135. For the special situation in Queensland, see G. P. Taylor, "Political Attitudes and Land Policy in Queensland, 1868-1894," *Pacific Historical Review* 37 (August 1968): 247-64.

19. Ward, *Australia,* pp. 90-94; Bernard Ringrose Wise, *The Making of the Australian Commonwealth, 1889-1900: A Stage in the Growth of the Empire* (London: Longmans, Green and Co. Ltd., 1913), pp. 236-37.

Victoria, Queensland and Tasmania were somewhat suddenly placed in the same position of political equality . . . as their South Australian and West Australian sisters." The granting of federal franchise undercut those forces blocking state franchise, and within a few years it had been extended in the remaining states.[20]

If temperance and federalism facilitated the achievement of women's suffrage, it did not necessarily follow that women's suffrage and federalism would further the cause of prohibition. The Australian federal constitution left the control of liquor laws with the states, except for customs and excise duties, and specifically empowered the states to deal with interstate shipments and intrastate storage of liquor. The states, however, hedged statewide referendums with complicated restrictions. In various state elections voters faced a four-choice ballot: continuance of the status quo, increase in the number of licenses, reduction in the number of licenses, or no license. No license required a three-fifths majority and had to draw the equivalent of thirty percent or more of the registered voters. In New Zealand in 1910 an amendment act provided for a triennial poll on national prohibition; however, prohibition never received the required three-fifths needed for passage. As long as the prohibitionists argued for bare-majority elections, they did not prevail.[21]

If women's suffrage did not bring prohibition in its wake, neither did it change the direction of social development and social welfare legislation in the Australian states and in New Zealand. In spite of early enfranchisement a woman was not elected to parliament until 1922. Studies of the Australian family in the twentieth century tend to reinforce these impressions. In the urban families "the wife is generally the major source of authority." Australia's peculiar mixture of frontier heritage and federalism, of a "radical culture" with an egalitarian ideal, had, paradoxically, produced a society in which woman's legal rights were secure, her economic subordination ensured, and her primary social role ideologically and operationally maintained. In New Zealand and Australia, a woman's essential "right" was to be a wife, a mother, and a worker—in that order.[22]

---

20. Lady Holder, "Women's Suffrage in Australia," *The Independent* 56 (June 2, 1904): 1310; Henry, *North American Review* 183: 1274.

21. Cherrington, *SEAP:* for the histories of the separate colonies see the following entries: (New South Wales) 4: 1924-38; (Queensland) 5: 2239-45; (South Australia) 6: 2479-86; (Tasmania) 6: 2598-604; (Victoria) 6: 2758-65; (Western Australia) 6: 2819-25; (New Zealand) 5: 1972-74. See Sir Robert Stout and J. Logan Stout, *New Zealand* (London: Cambridge University Press, 1911), pp. 144-45.

22. Taft and Walker in *Advanced Societies,* Rose, ed., pp. 154, 163-68; Craig McGregor, *Profile of Australia* (Chicago: Henry Regnery Co., 1966), Chapter 3; Stout and Stout, *New Zealand,* pp. 136-43; W. B. Sutch, "Social Legislation" in *New Zealand,* Horace Belshaw, ed., (Berkeley: University of California Press, 1947), pp. 198-203. Dan L. Adler has coined the term "matriduxy" to describe the mother's strong leadership role in the Australian family. Her predominance in the home is a function of her subordination in the society and the alternatives that the mateship culture offered the man outside the home (particularly in sports and drinking patterns). See Dan L. Adler, "Matriduxy in the Australian Family," in *Australian Society: A Sociological Introduction,* A. F. Davies and S. Encel, eds. (New York: Atherton Press, 1965), pp. 149-55.

AMERICA AND ITS WEST, 1890–1906

If in Australia the factors of egalitarianism, federalism, and political instability helped to foster women's suffrage and frustrate prohibition, in the United States the impact of the same factors was nearly the opposite for the same time period. In the women's suffrage campaign "from 1870 to 1910 there were exactly seventeen state referenda held, bunched in eleven states (all but three west of the Mississippi) of which just two were victorious."[23] From 1870 to 1910 twenty-six states made decisions on prohibition: eighteen states rejected it while eight adopted statewide prohibition (of which four later repealed their enactments). In the states west of the Mississippi, seven specifically rejected prohibition while, of the five Western states that had approved prohibition, two repealed their earlier enactments. Only Kansas, North Dakota, and Oklahoma remained "faithful" to prohibition.[24]

Many reasons have been offered for the few, but strategically important, suffrage and prohibition "victories in the West" during the late 1880s, the 1890s, and the early 1900s: the chivalry of western men, the impact of the Panic of 1893, the "radicalism" of the Populists, the "coercive reform" psychology of the prohibitionists, the leadership of the small-town elites in the post-frontier areas, the hostilities of native-born Anglo-Saxons of the Puritan tradition toward foreigners and urban mores, and the political needs of various parties. All such interpretations need to be qualified, however, by an analysis of the role of the egalitarian concepts, federalism, and political instability on the success *and failure* of prohibition and women's suffrage campaigns in the Great Plains, Rocky Mountain, and Pacific Slope states in the late nineteenth century.[25]

The concept of equality had changed subtly during the second half of the nineteenth century. The women's rights and suffrage movements had reached a brief period of intellectual vigor in the 1860s and 1870s in the heyday of Radical Republicanism, when the concept of equality was an operative principle for a strategic political elite. Equality was more than a slogan; it was an articulate philosophy with many dimensions: equality before God (moral worth of the

---

23. Eleanor Flexner, *Century of Struggle: The Woman's Rights Movement in the United States* (Cambridge, Mass.: Harvard University Press, 1959), p. 175.

24. Information derived from an analysis of state histories in E. H. Cherrington, *SEAP*. In the West, statewide prohibition was adopted in Kansas (1880), Iowa (1882), North Dakota (1889), South Dakota (1889), and Oklahoma (1907). It was rejected or repealed in Texas (1887), Oregon (1887), Nebraska (1890), Iowa (1896), South Dakota (1896), and Missouri (1910).

25. Susan B. Anthony and Ida Husted Harper, *History of Woman Suffrage*, vol. 4, *1887-1900* (Rochester, N.Y.: Susan B. Anthony, 1902), pp. 518-19 (hereinafter cited as Anthony, *HWS, 1887-1900*); Andrew Sinclair, *The Better Half: The Emancipation of the American Woman* (New York: Harper & Row, Publishers, 1965), Chapter 19; Joseph R. Gusfield, *Symbolic Crusade: Status Politics and the American Temperance Movement* (Urbana: University of Illinois Press, 1966), Chapter 4; and Alan P. Grimes, *The Puritan Ethic and Woman Suffrage* (New York: Oxford University Press, Inc., 1967), Chapter 4.

individual); equality of status before the law (the legal meaning of the abolition of slavery); equality of political rights (the basis for Negro enfranchisement); and equality of opportunity (the economic and social components of antimonopoly and homestead laws, public education, and civil rights acts). An appeal by Elizabeth Cady Stanton, Susan B. Anthony, or Anna Dickinson to the standard of equality could strike a responsive chord with Radical Republicans and "equal rights" Democrats alike, even if it did not always produce the desired results. Such men found it hard to deny the moral basis of the women's claim however much they might plead expediency or counsel patience for the moment.[26]

By the end of the nineteenth century the various dimensions of the concept of equality had been eroded by events and subverted by new ideas. The equality of every man in the eyes of God, the moral worth of the individual, had been undercut by the materialism of the age. A man's claim to existence rested on his economic contribution to society; progress meant material accumulation, not moral perfection. Lynch law, industrial accidents, and the slaughter of Indians made life seem cheap. Naturalistic science seemed indifferent to man's fate; theistic religion inadequate to the task of redefining man's place in the universe. A few labor reformers, Christian socialists, and sensitive theologians and writers struggled to keep alive and proclaim a vision of man's uniqueness and humanity.

The legal revolution that had been wrought by the Thirteenth, Fourteenth, and Fifteenth Amendments to the Constitution—the writing of equality into the fabric of federalism—had been slowly overturned by the Supreme Court. The slaughterhouse cases in 1873 undercut the antislavery, egalitarian basis of the Fourteenth Amendment; the civil rights cases of 1883 restricted the prohibition of discrimination to the states only and left individuals free to impose inequality on others; and the school segregation cases, ending in *Plessy* v. *Ferguson* (1896), put the seal of constitutionality on inequality with the slogan of "separate but equal."

Equality of political rights, the guarantor of legal and social equality, had been undermined first by the disfranchisement laws of Reconstruction, the cynical manipulation of Negro voters, and the systematic corruption of the ballot box by ward bosses and campaign directors. With the failure of populism came the disfranchisement of the Negro and the movement to restrict the ballot.[27]

Equality of opportunity in the economic and social spheres had undergone a number of distortions. The various economic connotations of the term had been challenged by events: the right to labor by cyclical unemployment; the freedom

---

26. For an excellent summary of the relationship between the concept of equality and Radical Republicanism, see W. R. Brock, *An American Crisis: Congress and Reconstruction, 1865-1867* (reprint ed., New York: Harper & Row, Publishers, 1963), pp. 74-75, 93-94, 285-94.

27. C. Vann Woodward, *The Strange Career of Jim Crow,* 2nd rev. ed. (New York: Oxford University Press, Inc., 1966), Chapter 3; Jacobus ten Broek, *Equal Under Law,* rev. ed. (London: Collier-Macmillan Ltd., 1965), Introduction to Revised Edition; Rayford W. Logan, *The Betrayal of the Negro: From Rutherford B. Hayes to Woodrow Wilson,* rev. ed. (London: Collier-Macmillan Ltd., 1965), Chapter 6.

to enter business by the growth of "trusts" and "monopolies" (more correctly called oligopolies); and the hope of reasonable return on investment by declining interest rates and periodic panics. Social equality was blunted by growing social exclusiveness and racism.[28]

The nature of American federalism as it affected the West also underwent change. American federalism in the late nineteenth century was subjected to a number of strains: a lingering tradition of states' rights and a judicially elaborated doctrine of the "police powers" of the states. In addition, the "blind spot" of American federalism—Congressional control of the territories—continued to create problems even after the formal settlement of the slavery question in the Thirteenth Amendment. The bulk of the West existed under territorial status from the end of the Civil War until the end of the 1880s. Although popularly elected legislatures enacted laws, Congress and the President effectively controlled patronage and Congress could legislate directly for the territories. Presidentially appointed governors could veto the laws, and federally appointed judges could overturn local laws. Congress also had, in effect, a veto over state constitutions when the territory applied for statehood. After the forced-draft admission of Nevada in 1864 (to ensure the passage of the Thirteenth Amendment and a Republican victory in the presidential election),[29] "the prospects for further admissions dimmed, while Republicans and Democrats in Congress, in effect, vetoed each other's nominees for statehood, agreeing only in opposing Utah."[30]

The issue in Utah was ostensibly the Mormon practice of polygamy, or plural marriage, but it was actually the political power of the Mormon hierarchy. When the Cullom Bill outlawing polygamy had been introduced in Congress in 1869, the Mormon leadership had countered with the enfranchisement of women to augment their political power.[31] The Cullom Bill failed to pass the Senate. Congressional opposition to Utah continued in the 1870s, and in 1882 Congress passed the anti-polygamy Edmunds Law and created an electoral commission to administer voter registration. When the stringent anti-Mormon Edmunds-Tucker law of 1887 contained a Congressional rider revoking women's suffrage in the Utah territory (at the same time as the Senate defeated the Anthony amend-

28. John A. Garraty, *The New Commonwealth, 1877-1890* (New York: Harper & Row, Publishers, 1968), Chapters 5, 8.

29. Gilman M. Ostrander, *Nevada: The Great Rotten Borough, 1859-1964* (New York: Alfred A. Knopf, Inc., 1966), pp. 35-39.

30. Earl Pomeroy, *The Pacific Slope: A History of California, Oregon, Washington, Idaho, Utah, and Nevada* (New York: Alfred A. Knopf, Inc., 1965), p. 71. Nebraska was admitted in 1867 during Radical Republican control of Congress. Women's suffrage was defeated in Nebraska in 1882. Flexner, *Century of Struggle,* p. 175. Colorado was admitted in 1876 with a constitution that authorized a referendum on women's suffrage. The referendum was held in 1877 and defeated. Anthony, *HWS, 1876-1885,* 3:.723.

31. Grimes, *Puritan Ethic,* pp. 33-34; Gustive O. Larson, *The "Americanization" of Utah for Statehood* (San Marino, California: The Huntington Library, 1971), pp. 65-69. A recent article challenges the idea that women's suffrage was a move to enhance Mormon power. See Thomas G. Alexander, "An Experiment in Progressive Legislation: The Granting of Woman Suffrage in Utah in 1870," *Utah Historical Quarterly* 38 (Winter 1970): 20-30.

ment for national women's suffrage), the National Woman Suffrage Association charged Congress with perpetrating an antisuffragist scheme.[32]

That Congress was more anti-Mormon theocracy than anti-women's suffrage was demonstrated in its handling of other territories. In 1890 Congress was confronted with the question of statehood for Wyoming and Idaho. The all-male state constitutional convention in Wyoming had written women's suffrage into the draft constitution in 1889. Democrats in the House of Representatives, wanting to block the admission of another Republican state, offered an amendment to limit suffrage to males. The territorial delegate telegraphed the legislature that the price of statehood might be the abandonment of women's suffrage. The legislature remained firm and replied, "We will remain out of the Union a hundred years rather than come in without woman suffrage." Congress gave way, and statehood was ratified in June 1890. Idaho presented fewer problems and was also granted statehood.[33] If in the 1880s Congressional control of the territories had disfranchised women voters in Utah and acted as a restraint on those seeking statehood in the Dakotas, it proved to be an insufficient check in the 1890s.

The emergence of the People's Party (Populists) raised the hopes of the suffragists and prohibitionists. Frances Willard of the WCTU tried in vain to unite the Prohibition party and the Populist party. Susan B. Anthony and Anna Howard Shaw failed to secure endorsement for women's suffrage from the Populists. In Kansas, where women had won municipal suffrage in 1887 with WCTU support, the Populists pushed a women's suffrage bill through the Kansas House in 1891 only to see it defeated by the Republicans in the Senate. The performance was repeated in 1894 when the suffrage leaders put their allegiance to the Republican party above their allegiance to the suffrage cause.[34]

In Colorado, the Populist party had included a women's suffrage plank in its state platform and supported a referendum bill with their votes in the state legislature. The motives of the Populists are unclear; perhaps they hoped to reap the electoral rewards of befriending the women. Whatever the reasons, the Populist governor, Davis H. ("Bloody Bridles") Waite signed the bill and set the stage for a final vote in the 1893 elections. The few organized women's suffrage supporters sent a delegate to the Women's Congress at the Chicago World's Fair and pleaded for assistance in their campaign. The eastern leadership of the newly formed National American Woman Suffrage Association was preoccupied with

32. Pomeroy, *Pacific Slope,* p. 72; Flexner, *Century of Struggle,* p. 163, 174-75; Anthony, *HWS, 1887-1900,* 4: 939-40, 969; Larson, *"Americanization" of Utah,* pp. 95-114, 210.

33. Flexner, *Century of Struggle,* p. 178; quote from Alma Lutz, *Susan B. Anthony: Rebel, Crusader, Humanitarian* (Boston: Beacon Press, 1959), p. 252. T. A. Larson argues that Wyoming men were willing to continue women's suffrage because of its marginal impact. In short, equal suffrage had not meant the achievement of equal rights. See T. A. Larson, "Woman Suffrage in Wyoming," *Pacific Northwest Quarterly* 56 (April 1965): 63.

34. Anthony, *HWS, 1887-1900,* 4: 653-54; Flexner, *Century of Struggle,* p. 223; Jack S. Blocker, Jr., "The Politics of Reform: Populists, Prohibition, and Woman Suffrage, 1891-1892," *The Historian* 34 (August 1972): 614-32; Grimes, *Puritan Ethic,* p. 81.

the New York constitutional convention and a Kansas amendment but agreed to send one of their younger workers, Mrs. Carrie Chapman Catt.[35]

Mrs. Catt represented the new breed of suffrage leaders. Western born and college educated, she had been a successful educator in Iowa and had been tempered by the adversity of an early widowhood in California. A shrewd leader who never fully trusted the promises of politicians or the staying power of simple enthusiasm, she had carefully analyzed the reasons for the failure of the women's suffrage campaign in 1890 in South Dakota. She applied these lessons well in Colorado in 1893. First, an efficient statewide organization was created backed by an adequate campaign fund. Special effort was devoted to the urban areas in Denver. All three major parties, the Knights of Labor, the WCTU, and numerous civic groups endorsed the proposal. Even a visiting Englishwoman was pressed into service for a speech. In spite of opposition from the liquor interests, the referendum was successful. By contrast, also in 1893, women's suffrage was defeated in Kansas and municipal suffrage for women was defeated in Nebraska in spite of Populist support.[36]

Idaho in the 1890s represented another challenge for Mrs. Catt's organizational strategy. The Populists had organized in 1892 and had supported the miners in the Coeur d'Alene area in their struggles with the mine owners. They made a good showing in the 1894 elections but were unable to dominate the legislature or to pass the labor legislation that they wanted. The Republicans, pressed for votes, reenfranchised the Mormons and turned a sympathetic ear to the advocates of women's suffrage. The Republican-dominated legislature passed a resolution on January 17, 1895, authorizing a referendum on women's suffrage in 1896. The state women's suffrage group, organized only in 1893, requested and received help from the NAWSA. First, Mrs. Emma S. DeVoe of Illinois arrived and then, in August 1896, Mrs. Catt. The situation in Idaho was unique: all four major political parties—Republican, Democrat, Populist, and Silver Republican—had endorsed women's suffrage. In addition, "a strong factor in the campaign was the large colony in the Southern part of the State who were residents of Utah when women voted there and who believed in their enfranchise-

---

35. Anthony, *HWS, 1887-1900*, 4: 509-14. The role of the Populists in passing the bill is indicated in the following vote tabulation:

	Populist		Republican		Democrat	
	Yes	No	Yes	No	Yes	No
House (March 8, 1893)	22	3	11	21	1	3
Senate (April 3, 1893)	12	1	8	4	0	5

(The National American Woman Suffrage Association is hereinafter cited as NAWSA.)

For the changing position of Populist governor Waite, see John R. Morris, "The Women and Governor Waite," *Colorado Magazine* 44 (No. 1, 1967): 11-19.

36. Mildred Adams, *The Right to Be People* (Philadelphia: J. B. Lippincott Co., 1967), pp. 84-94; Anthony, *HWS, 1887-1900*, 4: 514-19, 654, 806.

ment." The referendum was carried successfully in November 1896 and was subsequently sustained by the state supreme court.[37]

When Utah, which had reorganized politically along Republican-Democratic lines in the 1890s, petitioned for statehood in 1895 with women's suffrage in its constitution and protestations from the Mormons that they had abandoned plural marriage, Congress passed the enabling act without major delays. President Cleveland signed the bill in January 1896 in spite of his well-known personal objections to women's suffrage.[38]

In summary, no single factor was responsible for the fate of women's suffrage and prohibition in the American West in the late 1880s and 1890s. Neither changing conceptions of equality, nor lingering issues of federalism and states rights, nor the political upheaval of the Populist party could account for the pattern of victories and defeats. Clearly another factor was also at work in interaction with these forces. For example, the success of women's suffrage in Wyoming, Colorado, Idaho, and Utah could be attributed to superior organization or collective determination, or both, confronting weak, divided, or indifferent opposition. Whenever the opposition to women's suffrage was crystallized by the temperance question, whether by the "liquor interests" in the 1880s or by the prohibitionists in the 1890s, the outcome was bound to be unfavorable. Hence the continual lament of the suffragists about opposition by the "liquor interests" and growing doubts by the NAWSA leadership about the wisdom of the tie with the prohibitionists. Whenever a political party felt that the need to preserve its political power would be threatened by extension of the franchise to women, it opposed it until the situation changed in its favor. Republicans in Kansas in 1891, Colorado in 1893, and Idaho in 1894 are examples of this trend. The role of organized opposition can be illustrated by events in California, Massachusetts, and Oregon.

The California electorate had been embroiled in temperance and suffrage campaigns for two decades beginning in 1874 with a women's crusade and culminating in a local-option campaign that had reached its peak in 1894. The alliance between the temperance cause and women's suffrage was symbolized by the career of Sallie Hart, a fiery, red-headed suffragist who specialized in stump oratory and narrow escapes from drunken antitemperance mobs. The WCTU had lobbied for women's school suffrage in 1889, for municipal suffrage in 1889, and for full suffrage in 1891. The state Senate, strongly Republican in composition, refused to pass a women's suffrage law because of constitutional questions; but finally, in March 1895 it did agree to submit to the voters an amendment striking the word "male" from the Constitution.

---

37. William J. Gaboury, "From Statehouse to Bull Pen: Idaho Populism and the Coeur d'Alene Troubles of the 1890's," *Pacific Northwest Quarterly* 58 (January 1967): 14-22; Dennis L. Thompson, "Religion and the Idaho Constitution," *Pacific Northwest Quarterly* 58 (October 1967): 178; Anthony, *HWS, 1887-1900,* 4:589-93 (quotation from pages 592-93). The vote on women's suffrage was 12,126 for and 6282 against.

38. Anthony, *HWS, 1887-1900,* 4: 948-49; Pomeroy, *Pacific Slope,* p. 72; Larson, *"Americanization" of Utah,* Chapter 14.

"The action of the Legislature of 1895 in submitting an amendment to the voters, instead of conferring the franchise by statute, was somewhat of a disappointment to the women as it precipitated a campaign which would come at the same time as that for President of the United States, *and for which there was not sufficient organization*"[39] [italics added].

While the women's suffrage forces were in disarray, the liquor industry was just feeling the strength of a united effort. "Until the 'nineties, a 'united saloon power' had not existed outside San Francisco, except in the minds of temperance men," a historian of California prohibition has noted; ". . . but it was not until 1894 that a state-wide liquor organization was successfully completed." By 1896 both wholesale and retail liquor dealers had joined the California Protective Association and in three years they had revoked or nullified most of the county prohibition ordinances.[40]

In the 1896 campaign for the women's suffrage amendment (i.e., the campaign to remove the word "male" from the Constitution), the liquor organizations exerted pressure on the Republicans to ignore their previous endorsement and vote no. At the same time the tensions of the presidential campaign had divided the supporters of the amendment. The Populists (who endorsed the amendment) had fused with the Democrats (who opposed the amendment) and began to tone down their public statements. The anti-Catholic American Protective Association aroused the united opposition of the strong Catholic contingent in California and "both feared the effect of the enfranchisement of women, although at the beginning the former seemed wholly in favor."[41]

The amendment was defeated in the November 1896 elections by a vote of 110,355 for to 137,099 against. Looking back over the campaign, the historians of the NAWSA concluded that

"the women made a brave fight but these political conditions, added to insufficient organization, too small a number of workers, lack of necessary funds, the immense amount of territory to be covered, the large foreign population in San Francisco and the strong prejudices in general . . . made defeat inevitable."[42]

They designated the opposition of the liquor dealers as the "final blow" in this chain of adversity. The main center of opposition had been San Francisco. Both the poorest and the richest wards had opposed the amendment—a sign of things to come.

---

39. Anthony, *HWS, 1887-1900*, 4: 484-86; Gilman M. Ostrander, *The Prohibition Movement in California, 1848-1933* (Berkeley: University of California Press, 1957), Chapters 3, 4.

40. Ostrander, *Prohibition in California*, pp. 78 (quotation), 83-84.

41. Anthony, *HWS, 1887-1900*, 4: 492.

42. Anthony, *HWS, 1887-1900*, 4: 492.

In Massachusetts, where school suffrage had been granted to women in 1879, similar cleavages appeared. In the 1880s women voters became embroiled in a Protestant-Catholic public-parochial school controversy. "Catholic leaders not only warned their people against woman suffrage but also sought to influence the political process in order to prevent its extension" by the presentation of antiwomen's suffrage petitions and pamphlets to the General Court.[43] After a school crisis in Boston in 1887–88, the nonpartisan Massachusetts School Suffrage Association split and a nativist association, along with the WCTU, urged Protestant women to vote in massive numbers. The question of-the extension of women's suffrage to municipal and state levels in the early 1890s polarized the situation. A unique opinion referendum open to both sexes was scheduled for 1895. A Man Suffrage Association, with prominent Catholic leadership, was determined to turn out a large *no* vote. The Massachusetts Association Opposed to the Further Extension of Suffrage to Women was organized among upper-class women. The results—86,970 males for, 186,976 against; 22,204 females for, 861 against—were eloquent testimony to the power of counterorganization and provided ammunition for the antiwoman suffragists for the next decade.[44]

Massachusetts temperance forces had also learned the value of better organization. A prohibition law had been repealed in 1875 and a license act had been substituted for it. In 1881 this law had been amended to provide for annual local-option elections in cities and towns. In 1888 a high-license provision was added; in 1889 prohibition was defeated. At first the no-license advocates, composed of the "better elements" and more skilled, unionized workers, had suffered a series of defeats. In Cambridge a successful organizational technique was worked out in the middle 1880s in cooperation with the churches and the WCTU, and victory was secured in 1886. An effective Citizen's Law Enforcement Association followed up the victory with a campaign to keep the public informed and to keep the pressure on local law enforcement officials. By 1897 the no-license and total abstinence groups composed the backbone of the Massachusetts temperance movement until the formation of the prohibitionist Anti-Saloon League.[45]

The new tide of counterorganization and alternate temperance strategies hit the West in the decade following the Massachusetts and California suffrage referenda. The new pattern emerged first in the state of Washington, where a

---

43. James J. Kenneally, "Catholicism and Woman Suffrage in Massachusetts," *The Catholic Historical Review* 53 (April 1967): 45.

44. Ibid., pp. 44-49, 49 n. 29; Frank Foxcroft, "The Check to Woman Suffrage in the United States," *Nineteenth Century and After* 333 (November 1904): 838-40. Similar antiwomen's suffrage associations were organized in New York, Illinois, Maine, Rhode Island, Iowa, Oregon, and Washington.

45. Cherrington, *SEAP*, 4: 1713, 1720; Frank Foxcroft and others, *Ten No-License Years in Cambridge: A Jubilee Volume* (Cambridge, Mass.: John Wilson and Sons, 1898), pp. 89-113. Frank Foxcroft, a leading figure of the no-license movement, was also a leading opponent of women's suffrage. For an excellent analysis of the motives and background of men such as Foxcroft and their role in reform in the 1880s, see Geoffrey T. Blodgett, "The Mind of the Boston Mugwump," *Mississippi Valley Historical Review* 48 (March 1962): 614-34.

women's suffrage referendum was defeated in November 1898 in spite of support by the Populist-Silver Republican fusion party. The Anti-(Women's) Suffrage Association of New York had sent an agent to lobby against the bill. The bill had passed the legislature in 1897, but the equal suffrage forces were poorly organized, the time for the campaign was short, and the public was distracted by the Spanish-American War and the Yukon gold rush. The same year (1898) saw the formation of the Anti-Saloon League of Washington.[46]

In neighboring Oregon, no organized suffrage work had been carried on between the defeat of women's suffrage in 1884 and July 1894, when the indomitable suffragist pioneer, Abigail Scott Duniway, formed a committee in Portland. In January 1895 the legislature passed a bill to submit a suffrage amendment to the electorate. In spite of a Woman's Congress held in July 1896 to support a legally required second passage of the submission bill, the legislature deadlocked in 1897 and nothing was accomplished. By 1899, when the issue came up again, lobbyists for the New York and Massachusetts Anti-Suffrage Association canvassed the state and inundated the legislature with documents. The amendment was defeated in June 1900 by two thousand votes.[47]

The defeat in 1900 was a severe test for the Oregon suffragists. Abigail Scott Duniway had long been a vocal critic of the informal alliance between the prohibitionists and women's suffragists because she believed that this factor aroused the liquor interest to active opposition. In desperation the suffragists cast about for a new tactic to give the cause of women's suffrage a new public image. One of them, Mrs. Eva Emery Dye, decided that women needed the inspiration of a heroine to symbolize their cause. In a novel published in 1902 she created the myth of Sacagawea, the Indian maiden who supposedly guided the Lewis and Clark expedition. The NAWSA picked up the theme and used a Lewis and Clark Centennial in 1905 as a sounding board for another attempt at securing women's suffrage. But the male voters of Oregon were no more ready to follow the lead of the modern day "Sacagaweas" and enter into the Columbian Valley of Equal Suffrage than their predecessors had been willing to listen to Abigail Scott Duniway's tirades over the previous quarter-century. Women's suffrage was defeated again in 1906.[48]

The Oregon defeat in 1906 was emblematic of the doldrums into which the women's suffrage movement had fallen. Susan B. Anthony died in that year, and no one seemed qualified to fill her place. The NAWSA was plagued with organizational problems, personal feuds, and inadequate finances. In 1904, Frank Foxcroft, an unfriendly critic, summarized the status of the women's suffrage movement in a popular journal:

"These, then, are the fruits of more than half a century of persistent agitation

---

46. Anthony, *HWS, 1887-1900*, 4: 971-73; Cherrington, *SEAP*, 6: 2803.

47. Anthony, *HWS, 1887-1900*, 4: 891-96.

48. Ronald W. Taber, "Sacagawea and the Suffragettes," *Pacific Northwest Quarterly* 58 (January 1967): 7-13.

for women's suffrage in the United States. Of the forty-five states in the Union, twenty do not give women any form of ballot; twenty give them the lightly-regarded school ballot or the still less important and infrequently-exercised (taxpayers) ballot, on questions submitted to taxpayers; one admits them to municipal suffrage, but refuses them anything more; and four give them the full ballot."[49]

In searching for an explanation for the fact that the suffrage movement had come to a standstill, the author pointed to the growth of antisuffrage organizations, "the indifference or active hostility of the great majority of American women," and the infrequent use of the ballot by those who possessed it.[50]

Foxcroft's analysis was accurate, but he did not speculate on the causes of the seemingly widespread indifference of women to both the possession and the use of the ballot. In part, the failure of the women's suffrage movement was related to the modest gains of women's rights in the preceding seventy years; in part, it was related to the changing conceptions of equality and democracy. Married women's property rights had been expanded, educational advantages had been secured for an ever increasing number of women, access to some professions had been grudgingly granted, and minor changes had been made in divorce, custody, and alimony laws. Women's clubs and organizations flourished and provided alternative claims on the time of potential converts. At the same time, the very changes brought new problems. Sweatshops, exploitation, and subordination of women workers followed in the wake of extended economic "equality of opportunity." The middle-class character of the women's suffrage organizations cut them off from valuable recruits in the minuscule Women's Trade Union League and in the rest of the labor force. Anti-immigrant arguments used by some suffrage leaders created hostility in politically important ethnic groups. In short, American society had changed; the women's suffrage movement had not. Gradually, after 1890, the suffrage movement adapted its ideology to the prevalent elitism and racism.[51]

In sum, in appealing to the concept of equality in the late nineteenth century, the women's suffrage advocates had appealed to a tarnished image. Small wonder, then, that institutional changes had been secured mainly in the West whenever there was little organized opposition. The ideological sanction to change was too weakened by the erosion of the understanding of equality to override the more traditional and better organized opposition in the older areas of the country (where the ideological barriers were also the strongest). If the women's suffrage cause was to succeed in the twentieth century it needed either a

49. Foxcroft, Nineteenth Century and After 333: 837.

50. Ibid., pp. 838-41.

51. Flexner, Century of Struggle, Chapters 17, 18; Sinclair, Better Half, Chapter 22; Aileen S. Kraditor, The Ideas of the Woman Suffrage Movement, 1890-1920 (New York: Columbia University Press, 1965), Chapters 6, 7; Anne Firor Scott, The Southern Lady: From Pedestal to Politics, 1830-1930 (Chicago: The University of Chicago Press, 1970), Chapter 7.

refurbished ideology with widespread appeal or better organization and tactics, or both.

In a similar manner, the prohibition advocates pegged their case in the late nineteenth century to a particular concept of democracy—and suffered the consequences. In the formative years of the National Prohibition party (1868 to 1876), for example, the party acted as an avenue for the moral reform energies that were thwarted in the Republican party of the Grant era and provided leadership in the espousal of reform causes. In effect the prohibitionists kept alive the "higher law" doctrine of the prewar Republicans: the notion that a moral law overrides the decisions of the state or of a majority. Democracy must be restrained by a higher morality; government has no right to sanction a social wrong. "We have never yet ruled a great city on the principle of self-government," argued Wendell Phillips in 1870 when he accepted the Prohibition party nomination for governor of Massachusetts. "Republican institutions undermined by intemperance are obliged to confess that they have never governed a great city here, on the basis of universal suffrage, in such way as to preserve order, protect life, and secure free speech. . . ."[52] Since intemperance undermined the basis of democracy and was destructive of the ends for which the state was instituted among men, then intemperance must be eliminated by the power of the law—this was their argument.

The drive for state constitutional amendments in the 1880s and 1890s was prompted, in part, by a desire to place prohibition beyond the reach of the currents of public opinion. The "solemn sanction of the people" was requested only once—in endorsing constitutional prohibition. Thereafter their role would be the passive one of refraining from violating the law or of repealing the amendment. Frances Willard of the WCTU exclaimed, "We have seen that the principle of prohibition must be grounded in organic law beyond the reach of demagogues and that this must be done through nonpartisan methods by means of a constitutional amendment."[53]

This peculiar strategy of using democracy to delimit democracy arose from the relationship between "society" and the "state" that was sought by the prohibitionists. In attempting to define the nature of the community they sought to protect, the prohibitionists divided the community and precipitated social and political conflict. When the rhetoric of town-boosting and the argument that prohibition was "progress" could no longer conceal the divisions that they had wrought in the fabric of local society, the prohibitionists sought a higher level of political power in order to achieve their objective.[54]

---

52. James C. Malin, *A Concern About Humanity: Notes on Reform, 1872-1912, at the National and Kansas Levels of Thought* (Lawrence, Kan.: by the author, 1964), pp. 5, 9; D. Leigh Colvin, *Prohibition in the United States: A History of the Prohibition Party and of the Prohibition Movement* (New York: George H. Doran Company, 1926), p. 84.

53. Ibid., p. 280. For a discussion of the limitations of the state amendment idea, see pp. 219-20.

54. For the impact of prohibition on local, state, and national politics, see Robert R. Dykstra, *The Cattle Towns* (New York: Alfred A. Knopf, Inc., 1968), Chapter 7, Conclu-

If a consideration of the "frontier" situations of Australia, New Zealand, and the United States in the 1890s has revealed the importance of their respective conceptions of equality and traditions of political democracy, it has also shown the weaknesses of their women's suffrage and prohibition movements. Their needs for a refurbished egalitarian ideology, for new political tactics and better organizational techniques, and for a more comprehensive conception of the nature of society were all apparent at the beginning of the twentieth century. Subsequent events on the Scandinavian "frontier" and elsewhere would show how such changes could be stimulated, in part, by the impact of nationalism and the needs of wartime social control and social cohesion.

sion, and Appendix A; Richard Jensen, *The Winning of the Midwest: Social and Political Conflict, 1888-1896* (Chicago: The University of Chicago Press, 1971), Chapters 3, 4, 7, 10. Jensen's and Dykstra's insights into the role of the prohibition issue in the local, state, and national politics of the 1880s and 1890s have important implications for the understanding of political developments in the West during the period covered by this chapter.

7

Nationalism and
Social Control

FINLAND AND THE RUSSO-SCANDINAVIAN FRONTIER

The casual observer of the status of women's suffrage and prohibition after
1906-07 might well have concluded that these two causes had regained momentum. A brief flurry of excitement in 1906 accompanied the election of reform-
minded Liberal party governments in England and Sweden.

The sensitive observer would have noted that a number of new groups
had been organized and that new tactics were being employed. In England,
Emmeline Pankhurst and her daughters, who had organized the Women's Social
and Political Union in 1903, embarked on a campaign of militancy in 1905-06
designed to embarrass the reigning governments into granting women's suffrage.
The WSPU suffragettes (as they were called to distinguish them from the conventional suffragists) heckled speakers, disrupted meetings, courted arrest, and
exploited the resulting publicity. When arrested, the suffragettes went on hunger
strikes. The government fed the prisoners forcibly and made them martyrs in the
eyes of other women.[1]

In the area of temperance and prohibition, new tactics and techniques were
also emerging. In Sweden the Gothenburg system of control of *krogs* (similar to
English "pubs") by private monopolies was made mandatory in 1905 for cities
by act of the *Riksdag*. The purpose of the Gothenburg system was to control,
not eliminate, the sale of *brännvin* by eliminating the profit motive and by providing a more "wholesome" atmosphere for the working class than was found in
the ordinary krog. The Gothenburg system had numerous defects, however, and
prohibitionist sentiment continued to grow. During a general strike in 1909,
the government was compelled to impose temporary prohibition. To counteract

---

1. Constance Rover, *Women's Suffrage and Party Politics in Britain, 1866-1914* (London:
Routledge and Kegan Paul, Ltd., 1967), Chapter 7; David Mitchell, *The Fighting Pankhursts:
A Study in Tenacity* (New York: The Macmillan Company, 1967), Chapter 2; Dankwart A.
Rustow, *The Politics of Compromise: A Study of Parties and Cabinet Government in Sweden*
(Princeton, N.J.: Princeton University Press, 1955), Chapter 2.

the growing prohibitionist sentiment, a young Stockholm doctor, Ivan Bratt, proposed an alternate system of liquor control. The Bratt system (sometimes called the Stockholm system) used a semirationing system: passbooks, monthly quotas, revocation of privileges for offenders, social therapy for habitual offenders, and a program of public temperance education. The Bratt system promised to preserve individual freedom while achieving a modicum of social control.[2]

Significant victories for women's suffrage and prohibition came neither in England nor in Sweden, however. Rather, world attention was captured by dramatic events in Finland. There, on the frontier between Swedish culture and Russian political power, a tiny nation was struggling to find its identity. The interaction of geography, culture, and politics had shaped the people. A geographer has noted: "Settlement of Finland by Finn and Swede has been from the littoral to the interior and, in general, from south to north. It has continued independently of the intermittent swing of political frontiers across the land, though their shifts have disturbed and sometimes diverted it." But the pioneer of the remote frontier areas of Finland had little in common with his American and Australian counterparts except, perhaps, a certain hostility to central governmental authority. Moody, taciturn, and somewhat mystical in his religious outlook, the Finnish "backwoodsman" was given to "extreme mental attitudes which express themselves in, for example, strong local patriotism, communism and pietism."[3] During the 1880s and 1890s Finland developed its timber and textile export industries and laid the base for a labor movement. So rapid was Finnish industrial growth that Russian industrialists clamored for protection and secured Russo-Finnish tariff revisions in their favor in 1885 and 1897.[4]

In 1898 Czar Nicholas II and his ministers decided to integrate Finnish manpower into the Russian military system. The proposal was submitted to the Finnish Diet for their advice, but not for their consent. The Diet rejected the bill unanimously. A constitutional crisis had been precipitated. The Czar responded with the February (1899) Manifesto declaring that the Diet was abolished and that, henceforth, the Czar would rule directly with the aid of an appointive, consultative senate. The Diet rejected the Manifesto. A massive protest by the Finnish citizens and a petition, "Pro Finlandia," signed by leading intellectuals in Europe failed to change the Czar's mind. The Czar suspended the Finnish constitution in April 1903, and the stage was thus set for a massive confrontation between Finnish nationalism and Russian absolutism.

The controversy with Russia had a number of important effects within Finland. Rather than healing the divisions left over from the language struggles,

2. Walter Thompson, *The Control of Liquor in Sweden* (New York: Columbia University Press, 1935), Chapter 2; M. Marcus, "The Liquor Control System in Sweden," in *Drinking and Intoxication: Selected Readings in Social Attitudes and Controls,* Raymond G. McCarthy, ed. (New Haven: Yale Center of Alcoholic Studies, 1959), pp. 347-48.

3. W. R. Mead, "Frontier Themes in Finland," *Geography* 44 (July 1959): 154-55.

4. Eino Jutikkala, *A History of Finland,* trans. Paul Sjöblom (New York: Praeger Publishers, Inc., 1962), p. 228; Hugh Seton-Watson, *The Russian Empire, 1801-1917* (London: Oxford University Press, 1967), pp. 498-99.

it widened them. The Swedish-speaking party and the "Young Finns" (liberal nationalists) went into the opposition "Constitutionalist" camp that advocated a program of passive resistance and constitutional obstruction of the Russification program. The "Old Finns" (Finnish-speaking conservatives), now known as the "Compliants," were willing to man government posts under the Russian Governor-General Bobrikov in order to protect the Finnish language gains of the previous decades. Also under the impact of the Russification campaign, the Finnish Labor party turned leftward, changed its name to the Social Democratic party, and adopted a modified Marxian socialism in 1903. A Red Guard faction prepared to take up the instruments of class warfare. A small, clandestine group turned to violence, and one of its members assassinated Governor-General Bobrikov on June 16, 1904.[5]

The Czar, meanwhile, had troubles enough in Russia to occupy his attention. The defeat of Russian arms in the Russo-Japanese war discredited the ruling autocracy and fed the fires of rebellion and reform. "The Russian government decided to conciliate the Finns, and in March 1905 repealed the Conscription Law of 1901 and restored the irremovability of judges. This did not satisfy the Finns."[6] The Social Democrats sent petitions to the Diet of Four Estates advocating universal adult suffrage. The Diet debated the issue for a full day in April but was unable to come to any conclusions. By October the Russian General Strike spread to Finland. Red Guard militants appeared in force. Social Democratic demands for parliamentary reform and Constitutionalist support of the strike forced the Czar to grant further concessions. On November 4, 1905, he

---

5. Jutikkala, *Finland*, pp. 228–37; Seton-Watson, *Russian Empire,* p. 499. The Social Democrats in Finland occupied a peculiar position *vis-à-vis* classical socialism and Marxism. Although they borrowed the Erfurt program of the German Social Democrats with its strident Marxist goals, the Finnish Social Democrats were revisionists in their emphasis on immediate measures and democratic access to power long before the German socialists followed the same route. This reflected the fact that the Finnish Social Democrats were strongest among the lumberjacks, farm tenants, and teetotaling trade unionists rather than among the classic urbanized industrial proletariat of Marxist rhetoric.

For the background of German Social Democracy see Guenther Roth, *The Social Democrats in Imperial Germany: A Study in Working-Class Isolation and National Integration* (Totowa, N.J.: The Bedminster Press, Inc., 1963), Chapters 2, 7; Ralf Dahrendorf, *Society and Democracy in Germany* (New York: Doubleday & Company, Inc., 1967), pp. 190-93; Jacqueline Strain, "Feminism and Political Radicalism in the German Social Democratic Movement, 1890-1914" (Ph.D. diss., University of California, Berkeley, 1964). The sources used for the above generalizations on the Finnish Social Democratic movement were: P. Rommi review of Hannu Soikkanen, *Sosialismin tulo Suomeen: Ensimmäisiin yksikamarisen eduskunnan vaaleihin asti [The Arrival of Socialism in Finland: Until the Election of the First One-Chamber Diet]* (Helsinki: Soederstroem Osakeyhtiö, 1961) in *Politiikka* (Helsingfors, Finland) 3 (No. 3, 1961): 153-55 [trans. from Finnish by Raija Koponen, University of Minnesota]; Erik Allardt, "Patterns of Class Conflict and Working-Class Consciousness in Finnish Politics," in *Cleavages, Ideologies and Party Systems: Contributions to Comparative Political Sociology,* Erik Allardt and Yrjö Littunen, eds. (Helsinki: The Academic Bookstore, 1964), pp. 97-131; Anna Bondestam, "Den Finlandssvenska arbetarrörelsens uppkomst," *Historiska och Litteraturhistoriska Studier* 41 (1966): 284-331.

6. Seton-Watson, *Russian Empire*, pp. 610-11.

abrogated the February Manifesto and charged the Finnish senate with the task of drafting a law for a new legislature.[7]

As a consequence of the General Strike, the old senate, composed of Compliants (Old Finns), resigned, and a new one controlled by the Constitutionalists took up the task of drafting the new law for a unicameral legislature or *lantdag*. The socialists refused to participate in this "bourgeois" government and thus did not directly participate in the decisions. A working committee presented its preliminary report on February 28, 1906, and provided:

"Paragraph 5. Every Finnish citizen, man as well as woman, who has reached the age of twenty-four before the election year is entitled to vote in *lantdag* elections. *Paragraph 6.* Entitled to stand for election are, without reference to place of residence, all who are entitled to vote."[8]

When the law was promulgated by the Czar in July 1906, women in Finland were given the right to vote and to be elected to the *lantdag*.

Compared to England or the United States, little organized suffragist agitation had preceded the sudden victory. In 1897, the Finnish Women's Association, headed by Baroness Gripenberg, had petitioned the Diet for the suffrage. In 1904 the Association, the Women's Union of Finland, and the Social Democratic members of the Diet had petitioned again for women's suffrage.[9] As Baroness Gripenberg reported to the Danish Women's Society:

---

7. Jutikkala, *Finland,* pp. 240-41; Rosalind Travers, *Letters from Finland* (London: Routledge and Kegan Paul, Ltd., 1911), p. 389. The Social Democratic party had over 45,000 members in 1905, of whom about 10,000 were women.

On December 29, 1905, the Czar wrote: "Once the Finns have had their rights and privileges restored to them, they must be continued in the same spirit and promises must be kept; otherwise it will be half-measures again—and that is never any good." Although he was disturbed by subsequent events, he did not deviate from this attitude toward Finland. Edward J. Bing, ed., *The Secret Letters of the Last Tsar: Being the Confidential Correspondence between Nicholas II and His Mother, Dowager Empress Maria Feodorovna* (New York: Longmans, Green and Company, 1938), p. 207.

8. *"Lantdag* Law for the Grand Duchy of Finland Given at Peterhof, July 20, 1906, by Czar Nicholas II"; printed in appendix 11 to C. A. Reuterskiöld, *Politisk rösträtt för kvinnor* (Stockholm: Almqvist & Wiksell/Gebers Foerlag AB, 1911), pp. 340-43. [Translation from Swedish by Professor Nils J. Anderson, Augustana College.] During the General Strike of 1905, the Constitutionalists and Social Democrats had joined forces under the chairmanship of P. E. Svinhufvud. The Constitutionalists demanded abrogation of the Czar's February Manifesto and all subsequent decrees, the dismissal of the Compliant (Old Finn) senate, and resignation of the Minister Secretary of State. The Social Democrats demanded reform of the Diet of Four Estates and won a pledge from the Constitutionalists to support it. The Social Democrats wanted reform, however, via a revolutionary national assembly while the Constitutionalists (and later the Old Finns) favored change by constitutional means. Thus, although the Social Democrats advocated reform and proposed universal suffrage, proportional representation, and unicameralism at various times, they cannot be credited with working out the reforms or with significant participation in the senate deliberations. Jutikkala, *Finland,* pp. 240-41.

9. Ilmi Hallsten, *The Position of Woman in Finland* (Helsinki: The Government Printing Office, 1925), pp. 18-19.

"Until the new election law, prepared by the Estates, received the Emperor's confirmation, we women could hardly believe that we would actually receive the right to vote. Not only the right to vote, but the right to stand for election to the *lantdag*, and what's more *married* women would share in the reform, and *all* women . . . would hereafter have in their hand that powerful weapon, the election ballot! And almost immediately after the sanctioning of the law the activities of the women began"[10] [italics added].

The immediate task of the women's groups was to educate the Finnish women in the use of the ballot; the immediate task of the political parties was to attract the woman voter. Baroness Gripenberg indicated in 1907 some of the concerns of the women's rights advocates: "the abolition of the husband's guardianship over his wife in marriage, greater rights for the married mother over her children, the same wages for the same work without respect to sex, the right of the woman to choose the kind of work she wants to do, the revision of the law respecting the rights of children born out of wedlock." On the latter issue the women divided along party lines: the Social Democrats favoring the proposed law and the more conservative Old Finns opposing it. The one issue on which the women were united was that of temperance.

Total abstinence and prohibition were expected to be the primary beneficiaries of the extension of the franchise as both women's groups and the Social Democrats supported these measures. The total abstinence forces, led by the Friends of Temperance, had secured some legislative victories in the 1890s but had failed to achieve gradual prohibition through local option because of opposition in the Diet of Four Estates. In 1906 the Friends of Temperance dispatched an investigator to the United States to gather information on prohibition. When the new, reformed *lantdag* met in 1907, the Friends of Temperance introduced a draft bill for prohibition.[11]

The Social Democrats had a long tradition of support for prohibition and total abstinence reflecting in part an antiaristocratic, working-class bias and also the fact that much of the support for the party came from pietistic peasants and landless agrarians. Workers in southern Finland had participated in "drink strikes" in the late 1890s; the Workers party of 1901 had endorsed prohibition. The Uleaborg Program of the Social Democrats, adopted in 1906, enjoined strict temperance on all party representatives and endorsed prohibition.[12]

Who was responsible for the inclusion of women's suffrage in the new *lantdag* law? Several factors indicate that the inclusion was the work of academic

---

10. Alexandra Gripenberg, "From Finland," *Woman and Society* (Danish Women's Society), February 28, 1907, reprinted in Reuterskiöld, *Politisk rösträtt för kvinnor*, appendix 11, p. 350; G. H. Blakeslee, "Woman Suffrage in Finland," *The Outlook* 87 (September 7, 1907): 37.

11. John H. Wuorinen, "Finland's Prohibition Experiment," *Annals of the American Academy of Social and Political Science* 163 (September 1932): 216-17.

12. Travers, *Letters from Finland,* Appendix II, p. 391; John H. Wuorinen, *The Prohibition Experiment in Finland* (New York: Columbia University Press, 1931), pp. 35-37.

liberals and the leading nationalists. The members of the committee that drafted the law were mainly Constitutionalists.[13] The adoption by the committee of unicameralism reflected the Constitutionalist concern with constitutional rule and orderly change. The committee's memorandum on the *lantdag* law noted:

". . . the majority of the Committee is of the opinion that a unicameral *lantdag* offers greater guarantees for unity of action and satisfying the interests of a broad spectrum of the population. Neither has the Committee been able to ignore the fact that a strong public opinion within the country has declared itself in favor of a unicameral system, as expressed by at least two of the popularly elected Estates of the present *lantdag*, which are represented by a small number here and who are in favor of such a system. Also, the Committee has considered it important that the educated elements which are [best] qualified to hold positions in the government and for whom one would normally assure a place in the first chamber of a bicameral assembly, instead of occupying an exclusive position, will have the opportunity to influence directly the representative assembly as a whole, which is possible only if the assembly is not divided into two chambers.

The important point is that these elements, as is true of the country's best

---

13. "Statement of the Finnish Representative Reform Committee February 28, 1906," reprinted in Reuterskiöld, *Politisk rösträtt för kvinnor* [trans. Professor Nils J. Anderson]. The members of the committee were

Robert Hermanson	T. J. Boisman	Th. Rein
Santeri Alkio	J. K. Passikivi	Felix Heikel
Heikki Lindroos	P. E. Svinhufvud	Emil Schybergson
E. N. Setälä	J. R. Danielson	Juho Torpaa
Yrjö Sirola*	Edvard Walpas-Hänninen*	Vilhelms Blåfield

*Did not sign final report.

Academic influences in the committee were evident in the careers of several members. Hermanson was a professor of law who had been influenced by German ideas. Danielson, the vice-chancellor of Turku University, was a respected historian and member of the Old Finn party; Rein was a professor of philosophy and had also served as vice-chancellor. Setälä was a philologist and professor of Finnish language and literature. Alkio rose from the peasantry as a self-educated folk writer and later supported the Agrarian party. Heikel and Schybergson wrote on political economy and had interests in the banking system. Two of the members were known primarily as leading political figures: Svinhufvud, judge of the Turku Court of Appeals, was leader of the Young Finns and was supported by the Social Democrats; Passikivi, a historian (he had been a student under Danielson), was a supporter of the Compliance policy and a leading member of the Old Finn party. The two Social Democrats, Sirola, a priest, and Walpas-Hänninen, a publicist and orator, were representative of the first generation of Social Democratic leaders and were not comfortable in parliamentary roles.

Sources for the above information included L. Mechelin, ed., *Finland i 19DE Seklet: framstäldt i ord och bild* (Stockholm: Hugo Gebers Förlag, 1893), pp. 137, 235; Edvard Hjelt, ed., *Finland: The Country, Its People and Institutions* (Helsinki: Otava Publishing Company, 1926), pp. 447, 478–79, 483–85, 493, 561; Jutikkala, *Finland,* pp. 235, 240, 244; Travers, *Letters,* p. 386; Marvin Rintala, *Four Finns: Political Profiles* (Berkeley: University of California Press, 1969), pp. 51-52, 96-97.

talents generally, should not be excluded from the new representative assembly, even though the decision-making may be reserved for the great majority."[14]

Furthermore, the adoption of the complex d'Hondt system of proportional representation indicated the strong influence of the academic liberals' desire to restrain the "tyranny of the majority" in a democratic polity.[15]

The committee's memorandum was candid on the subject of women's suffrage but somewhat vague on the matter of responsibility for the final version of the law:

"The granting of suffrage to women, involving as it does a one hundred percent increase in the electorate, would, of course, influence election results to an extraordinary degree. We do not believe that men and women will align themselves against each other in separate political parties, but rather that in the majority of cases women will group themselves on the same basis as men. *Especially with regard to the matters of prohibition, morality, and education, to which women,* up to now, except for the woman question itself, *have devoted most of their energy,* their influence on the composition of the representative assembly can only be characterized as beneficial. But with respect to other matters some members of the Committee, on one hand, have pointed out that women are inclined to align themselves with extreme parties, political and social radicalism, or, as in Catholic countries, extreme reaction, while, on the other hand, another faction asserts that married women, who make up the majority, have as a result of their experiences in life learned to weigh arguments pro and con, and, for that reason, are in most questions likely to adopt a moderate point of view. The Committee believes that, of these opposed views, the latter is the correct one, and it has, for this reason and others mentioned above, added suffrage for women, married or unmarried, to its proposal for a new *lantdag* law. . . .

In the matter of women's suffrage, the overwhelming majority of the Committee has been of one mind. However, with respect to women's right to stand for election to the representative assembly, a greater difference of opinion has been revealed. A minority within the Committee has maintained that, though women nowadays receive the same education as men and have the right, along

---

14. "Memorandum on the *Lantdag* Law," reprinted in Reuterskiöld, *Politisk rösträtt för kvinnor* [trans. Professor Nils J. Anderson]. This emphasis on an educated elite was strong among the Young Finns. See Travers, *Letters from Finland,* p. 240. In the election of 1904 the Compliants (Old Finns) had suffered numerous defeats. The reference in the above quote is thus to the Constitutionalists who controlled the last Diet of Four Estates before the new law became effective. See Jutikkala, *Finland,* p. 239.

15. In the d'Hondt system, developed by the Belgian mathematician, Victor d'Hondt, seats were allocated according to rank order from lists prepared by the parties. Each party received a number of seats equivalent to its proportion of the total vote and allocated these seats to its own members in accordance with its own priorities. For the details of the d'Hondt system, see Donald J. Ziegler, *Prelude to Democracy* (Lincoln: University of Nebraska Studies, 1958), pp. 8–9.

with men, to hold many jobs both in public and private service, they must still be regarded as unproved with respect to holding public office, and since [it believes] that all reforms should proceed gradually, with short steps, this minority has rejected the proposal for the right of women to stand for election to the representative assembly. The majority of the Committee, however, has supported the point of view that the right to stand for election should be granted them for the same reasons it has been willing to grant them the right of suffrage. Moreover, the majority viewpoint is that it would be preposterous to exclude one-half of the electorate from the right to stand for election, when this half has the power to force through its will in this matter, and, by means of the ballot, elect representatives who would champion its cause"[16] [italics added].

Foreign observers subsequently argued that the extension of the franchise to women was a reward from the nationalists for the women's support during the passive resistance campaigns and the struggle with the Russians.[17]

The political parties offered a number of women candidates to the electorate. The results of the April 1907 election astonished the most seasoned political observers. The Social Democrats emerged as the strongest party with eighty seats; the Old Finns had fifty-nine; the Young Finns, twenty-six; the Swedish party, twenty-four; the Agrarians, nine; and the Christian Workers, only two. A total of nineteen women had been elected to the *lantdag;* nine Social Democrats, six Old Finns, two Young Finns, one Agrarian, and one Swedish party candidate. A post-election analysis revealed that the majority of voters in many key districts and cities had been women.[18]

The struggle with Russia was far from over, however. The Finnish *lantdag* was dissolved in April 1908 and new elections were scheduled. Russian Prime Minister Stolypin was not prepared to see Finnish nationalism and parliamentarism flourish on the doorstep of St. Petersburg. In a speech to the Russian Duma in May 1908, Stolypin called for the subordination of Finnish nationalism to Greater Russian nationalism. The Russian Council of Ministers now channeled all bills passed by the Finnish *lantdag* to a Committee on Finnish Affairs controlled by former supporters of Bobrikov. The Finnish voters responded in June 1908 to this threat to their autonomy by electing eighty-three Social Democrats, fifty-three Old Finns, twenty-six Young Finns, twenty-five Swedish party mem-

---

16. "Memorandum of the Finnish Representative Reform Committee," p. 3; reprinted in Reuterskiöld, *Politisk rösträtt för kvinnor* [trans. Professor Nils J. Anderson]. Anderson].

17. "Progress of Woman's Suffrage," *The Independent* 63 (July 4, 1907): 45-53; Blakeslee, *The Outlook* 87 (September 7, 1907): 35-39.

18. Jutikkala, *Finland*, p. 243; Hallsten, *Women in Finland*, pp. 20-21; Blakeslee, *Outlook* 87: 37. Some of these pioneer women legislators were: Baroness Alexandra Gripenberg (Old Finns), Mrs. Hedvig Gebhard (Old Finns), Miss Dagmar Neovius (Swedish party), Miss Lucina Hagman (Young Finns) and Miss Miina Sillanpää (Social Democrats).

bers, seven Agrarians, and two Christian Workers. Twenty-five women were elected to the new *lantdag*.[19]

In spite of significant support by women and Social Democratic legislators, a prohibition bill proposed by the Friends of Temperance in 1908 failed to pass "on the grounds that no provision was made for new sources of revenue" to replace lost excise taxes. Two years later another prohibition bill, also prepared by the Friends of Temperance, passed the *lantdag* but was not promulgated by the Czar. Similar laws in 1911 and 1914 also failed for lack of the Czar's support. Thus matters stood at a standstill until the Russian Revolution.[20]

In summary, Finland's experience in granting women's suffrage and in attempting to adopt prohibition illustrated the peculiarities of its "frontier" situation. Although the Finns possessed a high degree of racial homogeneity, they experienced deep cleavages related to ideological and class differences. The bitter civil strife between Red Guard and White Guard factions, the suspicions of the Social Democrats harbored by the bourgeois parties, and the continuing tensions of the language conflict between Finnish-speaking and Swedish-speaking segments —all these tensions were reflected in the women's movement. The only issue on which women from various class and ideological backgrounds could agree was the temperance issue. What held together the disparate elements of Finnish society was the force of nationalism fostered by the intrusion of Russian influence into this buffer zone of Scandinavian culture.

Rosalind Travers, an English suffragist traveling in Finland in 1908, recorded a conversation with a leader of the Finnish women's movement that throws an interesting light on the whole question:

"It seems, then, that the women in Finland have obtained all and more than they are asking for elsewhere. I naturally enquired, 'How did they get it? and how does it work out?'

---

19. Seton-Watson, *Russian Empire*, pp. 668-69; Travers, *Letters from Finland*, p. 98 and Appendix 1. The changes between 1907 and 1908 are summarized in the accompanying table:

FEMALE REPRESENTATIVES IN THE FINNISH LANTDAG

	1908			1907-1908	
Party	Reelected	Newly Elected	Total	Not reelected in 1908	Total
Social Democrats	7	6	13	2	9
Finnish Party	6	—	6	—	6
Young Finnish Party	1	1	2	1	2
Swedish Party	1	2	3	—	1
Agrarians	—	1	1	1	1
Christian Workers	—	—	—	—	—
Totals	15	10	25	4	19

Source: Reuterskiöld, *Politisk rösträtt för kvinnor*, Appendix 11, pp. 337-38.

20. Wuorinen, *Prohibition Experiment*, pp. 39-40.

'They got it by deserving it!' cried Helena Tott, which was splendidly final, but not quite clear. However, the main thesis of her discourse was this: Women are so strangely placed in modern civilization, suspended between privilege and slavery, as it were, that they will not gain their full citizen rights until they have shown that they deserve them by the steady performance of their full citizen duties. 'And here we think that every citizen's first duty is to support himself, to work for his own bread, and not live idle at the expense of his kindred, be they dead or alive!'"[21]

The idea that economic independence for Finnish women had paved the way for political emancipation reflected the nature of the Finnish conception of independence.

In the feminist literature, the search for independence was a persistent theme. In a popular Finnish novel published in the late nineteenth century, a jilted heroine "consoles herself by joining the great body of emancipated women whose ideal it is to become self-supporting whether their circumstances require it or not."[22] The great dream of Finnish nationalism—to be independent—found a parallel expression in the Finnish feminist's desire to be herself, to be independent of, rather than superior to, her male compatriots. In revolting against the social norm of female subordination, they opted not so much for female superiority as for feminine individuality—a kind of cultural "separate but equal" stance.

Because of this emphasis on independence, the Finnish women's rights movement emphasized *equity* more than equality in economic legislation. They desired access to professions and jobs not so much to achieve social mobility as to become self-supporting. Inequality in social rank was tacitly accepted; they

---

21. Travers, *Letters from Finland,* pp. 98-99. The emphasis on independence as a prerequisite for political rights was reflected in the provisions of the voting law in 1906. Those *not* entitled to vote were (1) those on active military duty, (2) those under guardianship, (3) those not registered in the previous census for three years, (4) those who neglected to pay taxes for two years because of indigence, (5) those receiving permanent public assistance, (6) those whose property had been surrendered to others under bankruptcy, (7) those who had been sentenced to the public workhouse for vagrancy within three years, (8) those under wardship of the courts, and (9) those who had accepted bribes in elections or disrupted elections by violence within the previous six years. "Lantdag Law for the Grand Duchy of Finland: Given at Peterhof, July 20, 1906" reprinted in Reuterskiöld, *Politisk rösträtt för kvinnor,* pp. 344-45.

22. Hermione Ramsden, "The Literature of Finland," *The Nineteenth Century and After* 56 (November 1904): 774. Because the literary feminist confronted strong cultural barriers, her rebellion tended to focus on the social institutions of marriage, the family, and customs more than upon political barriers. For a sensitive study of the way in which popular customs reinforced women's social role in traditional Swedish society, see Berndt Gustafsson, *Manligt-Kvinnligt-Kyrkligt: I 1800-talets svenska folkliv* (Stockholm: Svenska Kyrkans Diakonistyrelses Bokförlag, 1956). Radical feminist critiques of marriage and sexual mores reached a peak by 1910 and never extended outside the urban areas. Liberal and Marxist ideas were predominant in this critique. See Heikki Waris, "Finland" in *The Institutions of Advanced Societies,* Arnold Rose, ed. (Minneapolis: University of Minnesota Press, 1958), p. 219. For literary history and women writers, see Olof Enckell, *Modärn Finlandssvensk Prosa* (Stockholm: Fahlcrantz & Company, 1937); Erik Ekelund, *Finlands svenska litteratur: från Åbo brand till sekelskiftet* (Stockholm: Bonniers Foerlag AB, 1969), 2: 345-58.

sought not so much to rise out of their class as to enjoy equitable social rewards within it.

The granting of women's suffrage in 1906 was a means of unifying the "nation" in the face of an external threat. Since women constituted a majority in the politically significant age brackets, it was a way of binding their interests to the new Finnish state that was emerging around the resurgent *lantdag*.[23] "After all, the women are all good Finns and they were loyal in the passive resistance campaign"—this seemed to be the dominant mood among the men. Finnish welfare legislation rested on this premise of ethnic homogeneity. All citizens were entitled to certain standards of comfort or culture. This seemed to be the animating principle of their emerging welfare program. Unlike the Australian welfare system, the pioneering Finnish welfare laws were designed to free the woman for her primary social roles, not to entrap her in them.[24]

MILITANT TACTICS AND WARTIME CONDITIONS, 1906–1918

While women in Finland received the vote, an event in South Africa brought to prominence a figure destined to have an important impact on both the women's suffrage and prohibition causes in the twentieth century. In 1906 Mohandas Karamchand Gandhi, an Indian-born, British-educated Hindu, led a passive resistance campaign against an attempt by the Transvaal government to subjugate the Indian community in South Africa. Gandhi called his mass campaign of nonviolent noncooperation, "Satyagraha." In 1907 and 1908, Gandhi renewed his Satyagraha campaign and then journeyed to England in 1909 in hopes of influencing the colonial authorities. Thus, by a quirk of fate, four of the leading figures in future protest movements were in London in the summer of 1909: Mohandas Gandhi; Emmeline Pankhurst, the suffragette leader; and Alice Paul and Lucy Burns, her American disciples. The tactics of twentieth-century mass movements were already clear—civil disorder, whether peaceful or violent, coupled with an appeal to overarching moral or ideological principles.[25]

---

23. Arthur Reade, *Finland and the Finns* (New York: Dodd, Mead & Co., 1919), pp. 255-57. A similar set of circumstances had resulted in the enfranchisement of women in Norway. In 1905 Norway separated itself from Sweden. Women supported the nationalistic movement and demanded a voice in the plebiscite for the selection of a new king. The *storting*, in an emotional moment, received an address of loyalty signed by three hundred thousand women and in 1907 granted limited women's suffrage. Agnes Mathilde Wergeland, "Progress of the Woman Movement in Norway," in *Leaders in Norway and Other Essays*, Katharine Merrill, ed. (1916; reprint ed., Freeport, N.Y.: Books for Libraries, Inc., 1966).

24. Waris, "Finland," in *Advanced Societies*, Rose, ed., pp. 194-95; 215-16; Jaakko Nousiainen, *The Finnish Political System*, trans. John H. Hodgson (Cambridge: Harvard University Press, 1971), pp. 413-16.

25. Geoffrey Ashe, *Gandhi* (New York: Stein and Day, Publishers, 1968), pp. 96-118; Robert A. Huttenback, *Gandhi in South Africa: British Imperialism and the Indian Question, 1860-1914* (Ithaca, N.Y.: Cornell University Press, 1971), Chapters 5, 6.

Gandhi returned to South Africa in November 1909 to confront a deportation drive by the Transvaal government. He checked the deportations by court action; the confrontations slackened; and Gandhi retired to Tolstoy Farm with his faithful cadres to recuperate, meditate, and prepare for the next round of Satyagraha. On March 14, 1913, the Supreme Court of the Union of South Africa ruled "that Hindu, Muslim and Parsee marriages were invalid. Therefore Indian wives were concubines without status, liable to deportation, and the children were illegitimate."[26] Hell hath no fury like a woman scorned—or told that her children are bastards and that she is little better than a harlot.

Immediately, Satyagraha took on a new dimension. Women joined the ranks of the nonviolent protestors and were willingly arrested. Gandhi led a mass march, including women and children, and filled the jails with his followers. Before the onslaught of mounting world opinion, political pressure from India, and the personal intervention of Gandhi's friends, the Union government capitulated and met Gandhi's demands: the repeal of a head tax on free laborers, the recognition of non-Christian marriages, the mitigation of immigration and residence regulations, and an end to the indentured labor system. Gandhi prepared to return to India, which was increasingly restive under British rule.[27]

While Gandhi was developing his tactics in South Africa, Mrs. Pankhurst's suffragettes were improvising on their militant tactics. In the autumn of 1910, they had called a truce on militancy in hopes that a new suffrage bill and the General Election would result in an overwhelming victory for their cause. When the newly elected Liberal government once more delayed and equivocated, the suffragettes resumed militancy: ". . . so many of the suffragettes suffered violence during the six hours' struggle with the police on 'Black Friday' (18 November 1910) that there seems to have been a spontaneous decision amongst the rank and file of the WSPU to make their protest in future by attacking property, instead of suffering further personal harm through struggles in the streets."[28]

In renewing the militancy campaign, however, the suffragettes delayed the achievement of their goal. The major institutional barrier to electoral change —the veto power of the House of Lords—had been overcome in the 1910 General Election by the Liberal victory and was institutionalized by the Parliament Act of 1911. The Liberal party rank and file supported women's suffrage; the Liberal leader Asquith was personally hostile but had agreed to make the issue an "open" one for the party (that is, members, including the cabinet, could vote as they believed rather than following a party position). Yet Asquith "torpedoed" the "conciliation" bill by announcing on November 7, 1911, that the government would bring in a major franchise reform bill in the next session. Thereafter, the renewal of militancy by the suffragettes was counterproductive. The "back-

---

26. Ashe, *Gandhi,* pp. 119-22 (quotation on p. 122).

27. Ashe, *Gandhi,* pp. 123-26; Huttenback, *Gandhi in South Africa,* Chapter 8.

28. Rover, *Women's Suffrage,* pp. 81-82 (quotation); 194.

lash" to militancy destroyed the "conciliation" bill on its second reading in March 1912.[29]

If, by the end of 1912, the women's suffrage movement in England had been stalled by the reaction to militancy, in the United States the movement was gaining momentum. Washington, California, Arizona, Kansas, and Oregon had adopted women's suffrage laws or amendments; Illinois granted presidential suffrage by legislative enactment when the Progressive party shattered traditional political lines. Meanwhile, Lucy Burns and Alice Paul engineered a coup in the National American Woman Suffrage Association by having themselves appointed to its congressional committee.

Alice Paul and Lucy Burns, who had joined the suffragettes in England between 1907 and 1910, had learned the new tactics first hand—in Holloway Gaol. Even the moderate American suffrage leader, Carrie Chapman Catt, was impressed by the new militancy. In testimony before a Congressional committee in March 1908, she had remarked:

"The movement [for woman suffrage in England] was inaugurated there, as here, by what are commonly known as the middle classes. It has gone so far now that duchesses and countesses are a part of it upon the one side; and the new movement of the suffragettes has taken in a large number of the working women at the other extreme of society, until to-day we witness in England a curious condition which exists nowhere else in the world. All the emperors and kings of civilized nations are to-day escorted by police; even our President of the United States must have his cordon of police in order to protect his life from the possible bombs of anarchists. But the British members of the cabinet are protected also by the police, not from fear of the anarchists, but because of the fear of the imprudent and the saucy and the embarrassing questions of the suffragettes. The whole people of England declare that it can not be long before the parliamentary suffrage is granted there."[30]

English influences had also reached the United States via Harriot Stanton Blatch, the daughter of Elizabeth Cady Stanton, who had lived in England for twenty years. Upon her widowhood, she returned to the United States. Disgusted with the slow pace of the traditional suffrage organizations and their leisure-class leadership, Mrs. Blatch had organized the Equality League of Self-

---

29. Rover, *Women's Suffrage,* pp. 91-95; Barbara Bliss, "Militancy: The Insurrection that Failed," *Contemporary Review* 201 (June 1962): 306. Bliss noted that "the Pankhursts modelled their behaviour upon a misunderstanding of Parnell's strategy for winning Home Rule for Ireland and they never adapted themselves to changing conditions. Suffragettes made personal attacks with dog whips, pepper-pots, hatchets and stones, rang dinner bells at Liberal meetings, and did not hesitate to throw missiles through windows at audiences or into the homes of Liberals" (p. 307).

30. "Statement of Mrs. Carrie Chapman Catt, of New-York City, N.Y., before the Committee of the Judiciary, House of Representatives, March 3, 1908," reprinted in Reuterskiöld, *Politisk rösträtt för kvinnor,* Appendix 2, p. 123.

Supporting Women in January 1907. The Equality League tapped the dynamic
energy of self-supporting professional women, social workers, trade unionists,
and other young, college educated women. The Equality Leaguers held parades,
organized outdoor meetings, and barnstormed their states in automobiles and
trolley cars.[31]

When in March 1913, a Washington, D.C., women's suffrage parade organized by Lucy Burns and Alice Paul was attacked and harassed by hoodlums and
hecklers while the District police and some visiting national guardsmen stood
idly by, the women's suffrage cause reaped a windfall of publicity and public
sympathy. In April 1913, Lucy Burns and Alice Paul organized the militant
Congressional Union and announced their intention of conducting a vigorous
campaign for a federal women's suffrage amendment.[32]

Suffragists were not the only ones to adopt new tactics. The Anti-Saloon
League eschewed both the reliance on moral persuasion that had characterized
the older temperance groups and the emphasis on partisan political exertion
that had characterized the National Prohibition party. It found a way of uniting
the moral effort of the evangelical Protestant churches with the political power
of the overrepresented rural areas by stressing the classic mixture of nonpartisan-
ship, singleness of purpose, and centralization of authority. By concentrating
initially on local option as a strategy, the Anti-Saloon League made considerable
progress in the South where the resurgent white middle class was using the instruments of progressive democracy to disfranchise and repress the Negro population. On the strength of local-option success, the League increasingly shifted to
state prohibition. Prohibition became one more weapon in the arsenal of white
racism. From August 1907 to January 1909 five Southern states were swept into
the prohibitionist column by the Anti-Saloon League drive.[33]

31. Eleanor Flexner, *Century of Struggle: The Woman's Rights Movement in the United*
States (Cambridge, Mass.: Harvard University Press, 1959), pp. 249-54.

32. Flexner, *Century of Struggle,* pp. 259, 263, 265; Doris Stevens, *Jailed for Freedom*
(New York: Liveright Publishing Corporation, 1920), pp. 21-22.

33. For the traditional interpretation of these events, see Peter H. Odegard, *Pressure Politics:*
The Story of the Anti-Saloon League (New York: Columbia University Press, 1928), Chap-
ters 3, 4 (pp. 116-21); James Benson Sellers, *The Prohibition Movement in Alabama, 1702*
to 1943 (Chapel Hill: University of North Carolina Press, 1943), Chapter 6; Daniel Jay
Whitener, *Prohibition in North Carolina, 1715-1945* (Chapel Hill: University of North
Carolina Press, 1945), Chapters 9, 10. The following states adopted state prohibition:
Georgia (1907), Mississippi (1908), North Carolina (1908), and Tennessee (1909). Alabama
adopted statewide prohibition in November 1907 by legislative enactment but failed to
secure a prohibition amendment to the state constitution in November 1909. It thereupon
returned to local option until 1915.

A brief flurry of militant antisaloon behavior had erupted in 1900 when Carry Nation,
a Kansas Prohibitionist, decided to close down illegal saloons by smashing their contents and
fixtures. The technique was not emulated, however, on any extensive scale. Robert Lewis
Taylor, *Vessel of Wrath: The Life and Times of Carry Nation* (New York: The New American Library, Inc., 1966).

A number of recent studies have attempted to view the prohibition drive of the early
twentieth century as a social movement rather than as a pressure group or to interpret its
role in politics as an ethno-cultural issue. Peter G. Filene, "An Obituary for 'The Progressive

In exploiting the local-option strategy in the first decade of the twentieth century, the Anti-Saloon League had been able to maintain a democratic political stance. But predilection for a particular democratic device cannot be taken as dedication to democracy as a goal. On the question of such direct-democracy devices as initiative and referendum, the best that can be said for the Anti-Saloon League's record is that they favored such devices when they promised to achieve prohibition and they opposed them when they did not.[34]

The "conversion" of the Anti-Saloon League in 1913 from local-option and statewide prohibition to national prohibition through a federal amendment was thus a modification of means rather than a reconsideration of ultimate objectives. On December 10, 1913, a "Great Remonstrance" parade of four thousand prohibitionists marched down Pennsylvania Avenue to the Capitol to present a petition in favor of national prohibition. Unlike the suffragists of March, they were not manhandled by unrestrained spectators. During the following year the Anti-Saloon League launched a concerted drive to exert pressure on Congress by building a prohibition base in the states.[35]

The popular notion that prohibition was pushed through Congress by a militant minority in a moment of wartime madness while the achievement of women's suffrage was the inevitable result of a popular movement persists in spite of repeated scholarly refutation. The converse is closer to the truth. Prohibition was a popular cause in the prewar years and repeatedly won electoral victories in state legislatures and referendum elections. In 1914, five states adopted prohibition; in 1915, five more were carried; and in 1916, four more states joined the dry ranks. At the same time, women's suffrage was defeated in 1914 in five populous states and was passed in only two sparsely populated

---

Movement,'" *American Quarterly* 22 (Spring 1970): 20–34, challenged the conception of a unified Progressive movement and noted that prohibitionism divided the progressive electorate. Robert A. Hohner, "The Prohibitionists: Who Were They?" *South Atlantic Quarterly* 68 (Autumn 1969): 491–505, called attention to the Southern origins of the new prohibition drive and analyzed urban support of prohibitionism. Margaret Nelson, "Prohibition: A Case Study of Societal Misguidance," *American Behavioral Scientist* 12 (November–December 1968): 37–43, applied the sociological theories of Amitai Etzioni to the Anti-Saloon League to explain the effectiveness of their techniques. John Hammond Moore, "The Negro and Prohibition in Atlanta, 1885–1887," *South Atlantic Quarterly* 69 (Winter 1970): 38–57, called attention to Negro support of prohibition in the 1880s, but follow-up studies on later periods are lacking. The studies of religion and politics in the period throw some light on the new prohibition drive but are too fragmentary to support broad generalizations at this time. See Robert A. Hohner, "Bishop Cannon's Apprenticeship in Temperance Politics, 1901–1918," *Journal of Southern History* 34 (February 1968): 33–49; C. C. Pearson and J. Edwin Hendricks, *Liquor and Anti-Liquor in Virginia, 1619–1919* (Durham, N.C.: Duke University Press, 1967); and Paul E. Isaac, *Prohibition and Politics: Turbulent Decades in Tennessee, 1885–1920* (Knoxville: University of Tennessee Press in cooperation with the Tennessee Historical Commission, 1965).

34. Odegard, *Pressure Politics*, pp. 121–22.

35. Ibid., pp. 151–53; D. Leigh Colvin, *Prohibition in the United States: A History of the Prohibition Party and of the Prohibition Movement* (New York: George H. Doran Company, 1926), p. 430.

western states. In 1915, women's suffrage was defeated in four eastern states. In light of the militant tactics in 1914–16 of the Woman's Party (successor to the Congressional Union) and the lobbying role of the NAWSA, it is the adoption of women's suffrage, not prohibition, that needs to be explained in terms of pressure politics.[36]

Wartime conditions and nationalism strengthened demands for a more democratic suffrage. The task of the wartime governments became clearer as the war progressed. Support and loyalty could not be assumed; they had to be mobilized and organized for the long haul. In the extreme situation of wartime, the extension of the franchise acted not only as a channel for the expression of diverse interests but also as a chain to link the citizens together in an expression of their common interests. Voting, in this sense, became an expression of the essential equality of citizenship and a means of helping to define the nature of the state.

Such was the case in England, for example, in December 1916 when David Lloyd George became the prime minister of the coalition government. The problem of disfranchised servicemen had plagued the Asquith government for some time. A special committee rendered a report in January 1917 that recommended a general electoral reform, including women's suffrage. The Representation of the People bill, introduced in 1917, adopted by Parliament, and given the royal assent in February 1918, extended the franchise. It included women over thirty who were householders or wives of householders, occupiers of property of an annual value of £5, or holders of university degrees (or persons with an equivalent education). The terms were not generous and ignored the claims of the working women who had done so much to support the war effort; however, the changes were an opening wedge for an inevitable extension of suffrage later.

The leaders of the British suffrage movement had played their strategy correctly. Mrs. Pankhurst had called off the militant campaign of her suffragettes and had turned her energies toward arousing public support for the war. Mrs. Fawcett, the leader of the more moderate suffragists, had persisted in keeping quietly effective pressure on Parliament. The real heroines, however, were the ordinary women of England, Scotland, and Wales who worked in the munitions factories, drove "lorries," tended the sick and wounded, served in the armed forces as nurses, and performed the myriad other wartime tasks. Led on by the carrot of such generous service and threatened by the stick of an implied intention to renew militancy and political agitation after the war, political leaders were finally moved to act.[37]

The key role of political leadership in the situation was highlighted by events in the United States. Whereas David Lloyd George was a firm advocate

---

36. Colvin, *Prohibition in the U.S.*, pp. 430–31; Flexner, *Century of Struggle*, pp. 268–70. The militants had opposed Democratic candidates in the 1914 and 1916 elections on the theory that the ruling, majority party should be denied feminine support because it had failed to pass women's suffrage. See Aileen S. Kraditor, *The Ideas of the Woman Suffrage Movement, 1890–1920* (New York: Columbia University Press, 1965), pp. 231–37.

37. Rover, *Women's Suffrage*, pp. 206–7; David Mitchell, *Monstrous Regiment: The Story of the Women of the First World War* (New York: The Macmillan Company, 1965).

of both prohibition and women's suffrage, Woodrow Wilson believed strongly in neither cause. (His southern background, his academic liberalism, his practical progressivism created contradictory influences that made him reluctant to deal with these issues.) During the 1916 presidential election, the Woman's Party had campaigned against Wilson in the western women's suffrage states. The results were meager but the lesson was clear. Wilson could no longer equivocate on the issue. The militant Woman's Party would not wait. On January 10, 1917, women pickets appeared at the gates to the White House with banners reading, "Mr. President! How Long Must Women Wait for Liberty?" Day after day they stayed at their posts.

By April 1917 the United States had entered the war against Germany, and the public mood had changed. Where friendly crowds had once encouraged the pickets, and even President Wilson had tipped his hat as he drove by, now the pickets encountered hostilities and locked gates. In June local authorities began to arrest the women pickets and to hand down short-term sentences in the notorious Occoquan workhouse in Virginia. The stage was thus set for a repetition of the scenes in Holloway Gaol in prewar England. Mob attacks on the pickets, mass arrests, hunger strikes, and forced feeding followed in short order.

The women kept before the public eye the contradiction of the situation: while the United States was embarked upon a war to make the world safe for democracy, it was denying democracy at home. In this highly charged emotional atmosphere, a Senate committee reported favorably on women's suffrage (reportedly after its chairman had secretly visited the suffragette prisoners in jail). The way was clear for submission of a women's suffrage amendment. Having failed to compel the women to abandon their demands and to support the war effort unequivocally, Congress now refused to grant concessions in order to secure unity. In October 1918 the Senate failed to ratify the amendment by two votes.[38]

The war was officially over with the armistice in November 1918, but the emotions stirred by the war did not die. The same carrot-and-stick strategy that had worked in England was applied in the United States. While the militants continued to apply pressure with watchfire demonstrations, more arrests, and hunger strikes, the moderates assiduously cultivated President Wilson's support and lobbied in Congress. The Republicans had won control of both houses of Congress in the November 1918 elections but would not take command until 1919. With postwar tension dividing the nation and with both parties casting anxious eyes on the women's vote in the 1920 presidential election, Congress met in special session on May 19, 1919, and finally sent the women's suffrage amendment on its way to the states for ratification.[39]

---

38. Stevens, *Jailed for Freedom,* pp. 63-158; Flexner, *Century of Struggle,* p. 287.

39. Stevens, *Jailed for Freedom,* pp. 336-43; Flexner, *Century of Struggle,* pp. 314-24. For the complicated factors involved in the ratification of the amendment, see David Morgan, *Suffragists and Democrats: The Politics of Woman Suffrage in America* (East Lansing: Michigan State University Press, 1972), Chapter 10; John D. Buenker, "The Urban Political Machine and Woman Suffrage: A Study in Political Adaptability," *The Historian* 33 (February 1971): 264-79.

In the heady international atmosphere of the postwar years, the themes of self-determination, nationalism, and experimental democracy and socialism frequently found expression in the creation of new republics or democratic governments. The necessity of securing support from disparate populations for these new governments frequently led to the adoption of women's suffrage. Between 1917 and 1919 women's suffrage was adopted in Russia, Austria, Czechoslovakia, the Weimar Republic of Germany, Hungary, and Poland. With the barriers broken in England, women's suffrage was speedily inaugurated in 1918–19 in Canada, British East Africa, Ireland, Rhodesia, Scotland, and Wales. Even the governments that survived the war did not remain untouched. Belgium granted suffrage in 1919 to widows and mothers of soldiers and civilians killed in the war. Holland, Iceland, Luxembourg, and Sweden also extended the franchise to women.[40]

If wartime conditions and nascent nationalism carried women's suffrage forward, prohibitionists were willing to use the same forces to further their cause. In short order Congress, in 1917, passed the Lever Food and Fuel Control Act (forbidding the use of foodstuffs for distillation and regulating beer and wine production); the Eighteenth Amendment for national prohibition; and, in 1918, the War Prohibition Act, outlawing the manufacture and sale of beer and wine. The Eighteenth Amendment had achieved the ratification of the necessary two-thirds of the states by January 1919. "Enjoying majorities of over eighty percent in the ratifying states, the amendment was rejected by only three: New Jersey, Rhode Island, and Connecticut."[41] Wartime food shortages, the need for efficiency, anti-German sentiment, patriotism, and middle-class fears of immigrant, Indian, and Negro drinking habits were all factors in the political groundswell that accompanied the prohibition drive.

The comparative method, however, directs the attention of the student of history to another set of factors. Instead of the traditional question, "*Who* supported prohibition, and *why?*" the comparative perspective focuses on the question, "Why *prohibition?*" The impact of war, the need to conserve food

---

40. Stevens, *Jailed for Freedom,* p. 350. For the background to these developments, see Louis Fischer, *The Life of Lenin* (New York: Harper & Row, Publishers, 1964), Chapters 16-20; C. A. Macartney, *The Hapsburg Empire 1790-1918* (New York: The Macmillan Company, 1969), Chapter 18; Catherine Lyle Cleverdon, *The Woman Suffrage Movement in Canada* (Toronto: University of Toronto Press, 1950); Douglas V. Verney, *Parliamentary Reform in Sweden, 1866-1921* (London: Oxford University Press, 1957), Chapter 11; Knut Gjerset, *History of Iceland* (New York: The Macmillan Company, 1924), pp. 439-45.

41. James H. Timberlake, *Prohibition and the Progressive Movement, 1900-1920* (Cambridge, Mass.: Harvard University Press, 1966), p. 178. See also pages 172-83. Recent studies have modified the traditional rural versus urban interpretation of the prohibition victory by showing that class and religion were more determinative of attitudes than area of residence per se. See Norman H. Clark, *The Dry Years: Prohibition and Social Change in Washington* (Seattle: University of Washington Press, 1965), pp. 115-26; Richard Jensen, *The Winning of the Midwest: Social and Political Conflict, 1888-1896* (Chicago: The University of Chicago Press, 1971), Chapter 7. Although Jensen's study ends in 1896, his conclusions would explain the influences that shaped later voting behavior in the Midwest.

supplies, and the example of other nations are frequently cited as reasons for the adoption of wartime prohibition, but this analysis is seldom carried far enough. A brief survey of the patterns of temperance and prohibition legislation in other countries during and immediately after World War I will put the American case into its proper perspective.

In England, David Lloyd George, Chancellor of the Exchequer in the Asquith ministry and Minister of Munitions in the wartime coalition government, advocated higher taxes on beer and wartime prohibition. He proposed that the government nationalize the liquor trade with compensation to the original owners and run it under regulations designed to divert the least amount of grain and sugar from the food supply. The proposals were vigorously attacked as an attempt to "Prussianize" England and to enforce teetotalism in a reluctant nation. G. K. Chesterton criticized it as "a scheme too witless for Wonderland; a scheme for abolishing hats while preserving hatters." In spite of Lloyd George's sensational remarks on the adverse effects of the workers' consumption of alcohol on munitions production, and in spite of genuine concerns for food shortages, only partial prohibition was enacted for the duration of the war. In 1921 a Licensing Act was passed returning England to its prewar system of liquor control.[42]

In Russia, the prewar temperance movement represented a unique mixture of autocratic humanitarianism and working-class prohibitionism. The government owned and operated a monopoly that produced vodka and returned a substantial revenue to the treasury through sales in government shops. Temperance leaders among the peasant deputies in the Duma pressed for reduction in the number of shops, restrictions on private sales of liquor, and local option (with women being allowed to vote on the issue in the village councils). But the outbreak of war interfered with the implementation of these demands. Grand Duke Nicholas, Commander in Chief of the military, decreed partial prohibition during mobilization and in a *ukase* (imperial decree) in September 1914 extended the prohibition on vodka for the duration of the war. In July 1916 the Duma extended the ban to all beverages containing over 1½ percent of alcohol.[43]

In Finland, the adoption of prohibition was not without its ironies. For years the Social Democrats and Agrarians in the *lantdag* had advocated prohibition. Numerous prohibition laws had been passed between 1907 and 1914

---

42. D. C. Lathbury, "Drink and the War," *The Nineteenth Century* 77 (May 1915); 1004–14; Harry Jones, "What Lloyd-George Accomplished Against Liquor," *The World's Work* 30 (August 1915): 433–37; E. H. Cherrington et al., *Standard Encyclopedia of the Alcohol Problem* (Westerville, O.: American Issues Publishing Company, 1925–1930), 3:935–36 (hereinafter cited as *SEAP*).

For the background of wartime regulation in England, see E. M. H. Lloyd, *Experiments in State Control: At the War Office and the Ministry of Food* (London: Oxford University Press, 1924).

43. G. W. Frodsham, "Temperance Reform in Russia," *The Nineteenth Century* 77 (February 1915): 401–8; James Middleton, "A 'Teetotal' War," *The World's Work* 30 (June 1915): 206–10; Cherrington, *SEAP*, 5: 2334–35; William E. Johnson, *The Liquor Problem in Russia* (Westerville, O.: American Issue Publishing Company, 1915), Chapters 10, 11.

by the new *lantdag* only to fail because of opposition by the Czar. During the early stages of the European war, the partial prohibition decreed by the Czar was extended to Finland. Then in March 1917 the Russian Revolution posed a constitutional crisis for Finland. Did the provisional government of Kerensky automatically assume the sovereign powers over Finland that had been exercised by the Czar? "Finland gave *de facto* recognition to the provisional Russian government as the power that exercised 'supreme authority' by carrying out its rulings."[44] On May 29, 1917, the Russian provisional government approved a strict prohibition law for Finland that would go into effect on June 1, 1919. The Social Democrats, who controlled the *lantdag* and dominated the senate, attempted a constitutional coup d'etat in July 1917. In the Power Act, they declared that "supreme authority" rested in the Finnish parliament (except for foreign policy and military affairs). The Kerensky government refused to ratify the Power Act and dissolved the Finnish parliament. In the ensuing election the Social Democrats lost their majority. Thus Finland owed its prohibition law not so much to its supporters as to its enemies.[45]

In contrast to Finland's adoption of prohibition was Sweden's handling of the liquor problem. Sweden, too, had encountered a constitutional crisis in the spring of 1917. Inflation, food shortages, and labor troubles plagued the country as a result of the European war. Although the Conservative ministry under Hammarskjöld had followed a policy of strict neutrality in foreign affairs, it could not isolate the country from the effects of the war, particularly the naval blockades. The Hammarskjöld ministry resigned and new elections were set for September 1917. The Social Democrats emerged as the largest party in the Second Chamber (lower house) in spite of a secession by its pro-Bolshevik faction. Could the Social Democrats and Liberals form a Left coalition and rule the country? "The traditional disinclination of the Social Democrats to accept the responsibility of Government was only one of the obstacles in the way of a Left coalition. The other was the attitude of Gustav V towards leaders of a party which was pledged to republicanism at home and to a pro-Entente policy

---

44. Jutikkala, *Finland*, p. 250.

45. Wuorinen, *Prohibition Experiment,* p. 40; Jutikkala, *Finland,* pp. 251-52. The Bolshevik seizure of power in Russia in November 1917 compounded the problems in Finland. The Finnish socialist movement once again split into a revolutionary Red Guard wing and a parliamentary wing; the bourgeois parties rallied around the White Guards but disagreed as to republican or monarchical forms of government. The result was a bloody and debilitating civil war that lasted from January to May 1918. With the help of German troops, the White Guard army suppressed the Red Guards and reunited the country. The Social Democrats were stigmatized by the action of their revolutionary wing and lost some seats in the post-civil war elections held in March 1919. It was against this background of civil war, political upheaval, runaway inflation, and postwar depression that the prohibition law was put into effect in June 1919. Jutikkala, *Finland,* pp. 252-67; Wuorinen, *Prohibition Experiment,* pp. 59-61.

For the impact of wartime conditions in Finland on alcoholic consumption and regulation, see Leo Harmaja, *Effects of the War on Economic and Social Life in Finland* (New Haven: Yale University Press, 1933), pp. 73, 115-16.

abroad. He feared for his crown and for the neutrality of Sweden."[46] Should the king hold out for a center-right coalition or acquiesce in accepting a left coalition that represented the majority parties? The king bowed to necessity, a left coalition government took office, and the constitutional crisis was passed.

In the midst of this constitutional crisis the *Riksdag* had struggled with the question of liquor control. The basic outlines of the Bratt system of liquor regulation had been presented to the *Riksdag* in 1914 in a massive report entitled *Alkoholen och Samhället [Alcohol and Society]*. These proposals became the basis of a general liquor law enacted in 1917, known as the *Rusdrycksförsälj-ningsförordningen* (or Rff) act. The new act would not go into effect, however, until January 1, 1919. In the meantime, the government had to deal with the immediate crisis of the food shortage. A temporary, wartime prohibition act was defeated by the First Chamber (upper house), but the government did suspend sales until June 1 and then limited individual liquor purchases to two liters every three months (raised to sixteen liters on July 1). In August 1917 the distillation of spirits was temporarily suspended because of the acute grain shortage. In effect, wartime rationing of liquor was simply continued when the mechanism of the Bratt system went into operation in 1919.[47]

In summary, no necessary correlation existed between wartime conditions and the adoption of permanent prohibition. On the contrary, those countries faced with the most immediate and serious threats of food shortages, invasion, and disruption of their economies seemed to be the ones least willing to adopt anything more than wartime regulation or temporary prohibition. Russia and Finland were exceptions to this generalization, but even in Russia prohibition proved to be short-lived. The specters of famine and wartime food shortages provided the prohibitionists with additional arguments; but they cannot explain the comparative pattern of liquor regulation and prohibition.[48]

---

46. Verney, *Parliamentary Reform in Sweden,* p. 202. For a quantitative analysis of Social Democratic strength, see Olle Johansson, "Socialdemokratins väljare 1911 och 1914: En kvantitativ analys ar regional och social gruppering och struktur," *Historisk tidskrift* 87 (March 1967): 297–356. For detailed background of political changes, see Yngve Larsson, *På marsch mot demokratin: från hundragradig skala till allmän rösträtt, 1900–1920* (Stockholm: Almqvist & Wiksell/Gebers Foerlag AB, 1967).

47. Thompson, *Control in Sweden,* pp. 26–29; Cherrington, *SEAP,* 6: 2565. Regulation of beer was handled by a separate law (known as *pilsnerdricksförsäljningsförordningen*) enacted in 1919. See Thompson, *Control in Sweden,* Chapter 8.

48. A survey of the western countries in World War I indicated the following pattern of anti-liquor legislation (source: Cherrington, *SEAP*).

Austria	Wartime prohibition in mobilization areas; reduced production and higher taxes (1: 238).
Belgium	Prohibition in zone of allied troops decreed by king November 23, 1914; German forces enforced regulation and reduction of production (1: 315-16).
Denmark	Wartime restriction and higher taxes (2: 793-94).
England	Wartime prohibition in mobilization areas; restrictions on hours of public houses and sales (3: 935-36).
Finland	Wartime prohibition made permanent in 1917 (3: 238).

Why, for example, did Finland and the United States adopt permanent *prohibition* while England and Sweden instituted new systems of *regulation?* Regulation of deviant social behavior implies a certain tolerance of subcultures and may reflect a sense of security on the part of the ruling elite, class, or majority. It may indicate that a pluralistic social model of community is held by those who make the law. Prohibition, on the other hand, may reflect an uneasiness, a sense of insecurity, on the part of the ruling group and an unwillingness to tolerate deviation from its norms (which it identifies with defiance of its authority). The model of the community implicit in such a stance is unitary rather than pluralistic. The nature of the community is defined partly by negation (that is, by establishing parameters of deviance and punishing violations of them) and partly by definition (that is, by embodying the mores of the ruling group in law).[49]

In the period between 1910 and 1920, prohibition was part of an attempt to define the nature of the community in the face of external threats and internal divisions. Both Finland and the United States faced internal tensions related to factors of heterogeneity in their societies. Finland had the lingering language conflicts between Swedish-speaking and Finnish-speaking groups and the societal and ideological conflict of socialistic and capitalistic elements that led to civil war in 1918. The United States had experienced ethnic conflicts and cultural dislocations because of immigration, rapid urbanization, and rural overrepresentation in political structures. The United States between 1917 and 1919 was still an "unfinished country," as the Red Scare of 1919 demonstrated. Finland was a nation that had just declared its independence and had yet to establish its stability or its identity.[50]

France	Prohibition of absinthe; wartime prohibition in mobilization areas and war zones; requisitioning of industrial alcohol by government; restrictions and reduced production, higher taxes (3: 1031-37).
Germany	Regulation of production during wartime (3: 1093-98).
Iceland	Prohibition adopted 1912 to become effective in 1915 (3: 1279-80).
Italy	Reduction in number of public houses; no restrictions or prohibition (3:1365).
Norway	Wartime prohibition decreed in 1916 and extended for duration in 1917 (5: 2026).
Russia	Wartime prohibition decreed in 1914 and later extended by action of Duma to total prohibition; continued by Bolsheviks (5: 2334).
Sweden	Wartime restrictions but not prohibition (6: 2566).

49. For a brief discussion of some of the problems involved in the use of deviancy models and cross-cultural comparisons in social science research as it relates to the problem of alcoholism, see David J. Pittman, "International Overview: Social and Cultural Factors in Drinking Patterns, Pathological and Nonpathological," in *Alcoholism,* David J. Pittman, ed. (New York: Harper & Row, Publishers, 1967), pp. 3-20; David J. Pittman and Duff G. Gillespie, "Social Policy as Deviancy Reinforcement: The Case of the Public Intoxication Offender," in *Alcoholism,* Pittman, ed., pp. 106-24.

50. Norway too had language and ideological conflicts. In spite of ethnic homogeneity, Norwegian society was characterized by deep social and political cleavages. The election of 1918 ushered in a period of multiparty instability, growing distrust of parliamentarianism, and disintegration of the ruling Liberal party. A referendum on prohibition in 1919 secured

Sweden and England, on the other hand, opted for regulation rather than prohibition. Sweden, with its homogeneous society, its lack of external threats because of strict neutrality, and the accommodation of the majority of its Social Democrats to parliamentary evolution rather than paramilitary revolution in 1917, did not have to define the nature of its community in the same fashion as did other Scandinavian countries. Sweden was therefore free to adopt the Bratt system as part of an emerging welfare state. In England the severity of the external threat acted as an effective check to the attempt of its radical-dissenter groups to impose their concept of community upon the rest of the society. The monarchy and parliamentarism already symbolized the concepts of community that appealed to the instinctual conservatism of the British working class. Social, religious, and political toleration within tacitly agreed limits had already been institutionalized. Regulation and strict license, in short, were the traditional English way of handling the "drink problem" without creating open social conflict, and the ruling groups were not about to experiment with "radical" changes.[51]

---

the necessary majority but revealed the regional concentration of prohibition support. Temperance and prohibition enjoyed their strongest support in the pietistic rural areas of the South and West. See Stein Rokkan and Henry Valen, "Regional Contrasts in Norwegian Politics: A Review of Data from Official Statistics and from Sample Surveys," in *Cleavages, Ideologies and Party Systems: Contributions to Comparative Political Sociology,* Erik Allardt and Yrjö Littunen, eds. (Helsinki: The Academic Bookstore, 1964), pp. 184-89, 205, 221, 231; Henry Valen and Daniel Katz, *Political Parties in Norway: A Community Study* (London: Tavistock Publications, 1964), pp. 25-29; Harry Eckstein, *Division and Cohesion in Democracy: A Study of Norway* (Princeton, N.J.: Princeton University Press, 1966), Chapters 5, 7, 8.

In Iceland, which also adopted prohibition, temperance and total abstinence had been associated in the 1870s with nationalistic resistance to Danish taxation and control. In the 1880s and 1890s temperance and prohibition sentiment increased with the coming of the Good Templars lodge and the WCTU. Prohibition of liquor was proposed in 1905 and strongly supported by the leaders of the independence party. A prohibition law was passed by the *Althing* (parliament) in 1909 and signed by the Danish king in June 1909. Denmark, which exercised legal control over Iceland, was more influenced by German culture and adopted regulation, rather than prohibition, in 1912. Denmark was thus closer to Sweden in dealing with drunkenness than it was to Norway, Finland, or Iceland. See Cherrington, *SEAP,* 3: 1278-80; Knut Gjerset, *History of Iceland* (New York: The Macmillan Company, 1924), pp. 438-40; J. S. Dich, G. Drachmann, H. H. Koch, S. Wechselmann, eds., *Social Denmark: A Survey of the Danish Social Legislation,* trans. W. E. Calvert (Copenhagen: Socialt Tidsskrift, 1945), pp. 237-39.

For the situation in the United States, see Robert K. Murray, *Red Scare: A Study in National Hysteria, 1919-1920* (reprint ed., New York: McGraw-Hill Book Company, 1964); Otis L. Graham, Jr., *The Great Campaigns: Reform and War in America, 1900-1928* (Englewood Cliffs, N.J.: Prentice-Hall, Inc., 1971), Part 3.

51. For the debate on liquor control in England, see H. D. Rawnsley, "Liquor Control and the Carlisle Experiment," *The Hibbert Journal* 18 (February-March 1920): 557-71; "'Down Glasses'—The Test Case," *Living Age* 292 (February 17, 1917): 434-37; Cherrington, *SEAP,* 3: 935. The Conservative administration in 1904 had adopted a plan for reduction of "pub" licenses with compensation; the Asquith government had secured passage in 1908 of a bill for reduction of licenses over a fourteen-year period but the bill had been vetoed by the House of Lords.

From this historical perspective, prohibition was a means of social control and an aspect of heightened nationalism. In the United States, resurgent elements in the middle class had been using the prohibition movement as an instrument for reasserting their control over American urban life. In effect, they were willing to use the power of the state to create or sustain a particular conception of community. They had made the intellectual shift from the primarily negative conception of the state prevalent in the nineteenth-century temperance campaigns (the law ought not to *sanction* the liquor trade) to the more positive conception of the state inherent in the prohibition movement (the state ought to *suppress* the manufacture of alcoholic beverages). They had not, however, made the corresponding shift from the religious and absolutistic style of politics characteristic of the nineteenth century to the secular and pluralistic style more typical of the twentieth century. Furthermore, the political pressures generated from within the society by ethnic and other pressure groups constantly threatened to reshape the state and to redirect its power. Hence the frantic drive to place prohibition in the Constitution beyond the reach of mere majority rule.

In the socialist tradition (in Finland and Russia, for example), prohibition was important as a means of social control and as an aspect of cultural nationalism. The willingness of the Bolshevik regime in Russia to continue the Czarist policy of wartime prohibition may have been related to its insecure hold on the country and to its unitary ideological model for society. Also, there was a strong strain of asceticism and "puritanism" in Lenin, as is frequently the case with hard-core revolutionaries. In Finland, prohibition was one more weapon in the arsenal of the working-class lumberjacks, artisans, farm workers, and small farmers in their struggle for power with the bourgeois parties. Even into the 1920s, the Social Democrat and Agrarian parties in Finland persisted in interpreting the prohibition issue in terms of a conflict between the socialistic and pietistic masses and the capitalistic and aristocratic classes. Significantly, these same two parties consistently opposed any attempt to hold a plebiscite on prohibition. Prohibition was one part of the attempt by a worker-farmer alliance to define Finnish culture in its own terms and to impose it upon the rest of the society.[52]

In the comparative perspective, the adoption of prohibition and the extension of women's suffrage during the period between 1910 and 1920 represented interrelated aspects of cultural nationalism. Prohibition was a means of achieving

52. For the antialcohol tradition in socialism, see Ernest Gordon, *The Anti-Alcohol Movement in Europe* (New York: Fleming H. Revell Co., 1913). For the relationship of the Bolsheviks to prohibition as a means of social control, see William Hard, *Raymond Robins' Own Story* (New York: Harper & Row, Publishers, 1920), p. 189. On the temperance bias of Social Democratic and Agrarian legislators, see Marti Noponen and Pertti Pesonen, "The Legislative Career in Finland," in *Cleavages, Ideologies and Party Systems: Contributions to Comparative Political Sociology,* Erik Allardt and Yrjö Littunen, eds. (Helsinki: The Academic Bookstore, 1964), pp. 455-56.

social control; women's suffrage was a means of enhancing social cohesion. Both presumed an identity of interest between "society" and the "state" that was in keeping with current trends of political thought in both socialist and liberal-democratic traditions.[53]

53. An authority on Russian local government has summarized the issue as follows: "The (Russian) empire created a political tradition which revolved around the dichotomy of state and society; the two were considered separate and unequal entities. The basic premise of the Soviet regime's political philosophy has been the identity of state and society. Both regimes apotheosized the state: the empire identified it with the most vital aspects of social welfare, and the Soviet regime equated it with the totality of social life." Alexander Vucinich, "The State and the Local Community," in *The Transformation of Russian Society: Aspects of Social Change Since 1861*, Cyril E. Black, ed. (Cambridge, Mass.: Harvard University Press, 1960), p. 207.

8

Social Control, Equality, and Social Cohesion

PROHIBITION AND WOMEN'S SUFFRAGE: 1920s–1930s

The strands of shared images of woman's role and common tactics that had united women's rights and temperance movements unraveled further in the 1920s and 1930s. The "new woman" wanted freedom from social control, equality with men in moral standards, and an equitable share of the prosperity promised by postwar conditions. As developments along these lines undercut the basis of the Victorian compromise, the old feminism of moral superiority faded and a new feminism was proclaimed. The "flapper," the "emancipated woman," the "new socialist woman" explored new sexual standards, drank cocktails, flaunted convention, or tried to be the ideal revolutionary comrade. The heavy emphasis on economic independence in the women's rights movement and among feminist and socialist thinkers had undercut the primacy of the family.[1] Women could hardly claim to be the moral protectors of the home at the very moment when they were leaving it in massive numbers or when they were being called upon

---

1. By the time women's suffrage achieved its goal, the images of woman that had characterized the formative periods of suffrage thought had either become the ruling orthodoxy of the day or they had been so modified as to accommodate themselves to orthodox fears and stereotypes. The task of articulating new feminist visions and images of woman had fallen to the socialists, the birth control advocates, the new professional women, and the experimental novelists, some of whom maintained a tenuous connection with the suffrage movement.

For the background and progress of these ideological developments in the United States, see Aileen S. Kraditor, *The Ideas of the Woman Suffrage Movement, 1890-1920* (New York: Columbia University Press, 1965), Chapter 3; David M. Kennedy, *Birth Control in America: The Career of Margaret Sanger* (New Haven: Yale University Press, 1970), Chapters 3-5; William L. O'Neill, *Divorce in the Progressive Era* (New Haven: Yale University Press, 1967), Chapters 4, 5; Carl N. Degler, "Charlotte Perkins Gilman on the Theory and Practice of Feminism," *American Quarterly* 8 (Spring 1956): 21-39; Erwin O. Smigel and Rita Seiden, "The Decline and Fall of the Double Standard," *Annals of the American Academy of Political and Social Science* 376 (March 1968): 7-17; Arnold W. Green and Eleanor Melnick, "What Has Happened to the Feminist Movement?" in *Studies in Leadership: Leadership and Democratic Action,* Alvin W. Gouldner, ed. (New York: Harper & Row, Publishers, 1950), pp. 277-302; Kenneth A. Yellis, "Prosperity's Child: Some Thoughts on the Flapper," *American Quarterly* 21 (Spring 1969): 44-64; William L. O'Neill, *Everyone*

to forsake it for the goal of socialist reconstruction. The literary feminism of the interwar period was more private, less programmatic, than the feminism of the 1910s. This trend could be seen in the novels and essays of Virginia Woolf in England, in the novels of Elin Wägner in Sweden and Sigrid Undset and Cora Sandel in Norway, in the poetry of Edith Södergran in Finland and Edna St. Vincent Millay in the United States.[2]

Was Brave: The Rise and Fall of Feminism in America (Chicago: Quadrangle Books, Inc., 1969), Chapters 7-9.

    For developments in Russia relating to socialist feminism and ideology, see H. Kent Geiger, The Family in Soviet Russia (Cambridge, Mass.: Harvard University Press, 1968), Chapters 3, 4; Urie Bronfenbrenner, "The Changing Soviet Family," in The Role and Status of Women in the Soviet Union, Donald R. Brown, ed. (New York: Teachers College Press, 1968), pp. 98-117; Vera Sandomirsky Dunham, "The Strong-Woman Motif," in The Transformation of Russian Society: Aspects of Social Change Since 1861, Cyril E. Black, ed. (Cambridge, Mass.: Harvard University Press, 1960), pp. 459-83; Joan Mellen, "From Revolutionary Feminism to Accommodation," review of Alexandra Kollontai, The Autobiography of a Sexually Emancipated Communist Woman (New York: Herder and Herder, Inc., 1971) in New Politics 9 (No. 3, 1971): 80-86; Jan Gorecki, "Communist Family Pattern: Law as an Implement of Change," The University of Illinois Law Forum 1972 (No. 1, 1972): 121-36.

2. The literary feminism of the 1920s and 1930s must be followed in individual careers. Virginia Woolf's feminist essays and tracts (A Room of One's Own and Three Guineas) reiterated her belief that masculine rationality must be united with feminine intuition in the "androgynous mind" but advocated individualistic solutions to feminist problems. See Herbert Marder, Feminism and Art: A Study of Virginia Woolf (Chicago: The University of Chicago Press, 1968), Chapters 1, 4, 5. For contemporary opinion, see R. Brimley Johnson, Some Contemporary Novelists (Women) (reprint ed., Freeport, N.Y.: Books for Libraries, 1967, orig. ed. 1920), Introduction, Chapter 9.

    The shift in Scandinavian feminism can be seen by comparing the early novels of Sigrid Undset, such as Jenny (1911), or of Elin Wägner, such as Norrtullsligan (The Norrtull Gang, 1908), or Pennskaftet (The Penholder, 1910), with their emphasis on the fate, and feminist solidarity, of working women or women in the "movement," to their novels of the 1920s. Then Sigrid Undset turned to Roman Catholicism and history and Elin Wägner explored humanitarian and pacifistic themes or explored in semiautobiographical works the dissolution of unhappy marriages. Cora Sandel also explored the meaning of growing up female in Norway in a trilogy published in the 1920s and 1930s. See Alrik Gustafson, A History of Swedish Literature (Minneapolis: University of Minnesota Press, 1961), pp. 376-79; Otlu Alsvik, review of Odd Solumsmoen, Cora Sandel, en dikter i ånd og sannhet (Oslo: Aschehoug & Co. [H.], 1957) in Humaniora Norvegica 5 (1957-1958): 287; Harald Beyer, A History of Norwegian Literature, trans. Einar Haugen (New York: New York University Press, 1956), pp. 298-99, 305-8, 320-21, 327.

    The poetry of Edith Södergran, popularized by her friend Hagar Olsson in the magazine Ultra, ranged from a nonpolitical Nietzchian will-to-power to a religious reconciliation with life and death. Her poetry inaugurated a modernist movement in Finland (among the Swedish-speaking population) that ultimately spread to other Scandinavian countries. Nils-Børje Stormbom, "Twentieth Century Swedish Literature in Finland," in Scandinavia Past and Present: Through Revolutions to Liberty, Jørgen Bukdahl et al. (Copenhagen: Arnkrone, 1959), pp. 1112-14; Erik Kihlman, ed., Ur Finlands svenska lyrik: antologi (Stockholm: Björck & Börjesson, 1923), pp. 113-15; 518-25 [Translation from Swedish by Avis Nelson Paulson].

    Edna St. Vincent Millay's reputation as the poet of the "new woman" rested largely on the success of A Few Figs from Thistles (November 1920) with its famous image of the candle burning at both ends. She regarded her work as broader in scope than this work indicated and explored a wide range of themes in the 1920s and 1930s. See Jean Gould, The Poet and Her Book: A Biography of Edna St. Vincent Millay (New York: Dodd, Mead, & Co., 1969), pp. 122-28; 135-36; 159-62; 200-203.

Once the women's suffrage and prohibition movements had achieved their primary goals in the United States and in the Scandinavian countries, they had no political need for each other. The fate of the "noble experiment" (prohibition) in the 1920s and 1930s thus reflected the cross currents of postwar economic developments, social turmoil, and the emergence of new feminist and political ideologies. In Norway, where prohibition had been endorsed by a majority of voters in a plebiscite in 1919, preferential treaties between Norway (a fish-exporting country) and France, Spain, and Portugal (wine-exporting countries) were threatened. Gradually the Norwegian government abandoned its strict prohibition rather than jeopardize its economic stability.[3] A plebiscite in Norway in 1926 showed a complete reversal of opinion. "A comparison of the votes taken

---

3. In Norway, where the number of small farms had *increased* in the decade prior to World War I, support of temperance and prohibition was associated primarily with the pietistic, *landsmål*-speaking (rural language), parochial areas of the South and West and secondarily with urban labor elites. The 1919 referendum on prohibition, coming at a time of war-induced social turmoil, showed the following percentage pattern as compared to the 1926 referendum:

	Cities and Towns:		Rural Communes:	
	For	Against	For	Against
1919	44.5	55.5	70.1	29.9
1926	30.3	69.7	51.7	48.3

The regional variations in the 1926 vote are especially indicative of the sources of strength:

Area	Vote for prohibition	Area	Vote for prohibition
Oslofjord	26.2	South	74.8
East Inland	35.4	West	76.3
North	53.2	Trøndelag	60.8

[Source: Harry Eckstein, *Division and Cohesion in Democracy: A Study of Norway* (Princeton, N.J.: Princeton University Press, 1966), p. 212.]

For the background and interpretation of the prohibition and temperance issue in Norwegian politics in the 1920s, see Stein Rokkan and Henry Valen, "Regional Contrasts in Norwegian Politics: A Review of Data from Official Statistics and from Sample Surveys," in *Cleavages, Ideologies and Party Systems: Contributions to Comparative Political Sociology*, Erik Allardt and Yrjö Littunen, eds. (Helsinki: Academic Bookstore, 1964), pp. 184–86, 188–89, 196, 221; Karen Larsen, *A History of Norway* (Princeton, N.J.: Princeton University Press, 1948), pp. 506, 511, 521; G. Gathorne Hardy, *Norway* (New York: Charles Scribner's Sons, 1925), pp. 303–9.

Women in the rural working-class and small-holder households in the South and West tended to be more involved in religious associations (including temperance), to constitute a high proportion of the labor force, and to resist socialist appeals more than women in other areas. They had probably constituted the base for prohibition votes in these regions. See Rokkan and Valen, pp. 175 n. and 188.

In Iceland, prohibition had also been endorsed in a popular poll in 1908 and took effect in 1912. Similar problems were encountered in the 1920s as in Norway. Spain forced a modification of the prohibition law (to allow the importation of wine) by threatening to ban the importation of Icelandic codfish. In the 1920s reinstatement of full prohibition was supported in Iceland by the clergy, the Women's Franchise League, the National Union of Teachers, and the Socialist party. Ernest H. Cherrington, et al., eds., *Standard Encyclopedia of the Alcohol Problem* (Westerville, O.: American Issue Publishing Company, 1927-1930), 3: 1280–81 [hereinafter cited as Cherrington, *SEAP*].

In Sweden, a referendum on prohibition was held on August 27, 1922. The official vote was 886,232 for prohibition and 922,122 against prohibition. Observers noted that the women of Stockholm, Goteborg, and Malmö, the largest cities, had voted heavily against

in the two plebiscites shows that a smaller proportion of women participated in the 1926 plebiscite than in the 1919 plebiscite, which indicates that many of the women had lost interest in the controversy. There was also a marked decrease in the rural vote for prohibition."[4]

In Finland, where the career of prohibition paralleled that of the United States, the changing attitudes of women were revealed in a unique referendum on prohibition held in 1931. Women's votes were cast on red ballots, men's on white ballots. Only 44 percent of the electorate bothered to declare their opinions (52.2 percent of the men; 37.2 percent of the women). "The number of votes cast for the continuation of prohibition was 217,208. Of this total, the vote of the women was somewhat more than one half, or 115,684. Modification obtained only 10,947 votes, of which 4,914 were cast by women. Outright repeal found favor with 546,332 voters, of whom 226,820 were women." Political observers were startled to note that "the number of women favoring repeal was considerably greater than the total vote in favor of prohibition."[5]

---

prohibition. The failure of the referendum split the Liberal party into its component elements. The urban liberals (rationalistic, secular, and antiprohibition) formed the *Sveriges Liberala* party; the rural liberals (pacifistic, religious, pietistic, and prohibitionist) supported the *Frisinnade folkpartiet*. The percentage of the vote received by the prohibitionist Liberals declined in the 1920s from 13 percent in 1924 to 9.8 percent in 1932. In 1923 some liberal women attempted to enter a "women's list" in the general elections but the results were disappointing. A separate women's party was formed in Stockholm in 1926 but received only .6 percent of the vote, mainly from salaried women. Sources: Cherrington, *SEAP*, 6: 2566; Dankwart A. Rustow, *The Politics of Compromise: A Study of Parties and Cabinet Government in Sweden* (Princeton, N.J.: Princeton University Press, 1955), pp. 86-87, 241; Jarl Torbacke, "Kvinnolistan 1927-1928—ett kvinnopolitiskt fiasko," *Historisk tidskrift* 89 (No. 2, 1969): 145-84.

4. Association Against the Prohibition Amendment, *Norway's Noble Experiment* (Washington, D.C.: Association Against the Prohibition Amendment, 1931), p. 16.

5. John H. Wuorinen, "Finland's Prohibition Experiment," *Annals of the American Academy of Political and Social Sciences* 163 (September 1932): 223. For a more detailed account, see John H. Wuorinen, *The Prohibition Experiment in Finland* (New York: Columbia University Press, 1931). In the latter work, Wuorinen noted that prohibition in the 1920s was strongly supported by the Social Democratic and Agrarian parties. These two parties constituted a majority in every *lantdag* between 1919 and 1929 (except for 1922) and opposed a referendum (pp. 171-173). The National Progressive party (representing the forces of liberalism) supported the idea of a referendum as did the National Coalition party (representing the conservative Finnish-speaking population). The Swedish-speaking minority constituted a conservative, upper-class elite with disproportionate economic power. They opposed prohibition and advocated moral suasion rather than legal coercion in dealing with intemperance. Political scientists have discovered that Swedish-speaking women in Finland have a higher rate of voting turnout than Finnish men and that predominately Swedish-speaking voting districts (over 75 percent Swedish-speaking) have a consistently higher rate of voter turnout than predominately Finnish-speaking or mixed districts. Thus, the probability is that Swedish-speaking women played a key role in the antiprohibition vote. See Seymour M. Lipset, *Political Man: The Social Bases of Politics* (New York: Doubleday & Company, Inc., 1960), pp. 199-207; Wuorinen, *Prohibition Experiment in Finland*, pp. 192-198. On the other side of the issue, recent studies have shown that in Finland politics have been more class based than in Norway or Sweden. The Social Democratic party interpreted the prohibition problem in class struggle terms in the 1920s and appealed to class solidarity. They

| In the United States, the declining support of prohibition among women was indicated by the changing fortunes of the leading prohibition organizations. Sociologist Joseph Gusfield, in his study of the WCTU, has found that "between 1925 and 1950 the local leadership of the WCTU changed in its social characteristics. The percentage of women from upper middle-class background declined while the percentage from lower middle- and lower-class backgrounds increased."[6] Upper middle-class women activists and socially prominent women opinion molders gravitated to the Association Against the Prohibition Amendment and its Woman's Organization for Repeal of National Prohibition, to the Women's Organization for National Prohibition Reform, or to the League of Women Voters. Financial scandals plagued the Anti-Saloon League in the 1920s and discredited its claims of moral superiority and public confidence. Even the Federal Council of Churches, which had endorsed the prohibition movement and urged compliance with the law, soon diminished its support for prohibition. Social work offered an appealing field for feminine idealism in the 1920s and, even as late as 1928, social workers found it hard to repudiate prohibition. Yet by the time of the Great Depression, the forces of antiprohibition repeal, women's rights, and social welfare could be found in the same New Deal coalition.[7]

Prohibition was occasionally found in conjunction with advances in

were hindered by left-wing splits in the 1920s and by official repression of the Communists. Since the Social Democrats nominated more women candidates for the *lantdag* than any other party, anything that reduced their support would also reduce the role of women in political life. In 1919 the Social Democrats drew 38 percent of the vote; in 1922, following a left wing (Communist) split, their percentage fell to 25 percent and did not reach 30 percent again until 1930. Also, the percentage of *all* women voting fell from 65 percent in 1919 to 52–54 percent during the 1920s and did not exceed 60 percent until after 1930. See Jaakko Nousianinen, *The Finnish Political System,* trans. John H. Hodgson (Cambridge, Mass.: Harvard University Press, 1971), pp. 40–41, 175–77; Erik Allardt, "Patterns of Class Conflict and Working Class Consciousness in Finnish Politics," in *Cleavages, Ideologies and Party Systems: Contributions to Comparative Political Sociology,* Erik Allardt and Yrjö Littunen, eds. (Helsinki: The Academic Bookstore, 1964), pp. 97–131; Wuorinen, *Prohibition Experiment in Finland,* p. 171.

6. Joseph R. Gusfield, *Symbolic Crusade: Status Politics and the American Temperance Movement* (Urbana: University of Illinois Press, 1963), pp. 129 (quotation)-130 (tables).

7. John C. Gebhart, "Movement Against Prohibition," *Annals of the American Academy of Political and Social Science* 163 (September 1932): 174, 177; Raymond G. McCarthy and Edgar M. Douglass, "Prohibition and Repeal," in *Drinking and Intoxication: Selected Readings in Social Attitudes and Controls,* Raymond G. McCarthy, ed. (New York: The Free Press, 1959), pp. 379-80; Peter H. Odegard, *Pressure Politics: The Story of the Anti-Saloon League* (New York: Columbia University Press, 1928), pp. 236-40; Donald B. Meyer, *The Protestant Search for Political Realism, 1919-1941* (Berkeley: University of California Press, 1961), pp. 11-12, 118-29, 178-79; Paul Carter, *The Twenties in America* (New York: Thomas Y. Crowell Company, 1968), p. 69.
    The above interpretation is not meant to imply that declining female support was the primary cause of the repeal of prohibition. For the many complicated factors involved in the failure of prohibition and the causes of repeal, see Carter, *The Twenties in America,* Chapter 3; Charles Merz, *The Dry Decade* (New York: Doubleday & Company, Inc., 1931); Kenneth Allsop, *The Bootleggers and Their Era* (New York: Doubleday & Company, Inc., 1961).

women's rights in the 1920s in those countries where the need for social control
or the demands of cultural nationalism were temporarily predominate. In Russia,
for example, the Bolsheviks confronted the turmoil of postwar depressions,
civil war, and massive social experimentation. They continued the wartime prohibition policy as part of their "War Communism," 1918–1921. They hoped that
such a policy would not only save grain but that it would benefit the workers as
well as maintain public order. But the peasants converted their surplus grain into
home-brewed vodka and sold it on the black market to the city dwellers. Finally,
between 1921 and 1925, under the so-called New Economic Policy, the government abandoned prohibition and reinstituted the prewar policy of a government-
owned monopoly for the production and distribution of wine, beer, and vodka.
At the same time, the Bolsheviks had embarked on an ambitious experiment
in family law and women's rights. The family code of 1918 and various decrees
abolished inheritance and community property, established divorce by mutual
consent, gave judicial recognition to free unions ("common law" marriage in
Western terms), permitted abortions, and made marriage a civil rather than
religious act. But ideological ambiguities about the meaning of sexual freedom
in the Marx-Engels canon contributed to a period of instability in sexual patterns
of behavior not unlike the simultaneous "revolt of youth" in the western countries. However, the equal obligation to labor, coupled with the failure of the
soviet regime to provide adequate day care and communal facilities, meant
that the women had to bear a double burden while some of the men "went off
whistling" (in the Russian phrase) and left the state to bear the expense of caring
for their children. Gradually the courts reinstated some former practices, the
theoreticians repudiated "free love" ideas, and family laws and policies were reversed in the 1930s. The conjunction of prohibition and women's rights was thus
partly fortuitous and, except for a few highly placed women Communists such as
Alexandra Kollontai and Lenin's widow, Krupskaya, the bulk of the women had
little influence on the developments.[8]

---

8. Joseph Barnes, "Liquor Regulation in Russia," *Annals of the American Academy of
Political and Social Science* 163 (September 1932): 227-33; Edward Hallett Carr, *A History
of Soviet Russia* (New York: The Macmillan Company, 1951-1964), 5: 465-68. Stalin defended the reintroduction of the vodka monopoly on the grounds that it was better to raise
capital internally by such means than to borrow from foreign capitalists. Krupskaya was
critical of the move and helped to bring about a reduction of production in the late 1920s.
For the sources on women and the family in Russia in the 1920s and 1930s, see the sources
listed in footnote number 1 of this chapter. The Constitution of the Russian Socialist Federated Soviet Republic, adopted in July 1918, established equal suffrage for both sexes over
eighteen in the selection of delegates to local soviets but weighted representation in favor of
urban areas. A new constitution was adopted in 1923-1924 creating the Union of Socialist
Soviet Republics. Suffrage qualifications were largely unchanged, but increasing one-party
rule rendered them meaningless in the Western political sense of choice among opposing
parties or candidates. Some mobility for Communist women was provided by the International Women's Secretariat of the Communist International (1920-1926). Sidney Harcare,
Russia: A History, 4th ed. (Philadelphia: J. B. Lippincott Co., 1959), pp. 501, 535; Edward
Hallett Carr, *A History of Soviet Russia,* 7: 976-86.

Turkey also confronted revolution, foreign intervention, and civil war in the 1920s. The nationalist movement was pulled in one direction by the Islamic heritage of its past and in another by the westernizing ideas of its leader Mustafa Kemal (Atatürk) and some of the leading feminists: Eminé Semie Hanum, a revolutionary nationalist; Halidé Edjb, a journalist; Nakie Hanum, an educator, and Latife Hanum, Kemal's wife. In September 1920, the first nationalistic Grand National Assembly adopted prohibition of the import and general sale of liquor. Kemal, a hard-drinking professional soldier, personally ignored the law but did not overrule the strict Moslem deputies. Over the next four years the prohibition was extended as the nationalists gained increasing control of the country. With the proclamation of a republic in 1923, Kermal emerged as un-disputed leader and moved the country in a more secular, Western direction. Prohibition was abolished in 1924, in spite of protests by the Green Crescent Temperance Society, and a strict license law was adopted and a government mo-nopoly established. Kemal's personal support of reforms for women and pressure from women's groups brought about significant changes in the marriage laws (Civil Code of 1926), educational opportunities, and economic prospects of women. The mere mention of the possibility that women would be included in the census for representation under a new electoral law had brought the Assembly into an uproar in 1923, yet within a decade Kemal had, through dictatorial con-trol of his party and the government, brought in women's suffrage. Women voted for the first time in the national elections in February 1935, and helped to elect seventeen women to the Grand National Assembly. Thus only the driving force of Kemal's leadership and the religious base of a common cultural nationalism held together the divergent tendencies of traditionalist prohibitionism and modernist feminism, women's rights, and suffragism.[9]

India had similar problems in reconciling traditional, religious prohibition with modern, secular feminism. While England had tried to rule its portion of India without disturbing local customs in the nineteenth century, the impact of English economic policies had undermined the old village economy and had transformed the Indian economy into that of a market for English manufactures and a source of raw material for English factories. The gradual introduction of the English legal system (with its principle of equality before the law) and of English-language education and public administration also began the long process

---

9. Lord Kinross, *Atatürk: A Biography of Mustafa Kemal, Father of Modern Turkey* (New York: William Morrow and Company, Inc., 1965), pp. 299, 311-12, 390-91, 419-20, and Chapter 51; Donald Everett Webster, *The Turkey of Atatürk: Social Process in the Turkish Reformation* (Philadelphia: The American Academy of Political and Social Science, 1939), pp. 30-31, 110-11; Cherrington, *SEAP*, 6: 2685-87; Margaret Smith, "The Women's Move-ment in the Near and Middle East," *Asian Review* 24 (April 1928): 188-92.

For additional information on the women's movement, see Vahan Cardashian, "The Feminist Agitation in Turkey," *Travel* 23 (March 1914): 26-27; Beatrice Hill Ogilvie, "The New Woman of Turkey," *The Current History Magazine* 20 (August 1924): 805-13; Ruth Frances Woodsmall, *Moslem Women Enter a New World* (New York: Round Table Press, Inc., 1936); Daniel Lerner and Lucille W. Pevsner, *The Passing of Traditional Society: Modernizing the Middle East* (New York: The Free Press, 1958), Chapters 4, 5.

of modifying the Indian legal system (with its principle of hierarchical caste law) and introduced Western ideas of liberal reform. Christian missionaries, insisting that all souls were equally valuable in the sight of God, introduced pioneering educational ventures for women. Traditional Hindu social structure had confined men and women into tribes, castes, and subcastes with little chance for individual social mobility in the Western sense. While the village system provided security, stability, and customary protections, the law—both customary and written—condoned a number of practices that degraded women.[10]

Since the main thrust of both traditional Hindu society and British colonial rule was in the direction of inequality of status and hierarchical relationships, the growth of modern political nationalism (which rests on the essential equality of citizenship) had come from religious reform movements (both Hindu and Christian) that advocated a root moral worth (or equality) of all people or religions and from English-educated elites seeking to realize the egalitarian premises of English liberalism. When these formative influences were combined with a rediscovery of India's past and a renaissance of cultural nationalism, the Indian National Congress (the vehicle of political nationalism) assumed a more militant and aggressive stand. The British colonial bureaucrats and the politicians

---

10. For the impact of English concepts of legal equality on traditional Hindu law, see René David and John E. C. Brierly, *Major Legal Systems in the World Today: An Introduction to the Comparative Study of Law* (London: Collier-Macmillan, Ltd., 1968), pp. 411-39; Lloyd I. Rudolph and Susanne Hoeber Rudolph, *The Modernity of Tradition: Political Development in India* (Chicago: The University of Chicago Press, 1967), Part 3; Marc Galanter, "The Problem of Group Membership: Some Reflections on the Judicial View of Indian Society," in *Class, Status, and Power: Social Stratification in Comparative Perspective,* 2nd ed., Reinhard Bendix and Seymour Martin Lipset, eds. (New York: The Free Press, 1966), pp. 628-40; Bernard S. Cohn, "From Indian Status to British Contract," *Journal of Economic History* 21 (December 1961): 613-28.

For the economic aspects of equality and the impact of English rule, see W. H. Moreland and Atul Chandra Chatterjee, *A Short History of India,* 4th ed. (New York: David McKay Co., Inc., 1962), Chapter 44; Morris David Morris and Burton Stein, "The Economic History of India: A bibliographic essay," *Journal of Economic History* 21 (June 1961): 179-207; A. R. Desai, *Social Background of Indian Nationalism* (Bombay: Oxford University Press, Indian Branch, 1948), Chapters 3, 4, 7.

On the status of women in traditional Hindu society and attempts at reform in the late nineteenth and early twentieth century, see Pandharinath H. Prabhu, *Hindu Social Organization: A Study in Socio-Psychological and Ideological Foundations,* 4th ed. (Bombay: Popular Prakashan, 1963), Chapter 7; R. C. Majumdar, *The History and Culture of the Indian People* (Bombay: Bharatiya Vidya Bhavan, 1965), Vol. 10, *British Paramountcy and Indian Renaissance,* Part 2: 260-92; Desai, *Social Background,* Chapter 16.

Recent scholarship has shown that social mobility in India was primarily by groups, rather than individuals, and operated through the process of Sanskritization (the acceptance of Hindu tradition and emulation of higher castes). See M. N. Srinivas, "Mobility in the Caste System," in *Structure and Change in Indian Society,* Milton Singer and Bernard S. Cohn, eds. (Chicago: Aldine-Atherton, Inc., 1968), pp. 189-99; M. N. Srinivas, *Social Change in Modern India* (Berkeley: University of California Press, 1967), Chapters 1, 3.

I am indebted to Professor Ralph Radloff, Augustana College, for help in understanding the position of women in Hindu society. The focus on Hindu society in this chapter should not obscure the simultaneous problems in Muslim communities of India or deny the important role of the Muslim League in the nationalist movement. Since the purpose of this section was to deal with Gandhi's role, the concentration on Hindu culture was necessary to clarify the issues involved.

in London had attempted to curtail nationalist aspirations by strengthening imperial control through constitutional reforms. The 1909 Morley-Minto scheme (named after the Secretary of State for India, John Morley, and the Viceroy, Lord Minto) was designed to represent "interests," not individuals or territories, and thus to bind the "natural" oligarchies to the preservation of the government. But the cross-pressures of continued nationalist agitation and wartime support of the British Empire reopened the question of constitutional reform and, hence, of the relationship between traditional communities and customs (such as prohibition) and modernizing "collectives" and political rights (such as women's rights and franchise).[11] It was a question, in short, of the basis of community, the nature of social cohesion, and the means of achieving social control all in one.

The intricate relationship between prohibition, women's rights and women's suffrage, and nationalism was dramatically illustrated by events in India in the 1920s. In August 1917, the British cabinet had attempted to spell out its goals for India: "the increasing association of Indians in every branch of the administration and the gradual development of self-governing institutions with a view to the progressive realisation of responsible government in India as an integral part of the British Empire."[12]

The Secretary of State for India, E. S. Montagu, conferred in India with the Viceroy, Lord Chelmsford, on the details of the proposed changes. A delegation of women nationalists and suffragists had presented a memorandum to

---

11. Dietmar Rothermund, "Emancipation or Re-integration. The Politics of Gopal Krishna Gokhale and Herbert Hope Risley," in *Soundings in Modern South Asian History*, D. A. Low, ed. (Berkeley: University of California Press, 1968), pp. 131-58. Rothermund concisely summed up the issue as follows:

"The terms integration and emancipation may indicate in a more comprehensive manner the alternatives of social organization . . . . The role of an individual in an integrated system is determined by a code of conduct which provides him with a well-defined identity at every stage and station of life. The Indian system of *varnashramadharma* which regulates the duty (*dharma*) of every man according to his caste (*varna*) and age-grade (*ashrama*) is an ideal example of integration . . . . In an emancipated society, however, the authority exercised by an individual may concern only one of his many identities, e.g., his roles as a father, a citizen, an employee, etc., are distinct and compartmentalised. From this it follows that there will be different codes of conduct for different roles. In the field of public authority this means the rule of law and not of men, which may nevertheless manifest itself in a rule of men who represent the law, i.e. the bureaucrat and the elected representative" (pp. 132–33).

Thus prohibition would be an aspect of integration; women's suffrage an aspect of emancipation. The constitutional issue was whether the British colonial government could reintegrate society by basing representation on traditional communities or whether the nationalists could create a new basis of society by a secular emancipation (freeing of individuals) based on equal citizenship and representation.

On the relationship between religious reform, education, and nationalism, see Charles H. Heimsath, *Indian Nationalism and Hindu Social Reform* (Princeton, N.J.: Princeton University Press, 1964); Anil Seal, *The Emergence of Indian Nationalism: Competition and Collaboration in the Later Nineteenth Century* (London: Cambridge University Press, 1968).

12. R. Coupland, *The Indian Problem: Report on the Constitutional Problem in India* (London: Oxford University Press, 1944), 1: 52.

Mr. Montagu, demanding the vote for women, but the colonial officials were wary of the issue. The Montagu-Chelmsford report of 1918 (embodied in the Government of India Act of 1919) left the issue of women's suffrage to the Indian provincial legislatures for decision as a domestic matter.[13]

The Montagu-Chelmsford report had also placed prohibition and liquor control on the list of "transferred powers" to be given over to the legislative councils of the provincial governments. This move was subsequently criticized for placing the prohibition issue in the hands of high-caste Hindus and wealthy Muslims, who were opposed to drinking. This discriminated against "the working classes, the low castes, and aboriginal and backward classes" who did most of the drinking or who were involved in illegal distillation. In attempting to defer to the realities of the Indian caste and class system, the Montagu-Chelmsford report offended both the nationalists' desire for modernization and the civil service bureaucrats' desire for administrative efficiency.[14]

Both the critics and supporters of the Montagu-Chelmsford plan reckoned without Gandhi, for Gandhi was the personification of the ideals of the new India; the Indian National Congress his chosen instrument of reform. Just as the Declaration of Independence is the touchstone of American ideals of equality, so Gandhi is the epitome of Indian idealism. Deeply religious, shrewdly practical, slightly quixotic, he made the spinning wheel and hand-woven cloth symbols of

---

13. Hannah Sen, "Our Own Times," in *Women in India,* Tara Ali Baig, ed. (Delhi: Ministry of Information and Broadcasting, 1958), p. 35. The women's suffrage supporters included a number of women of Anglo-Irish background who had participated in the Irish Home Rule agitation: Margaret Noble (known as Sister Nivedita), Margaret Cousins, and Annie Besant (a former Fabian socialist). Annie Besant, a leader of the Theosophy movement, had advocated universal suffrage for the local *panchayats* (local village or caste councils) in 1915 and had established the All-India Home Rule League in 1916 to outmaneuver moderate elements in the Indian National Congress. The government had interned her in 1917. When she was released from detention, she was a martyr figure for the nationalists and was elected president of the Congress. The women's deputation to Montagu and Chelmsford thus put women's suffrage in a strong nationalist context. Sarojini Naidu, an Indian woman nationalist, was spokeswoman for the deputation. See Hannah Sen, "Our Own Times," pp. 33-36; H. F. Owen, "Towards Nation-Wide Agitation and Organization: The Home Rule Leagues, 1915-18," in *Soundings in Modern South Asian History,* D. A. Low, ed. (Berkeley: University of California Press, 1968), pp. 159-95.

The Montagu-Chelmsford report had attempted to undercut the basis of suffrage arguments by pointing out that only 11 percent of the men and 1.1 percent of the women in British India were literate enough to read or write a letter. Coupland, *The Indian Problem,* 1:55.

The Government of India Act (1919) established the following criteria for voting in provincial elections: Male British subjects over 21 years of age with 12 months' residency and either payment of municipal taxes, annual rental, or income tax of specified amounts (urban constituencies) or ownership of agricultural land of specified value. It further stipulated: "Women (or any class of women), possessing the necessary qualifications otherwise, may be admitted to registration as electors by resolution of the legislative body concerned, . . ." E. A. Horne, *The Political System of British India* (London: Oxford University Press, 1922), p. 109 n.2.

14. F. Slocock, "Prohibition in India: A Sidelight on the Working of the Montagu-Chelmsford Scheme," *English Review* 59 (December 1934): 696-701.

the Indian quest for freedom from foreign domination through a cultivation of self-reliance, mutual aid, and mutual forbearance. He made women partners in his quest and thereby insured their rights in the new India.

Gandhi cultivated the support of women, sent them out to picket liquor shops, and set them to looming homemade fabrics to replace imported textiles in India. "For his village audiences he hit on a visual aid. Holding up his left hand with fingers outspread, he would check them off with his right forefinger. 'This is equality for Untouchables; this is spinning; this is keeping off drink and drugs; this is Hindu-Muslim friendship; this is equality for women. And the wrist is non-violence.'"[15] But the masses were not trained for nonviolent noncooperation, and violence erupted in 1921. Gandhi was imprisoned in 1922 and the Swaraj (Home Rule) movement temporarily abated. But Gandhi had brought the women into the Congress as supporters, delegates, and sources of funds for the nationalist movement.[16]

Between 1923 and 1926 some Congress members broke with Gandhi's non-cooperation program and began to stand for election to the legislative councils in the provinces under the name of the Swaraj party. The councils, which had been controlled by liberals or moderates, enacted a series of laws designed to implement their "transferred" powers. Women's suffrage was adopted in relatively quick order in United Provinces (1923), Assam (1924), Bengal (1925), Central Provinces (1926), Madras (1926), and the Punjab (1926).[17]

In 1921, the legislative council of the Central Provinces had demanded that the minister in charge of excises institute complete prohibition by withdrawing licenses, raising taxes, and reducing illegal liquor trade. While this program did reduce consumption somewhat, it also increased illegal distillation; and imprisonment rates rose alarmingly. However, it was not until after the passage of the Government of India Act in 1935 that the Congress could implement its

15. Geoffrey Ashe, *Gandhi* (New York: Stein and Day, Publishers, 1968), p. 243. For the role of women and temperance in Gandhi's activities in the early 1920s, see pages 211, 220, 272, 289, 295. For a psychoanalytic approach to Gandhi, see Erik H. Erikson, *Gandhi's Truth: On the Origins of Militant Nonviolence* (New York: W. W. Norton & Company, Inc., 1969).

16. Gopal Krishna, "The Development of the Indian National Congress as a Mass Organization, 1918-1923," in *Modern India: An Interpretive Anthology,* Thomas R. Metcalf, ed. (London: Collier-Macmillan Limited, 1971), pp. 264-68. The number of women delegates reached a high of 144 in 1921 and constituted 3 percent of the annual Congress; 12 women served on the All-India Congress Committee (the Parliament of the movement) in 1922.

17. B. M. Sharma, *The Republic of India: Constitution and Government* (New York: Asia Publishing House, 1966), p. 39 n.18. The situation in Madras was somewhat unique. The non-Brahmin (anti-Congress) Justice party won the election in 1920 and dominated the legislature. A resolution concerning women's enfranchisement passed the Madras Assembly in April 1921, but failed to achieve enactment in the Council. Significantly, women's suffrage was achieved after the decline of the Justice party in 1925 and the emergence of the Swaraj (pro-Congress) party. See Eugene F. Irschick, *Politics and Social Conflict in South India: The Non-Brahman Movement and Tamil Separatism, 1916–1929* (Berkeley: University of California Press, 1969), pp. 172–81, 311–25; R. C. Majumdar, ed., *The History and Culture of the Indian People* (Bombay: Bharatiya Vidya Bhavan, 1951–1969), 11: 384.

Gandhian pledge of prohibition on a widespread scale. In 1938–39, prohibition was established in parts of Madras, Ahmedabad, Bombay, and other scattered areas under Congress control. The outbreak of war, the resignation of Congress ministries in 1939, and the outlawing of the Congress party during World War II interrupted further progress in these lines until after independence.[18]

In the area of women's suffrage, the Congress leaders had pressed for further extensions in the 1928 Nehru report and in the 1930–31 Round Table Conferences in London. At the same time, the Simon Commission (1929) recommended an increase in the ratio of women voters. A franchise committee under Lord Lothian visited India in 1932 in preparation for the third Round Table Conference in November 1932. From these deliberations came the Government of India Act (1935) which increased the adult electorate from 2 percent of the total population to approximately 10 percent. Whereas only 315,000 women had enjoyed the franchise under the 1919 act, more than 6 million were enfranchised by the 1935 act. In addition, women "were allotted 6 seats out of a total of 156 reserved for British India in the Federal Council of State and 9 out of a total of 250 so reserved in the Federal Assembly. So far as Provincial Assemblies were concerned, women had reserved to them 8 seats in Madras, 6 in Bombay, 5 in Bengal, 6 in the United Provinces, 4 in the Punjab, 4 in Bihār, 3 in the Central Provinces and Berar, 1 in Assam, 2 in Orissa and 2 in Sind."[19] The use of reserved seats and special communal electorates based on religion represented a deviation from the egalitarian premise of nationalistic suffrage (one citizen = one vote). However, they were necessary to accommodate democracy to the realities of Indian social structure and religious diversity. They provided some protection of minority rights as against the "tyranny of the majority" and thus fulfilled the same role in India as proportional representation had played in European and Scandinavian franchise schemes.

Gandhi had helped to expand the social reform aspects of the Congress movement. With the support of the educated elites in the Indian Civil Service

---

18. Slocock, *English Review* 59 (December 1934): 696-97; T. A. Raman, "Prohibition Campaign in India: Congress Declares a Moral War," *Great Britain and the East* 50 (January 20, 1938): 69; E. A. Mackenzie-Bell, "The Economics of Prohibition," *Great Britain and the East* 52 (April 6, 1939): 389-91; "Prohibition Policy in Bombay," *Great Britain and the East* 52 (April 13, 1939): 420; R. Coupland, *The Indian Problem,* 2: 141-43.

Prohibition in Bombay brought protests from the Parsi community (Zoroastrians descended from Persian refugees) which controlled the licenses for distillation of palm "toddy" and the distribution of liquor to the tourist trade. To make up for lost excise revenue, the Congress ministry imposed an urban real estate tax. This, in turn, angered the Moslem religious foundations that invested in land. Serious disorders in August 1939 resulted in casualties and the proclamation of a curfew. Thus an experiment in social control threatened the social cohesion of the community that Gandhi was trying to turn into a nation. E. A. MacKenzie-Bell, *Great Britain and the East* 52 (April 6, 1939): 391; 53 (August 10, 1939): 144.

19. R. C. Majumdar, H. C. Raychaudhuri, and Kalikinkar Datta, *An Advanced History of India,* 3rd ed. (New York: St. Martin's Press, Inc., 1967), pp. 954-55. For the background and details of the Government of India Act [1935], see Coupland, *The Indian Problem,* I: Chapters 7, 8, 9, 10; Sharma, *The Republic of India,* Chapter 24.

and backed by the political power of women voters, the women's rights cause made considerable progress in the 1920s and 1930s. A Women's Indian Association was started in Madras in 1923; a Birth Control League in Bombay in 1924. A Civil Marriage Act (restricted to Hindus) was defeated in 1922 and passed in a modified form in 1923, but bills to establish monogamy and divorce were less successful. The most significant gains were registered in education where, between 1921 and Independence, the number of girls and women in the schools and colleges trebled while the number of boys and men doubled in the same time period. Summing up the cumulative effect of these changes (and the impact of World War II), a noted Indian historian has observed: "The abolition of *purdah*, free social intercourse between men and women, co-education, use of public transports along with men, increase in marriageable age of boys and girls, and practical monogamy of men—these and many other revolutionary changes were carried out almost imperceptibly and without any protest."[20]

What held together the various aspects of women's rights, women's suffrage, temperance, and prohibition was Gandhi's vision of India's future. Indian society would be reconstituted on the basis of self-sufficient peasant villages; revived physically and spiritually on the basis of prohibition of opium and alcohol (social control), the abolition of untouchable caste status and the elevation of women (equality), and the teaching of a common language, Hindi, in an atmosphere of Hindu-Muslim trust (social cohesion); and redirected from a deadening emulation of Western materialism toward a quickening exemplification of Eastern mutalism. Gandhi's vision was not the only one that stirred the nationalists, however. A more secular, rationalistic, and modernist vision was proclaimed in the 1920s and 1930s by Jawaharlal Nehru. Combining British scepticism, secularism, and humanism with Marxian socialism (and a belated appreciation of India's past), Nehru moved the nationalist movement toward an acceptance of industrialism, socialism, and the trappings of a modern state. Both conceptions were institutionalized in the Constitution of 1950 that proclaimed independent India to be a secular, national state. Since the achievement of Independence, some aspects of the Gandhian legacy have been tried and found wanting (such as the gradual abandonment of prohibition) but other aspects have flourished (such as the enhanced role of women and the functioning of mass democracy). The total Gandhian vision remains, however, as a legacy from the past and is periodically rediscovered by Indian intellectuals, politicians, and spiritual leaders.[21]

---

20. Majumdar, Raychaudhuri, and Datta, *Advanced History of India,* pp. 953-56; George Rosen, *Democracy and Economic Change in India* (Berkeley: University of California Press, 1966), pp. 54, 60, 63; Majumdar, *History and Culture of the Indian People,* 11: 999 (quotation).

21. Donald Eugene Smith, *India as a Secular State* (Princeton, N.J.: Princeton University Press, 1963), Chapters 3, 4, 5; Milton Singer, *When a Great Tradition Modernizes: An Anthropological Approach to Indian Civilization* (New York: Praeger Publishers, Inc., 1972), Chapters 7, 8; Barrington Moore, Jr., *Social Origins of Dictatorship and Democracy: Lord and Peasant in the Making of the Modern World* (Boston: Beacon Press, 1966), pp. 370-78; Donald Eugene Smith, *Nehru and Democracy: The Political Thought of an Asian Democrat* (Bombay: Orient Longmans Private Ltd., 1958), Chapters 5, 6, 7; M. N. Das, *The Political*

CONCLUSION

In the perspective of history, the interrelated factors of feminism, women's rights, and women's suffrage, and the correlated movements for temperance, total abstinence, and prohibition, had represented separate aspects of the search for equality and for democratic social control in the accommodation of traditional social and political structures to the imperatives of industrialization, urbanization, and modernization. During the hundred years between the political revolutions and economic upheavals of the 1830s and the nationalistic developments and post-war adjustments of the 1920s and 1930s, the two streams had flowed together, intermingled, and then separated again. Comparative analysis has revealed that certain landmarks stood out above the wreckage left by the floodtides of historical forces. Like rocks polished by the rushing waters, each factor revealed hidden flaws and unexpected facets.

Temperance, for example, was primarily a socio-cultural phenomenon. The root cause behind the temperance movement in the early nineteenth century was the problem of drunkenness, of public disorder, that emerged from the conflict of groups, races, and classes that accompanied social change in the United States, England, and the Scandinavian countries. Folk cultures characterized by strict social hierarchies and rigid social norms have traditionally ritualized drunkenness into periodic festivals or permissible occasions (births, marriages, deaths, athletic or military victories) when the normal rules of behavior and social roles were temporarily suspended. But the drunkenness of the early nineteenth century, whether related to the technological innovations that increased the supply of intoxicants, the trade policies of financially pressed governments, the dislocations of growing urban centers, or the disintegration of traditional rural life, seemed random in incidence, uncontrolled in intensity, and persistent in duration. Drunkenness was defined as a moral failing, a willful departure from that mutually supporting discipline that enhances community and minimizes disharmony. Those religious groups that emphasized personal responsibility for actions and the ability through right conduct (pietism) to overcome moral weakness took the lead in the temperance movement.

Philosophy of Jawaharlal Nehru (New York: The John Day Company, Inc., 1961), Chapters 1, 3, 5.

The Indian Constitution of 1950 contained a "directive principle" calling for "prohibition of intoxicating drinks and drugs," but left enactment of legislation to the states. Only three states adopted total prohibition (Maharashtra, Madras, and Gujarat) while ten adopted partial prohibition; however, no more than a third of India's districts were dry by the middle of the 1960s. A reaction against prohibition set in after the mid-1960s until only Madras and Gujarat remained strictly dry. See Thomas F. Brady, "Noble Experiment, Indian Style," *New York Times Magazine*, February 16, 1964, pp. 24-34; *New York Times*, August 10, 1967, p. 22, col. 8; *New York Times*, August 13, 1972, p. 13, col. 8.

For the status of women's rights in India, see Khushwant Singh, "The Women of India," *New York Times Magazine*, March 13, 1966, pp. 24-42; S. R. Venkataraman, "Social Development in India, 1947-1966," in *India: Studies in Social and Political Development, 1947-1967*, A. Appadorai, ed. (New York: Asia Publishing House, Inc., 1968), pp. 3-33.

The problem that confronted the early temperance advocates was how to inculcate discipline in the absence or failure of traditional, organic means of reinforcing it. How, in short, to create new structures of moral order. For the temperance leaders, there were only two options: either everyone exercised *self-discipline* and thus obviated the need for state action, or the majority through the democratic processes available should cause the state to withhold or exercise its power of *social discipline* over all, particularly over those groups which the majority regarded as being "in" but not "of" the society (Indians, slaves, and occasionally immigrants). If the physiological and psychological causes of chronic drunkenness (alcoholism) were little understood, the approximate behavioral and sociological conditions that seemed to lead to it were highly visible and easily identifiable. By abstaining from drinking *any* intoxicating beverage and by avoiding any place that served them, the teetotaler was practicing that self-willed freedom that was deemed a prerequisite to the maintenance of moral order. In practical terms, such self-discipline might facilitate social mobility and provide the political base for criticism of more powerful groups or classes in society. This fragile structure of order was constantly threatened by the actions, or failures, of the state.

The relationship between temperance and democracy in the nineteenth century was not coincidental; it was instrumental. In the United States, where male suffrage was extensive, temperance demands moved rapidly from regulation and local option (1830s—1840s) to Maine Law prohibition (1850s). The majoritarian premise of early temperance politics—that the majority could define "evil" and move the state against it—was in keeping with the transcendental and romantic faith in democracy, but it ignored the possibility of a negative public sentiment until after the debacle of the 1850s. In Norway and Sweden, where the right to vote was still tied to land ownership or tax and class status, the temperance advocates confronted political structures that rested on archaic social definitions. The movement for restriction of home distillation and for local option became part of the political aspirations of pietistic farmers, urban workers (in the Marcus Thrane movement in Norway), and nationalistic professionals in the urban centers. These mid-century struggles contributed to the growing awareness that the structures of government would have to be modified if a new mode of public order was to be obtained. Temperance pressure contributed, in the late nineteenth and early twentieth centuries, to the process of adaptation of political structures that was achieved by nationalistic self-assertion in Norway and Finland and by working-class assertion in Sweden.

In England, Scotland, and Wales, teetotalism had tended toward the nonpolitical expressions of self-help religion and trade unionism. The attempt to rekindle the lagging political aspects of temperance in the 1850s and 1860s by the importation of Maine Law ideas and by the creation of the United Kingdom Alliance contributed to the growing criticism of the unrepresentativeness of Parliament and, after the reforms of 1867, to the realignment of local political factions. The union of prohibitionist and women's rights and suffrage societies in the later decades of the nineteenth century in the United States, England,

and the Scandinavian countries added new recruits to the drive for extension of
the franchise but revealed an intellectual dilemma. Increasingly, the goal of prohibitionism became a society characterized more by the enforcement of social
discipline than by the reinforcement of self-discipline. Democracy was a means
to achieve the goal of an orderly society but would be restricted by the constitutional status of prohibition once that goal had been achieved.

The twentieth century saw the combined pressures of immigration, wartime conditions, and nationalistic sentiment heighten the need to enhance social
cohesion as well as to maintain social discipline. The granting of women's suffrage
facilitated cohesion while the enactment of prohibition seemed to contribute
to discipline. The tensions between the freedoms promised by social cohesion
and the restraints imposed by social discipline were not easily reconciled, however. As nationalistic movements (or sensitivities) confronted either the diversity
of heterogeneous populations or the deep divisions in homogeneous populations,
the recognition of the need to find some common ground of citizenship (in the
granting of equal political rights or in the imposition of equal obligations) carried
with it the acknowledgment of cultural variations. Thus pluralism as a premise of
social cohesion made it increasingly difficult to maintain prohibition as a form
of social control. Whether in the United States, Australia, New Zealand, Finland,
or in India during the Congress period, the granting of women's suffrage poten-
tially armed "minority" groups (except where they were disenfranchised by
legal requirements) against "majority" attempts at unwanted social control.
How women did, in fact, use the vote varied in each country according to the
content of its feminist tradition, the status of the women's rights movement,
and the concepts of equality embodied in its institutional and intellectual life.

Feminism was a culturally radical assertion of women's superiority to all
social claims that tended to denigrate her worth, to thwart her potentiality, or
to smother her individuality. If some of the pioneering feminists tended toward
extreme statements or views, if they seemed to be sacrificing their very souls
to free their bodies from the silken chains of the maternal and familial ties, if
they sought an elusive sense of superiority in the intensity of their self-sacrifice
—was this not but an index of the tenacity of the traditions that they struggled
to break? Like the men and women of the Reformation who came out of their
cloisters and convents to proclaim a new vision of God's love and to seal it with
their bodies, the feminists found that in the eyes of their contemporaries they
were either the new saints or the ultimate rebels against man and God. Since
the feminists sought attitudinal changes, the historian can measure their achievements not by objective institutional innovations but by the more imprecise psychological moods of the literary monuments that have survived: the polemics of
Mary Wollstonecraft and Frances Wright, the brilliant essays of Margaret Fuller,
the novels of Fredrika Bremer or Virginia Woolf, and the scholarly research of
Charlotte Perkins Gilman. Every woman who breathes the pure, psychological
air of freedom today is, in some ultimate sense, the child of the feminists.

The history of the women's rights movement has been that of a perennial
struggle periodically renewed by changes in the human environment. The causes

espoused by the early advocates of women's rights—married women's property rights, earlier majority, freedom from guardianship, control of earnings, easier divorce, more liberal alimony, access to education, temperance legislation, anti-slavery, economic equality of opportunity, and equitable remuneration—were sometimes granted gradually, reluctantly, or unexpectedly as men, for various reasons, saw fit to grant them.

Women responded to equality as it was defined by their culture. In the Anglo-American culture of aspiration it was an equality of effort in which the woman was free to participate in the public life of the society only to the extent that she was willing to shoulder the burdens and risks of a highly competitive life-style. The only socially acceptable alternative to equality in the public sphere was a sentimental superiority in the domestic sphere that promised security rather than opportunity. Like an entrepreneur, she had to decide how best to invest and risk her emotional capital. Equality for the American or English woman meant primarily equality of opportunity; but opportunity was what she chose to make it. /

In the Scandinavian culture of achievement, women were allowed to participate in public life because the society was willing to help shoulder some of the burdens and risks that fell upon the family when she stepped outside its confines. Whether it was a law that allowed middle-class widows to open penny shops, a law that restricted street hawking to working-class wives, a law that helped mothers of illegitimate children, or a law that opened the professions to women, the intent of these early Scandinavian welfare laws was to protect the family rather than to foster feminine individualism per se. While individualism in England was confined within class mores and eccentricity was widely tolerated, and while in America individualism was fettered by the demand for conformity, in Scandinavia individualism was subordinate to the family (which was why the feminists rebelled against it). Equality existed between groups (or classes) and independence was achieved only within one's group.[22]

The coexistence of tacitly assumed social inequalities and explicitly stated goals of cultural equality did not seem contradictory to the Scandinavians. Since everyone was a member of the ethnically defined folk community (Swedes, Danes, Finns, and Norwegians), all persons ought to enjoy an equitable share of those cultural attributes (style of life) that made them a distinctive people. A strongly conservative cast characterized the Scandinavian women's rights organizations in the late nineteenth and early twentieth centuries. Leadership was drawn from the upper ranks of society. The subsequent development, in the

---

22. Significantly, the recent debate in Sweden over women's rights has turned on the questions of equality of roles *within* the family and of equity between women's primary roles in modern society. See Alva Myrdal and Viola Klein, *Women's Two Roles: Home and Work* (London: Routledge & Kegan Paul, Ltd., 1956); Edmund Dahlstrom, ed., *The Changing Roles of Men and Women,* trans. Gunilla and Steven Anderman (London: Gerald Duckworth & Co., Ltd., 1967); and Lars Gustafsson, *The Public Dialogue in Sweden: Current Issues of Social, Esthetic and Moral Debate,* trans. Claude Stephenson (Stockholm: Norstedt & Soener AB [P.A.], 1964).

second quarter of the twentieth century, of welfare programs under socialistic and center-left coalitions represented the working out of a socialistic conception of equality of status that had deep roots in the traditional culture of the Scandinavian countries.

The comparative experiences of the three frontier areas (Australia, the American West, and Finland) revealed significant differences in their conceptions of equality. In the Australian setting of racial homogeneity, economic scarcity, and harsh geography, equality meant "mateship," security, and an equitable enjoyment of social rewards. In the United States, with its racial and ethnic heterogeneity, economic abundance, and varied geography, equality meant an emphasis on the importance of individual effort, the presence of opportunity (or the conditions of competition), and the equity (proportionality) of rewards.

The Finnish (and Scandinavian) conception of equality had much more of a cultural base than the American or Australian conceptions. Whereas Australian mateship was primarily a masculine (man-to-man) concept of equality that coexisted with (or even required) female subordination, Finnish comradeship was a communal, bisexual (man-and-woman) concept of equality that laid the base for the gradual emergence of a welfare state. The Finnish (and Scandinavian) concept of cultural equality was, therefore, less competitive, and more cooperative, than the American concept of equality of economic opportunity. Because Finnish society was divided by linguistic duality, because the economy was still primarily agrarian, and because geography acted to isolate the people, equality in Finland carried connotations of economic independence, cultural unity, and social security. In many respects, the Scandinavian concept of equality was the most subtle, the American concept of equality the most simple, and the Australian concept of equality the most strenuous.

While the meaning of any particular change in the rights of women varied according to the country's concept of equality, the significance of the extension of the suffrage to women depended on the immediate historical situation, the goals of the men and women involved, and their understanding of their political traditions. The early grants of municipal, communal, school board (or poor relief), and local liquor control board suffrage did not necessarily mean that women had been admitted to equality with men; rather, it was frequently a way of paying deference to the concept of female superiority in the moral realm. The historical union of the women's suffrage and prohibition movements in the second half of the nineteenth century provided strategic support for the suffrage drive in Australia, the American West, and, to a lesser extent, in Scandinavia.

The granting of women's suffrage on the Anglo-American and Scandinavian frontiers occurred because the institutional barriers to change were weakened by extraordinary events at the moment when strong organizational or ideological pressure could be brought to bear. In Australia and New Zealand the impact of the political upheavals of the 1890s and the nature of the new federalism carried women's suffrage, but not prohibition. In the American West the weakening of Congressional opposition, the temporary support of Populists and prohibitionists, and better organization by the suffragists secured victories until they encountered

effective counterorganization by the brewers and distillers and by the antisuffragists. In Finland (and Norway), the feminist ideology was primarily economic and
cultural and the women's movement relatively recent, yet they secured women's
suffrage because strong nationalistic sentiments coincided with constitutional
crises that made it expedient for men to grant the concession.

/ In the twentieth century, the suffragists shifted the grounds of their
ideology from their traditional argument of "justice" (women ought to have
the ballot as a matter of right) to "expediency" (women need the ballot in order
to enhance their status, protect against exploitation, clean up politics, and so
forth). This shift reflected, in part, the impact of earlier changes in women's
rights. Now that some women had received college educations, had entered
professions, had moved out of the home into the sweatshops and factories, had
become self-supporting, they had new needs and specific goals. Their heightened
sense of expectation and frustration fed the fires of militant tactics and organized political pressure.[23]

The leading figures in the suffrage struggle had reflected not only their
own personalities but their cultures and national characters as well: Susan B. Anthony, stern, severe, "schoolmarmish"; Elizabeth Cady Stanton, petulant, spoiled,
and intellectually astute; Baroness Gripenberg, cool, aristocratic, conservative;
Mrs. Pankhurst and her daughters, egocentric, eccentric, "electric"; Carrie Chapman Catt and Millicent Fawcett, efficient, businesslike, parliamentary; Alice Paul
and Lucy Burns, idealistic, energetic, youthful; the followers of Gandhi, patient,
passionate, and resourceful. For them, the possession of the vote was not an
empty symbol or a temporary infatuation, but a pledge of better things to come.

What then was the relation of women's suffrage to democracy? Political
scientists, sociologists, and social commentators have for over fifty years been
compiling evidence and testing generalizations on the political behavior of
women. Their conclusions have not varied. They have only been elaborated with
time: women do not vote as a group, they form no distinctly significant political
party, they have not "redeemed" politics overnight. By and large, they divide
along roughly the same political lines as men; they respond to the same empty
slogans, glib half-truths, and ideological fantasies as men.[24]

A recent critic of American historians has raised the rhetorical issue that
if one asked:

" 'What is the most effectively conservative piece of legislation passed by the

---

23. For summaries of the arguments used by suffragists and their supporters, see Aileen S.
Kraditor, *The Ideas of the Woman Suffrage Movement, 1890-1920* (New York: Columbia
University Press, 1965); Aileen S. Kraditor, ed., *Up From the Pedestal: Selected Writings
in the History of American Feminism* (Chicago: Quadrangle Books, Inc., 1968); T. R. Smith,
ed., *The Woman Question* (New York: Boni and Liveright, Inc., 1918); June Sochen, ed.,
The New Feminism in Twentieth-Century America (Lexington, Mass.: D. C. Heath &
Company, 1971), Part 1.

24. Martin Gruberg, *Women in American Politics: An Assessment and Source Book* (Oshkosh, Wis.: Academia Press, 1968) is a convenient summary of this literature.

federal government in this century?' the answer . . . is both obvious and incontestable. It is the Nineteenth Amendment, extending the suffrage to women. . . . Yet in all our history books the Nineteenth Amendment is regarded as a progressive and liberal action, not at all as a conservative one."[25]

In the light of the comparative cases surveyed by this book, this "conservative" character of women's suffrage illustrated one facet of the nature of democracy in the modern world. One function of a democratic franchise has been to bind the citizen to the national state and thereby to preserve a particular government by providing peaceful channels for the pursuit of private interests and the public good. The granting of women's suffrage at the highest constitutional rank in a number of countries coincided with or followed nationalistic upheavals, constitutional crises related to internal social tensions, or the creation of unstable republics from wartorn countries and weakened colonial empires. If women voters were more cautious than men, if they did respond out of a calculus of instinctual conservatism and a preference for the known present or imagined past over an unknown and insecure future, perhaps they were fulfilling precisely that historical function for which they had been granted the right to vote. Whether this preservative function has been "progressive and liberal" depends on the institutionalized ideals that are thus preserved for another generation. The preservation and extension of the meaning of equality is surely a worthy contribution to any culture.

25. Irving Kristol, "American Historians and the Democratic Idea," *American Scholar* 39 (Winter 1969-70): 90; reprinted in Irving Kristol, *On the Democratic Idea in America* (New York: Harper & Row, Publishers, 1972), Chapter 4.

Epilogue:
The Past as Perspective

This book has followed the course of women's rights and temperance movements from the 1830s to the 1930s. It has shown how these two movements intersected in the mid-nineteenth century; influenced each other, particularly in the women's suffrage and prohibition issues; and then split apart. It remains to be shown how this understanding of the past provides a perspective on recent events.

Temperance and prohibition were different tactics for dealing with a persistent social problem, alcoholism. While temperance stressed self-control, prohibition stressed social control. The repeal or abandonment of prohibition in Norway, Iceland, Finland, the United States, and the Indian states, except Madras and Gujarat, left unsolved the basic question of how best to deal with alcoholism. Given the structure of American federalism, a few states such as Oklahoma and Mississippi persisted in enforcing statewide prohibition after the repeal of nationwide legislation and some, such as Iowa, adopted state monopoly systems for control of distribution. The oil-rich country of Kuwait enforced an Islam-sanctioned prohibition in the 1960s with the predictable result of creating a market for Middle Eastern smugglers.[1] Scandinavian countries combined state-owned monopolies for distribution with rationing or regulation programs.

While the use of prohibition as a means of social control declined, a significant change in the methods of dealing with alcoholism took place in the 1950s and 1960s in Scandinavia and Europe. The post-war revival of economies brought in its wake an increase in the consumption of alcoholic beverages, and traditional social welfare policies (incarceration, regulation, education, and rationing) seemed inadequate to deal with the resultant increase in alcoholism. The idea of deemphasizing police regulation and of stressing public rehabilitation was not new but it received significant new political support.

---

1. "Bootleggers Boom," *The Economist* 214 (February 6, 1965): 530; James Bacon, "Big Money for Bootleggers in 'Dry' India," *Moline* (Illinois) *Daily Dispatch*, May 1, 1970, p. 42, cols. 1-2. Mississippi became the last state to repeal its prohibition law in 1966.

"The year 1954 saw the inauguration of several new programs. An important event in France was the creation in that year, through the initiative of Mr. Mendes-France, of the Government High Committee of Study and Information on Alcoholism. In 1954, in the Soviet Union, the Ministry of Health issued directives on alcoholism education and treatment to doctors and medical personnel which led to the development of a nationwide program organized through the Central Research Institute of Health Education." [2]

A French law provided for treatment of all alcoholics who represented a danger to other persons. A similar move in Sweden resulted in an overhaul of the Bratt system in 1955. Local temperance boards were empowered "to interfere at an earlier stage with abuse of alcohol" thus making it possible "to offer remedial measures before a serious case develops." Noncriminal detoxification laws were passed in Poland (1956 and 1959), Germany (1958), Finland (1961), Czechoslovakia (1948 and 1962), South Africa (1963), Switzerland (various cantons between 1952 and 1968), New Zealand (1966), and Australia (1968). [3]

   In the United States, the idea that alcoholism is a disease rather than a crime had achieved the status of a truism among social workers, social scientists, and psychiatrists by the 1940s, but it had had little impact on the law or general public attitudes. The first state-sponsored alcoholism programs (Utah and Oregon, 1943, and Connecticut, 1945) focused on research, public education, and treatment within the public health agencies. The Yale Center of Alcohol Studies, the National Council on Alcoholism (1944), and the association of alcoholics' families, Al-Anon (1949), provided the public with information and exerted pressure on state legislatures and on Congress. In spite of progress in the 1950s, the historians of state alcohol programs concluded in 1962 that "state alcoholism

---

2. Archer Tongue, "What the state does about alcohol and alcoholism: an international survey," in *Society, Culture, and Drinking Patterns,* David J. Pittman and Charles R. Snyder, eds. (New York: John Wiley & Sons, Inc., 1962), p. 595. A comprehensive survey of Scandinavian welfare policies published in 1953 admitted that per capita consumption had risen since 1940 and that alcoholism remained a serious problem in spite of welfare legislation. See George R. Nelson, ed., *Freedom and Welfare: Social Patterns in the Northern Countries of Europe* (Denmark: Krohns Bogtrykkeri, 1953), pp. 354-57. For the background on Russian efforts, see Vera Efron, "The Soviet Approach to Alcoholism," in *Comparative Social Problems,* S. N. Eisenstadt, ed. (New York: The Free Press, 1964), pp. 26-31.

3. Arne Skutin, "Sweden: Sequel," in *Drinking and Intoxication: Selected Readings in Social Attitudes and Controls,* Raymond G. McCarthy, ed. (New York: The Free Press, 1959), p. 356 (quotation); Mark Keller and Shirley Sirota Rosenberg, eds., *First Special Report to the United States Congress on Alcohol and Health from the Secretary of Health, Education, and Welfare, December, 1971* (Washington, D.C.: Department of Health, Education, and Welfare, 1971), pp. 95-96. A 1953 law in Norway strengthened the temperance boards (which dated back to 1913) and made them mandatory for all towns and townships; a 1957 amendment added "narcomaniacs" to the jurisdiction of the temperance boards and authorized hospital treatment for alcoholism under the National Health Insurance system. Thomas D. Eliot, Arthur Hillman, et al., *Norway's Families: Trends, Problems, Programs* (Philadelphia: University of Pennsylvania Press, 1960), pp. 296-303.

programs are born against resistance, live surrounded by hostile and threatening forces, and only continue to survive by a constant interest and effort."[4]

To add treatment statutes to the law was one thing; to remove criminal statutes or punitive legal concepts was another. In a series of landmark cases, federal courts, including the United States Supreme Court, challenged the 350-year-old tradition of treating public intoxication as a criminal offense. In *Easter* v. *District of Columbia* (1966), *Driver* v. *Hinnant* (1966), and *Powell* v. *Texas* (1968) the courts held that, since alcoholism is a disease, the defendants could not be held responsible for public intoxication because their acts were involuntary and, therefore, criminal penalties could not constitutionally be applied. (Technically, the cases applied only to "homeless derelicts" but the broader implications were clear enough.) In the wake of these cases, a few states began to repeal their public intoxication statutes or to provide for court-ordered treatment of chronic alcoholics. In 1967 England amended its criminal code to abolish imprisonment for being drunk and disorderly but increased the maximum fine for the offense. A 1971 report called for the immediate provision of detoxification and treatment centers. A similar Swedish report in 1969 concluded that arrest and punishment of intoxicated persons was outmoded and called for detention in treatment centers rather than incarceration.[5]

In the United States, the federal government's changed attitude toward alcoholism and its treatment can be dated from President Lyndon Johnson's health message to Congress in March 1966. The Highway Safety Act of 1966 and the Economic Opportunity Amendments of 1967 focused on selected aspects of the problem. The most significant, and comprehensive, attempt to deal with alcoholism came with the Alcoholic Rehabilitation Act of 1968 in which Congress declared alcoholism to be a major health and social problem and called for community-based treatment programs. Two years of initial attempts at funding such centers under the community mental health programs highlighted the need for a more coordinated approach. Accordingly, in 1970 Congress established the National Institute on Alcohol Abuse and Alcoholism (under the Department of Health, Education, and Welfare) to coordinate all federal activities and to oversee grants to the states under state-initiated alcoholism plans. A massive campaign to influence public opinion was launched using television, radio, newspapers, and educational resources.[6]

In theory, the historian should be able to show how, as the emphasis on various ideas about the nature of alcoholism changed (from sin, to crime, to

---

4. Morris E. Chafetz and Harold W. Demone, Jr., *Alcoholism and Society* (New York: Oxford University Press, 1962), Chapter 6 (quotation, p. 118). The state of professional opinion in the early 1940s is summarized in E. M. Jellinek, ed., *Alcohol Addiction and Chronic Alcoholism* (New Haven: Yale University Press, 1942).

5. Keller and Rosenberg, *Alcohol and Health,* Chapter 7.

6. National Institute of Mental Health, *Alcohol and Alcoholism* (Washington, D.C.: National Clearinghouse for Mental Health Information, 1969), Chapter 13; Keller and Rosenberg, *Alcohol and Health,* Chapter 7.

disease), so the means of social control changed (from temperance, to prohibition, to treatment). But the correlations are not so exact in human affairs. Changes in law, public policy, or public opinion did not follow so automatically; counterarguments were heard and old issues were revived. While it was possible to argue that the causes of alcoholism were essentially private and preventable, observers noted that the consequences were frequently public and punishable, particularly in the area of traffic safety. The demand for more stringent law enforcement and the application of new technology to traffic safety and police procedures combined to produce better drunk-o-meters, experimental "drunk proof" auto ignition systems, and implied consent laws. One highly effective television campaign stressed the theme that the drunken driver had to be curbed first, and then given treatment, in the interest of public safety. Ironically, at the very moment when the United States seemed to be moving away from a reliance on punishment and toward a reliance on treatment, the Soviet Union showed signs of reinstituting a punitive attitude toward alcoholism.[7]

In a curious twist of history, the whole issue of prohibition as a means of social control was raised again in the 1970s by the public debate on drug abuse. The argument that, since the prohibition of alcoholic beverages had failed, the prohibition of drugs was destined to failure had achieved the status of an unchallenged truism among advocates of drug legalization, from law professors and psychiatrists to former drug users.[8] But such an either/or approach (either prohibition or legalization) rested on an incomplete analysis of the historical parallelism. If one were to move beyond the simplistic pragmatic question, "did prohibition work?" to the more sophisticated policy question, "under what conditions is prohibition (of anything) an effective means of social control?" the true complexity of the issue would be revealed.[9] For example, if massive public support of law enforcement efforts is a prerequisite for effective prohibition,

---

7. For the changing Soviet attitude toward alcoholism, see N. Troyan, "Harmful Indulgence," and A. Gertsenzon, "Such a Law Is Needed," in *American and Soviet Society: A Reader in Comparative Sociology and Perception,* Paul Hollander, ed. (Englewood Cliffs, N.J.: Prentice-Hall, Inc., 1969), pp. 356–59.

8. The prevalence of the truism can be illustrated from two diverse sources. Compare Lester Grinspoon, *Marihuana Reconsidered* (Cambridge, Mass.: Harvard University Press, 1971), p. 346, and the testimony of Sherwin De Graff, of the West Side Organization drug abuse program, before the Senate subcommittee on alcoholism and narcotics, Chicago, Illinois, May 17, 1971, in *Narcotics and Alcoholism, 1971: Hearings before the Subcommittee on Alcoholism and Narcotics of the Committee on Labor and Public Welfare, United States Senate, Ninety-Second Congress, First Session* (Washington, D.C.: U.S. Government Printing Office, 1971), Part 2, p. 623.

9. John Kaplan, *Marijuana—The New Prohibition* (New York: World Publishing Company, 1970), Chapters 1, 2, and 10 relied on Joseph Gusfield's study of prohibition as "status politics" to discuss the symbolic function of the law in legitimizing subcultural life styles. He united this approach with a cost-benefit analysis of law enforcement to conclude that the "criminalization" (i.e., prohibition) of marijuana was counterproductive and urged a licensing model for social control. Unlike those who argue from the failure of alcohol prohibition to the inefficacy of controls on *all* drugs, Kaplan had invoked criteria of sufficient

the important question is not only why the prohibition of alcoholic beverages lacked such support but also whether the prohibition of certain drugs can generate such support. As the history of the temperance and prohibition movements has illustrated, a specific means of social control can serve various functions in a given society over time.

While the question of social control was involved in the changing attitudes toward alcoholism and drug abuse, the question of equality was once again raised by changes in the areas of feminism, women's rights, and women's suffrage. The experiences of the quarter century that had followed the granting of women's suffrage had established certain general patterns. The goals for which women would use the ballot depended on their images of women's roles, the current ideological understandings of the purposes of political parties, and their perceptions of the nature of the democratic process. Where there was no unity among women along interest or ideological lines, separate political parties or lists of candidates were ineffective. In the United States, the militant National Women's party proposed an Equal Rights amendment in 1923 and supported women candidates in the 1924 elections. Neither the amendment nor their candidates found widespread support among organized women's groups. In Sweden, a separate party formed by salaried women entered the 1927 and 1928 elections, but the results were disappointing.[10]

When attention was shifted from women as candidates to women as civil servants or as public officials, the results were equally disappointing. The more closely one approached the center of political power, the fewer women one found in positions of authority. The pioneering women cabinet officers of the

---

specificity (cost-benefit analysis) to distinguish between various types of drugs and of sufficient flexibility to envision changes in public attitudes. He thus overcame the vagueness of the "status politics" theory.

Troy Duster, *The Legislation of Morality: Law, Drugs, and Moral Judgment* (New York: The Free Press, 1970), Chapters 1, 4, 5, 10, invoked the Gusfield study and the theories of the Danish sociologist, Svend Ranulf, to examine middle-class moral indignation as the basis of drug prohibition. He noted that the following argument is a tautology: "Only laws which are in keeping with public morality can be effectively enforced. Laws which are contrary to public morality (e.g. Prohibition) are doomed to failure. If an instance is cited where a law was passed which *seemed* to be contrary to public morality and was effective, then it was not *really* contrary to public morality after all" (page 102). He advocated basing moral judgments on a firm knowledge of the physiological effects of addiction and not on the social-legal categorization of addicts: "The moral beliefs upon which we have based our public policy are themselves founded on myths about both the physical effects of drugs and errors about the total quality of persons addicted" (p. 239). He advocated a clinic system to legalize and control drug distribution and to provide for rehabilitation. He noted that the American Bar Association and American Medical Association joint committee on narcotic drugs had concluded in 1961 that drug addiction was a sickness or disease, thus setting the stage for a reevaluation of public policy.

10. William L. O'Neill, *Everyone Was Brave: The Rise and Fall of Feminism in America* (Chicago: Quadrangle Books, Inc., 1969), pp. 274–94; William Henry Chafe, *The American Woman: Her Changing Social, Economic, and Political Roles, 1920-1970* (New York: Oxford University Press, 1972), Chapter 5; Jarl Torbacke, "Kvinnolistan 1927-28 — ett kvinnopolitiskt fiasko," *Historisk tidskrift* 89 (No. 2, 1969): 145-84.

1920s and 1930s were the exceptions that proved the rule. Finland, which had the highest proportion of women in its national legislature of any Scandinavian country, had approximately the same percentage of women members from 1940 to 1949 as it had had from 1907 to 1909 (about ten percent). Elsewhere the percentage had either declined over the years or showed growth mainly at the municipal level. A comparative study of Scandinavian voting patterns showed that, up to 1950, women's voting rates tended to be lower than men's voting rates.[11] Political scientists noted that women as *candidates* and *public officials* were more prominent on the left in the political spectrum, but that women as *voters* tended to favor the center or right in mid-century elections.[12]

In a mood of post-war idealism, the United Nations established a Commission on the Status of Women in 1946 and included a condemnation of sex discrimination in the 1948 Declaration of the Universal Rights of Man. The Commission on the Status of Women proposed a Convention on the Political Rights of Women which, after some delay, was finally adopted in 1952. "In essence it gave women equal rights with men to vote at all elections, to be eligible for all elected public bodies established by national legislation, and to occupy any public posts or offices created by such legislation"; however, as a noted authority has observed, "by 1964 only forty-two member States had ratified this convention, though many of these made reservations to Article 3 'access to public office.'" Surveying the major Western democracies since World War II, this authority concluded that the period was one of decreasing political power for women and that the United States, in this respect, was even more depressing than Italy.[13]

The revival of feminism and interest in women's rights in the 1960s in the United States, Sweden, and England invoked various concepts of equality, created new images of women's roles in society, and involved new understandings of the political process. These changes did not, at first, define new uses for women's suffrage because of the contexts in which the new debates had arisen.

In the United States, neofeminism and concern for women's rights emerged in the context of the civil rights debate. In December 1961, President John F. Kennedy, prompted largely by political considerations, signed an executive order creating a Commission on the Status of Women. The Commission's report, moderate in tone and limited in its recommendations, was released in late

---

11. Elina Haavio-Mannila, "Sex Roles in Politics," *Scandinavian Political Studies* 5 (1970): 209-16, 226-29, 232-34, 237-38.

The first women cabinet officers included Nina Bang, Minister of Education in Denmark, 1924; Miina Sillanpää, who joined the Finnish cabinet in 1927; Margaret Bondfield, Minister of Labour in England, 1929; and Frances Perkins, Secretary of Labor in the United States, 1933.

12. Maurice Duverger, *The Political Role of Women* (Paris: United Nations Economic and Social Council, 1955); Seymour Lipset, *Political Man* (New York: Doubleday & Company, Inc., 1960).

13. Evelyne Sullerot, *Woman, Society and Change,* trans. Margaret Scotford Archer (New York: McGraw-Hill Book Company, 1971), pp. 205-6, 217 (quotation), 222-23.

1963 when Betty Friedan's *The Feminine Mystique* was stirring public interest by attacking the suburban ideology of the 1950s. The Commission's efforts and the new awareness of women's rights contributed to the public debate that accompanied the passage of the 1963 Equal Pay Act and the inclusion of anti-sex discrimination in the 1964 Civil Rights Act (Title VII). Thus, the initial thrust of renewed interest in feminism and women's rights among reformist groups was in the direction of securing equality of opportunity in the economic realm and freedom from the cold-war ideology of conformity and consumption.[14]

If the civil rights movement in the United States provided a *context* for a revival of reformist concern for women's rights, it also provided some of the *content* of the radical feminist ideology that also emerged in the 1960s. The young veterans of the nonviolent student civil rights activism and the peace demonstrations, the militant new left, carried with them into the women's liberation movement much of the style, rhetoric, and neo-Marxist analysis of their earlier activities. Defining their goals as the restructuring of society and emphasizing the tactics of dissent, disruption, and demonstration, they had little use for the traditional means of political participation. Historian William L. O'Neill argued that the pursuit of women's suffrage in the nineteenth and early twentieth centuries had stifled the feminist critique of marriage and had thus inhibited their ability to propose genuine solutions (either a welfare state or the reorganization of domestic institutions). To some of the radicals, "suffragism" became synonymous with a conservative, male plot to keep women preoccupied with reformist nonsolutions.[15]

---

14. Judith Hole and Ellen Levine, *Rebirth of Feminism* (Chicago: Quadrangle Books, Inc., 1971), pp. 18–44; Betty Friedan, *The Feminine Mystique* (New York: W. W. Norton & Company, Inc., 1963). William Henry Chafe has argued that the feminism of the 1960s was an unintended *consequence* of economic and social changes in the 1940s and 1950s; that the increased participation of women in economic life was rationalized or accommodated to the prevailing orthodox images of woman; and that, therefore, "the debate over woman's place in the late 1940's and 1950's failed to result in a new definition of women's identity, as some had hoped." Chafe, *The American Woman,* Chapter 9 (quotation, p. 225).

Caroline Bird called attention to the fact that the ban on sex discrimination in the 1964 Civil Rights Act was the ironical result of an attempt by opponents of the bill to either delay or defeat it by offering "amusing" amendments. The significant point, however, is that once passed, the amendment was seized upon by women's organizations, particularly the National Organization for Women (NOW), which insisted on prompt enforcement. Without the interest aroused by the presidential commission and Betty Friedan's book, the amendment might have been forgotten. Similar tactics by antisuffragists in Australia in the 1900s had also backfired. See Caroline Bird and Sara Welles Briller, *Born Female: The High Cost of Keeping Women Down,* revised ed. (New York: David McKay Co., Inc., 1970), Chapter 1. The first edition was published in 1968 and received a sympathetic review by Barbara Miller Solomon in the *Saturday Review* in November 1968.

15. Hole and Levine, *Rebirth of Feminism,* pp. 108–66; O'Neill, *Everyone Was Brave,* pp. 21–48; Roberta Salper, "The Development of the American Women's Liberation Movement, 1967-1971," in *Female Liberation: History and Current Politics,* Roberta Salper, ed. (New York: Alfred A. Knopf, Inc., 1972), pp. 169–84.

As the civil rights movement splintered along black power, black separatist, and black consciousness lines, the question of the unique problems and potentials of black women became more acute. The assertion of black masculine leadership in the radical groups, on the

If the civil rights movement in the United States shaped the revival of interest in feminism and women's rights, in Sweden and England the issues arose in the context of the welfare state. In 1956 the Swedish sociologist Alva Myrdal and the English sociologist Viola Klein had published a comparative study, *Women's Two Roles: Home and Work*. They portrayed women as confronting a fundamental conflict in modern society: "On the one hand, they want, like everybody else, to develop their personalities to the full and to take an active part in adult social and economic life within the limits of their individual interests and abilities. On the other hand, most women want a home and a family of their own."[16] They advocated a moderate list of changes in individual attitudes, public policies, and economic practices designed to help men, women, and society achieve an accommodation with women's twin roles in a welfare state. This position was sharply criticized in 1961 by Eva Moberg in an article, "The Conditional Emancipation of Woman." Moberg dismissed the "two roles of women" concept and postulated a single, egalitarian role: to become fully human. There was no biological connection between child bearing (which only a woman could do) and child rearing (which either sex could do). It was not a question of women's rights or women's roles, she asserted, but of the "sex roles" created by society.[17]

The sex-role debate in Sweden took place largely within the tightly knit circles of the Swedish intelligentsia (or "rationalists," as they were sometimes called) that exerted a powerful influence on both the public media and the governmental policy of the ruling Social Democratic party. Since they accomplished some of their aims without recourse to the ordinary competition of party politics, the relationship between women and political power received scant attention. However, a Swedish feminist warned in the mid-1960s: "Unless the political parties and trade union organizations actively engage themselves in the matter, it will be difficult to explain the implications of the sex-role question to the

---

one hand, and the desire of some black women to achieve sufficient status and leisure so as *to be able* to devote more time to their homes, on the other hand, represented some of the diverse dimensions of the situation. See Gerda Lerner, ed., *Black Women in White America: A Documentary History* (New York: Random House, Inc., 1972); Joyce A. Ladner, *Tomorrow's Tomorrow: The Black Woman* (New York: Doubleday & Company, Inc., 1971); Linda J. M. LaRue, "Black Liberation and Women's Lib," Nathan and Julia Hare, "Black Women 1970," *Transaction* 8 (November-December 1970): 59-64; 65-68, 90; Frances M. Beal, "Double Jeopardy: To Be Black and Female," in *Sisterhood Is Powerful*, Robin Morgan, ed. (New York: Random House, Inc., 1970), pp. 340-53.

16. Alva Myrdal and Viola Klein, *Women's Two Roles: Home and Work* (London: Routledge & Kegan Paul Ltd., 1956), p. xii. See also Chapters 1, 9, 10.

17. Rita Liljeström, "The Swedish Model," in *Sex Roles in Changing Society*, Georgene H. Seward and Robert C. Williamson, eds. (New York: Random House, Inc., 1970), pp. 202-5; Edmund Dahlström, "Analysis of the Debate on Sex Roles," in *The Changing Roles of Men and Women*, Edmund Dahlström, ed., trans. Gunilla and Steven Anderman (London: Gerald Duckworth & Co. Ltd., 1967), pp. 176, 178-81; Lars Gustafson, *The Public Dialogue in Sweden: Current Issues of Social, Esthetic and Moral Debate*, trans. Claude Stephenson (Stockholm: Norstedt & Soener AB [P.A.], 1964), pp. 101-10.

public at large and to apply egalitarian ideas in practice."[18] New left critics also charged that the Social Democratic party had failed to extend democracy from the political realm to the social and economic realms, thereby causing "contradictions in the domestic system, from inequality in wages and women's rights to the alienation of individuals from bureaucratizing tendencies in politics and private organizations."[19] In short, the sex-role debate focused attention on social reconstruction first and political mobilization only secondarily.

In England, the ideological debate on women's roles was launched within the left intellectual circles by the publication of Juliet Mitchell's essay, "Women: The Longest Revolution" in the December 1966 issue of *New Left Review*. The country had just come through a general election in which the Labour party had received a mandate to deal with endemic economic problems. Parliament, in mid-year, was preoccupied with wage policies but did take time to debate an abortion bill. Only a year before, a committee of the Ministry of Health had finally announced that it had no objections to the marketing of oral contraceptives. The time was ripe for a broad discussion of women's rights. Mitchell argued that women's liberation depended on the transformation of four structures that determined women's inequality: production, reproduction, socialization of children, and sexuality. The greatest hope for authentic liberation was in the highly developed and industrialized nations of the West, particularly if all four structures could be transformed. The conjunction of official welfare policies and radical social critiques occurred in the areas of family, welfare, work, and female sexuality. This gave the ensuing discussion an economic and social cast.[20]

---

18. Anna-Greta Leijon, *Swedish Women—Swedish Men*, trans. Paul Britten Austin (Stockholm: The Swedish Institute, 1968), p. 132.
    Swedish Prime Minister Olof Palme characterized the official policy of his government during a visit to the United States in 1970 as seeking equality between the sexes and emancipation of men as well as women. He referred his incredulous listeners to the Swedish government's report on the status of women, submitted to the United Nations in 1968, for the basis of this policy. See Ingrid Fredriksson, "Sex Roles and Education in Sweden," *New York University Education Quarterly* 3 (Winter 1972): 17–24; *Rapport till förenta nationerna över kvinnoras status i sverige* (Stockholm: Norstedt & Soener AB [P.A.], 1968).

19. M. Donald Hancock, *Sweden: The Politics of Postindustrial Change* (Hinsdale, Illinois: The Dryden Press, Inc., 1972), p. 85.

20. Juliet Mitchell, *Woman's Estate* (New York: Random House, Inc., 1971), pp. 120-21. For background on the situation in England in the mid-1960s, see Pauline Gregg, *The Welfare State: An Economic and Social History of Great Britain from 1945 to the Present Day* (Amherst: The University of Massachusetts Press, 1969), pp. 118-20, Chapter 15; "What Women Want," *The Economist* 228 (July 6, 1968): 12-14; "On Equality," *The Economist* 230 (March 29, 1969): 22; Corinna Adam, "Britain's Submerged Sex," *New Statesman* 79 (January 16, 1970): 72; Corinna Adam, "Sisters versus Comrades," *New Statesman* 79 (March 6, 1970): 323-24; Corinna Adam, "Why Women Aren't Socialists," *New Statesman* 82 (July 9, 1971): 37–38. According to a study noted by Evelyne Sullerot, Englishwomen in Parliament in 1967 accounted for less than five percent of the members, and women in local government averaged twelve percent overall. Sullerot, *Woman, Society and Change*, pp. 222–23.

Mitchell's analysis was criticized by neo-Marxist, American feminists as being too idealistic, pessimistic, and individualistic (i.e., too concerned with questions of individual identity and sexuality). True equality for women could be found by looking to Communist China, the Soviet Union, Eastern Europe, or revolutionary Cuba or Algeria. Numerous polemical articles appeared in the United States attempting to relate women's liberation to Marxist analysis, to anticolonialism, and to revolutionary movements.[21] When social scientists engaged in comparative studies of women's status, they found the question of equality to be more complicated. A comparison of the time budgets of Hungarian and Finnish women, for example, found that while women in Hungary had achieved more formal equality under socialism, they had less equality in the everyday business of living and, therefore, bore a double burden. Similar studies of the Soviet Union and China came to similar conclusions: women's equal obligation to participate in society was matched by an unequal burden in the home. Women's two roles—home and work—had become women's twin burdens.[22]

In summary, concern for how women could use their vote to achieve the newly defined goals of equality emerged slowly in the United States, Sweden, and England in the late 1960s and early 1970s because of the initial contexts in which those goals had been defined. The United States was especially illustrative of this situation. Spurred by the legal and administrative obstacles to achieving the promised benefits of the 1964 Civil Rights Act (Title VII), stimulated by the ideological ferment of the women's liberation movement, shocked out of self-limiting stereotypes by consciousness-raising sessions, moderate egalitarian groups abandoned their historic hostility to the Equal Rights Amendment and began to reexamine the relationship between women and the political process. The evidence was not reassuring. In 1968 Martin Gruberg published a meticulous compilation of facts and generalizations on women's political behavior from

---

21. For the radical liberation critique of Mitchell, see Roberta Salper, ed., *Female Liberation*, pp. 169–72. For representative documents on the radical liberation movement, see Salper, *Female Liberation*, Part 2; Morgan, ed., *Sisterhood Is Powerful.*

22. Veronica Stolte-Heiskanen and Elina Haavio-Mannila, "The Position of Women in Society: Formal Ideology versus Everyday Ethic," *Social Science Information* 6 (December 1967): 169–88. These authors theorized that in countries "where the formal doctrine of equality 'forces' women into greater participation in society without at the same time decreasing their traditional obligations, women have to pay the price of their formal emancipation by sleeping less"; however, they noted that this might not completely explain the situation in Hungary where "women spend considerably less time on productive activity than men" (p. 183).

For the analysis of the Soviet Union, see Mark G. Field, "Workers (and Mothers): Soviet Women Today," in *The Role and Status of Women in the Soviet Union*, Donald R. Brown, ed. (New York: Teachers College Press, 1968), pp. 7–56; H. Kent Geiger, *The Family in Soviet Russia* (Cambridge, Mass.: Harvard University Press, 1968), Chapter 7; Paul Hollander, ed., *American and Soviet Society: A Reader in Comparative Sociology and Perception* (Englewood Cliffs, N.J.: Prentice-Hall, Inc., 1969), Chapter 4.

For a perceptive review of developments in China, see Charlotte Bonny Cohen, "Experiment in Freedom: Women in China," in Morgan, ed., *Sisterhood Is Powerful,* pp. 385–417.

current political science research while Peggy Lamson surveyed examples of the few women who had succeeded in politics. The most devastating attack on the political status quo, however, came in 1971 in Kirsten Amundsen's book, *The Silenced Majority: Women and American Democracy.*[23]

The renewed interest in political power that accompanied the changed attitudes toward the Equal Rights Amendment revealed an anomalous situation. From 1944 to 1964, the Equal Rights Amendment had been endorsed in every presidential election by the major political parties. It was replaced in the 1964 campaign by general antidiscrimination statements. It had been supported largely by old-line feminists and professional, salaried women (who hoped it would pass) and was endorsed by many professional politicians (who hoped that it would not pass but wanted to pacify the feminist lobbyists). It was opposed by organized labor and by women's rights advocates and groups (who feared that it would jeopardize welfare and protective labor legislation). After 1968, the Equal Rights Amendment gathered support from neofeminists and women's rights groups, was now opposed by many politicians, and was condemned by new left, militant feminists (who believed that it would divert attention from more radical, social reconstruction). The sudden switch in positions left much of the public confused and enabled opponents of the amendment to play on public fears and misleading stereotypes that had been created by media coverage of the "women's lib" phenomena.[24]

American feminists and women's rights advocates in the 1970s thus found themselves in the same situation as their predecessors in the 1870s. The women's movement was divided into radical and reformist camps; the public was alternately bemused, confused, and antagonized by the conflicting impressions of the women's activities; and the historic alliance with black aspirations and white humanitarianism (abolitionism in the 1860s; civil rights in the 1960s) had been shattered by partial success and numerous setbacks. If the achievement of equal rights and opportunities was to be the primary objective of the 1970s, then the logic of the situation required a broad political coalition, some accommodation within public images and expectations, and a repudiation of the tactics of extremists—in short, the politics of compromise, pluralism, and a new consensus. If, on the other hand, the primary goal was to be the reconstruction of society, or at least of basic social institutions such as marriage and the family, then the

---

23. Martin Gruberg, *Women in American Politics: An Assessment and Sourcebook* (Oshkosh, Wis.: Academia Press, 1968); Peggy Lamson, *Few Are Chosen: American Women in Political Life Today* (Boston: Houghton Mifflin Company, 1968); Kirsten Amundsen, *The Silenced Majority: Women and American Democracy* (Englewood Cliffs, N.J.: Prentice-Hall, Inc., 1971).

24. The case for the Equal Rights Amendment was spelled out most clearly in Barbara A. Brown, Thomas I. Emerson, Gail Falk, and Ann E. Freedman, "The Equal Rights Amendment: A Constitutional Basis for Equal Rights for Women," *The Yale Law Journal* 80 (April 1971): 872-985. See also Catharine Stimpson, ed., *Women and the "Equal Rights" Amendment: Senate Subcommittee Hearing on the Constitutional Amendment, 91st Congress* (New York: R. R. Bowker Co., 1972).

imperatives of the situation moved in another direction: a narrower, cultural-political coalition, confrontation with public stereotypes, cultivation of links with radical liberation movements, experimentation with counter-cultural life styles—the politics of cultural revolution. Whatever the final choice, the perspective of history was clear: the crucial element was the conception of equality and its meaning in the context of the American democratic tradition.

Index